D0574626

MONOGRAPHS OF
THE MEDIAEVAL ACADEMY
OF AMERICA
No. 7

ACADEMY PUBLICATIONS

No. 1, *A Concordance of Boethius*, by LANE COOPER

No. 2, *A Concordance to the Historia Ecclesiastica of Bede*, by P. F. JONES

No. 3, *A Survey of the Manuscripts of Tours*, by E. K. RAND, two volumes, text and plates

No. 4, *Lupus of Ferrières as Scribe and Text Critic*, by C. H. BEESON, with facsimile of *MS. Harley 2736*

No. 5, *Genoese Shipping in the Twelfth and Thirteenth Centuries*, by E. H. BYRNE (*Monograph No. 1*)

No. 6, *Greek and Syrian Miniatures in Jerusalem*, by W. H. P. HATCH, with reproductions

No. 7, *Harūnū'l-Rashīd and Charles the Great*, by F. W. BUCKLER (*Monograph No. 2*)

No. 8, *Alien Merchants in England, 1350 to 1377*, by ALICE BEARDWOOD (*Monograph No. 3*)

No. 9, *A Concordance of Prudentius*, by R. J. DEFERRARI and J. M. CAMPBELL

No. 10, *The Script of Cologne from Hildebald to Hermann*, by L. W. JONES, text and plates

No. 11, *Feudal Monarchy in the Latin Kingdom of Jerusalem, 1100–1291*, by J. L. LA MONTE (*Monograph No. 4*)

No. 12, *Alexander's Gate, Gog and Magog, and the Inclosed Nations*, by A. R. ANDERSON (*Monograph No. 5*)

No. 13, *The Administration of Normandy Under Saint Louis*, by J. R. STRAYER (*Monograph No. 6*)

No. 14, *The Cathedral of Palma de Mallorca*, by RALPH ADAMS CRAM

No. 15, *Borough and Town: A Study of Urban Origins in England*, by CARL STEPHENSON (*Monograph No. 7*)

BOROUGH AND TOWN

A STUDY OF
URBAN ORIGINS IN ENGLAND

CARL STEPHENSON

Professor of History
Cornell University

THE MEDIAEVAL ACADEMY OF AMERICA

CAMBRIDGE, MASSACHUSETTS

1933

The publication of this book was made possible by a fund granted the Academy by the Carnegie Corporation of New York

COPYRIGHT, 1933

BY

THE MEDIAEVAL ACADEMY OF AMERICA

Printed in U. S. A.

UNIVERSITY LIBRARY

116209 Lethbridge, Alberta

Composed, Printed and Bound by
The Collegiate Press
George Banta Publishing Company
Menasha, Wisconsin

TO

HENRI PIRENNE

WITHOUT WHOSE KINDLY INSPIRATION
THIS BOOK WOULD NEVER HAVE BEEN UNDERTAKEN

PREFACE

AS A definite project, this book owes its inception to a year's study under M. Pirenne in 1924–25. Much of the material that it contains, however, was to some extent assembled earlier, for in one way or another I have been dealing with boroughs ever since my initiation into graduate work at Harvard University. Charles Gross, just before his final illness forced him to abandon teaching, gave me a thesis subject connected with English municipal history, and so introduced me to many problems that reappear in the ensuing chapters. But my dissertation was little more than a hope when I came under the direction of another master. If in time I learned the meaning of scholarship and developed a liking for research strong enough to survive the toil of thesis-writing, it was as the pupil of Professor Charles Homer Haskins. To him my debt of gratitude is too great to be expressed here or elsewhere.

From my thesis I was led to consider the military and fiscal obligations of mediaeval townsmen generally, and although my original topic did not directly involve the fundamental problem of the borough, I was inevitably led to it. I became increasingly familiar with the pertinent sources and with the interpretations made of them by leading historians. I came to appreciate as fundamental to our knowledge of the Norman records the searching criticism of Round, whose essays, for the sheer power of straight thinking there exhibited, have been to me a constant joy and incentive. Also I came under the lasting charm of Maitland, whose marvellous sense of historical values, combined with an uncanny faculty of vivid expression, has given us our truest picture of early English institutions. On this book his influence will be apparent from title to concluding page.

Meanwhile, investigation of Continental materials taught me the value of examining English custom against a European background. Along with the writings of many other authorities, I read and admired the articles of Henri Pirenne, but because I gave the matter no concentrated attention, I failed to realize that his ideas might have especial significance for the history of the borough. Then came the opportunity of studying at the University of Ghent, and under the personal guidance of a great teacher, the half-understood reading of earlier days took on new meaning. Ill-assorted bits of information that I had already gained from the English sources clicked into place, suggesting the outline of the book that is herewith presented.

By sketching the history of the boroughs down to the opening of the thirteenth century, I have attempted, in the light of similar developments on the Continent, to explain the beginning of town life in England. I have made no effort to catalogue all the boroughs during this period or to give a complete account of any one of them. My essay, being thus a consideration of early boroughs in general, naturally stresses certain matters of theory; but for reasons stated above, I hope that it will not seem the mere justification of a preconceived doctrine. At every point I have tried first to give an impartial review of the evidence, and then to draw the conclusions thereby demanded. Conjectures I have sought to provide with honest labels. To proceed otherwise, assuredly, would be contrary to the spirit of the scholar to whom the study is dedicated.

As already remarked, many portions of this book are based on work begun long ago, but very little of it appeared in print before 1926 — only small sections of Chapters IV and VI, which formed part of an article in the *English Historical Review*, October, 1919.[1] A sketch of the central thesis here developed was read at the meeting of the American Historical Association in 1925 and published in the *American Historical Review*, October, 1926.[2] It is now incorporated in Chapters III and IV, which also include a sequel that appeared in the *English Historical Review*, April, 1930.[3] And much of Chapters V and VI was outlined in a paper read at the meeting of the American Historical Association in 1930 and published in the *American Historical Review*, April, 1932.[4]

At the suggestion of Professor Stuart A. Rice, I contributed to the case book, which he was editing for the Social Science Research Council, an article dealing with theories on the origin of mediaeval towns;[5] and this, with many amendments, now stands as Chapter I. On the other hand, Chapter II has been entirely written during the past year. It brings together material long familiar to specialists in the field, but scattered among dozens of volumes, some of them hard to obtain. I trust that, by helping to explain urban development in England, my summary will be as useful to the reader as the composition of it has been to me.

Chapter VII is likewise new, except in so far as its theme was briefly stated in a paper read at the last Anglo-American Historical Conference in London and since published in *History*, April, 1932.[6] It is at best the mere introduction of a subject that deserves a volume to itself — the

---

[1] 'The Aids of the English Borough,' *E.H.R.*, xxxiv, 457 ff.

[2] 'The Origin of the English Towns,' *A.H.R.*, xxxii, 10 ff.

[3] 'The Anglo-Saxon Borough,' *E.H.R.*, xlv, 177 ff.

[4] 'The French Commune and the English Borough,' *A.H.R.*, xxxvii, 451 ff.

[5] 'The Work of Henri Pirenne and Georg von Below with Respect to the Origin of the Mediaeval Town,' *Methods in Social Science* (Chicago: The University of Chicago Press, 1931), pp. 368 ff.

[6] 'Investigation of the Origins of Towns,' *History*, xvii, 8 ff.

topography of the primitive borough. But that volume cannot be written until the facts are made available by further research; and that research will hardly be undertaken until its worth is better appreciated. Though possessing neither the opportunity nor the technical training for much independent work in the archaeological field, I have been able to visit a number of boroughs and to supplement the study of books and maps by direct observation. Such casual exploration as my own hardly leads to results that can be set down in footnotes, but it has greatly quickened my understanding of the problems involved. By stating them now, may I not enlist collaboration for their solution in the future?

The study of urban development cannot be intelligently pursued without the aid of accurate maps. Most local histories, unfortunately, fail to provide them, and to make up for the lack in a general essay such as this is quite impossible. Nevertheless, a few plans — for the drawing of which I am indebted to the skill of Mr Malcolm J. Rand — have been inserted to illustrate the growth of the boroughs singled out for special treatment in Chapter VII and of two characteristic towns among those considered in Chapter II. These plans should not be regarded as more than graphic presentations, in very simplified form, of the main points discussed in the text; for more precise indication of topographical detail the reader should consult the works referred to in the pertinent notes.

When citing authorities, I have tried to supply the necessary information fully and clearly. Most of the chapters are based upon published materials already familiar to every student of mediaeval England. Only such standard works have been uniformly abbreviated. Wherever references of another sort have been demanded, especially throughout the first two chapters, complete bibliographical data have been placed in the notes, according to the plan usually followed in periodicals. Separate compilation of a long array of titles would, I believe, be of no additional value. Criticism of important works on the towns forms an integral part of this essay and may be traced in detail through the index of authors.

In transcribing Latin documents, many of which are published in record type, I have modernized the text as to punctuation and capitalization. For the sake of uniformity, I have paid no attention to the occasional use of *j* for *i*, and have written *u* or *v*, in the absence of any mediaeval standard, according to ordinary English usage. Pounds, shillings, and pence I have indicated respectively by *lib.*, *sol.*, and *den.*

In conclusion I wish to acknowledge the kindness of the editors and publishers who have granted me permission to reprint portions of the articles mentioned above. For the opportunity of European study, without which this book would have been impossible, I am deeply grateful to the C. R. B. Educational Foundation, to the John Simon Guggenheim Memorial Foundation, to the University of Wisconsin, and to the Heckscher Research Foundation of Cornell University.

Among the many persons to whom I am indebted for aid in securing valuable information while abroad, should be mentioned Professor Louis Halphen, of the University of Paris; Professor Karl Frölich, of the University of Giessen; Professor F. M. Powicke, of Oxford University; Professor C. W. Previté-Orton, of Cambridge University; Mr G. H. Stephen, City Librarian of Norwich; Mr Frank Hill, of Lincoln; and Mr George Benson, of York. And for their especial kindness in many ways, much more than this word of appreciation is due my good friends, Mrs T. F. Tout, Miss Nellie Neilson, and Professor J. F. Willard.

From the criticism of those who have read this book in manuscript — among them my colleague, Professor M. L. W. Laistner — I have gained many valuable suggestions.   In return I can only say that I wish them in all their undertakings assistance as generous and unfailing as I have had in mine.

CORNELL UNIVERSITY   CARL STEPHENSON
June, 1932

CONTENTS

xi

'above the line,' 83–84; tenurial heterogeneity, not a matter of prime importance for the early borough, 84–88.

CHAPTER V

3. The Social Transition in the Boroughs..............205–214

The familiarity to us of the twelfth-century borough, 205–206; difficulties encountered in explaining its origin, 206–207; the primitive borough judged according to contemporary sources, 207–208; transition from the military to the mercantile borough, 208–209; revolutionary effect of the Norman Conquest, 209–213; adaptation of the mercantile settlement theory to explain the beginnings of town life in England, 213–214.

APPENDICES

INDICES

PLATES

ABBREVIATIONS

A.H.R. — *American Historical Review.*

A.S.C. — *The Anglo-Saxon Chronicle*, ed. B. Thorpe (Rolls Series). London, 1861. (Reference is made to the translation, with the original cited by dates in parentheses.)

B.B.C. — *British Borough Charters.* Vol. i, ed. A. Ballard; Vol. ii, ed. J. Tait. Cambridge, 1913–23.

C.D. — J. M. Kemble, *Codex Diplomaticus Aevi Saxonici.* English Historical Society. London, 1839–48. (Reference is made to the documents by number, with the date in parentheses.)

D.B. — *Domesday Book.* Record Commission. London, 1783–1816.

E.H.R. — *English Historical Review.*

G. — F. Liebermann, *Gesetze der Angelsachsen.* Halle, 1903–16.

H.E.L. — F. Pollock and F. W. Maitland, *The History of English Law before the Time of Edward I.* 2nd ed. Cambridge, 1899.

P.R. — *Pipe Roll*
  31 Henry I. Record Commission. London, 1833.
  2–4 Henry II. Record Commission. London, 1844.
  5 Henry II (and following years). Pipe Roll Society. London, 1884 ff.

S.C. — W. Stubbs, *Select Charters Illustrative of English Constitutional History.* 9th ed., by H. W. C. Davis. Oxford, 1913.

V.H.C. — *The Victoria History of the Counties of England.* Westminster, 1900 ff.

BOROUGH AND TOWN
A STUDY OF URBAN ORIGINS IN ENGLAND

I

THE MEDIAEVAL TOWN IN HISTORICAL LITERATURE

1. Georg von Below and Earlier Writers

THE mediaeval town has long been a controversial subject. Since scholars of the romantic revival turned back to the Middle Ages, it has been realized that modern European culture is essentially an urban culture, that it did not exist a thousand years ago, and that its beginnings deserve intensive study. During the nineteenth century many historians, thus coming to appreciate the problem of municipal origins, offered many solutions; and in the absence of really valid evidence, each speculative effort was plausible enough to gain numerous adherents. Rival theories multiplied; polemic flourished; ultimate agreement of authorities seemed impossible. Nevertheless, as knowledge of the sources has improved, certain facts have won general acceptance. To that extent we may hope to grasp the truth; for although we rightly hesitate to regard our own ideas with utter complacence, we are sure that the second quarter of the twentieth century finds the scholarly world nearer accord than ever before on the early history of mediaeval towns. To sketch this *rapprochement* will be the object of the ensuing chapter.

With the gradual abandonment of the Romanist theory,[1] by which the persistence of urban institutions throughout the Dark Age was unthinkingly asserted, no less than seven substitute explanations came to be offered before 1900. These, to adopt a convenient order, were (1) the immunity theory of Arnold; (2) the *Hofrecht* theory of Nitzsch; (3) the gild theory of Wilda and others; (4) the *Marktrecht* theory of Sohm; (5) the *Landgemeinde* theory of Maurer and Below; (6) the *Burgrecht* theory of Keutgen; and (7) the mercantile settlement theory of Pirenne and Rietschel. To review them all in detail will not be necessary, for the

---

[1] Among recent works the strongest argument for the continuity of urban life in western Europe since Roman times will be found in A. Dopsch, *Grundlagen der Europäischen Kulturentwicklung* (2nd ed., Vienna, 1923–24), I, 100 ff.; II, 344 ff. Dopsch's principal contention, that the Germanic invasions resulted in no systematic destruction of the Roman cities, will hardly be objected to by any modern critic. But Dopsch goes much farther than this and, by indiscriminately throwing together evidence concerning *civitates, castella, burgi*, etc., minimizes the break between ancient and mediaeval culture. Such procedure, to my mind, is unwarranted and tends to obscure the true significance of the author's thesis. Especially in connection with Britain (II, 379 ff.), his discussion reveals inadequate knowledge of the sources.

summary made by Pirenne some thirty-five years ago needs neither ad-
vertisement nor recapitulation in these pages.   Furthermore, since the
first four theories on the list were quite discredited before the opening of
the present century, little need be said of them except by way of introducing the latter three, which still have significance for the history of
the English borough.

The first noteworthy clarification of what had become a very complicated problem was made by Georg von Below.   From research on the
princely authority in Jülich and Berg he was led, by way of taxation and
the burgher estate, to the nature of the mediaeval town in general.[1]   Two
articles on the subject were followed by two small books, and these in
turn by many other contributions.[2]   And although Below drifted somewhat readily into violent polemic, much of his work has since been regarded as definitive.   Arnold had pictured the towns as evolving out of
free communities in the Rhine and Danube valleys.   These communities,
he thought, had at first been subject to the great bishops who, through
grants of immunity, had come to share the public authority of the king.
Eventually, when the towns became independent of the bishops, they
merely took over functions that had previously belonged to the latter.
So municipal development was based on *öffentliches Recht*.[3]   But this
conclusion had been completely denied by Nitzsch.   In his opinion the
town had begun as a servile community, administered under manorial
jurisdiction (*Hofrecht*) by low-born agents of the lord (*ministeriales*).   It
was by no sudden revolution that the townsmen had achieved freedom,
but by a long slow process.   Eventually, however, autonomy was secured, and the *ministeriales* became an urban aristocracy.[4]

Below, following up the conviction to which he had been brought by
his previous study, proceeded first of all to demolish the *Hofrecht* theory.
Not only did he succeed in this undertaking, but he also proved the utter
inadequacy of Arnold's doctrine.   The mediaeval town, argued Below,
had from the outset been a free community, where liberty could be secured even by servile immigrants.   Such a settlement came to differ from
the contemporary village in four respects: it had a market; it was walled;

---

[1] G. von Below, *Die Landständische Verfassung in Jülich und Berg* (Düsseldorf, 1885–91).   For
Below's own account of how he came to deal with the town, together with a general criticism of
pertinent writings, see *Der Deutsche Staat des Mittelalters* (2nd ed., Leipzig, 1925), pp. 48 ff., 91 ff.;
cf. G. Schmoller, *Deutsches Städtewesen in Älterer Zeit* (Bonn, 1922), pp. 1 ff.

[2] 'Zur Entstehung der Deutschen Stadtverfassung,' *Historische Zeitschrift*, LVIII (1887), 193 ff.;
LIX (1888), 193 ff.   *Die Entstehung der Deutschen Stadtgemeinde* (Düsseldorf, 1889).   *Der Ursprung
der Deutschen Stadtverfassung* (Düsseldorf, 1892).   The first article was in part reprinted in *Terri-
torium und Stadt* (2nd ed., Berlin, 1923), pp. 213 ff.

[3] W. Arnold, *Verfassungsgeschichte der Deutschen Freistädte* (Hamburg, 1854).

[4] K. W. Nitzsch, *Ministerialität und Bürgertum* (Leipzig, 1859).

it constituted a jurisdictional unit; and it enjoyed special dispensation with regard to fiscal, military, and other political responsibilities. These four characteristics were necessitated by the new economic life of the town and were matters of public law, coming by virtue of state endowment. But they were not fundamental elements; they were accretions which, making a village into a town, still left the village at the heart of the new agglomeration. The urban community had at first been a village community, and to the *Landgemeinde* the *Stadtgemeinde* owed the germ of its constitution. Its unity, its liberty, its self-government did not arise from monarchical delegation, but from the primitive *Mark-genossenschaft*.[1]

Thus, with some slight amendment, it was the famous doctrine of Georg von Maurer that Below adopted.[2] To him, undoubtedly, it seemed a matter of common sense — and so it must continue to seem to any one who, like Below, starts with confidence in the attractive mark theory. For, it should be noted, Below never thought it necessary to test that idea; to his mind it had already been sufficiently proved. Maurer's *Stadtverfassung* had been sharply criticized for depicting eleventh-century conditions according to fifteenth-century evidence.[3] But Below insisted that the use of later records was necessary to supplement the fragmentary sources of an earlier age, and was justifiable, provided only that the younger were interpreted in the light of the older. So far as the town was concerned, its development from the village was clearly demonstrated by the many agricultural features that it preserved all through the later Middle Ages. It was only when historians wrongly limited their research to a few large and rapidly growing centres that they failed to discover this elemental connection between the urban and the rural community.[4]

Meanwhile the gild theory, originally propounded by Wilda, had been greatly developed by other writers in Germany and outside it.[5] According to their interpretation, the town had grown from a private association or club, which, though perhaps organized for social or religious purposes, was quickly adapted to mercantile or political interests. Particularly in England, where such societies were known to have existed

---

[1] A particular adaptation of this same theory by Vanderkindere derived the municipal magistracy of the Middle Ages from the popular leaders of the ancient rural commune. See below, p. 37, n. 1.

[2] The well known books of G. L. von Maurer began with the *Einleitung zur Geschichte der Mark-, Hof-, Dorf-, und Stadtverfassung* (Munich, 1854) and ended with the *Geschichte der Stadtverfassung* (Erlangen, 1869–71).

[3] See particularly A. Heusler, *Der Ursprung der Deutschen Stadtverfassung* (Weimar, 1872), pp. 157 ff., 236 ff.

[4] Below, *Stadtverfassung*, pp. 4 ff.

[5] W. E. Wilda, *Das Gildenwesen im Mittelalter* (Halle, 1831).

from an early time, and in France, where the gild was identified with the sworn commune, Wilda's doctrine won great popularity.[1] But it, too, failed to withstand more critical examination. Hegel, Gross, and, to a minor degree, Below joined in demonstrating what is now universally accepted: that while town and gild were often closely associated, they were always two quite distinct entities.[2]

At the same time a similar fate befell a much younger theory, that by which Sohm sought to identify *Stadtrecht* and *Marktrecht*.[3] Below, as we have seen, had himself attributed the more characteristic features of town life to an economic revolution, but had insisted that none the less, the town at heart remained a village community. In the promulgation of this doctrine he had considered himself as much the disciple of Sohm as of Maurer, for it was the former who had proved that the *Landgemeinde* had not been a *Gerichtsbezirk*, had never been made a political unit within the Carolingian state. To Below the market theory seemed a desertion of first principles, and he forthwith joined in the attack upon his old master.[4] It was at this point that a new turn was given to the discussion by the discerning criticism of a Belgian historian.

2. Henri Pirenne and Siegfried Rietschel

In 1889 Henri Pirenne had published his first book, a dissertation on the early history of Dinant, and two years later his well known edition of Galbert de Bruges. Various reviews had proved his thorough familiarity with the work of German scholars on the mediaeval town, while original research had led him to draw certain noteworthy conclusions of his own.[5] This comprehensive information was now displayed to the learned world by the classic essays of 1893 and 1895.[6]

First of all, Pirenne set out to explain for French readers the tangled controversy that had grown up round the beginnings of urban life in mediaeval Europe. With precision and clarity the conflicting views men-

---

[1] See below, pp. 13, 16.

[2] K. Hegel, *Städte und Gilden der Germanischen Völker im Mittelalter* (Leipzig, 1891); C. Gross, *The Gild Merchant* (Oxford, 1890); G. von Below, in *Jahrbücher für Nationalökonomie*, LVIII (1892), 1 ff.

[3] R. Sohm, *Die Entstehung des Deutschen Städtewesens* (Leipzig, 1890).

[4] For Below's attitude toward Sohm and Maurer, see particularly *Hist. Zft.*, LIX, 204; *Stadtgemeinde* pp. 1 ff.; *Stadtverfassung*, pp. 4 ff.; *Der Deutsche Staat*, pp. 48 ff., 95 ff.

[5] *Histoire de la Constitution de la Ville de Dinant au Moyen Age* (Ghent, 1889); Galbert de Bruges, ed. in *Collection de Textes pour Servir à l'Enseignement de l'Histoire*, x (Paris, 1891). A complete list of Pirenne's reviews will be found in *Mélanges d'Histoire Offerts à Henri Pirenne* (Brussels, 1926), I, xxxi ff.

[6] 'L'Origine des Constitutions Urbaines au Moyen Age,' *Revue Historique*, LIII (1893), 52 ff.; LVII (1895), 57 ff.

tioned above were in turn analyzed, appraised, and — in so far as each laid claim to finality — rejected. Pirenne accepted the restatement of the problem that Below had effected, but disagreed with the particular answer that he had given it. In an autonomous village of the early Middle Ages, whether called *Markgenossenschaft* or *Landgemeinde*, Pirenne refused, on the mere evidence of late mediaeval sources, to place confidence. The derivation, as a matter of juristic logic, of municipal institutions from such an imaginative reconstruction to him lacked historical reality. On the contrary, he believed that the mediaeval town was pre-eminently the product of social and economic forces which, in spite of all ethnic and political variation, had been fundamentally the same in both halves of the Carolingian Empire. To interpret European phenomena in terms of nationalism was wrong. Only by ignoring such artificial lines as those drawn at the partition of Verdun could the historian hope to arrive at the truth.

In his second article Pirenne presented his own ideas on the town. Starting with the *civitas* of the late Roman Empire, he showed how, with the advent of the Dark Age, it had ceased to be either an economic or a political entity. Important still as a fortress, administrative centre, and residence for bishop or temporal prince, it had lost all but an insignificant number of its original inhabitants and all but a few vestiges of its ancient industrial activity. Economically the city became dependent upon the agrarian countryside; politically it became a patchwork of rival jurisdictions.[1] True urban life no longer existed, and before it could be reborn, there had to be a revival of commerce.

Meanwhile western Europe had come to be dotted with abbeys and castles, round which towns occasionally grew. Such developments, however, were the exception rather than the rule and were in no instance due to the magnetism of the earlier institution, ecclesiastic or lay. Sohm had performed a noteworthy service in showing the existence of a mercantile element in *Stadtrecht*, but had exaggerated the importance of markets. Local centres of exchange had existed for centuries without attracting a permanent population. For a true urban concentration wider commerce was demanded. Towns grew up in mediaeval Europe as naturally as they have in modern America — on sites where the geographic location was favorable to trade and industry. And since the old Roman cities had originally been evolved in response to similar demands, it was to be expected that, when commerce revived, they too would revive. This was what happened throughout the larger part of Gaul, but in regions where

[1] In this connection Pirenne cited particularly J. Flach, *Les Origines de l'Ancienne France*, II (Paris, 1893), 215 ff., and Rietschel's first work, below, p. 9, n. 1.

ancient colonization had been slight, as in Flanders and in most of Germany, new towns arose to meet new needs.

Thus, no matter whose the soil or what its previous history, the mediaeval town was essentially a trading settlement, which commonly began as a stockaded quarter beside some older fortification. There, by virtue of the mercantile calling, personal freedom became the rule; seignorial obligations tended to disappear; a new land tenure, a new peace, a new law, a new status developed. And with the rapid expansion of these new elements, what had been the dominant features of the original settlement — agrarian, military, and official — were entirely submerged. It was not from them that the town sprang, but from the exigencies of a new society. Political institutions were also revolutionized. Inevitably, as the urban community developed, antiquated systems of finance, justice, police, and administration broke down. The town came to manage its own local affairs under elected magistrates. Nor were such practices derived from rural custom, for at that time there were no autonomous villages. Self-government was as new as the bourgeoisie itself.

While Pirenne was thus sketching a more comprehensive theory of municipal origins than had as yet appeared, the work of Below was being followed up in Germany by two younger historians, Friedrich Keutgen and Siegfried Rietschel — the one in remarkable agreement with Pirenne's ideas, the other in almost diametrical opposition. To Keutgen the town was primarily a legal concept. The Anglo-Saxon borough, he thought, might be treated as homogeneous with the German *Stadt*, because both had a Teutonic basis; but not the Roman *civitas* or the French *ville*. Below had rightly emphasized the distinction between *Gemeindeverfassung* and *Gerichtsverfassung;* whatever the origin of the town as a community, as a jurisdictional unit it began by formal act of the state. And in that respect the cities of the Rhine were remodelled after the creations of Henry the Fowler. The primitive German name for a town was *Burg; Stadtfriede* was originally not *Marktfriede*, but *Burgfriede*. The town as a legal entity was military rather than commercial, for it was founded on the king's *Burgbann*, which, by offering necessary protection, eventually attracted a trading population. Thus Keutgen did not deny the primitive communal element in the town, but his theory tended to make it insignificant. The continuity between village and town that had been stressed by Below was broken, according to the new argument, by an official revolution.[1]

[1] F. Keutgen, *Untersuchungen über den Ursprung der Deutschen Stadtverfassung* (Leipzig, 1894). See also his article 'Commune,' in the *Encyclopaedia Britannica*, 11th ed., of which the 14th ed. gives a mere condensation.

Rietschel, in the meantime, had re-examined the early history of the Rhine and Danube cities, and had come to conclusions which, so far as they went, coincided with those of Pirenne. Until the revival of commerce in the eleventh century, the mediaeval *civitas* lacked political autonomy, legal unity, and economic self-sufficiency. Socially its inhabitants were indistinguishable from those of the countryside. Nor did the early Germans imply that a *civitas* was a town when they called it *Burg*, for that was merely their name for any fortified enclosure. Neither dense population, nor mercantile life, nor municipal organization occasioned the usage, but solely the wall. In fact, the early Germans, whose society was thoroughly agrarian, could have had no conception of a town as an urban centre; that meaning of the word *Burg* was the product of later centuries.[1]

These ideas Rietschel further elaborated in a second book published three years later.[2] Still a believer in the mark, and in many respects a disciple of Below, he found little evidence for the derivation of the *Stadtgemeinde* from the *Landgemeinde*. On the other hand, he showed that the German town regularly grew from an independent source — from a mercantile settlement alongside a previously existing castle, church, village, or episcopal city. To the older institution the new one owed little but its name. Below had overestimated the importance of the primitive rustic element in urban evolution. The possession of forest and pasture rights by burghers did not imply that they lived by agriculture; merchants had to have horses, and artisans generally kept cows, goats, and pigs. Moreover, villages that in later ages secured rights copied from those of towns were of no value for explaining municipal origins. Both *Marktrecht* and *Burgrecht* had their influence in *Stadtrecht*, but the significance of market and wall must not be exaggerated. 'Die Stadt ist ein Markt, der zugleich Burg ist. Alle Städte sind Märkte, aber nicht alle Märkte sind Städte. Alle Städte sind Burgen, aber nicht alle Burgen sind Städte.'[3] The town could therefore not be accounted for in terms of any pre-existing institution. From the outset the novelty of its life was reflected throughout its law and organization.

With the close of the century it thus became apparent that such narrow and arbitrary interpretations of the sources as had once prevailed were quite discredited. To that extent the joint efforts of a new generation of scholars had proved decisive. And though on the constructive side there was no complete agreement, it could soon be seen that the really contro-

[1] S. Rietschel, *Die Civitas auf Deutschem Boden* (Leipzig, 1894), especially pp. 40 ff., 95 ff.
[2] *Markt und Stadt in ihrem Rechtlichen Verhältniss* (Leipzig, 1897).
[3] *Ibid.*, p. 150.

versial matters were rapidly shrinking. The debate still continued; old slogans were still repeated; but little by little viewpoints were shifted and the antagonists made notable concessions to each other's opinions.

Keutgen, as we have seen, had greatly emphasized the importance of fortification in municipal history, and his thesis, while rendering the factor of the *Landgemeinde* relatively insignificant, by no means denied it. Indeed, in later publications Keutgen posed as the great champion of Below's doctrine against the onslaught of Pirenne and Rietschel. Their fundamental contention had been that places called *civitates*, *urbes*, *castella*, or *burgi* in the ninth and tenth centuries were not necessarily towns: that the real origin of the latter lay in mercantile settlements attached to the old centres. Keutgen, however, could not see the point. In an article of 1900 he insisted that *Burgrecht* could mean nothing but *Stadtrecht*, and accused Rietschel of exaggerating the significance of artificial *Marktansiedelungen*.[1] Even if, he added in 1903, most towns had been thus founded, the truth neither of his own nor of Below's theory was in the least impaired.[2]

Below himself was more generous; in later writings he frankly accredited Rietschel with having accomplished a great simplification of the problem, and unreservedly adopted the new classification of the German towns. He had, he admitted, considerably overestimated the number of urban communities that had developed from village communities. After all, he had himself never denied the decisive influence of trade upon the town: he had sought to explain what it grew out of, not why it grew.[3] But although Below might thus find consolation by minimizing the ultimate significance of Rietschel's argument, the admissions to which he had been forced proved fatal to the *Landgemeinde* theory as originally promulgated; for once it was conceded that most towns developed quite apart from village communities, that factor was eliminated as essential to municipal evolution.

Pirenne, as was to be expected, gave warm support to the conclusions of Rietschel. In a brief article of 1898 he joined the German scholar in writing *finis* to the *Marktrecht* theory.[4] 'C'est parceque certains endroits

---

[1] F. Keutgen, in *Neue Jahrbücher für das Klassische Altertum, Geschichte*, etc., v (1900), 275 ff. Specific criticism of Pirenne and Rietschel is slight; earlier insistence upon nationalism as a governing factor for the study of the mediaeval town is somewhat relaxed.

[2] *Ämter und Zünfte* (Jena, 1903), pp. 110 ff.

[3] G. von Below, in *Vierteljahrschrift für Sozial- und Wirtschaftsgeschichte*, VII (1909), 413 ff.; also in *Jahrbücher für Nationalökonomie und Statistik*, cv (1915), 651 ff. And see especially *Probleme der Wirtschaftsgeschichte* (2nd ed., Tübingen, 1920), p. 474, n. 4: 'Ich habe früher die Zahl der Städte, die unmittelbar aus Landgemeinden hervorgegangen sind, erheblich höher angeschlagen, als ich es heute, namentlich durch die Forschungen Rietschels, eines Besseren belehrt, tue.' Cf. *Deutsche Städtegründungen im Mittelalter* (Freiburg im Breisgau, 1920), pp. 12 ff., 19.

[4] H. Pirenne, 'Villes, Marchés et Marchands au Moyen Age,' *Revue Historique*, LXVII (1898), 59 ff.

sont devenus de bonne heure le centre d'un commerce permanent que ces endroits sont devenus des villes. A ce point de vue, on peut dire que la ville est un marché, non pas, il est vrai, dans le sens de *mercatus*, mais dans le sens de *forum*.' Such a trading settlement in eleventh-century France, when surrounded by a palisade, was commonly called a *bourg* (*burgus*) and its inhabitants *bourgeois* (*burgenses*). In Flanders exactly the same sort of thing was often styled *portus* (hence *poorter*, meaning burgher), and it was from these colonies of merchants established beside the count's ancient castles that the great Flemish communes all developed.

This important fact, it should be remarked, was no recent discovery of Pirenne's. Though very lightly touched in his article of 1895, it had earlier been noted in his edition of Galbert de Bruges and had been learned from him by many pupils.[1] But from now on the fortress as a great factor in helping to produce the Flemish towns was more and more to be emphasized. Briefly sketched in the *Histoire de Belgique*,[2] Pirenne's ideas in this respect did not receive definitive treatment until 1905.[3] Since then they have been made very familiar, even in English-speaking countries, by many popular presentations.[4] To-day it may be taken as established that the old Flemish *burg* or castle was a military stronghold;[5] that the new *burg* or *port* was a trading colony; that by the twelfth century the new *burg* had entirely engulfed the old, had become a town where recently no town had been. The word *bourgeois*, in its changing meaning, epitomizes a social revolution.

In its wider application Pirenne's thesis may now be seen to have effected a great advance toward the clarification of a very obscure subject. As early as 1876 the great scholar, Waitz, departing from the doctrines of his contemporaries, had described the towns of the mediaeval Empire as evolving through colonization in and about markets.[6] The

---

[1] *Ibid.*, LVII, 74, n. 1; Galbert de Bruges, p. 15, n. 2, p. 49, n. 1. Cf. H. van Houtte, *Essai sur la Civilisation Flamande au Commencement du XIIᵉ Siècle d'après Galbert de Bruges* (Louvain, 1898), pp. 74 ff.; G. Des Marez, *Étude sur la Propriété Foncière dans les Villes du Moyen Age* (Ghent, 1898); G. Espinas, *Les Finances de la Commune de Douai* (Paris, 1902), now expanded as *La Vie Urbaine de Douai au Moyen Age* (Paris, 1913).

[2] First published as *Die Geschichte Belgiens* (Gotha, 1899); but see vol. I, 5th ed. (Brussels, 1922).

[3] 'Les Villes Flamandes avant le XIIᵉ Siècle,' *Annales de l'Est et du Nord*, I (1905), 1 ff.

[4] *Les Anciennes Démocraties des Pays-Bas* (Paris, 1910), tr. as *Belgian Democracy* (Manchester, 1915); *Mediaeval Cities* (Princeton, 1925), published in French as *Les Villes du Moyen Age* (Brussels, 1927). The latter is to be preferred to the American edition, having fuller notes and not suffering from obscurities and inaccuracies of translation. The title should be *Mediaeval Towns*, for in the text 'city' is used to mean the Roman *civitas*. See also Pirenne's chapter on the northern towns in the *C.M.H.*, VI, 505 ff.

[5] It should be noted that the early castle was rather a fortified place of refuge than the feudal type of stronghold that is so familiar; see below, pp. 23, 53, n. 2.

[6] G. Waitz, *Deutsche Verfassungsgeschichte*, VII (Kiel, 1876), 374 ff. With considerable justifica-

one point that his remarkable account chiefly failed to make clear, and
the one on which Sohm later went astray, was the distinction between
the market and the mercantile settlement. If both are called *Markt*,
ambiguity with regard to early municipal institutions is hard to avoid.
Depending upon which is meant, *Stadtrecht* may or may not be described
as *Marktrecht*. On this very subject Rietschel wrote his famous book,
and although it has been rightly considered an epoch-making work, in the
matter of fundamental definition it still left something to be desired.

The town was a *Markt* which at the same time was a *Burg*, said
Rietschel; and the essential characteristic of the latter was its wall.
Fortification legally created the town by establishing within its precincts
the royal *Burgfriede*. And since Rietschel understood *Ummauerung* to
imply stone construction, he was able to discover very few places in
twelfth-century Germany that came up to the standard. By 1200 not
more than a dozen walled towns had appeared, and of these nine were old
Roman cities.[1] As Gerlach proved, however, Rietschel's estimate, even
on the basis of his own definition, was much too small; and his definition
was much too arbitrary.[2] Indeed, as Pirenne had earlier shown, the
mediaeval town was the product of gradual evolution, rather than of
legal promulgation. During a time when fortification normally consisted of embankments and stockades, there could be no meticulous standard of *Stadtrecht* based solely on the erection of stone walls. And how,
in determining the meaning of such terms as *burgus* and *burgenses*, could
the data of merely German sources be considered self-sufficient?[3]

In general, the passing of an age of controversy over town origins was

tion Seeliger (below, p. 13, n. 1) hails Waitz as the founder of the *Marktansiedelung* theory. Waitz
noted the fact that the ancient Germans knew no real towns; emphasized the importance of the
Roman cities and of the newer *Burgen* as fortifications; sketched the later developments in connection
with the founding of markets; traced the acquisition of special privileges by the merchants of the
older places; and described the foundation of *Marktstädte*. In his treatment he did not restrict his
attention to Germany proper, but considered also the towns of the Low Countries. His conclusions
regarding the sworn commune, the gild, and the nature of urban liberty were extraordinarily sane.
He even remarked the distinction between the old *civitas* and the commercial quarter outside it.
From reading his work one gets the impression that his understanding of the subject was clearer than
his written exposition.

[1] *Das Burggrafenamt und die Hohe Gerichtsbarkeit* (Leipzig, 1905), pp. 323 ff.

[2] W. Gerlach, *Die Entstehungszeit der Städtebefestigungen in Deutschland* (Leipzig, 1913), especially
pp. 21, 36, 74. Gerlach has made equally sensible protest against other unduly narrow definitions
of *Stadt: Historische Vierteljahrschrift*, xvii (1914–15), 508 ff.; xix (1919–20), 331 ff. See also
Seeliger, as cited below, p. 13, n. 1. It is worth remarking that all agree in regarding the famous
Burgen of Henry the Fowler as forts, not towns. Cf. Pirenne, in *Revue Historique*, lvii, 65; also the
article by Koehne, below, p. 13, n. 2.

[3] Above, p. 10, n. 4. A recent discussion of the same question, although the author does not cite
Pirenne's work, arrives at similar conclusions: F. Beyerle, in *Zeitschrift der Savigny-Stiftung für
Rechtsgeschichte*, Germ. Abt., l (1930), 1 ff.

clearly marked by 1918, when Seeliger published his admirable summary.[1] Although, he said, the theory of the *Landgemeinde* might still be encountered in a modified form, that of the *Marktansiedelung* had come to be accepted by virtually all scholars. Adding to it the support of his own lucid exposition, he indicated as unsettled questions only such matters as the antiquity and significance of artificial town-planning, or the relation of urban foundation to the beginnings of self-government. And a glance at the more recent literature on the mediaeval German town shows how fully Seeliger has been justified in his analysis. Discussion continues to follow the lines that he suggested, and the major contentions of Rietschel are taken for granted by all parties.[2]

3. French Historians

In France, meanwhile, the violent controversies among German scholars had had but slight echoes. French historians, when forced by lack of evidence to abandon a Roman origin for their municipalities, could hardly be expected to substitute explanations intelligible only to German jurists. Nevertheless, Thierry, the first great writer on the subject in France, was willing to go a considerable way toward compromise with the Germanist school. According to him, the chief agents in the rise of the Third Estate were the revolutionary communes of the North; and they, in contradistinction to the consulates of the Midi, which had been founded under Italian influence, had sprung from the Teutonic gild.[3]

---

[1] G. Seeliger, 'Stadtverfassung,' in J. Hoops, *Reallexikon der Germanischen Altertumskunde,* IV (Strasbourg, 1918), 244 ff.

[2] A controversy of secondary interest has been waged over a theory launched by W. Sombart in his well known work *Das Moderne Kapitalismus* (Leipzig, 1902), I, 282 ff. Arguing that all the profits of mediaeval trade were immediately consumed by the traders, he found the origin of bourgeois capital in enhanced ground rents — in the unearned increment accruing to urban soil. This thesis was at once attacked by many scholars, particularly by Georg von Below (*Probleme der Wirtschafts-geschichte,* pp. 399 ff.), and was consequently amended by Sombart in the second edition of his book (Leipzig, 1916), I, 142 ff. To support his ground-rent theory, he now insisted that the mediaeval town was primarily an administrative centre, a place of official residence, a garrisoned fortification. Below also objected to the revised version (*op. cit.,* pp. 496 ff.), but Karl Koehne has shown (*Historische Zeitschrift,* CXXXIII, 1 ff.) that there is much truth in this idea if it is applied to the early *Burg,* rather than to the later mercantile settlement. Koehne recognized the fact that this distinction is fundamental to our understanding of urban development in Flanders and Germany; but was prevented from applying it to the history of the English boroughs by Liebermann's mistranslation of the dooms (see below, pp. 67 ff.). The recent work of two other German historians may be singled out for special notice because they likewise have emphasized the importance of considering the town something more than a Germanic institution. F. Beyerle, in the article noted above (p. 12, n. 3), gives an admirable review of urban institutions in Burgundy and thus explains certain peculiarities in connection with the founding of Frieburg im Breisgau. K. Frölich (in the same periodical, LI, 628 ff.) gives welcome recognition to Pirenne's *Villes du Moyen Age* and makes a plea for wider recognition of the problems common to the history of towns throughout western Europe.

[3] A. Thierry, *Considérations sur l'Histoire de France,* ch. VI; see above, p. 4.

With some modifications, Thierry's doctrine reappeared in the well known books of Luchaire. The latter, it is true, declared that Thierry had exaggerated the importance of the communes and underestimated that of the lesser bourgeoisie, but in his own work the commune continued to hold first place and *la révolution communale* remained a favorite expression.[1]

So far as origins were concerned, Luchaire pushed the question to one side as fundamentally insoluble, devoting to it only a few vague remarks. The Germanists, he said, had been scarcely more accurate than the Romanists. Although the gild had played an important part in the formation of the commune, there was nothing essentially Teutonic in the principle of association as worked out in the towns. The word consulate may have been borrowed from Italy, but the institution was indigenous; it was merely the commune under another name. Thus the communal revolution was truly *un événement national*. It was but one phase of a political and social reaction engendered by the excesses of the feudal system. As feudalism was French, so, Luchaire would apparently have us believe, was the commune. And to strengthen this argument, he adopted the concept, earlier formulated by Giry, that the commune was a member of the feudal hierarchy, a *seigneurie collective*.[2]

Mediaeval French towns, said Luchaire, fell into two primary groups: *villes franches* and *villes libres*. Between them, so far as social privilege was concerned, there was no difference. Nor was the basis of the distinction political autonomy, for many of the *villes franches* had more complete self-government than some of the *villes libres*. The mark of the really free town, whether northern commune or southern consulate, was the sworn association which underlay its constitution and gave it the legal status of a vassal. That this theory possessed indisputable charm is attested by its repetition in countless books and articles. For nearly half a century it has been constantly cited as an authoritative statement of fact. Nevertheless, as must be at once apparent, it is hard to reconcile with any explanation of urban revival as a development common to western Europe. In such a synthesis as Pirenne's it finds no place. And close analysis shows it neither consistent in structure nor intelligible in final purport. However plausible as an abstract doctrine, attempts to apply it to the interpretation of specific sources have generally led to confusion.[3]

Accordingly, before the publication of Pirenne's articles in the *Revue*

---

[1] A. Luchaire, *Les Communes Françaises* (1st ed., Paris, 1890), introductory chapters and conclusion; *Manuel des Institutions Françaises* (Paris, 1892), pp. 406–09, 430.

[2] See Appendix I.

[3] Luchaire, *Manuel*, pp. 378 ff., 393, 402; below, pp. 27 ff., 173 ff.

Historique, remarkably little had appeared in French to elucidate the problem of town development.[1] Since then the mercantile settlement theory has gradually come to dominate the field, for Viollet,[2] Halphen,[3] Prou,[4] Coville,[5] and Sée[6] have all given it their approval. On the other hand, in a general review of literature on the towns in 1903, Bourgin expressed a decided leaning toward the Maurer-Below doctrine.[7] The reason, evidently, was the prominence of agriculture in the Soissons group to which the author had been devoting his attention.[8] But, as will appear below, something still remains to be said concerning the significance of the Soissons customs,[9] and in the meantime Bourgin has published other statements of a less irreconcilable character.[10] In France, therefore, the present state of opinion is much the same as in Germany.

4. ENGLISH HISTORIANS

Turning now from the Continent to England, we encounter a number of familiar views. Again the Romanist doctrine is for a time held and

[1] An admirable beginning in this direction, presumably inspired by Réville, was made in chapter VIII of Lavisse et Rambaud, *Histoire Générale*, II (Paris, 1893), but the effect was marred by Giry's theory of the commune (see Appendix I). The same lack of cohesion appears in the chapter on the French towns by Eleanor Constance Lodge in the *C.M.H.*, V, 624 ff. Flach's brilliant description of the Roman city in Frankish Gaul (*Origines de l'Ancienne France*, II) was followed by a much less successful attempt to explain the revival of urban life. See the comments of Pirenne, (above, p. 6, n. 6), Bourgin (below, n. 7), and Ashley (below, p. 19, n. 1). More recently F. Funck-Brentano in his popular history, *Le Moyen Age* (Paris, 1922), ch. II, has gone beyond Flach in identifying *château* and *ville*, but his patriarchal-feudal theory is not to be taken seriously.

[2] P. Viollet, 'Les Communes Françaises au Moyen Age,' *Mémoires de l'Académie des Inscriptions et des Belles-Lettres*, XXXVI (Paris, 1898), 401. This sketch, it should be noted, is much superior to the more famous exposition by Luchaire. Viollet's definition of the commune is arbitrary but sensible, and his interpretation of the sources is not made to fit an *a priori* conviction.

[3] L. Halphen, Introduction to Luchaire's *Communes Françaises* (2nd ed., Paris, 1911); *L'Essor de l'Europe* (Paris, 1932), pp. 79 ff.

[4] M. Prou, 'Une Ville-Marché au XIIe Siècle,' *Mélanges d'Histoire Offerts à Henri Pirenne*, II, 379 ff.

[5] A. Coville, 'Les Villes du Moyen Age,' *Journal des Savants*, 1928, 15 ff., 72 ff.

[6] H. Sée, *Esquisse d'une Histoire Économique et Sociale de la France* (Paris, 1929), p. 92. Cf. F. Lot, *La Fin du Monde Antique et le Début du Moyen Age* (Paris 1927), pp. 423 ff.

[7] G. Bourgin, 'Les Études sur les Origines Urbaines au Moyen Age,' *Revue de Synthèse Historique*, VII (1903), 317: 'Néanmoins la théorie Maurer-Below nous paraît avoir eu cet avantage de nous rappeler que le caractère essentiel de l'économie médiévale est agricole: dissocier cette économie et la révolution communale est une erreur fondamentale de ceux-là même qui ont vu dans l'état économique de la société aux XIe et XIIe siècles la cause profonde de cette révolution.'

[8] *La Commune de Soissons et le Groupe Communale Soissonais* (Paris, 1908). This book was subjected to sharp criticism by Espinas in *Le Moyen Age*, XXII (1909), 309 ff.

[9] See below, p. 38, n. 2.

[10] 'L'Évolution des Villes,' *Scientia*, XV (1914), 1 ff. In this essay Bourgin insists upon the economic viewpoint as best providing a synthesis of mediaeval urban civilization, and seems to indicate commerce as the basis of that civilization; for the function of the town, whether an old Roman city or a later agglomeration, was 'celui d'organizer la production et la répartition.' One may also heartily agree with Bourgin's criticism of Luchaire and with his comments on the lack of synthetic study on the English towns.

then abandoned.   The mark system is well advertised, and by many made the basis of municipal history.   The gild is prominent, and to a lesser degree the commune.   The *Burg* reappears as the borough.   Some of the Continental theories, it is true, are disregarded; but the situation is from the outset complicated by attempts to evaluate the respective importance of the French and Germanic elements that merged to form the institutions known as English.

The first really judicious attempt to explain the origin of towns in England was made by the eminent William Stubbs.[1]   He, as was to be expected, rejected the Romanist doctrine and in its place, though with a caution that at times verged on contradiction, put the mark theory of Georg von Maurer.[2]   Thus, he says, in spite of the fact that the mark system cannot be historically shown ever to have existed in England, the township, the self-governing village community, represents the 'principle of the mark' and underlies all English constitutional development.   The Anglo-Saxon *burh* was 'simply a more strictly organized form of township.'   The early Germans did not settle in the Roman cities, but some of the latter continued to be used as 'fortified camps' and 'civil centres.'   'Other towns grew up round the country houses of the kings and ealdormen, round the great monasteries in which the bishops had their seats, and in such situations as were pointed out by nature as suited for trade and commerce.'   All urban variations from the normal township system were subsequent developments due to changing environment. For example, the later dominance of the gild or of its French counterpart, the sworn commune,[3] was in the nature of an encroachment upon the 'ancient rights of free inhabitants.'   The governing corporations of the thirteenth century may have evolved from gilds, but the boroughs did not.

---

[1] *Constitutional History of England* (6th ed., Oxford, 1903), I, 53 ff., 88 ff., 99 ff., 455.   The first edition was published in 1873.   In *The Saxons in England* (London, 1849), bk. II, ch. VII, Kemble had devoted some time to refuting the Romanist theory and, in spite of his devotion to the mark, had then followed Thierry in deriving the tenth-century boroughs from gilds.   To-day Kemble's discussion is of interest mainly because it shows how very little he (or his contemporaries) knew about the subject.   Nine-tenths of his account is sheer imagination.

[2] Down to the date of its publication the well known essay of Petit-Dutaillis furnishes an admirable guide on this whole question: C. Petit-Dutaillis, *Studies and Notes Supplementary to Stubbs' Constitutional History* (1st ed., Manchester, 1908), ch. VIII.   The last edition, published together with certain contributions by Georges Lefebvre, is that of 1930.   But since the pagination of the early part is the same, reference will be made merely to Petit-Dutaillis, *Studies*.

[3] Stubbs understood the commune to have been a perfected municipality or incorporated town, secured at London by insurrection (*S.C.*, p. 304).   But the commune was only 'the old English guild in a new French garb' (*Const. Hist.*, I, 459), like the former exercising usurped authority.   And yet, in another connection (*ibid.*, I, 446), Stubbs says that the acquisition of the *firma burgi* turned a township or gild into a *communio*, 'a partnership or corporate society.'

After these words from the master, it was but natural that the disciples of Stubbs should readily accept the conclusions of Below for the Continent. All English scholars, however, were not to prove so orthodox. At the same time that Maitland was being led to question the self-governing township, Keutgen's *Stadtverfassung* inspired him with a new theory for the origin of the borough.[1] So far as the township was concerned, Maitland found himself unable to accept an institution for which the entire Anglo-Saxon period afforded no evidence. The village might be a community in so far as co-operative agriculture made it so, but this, he believed, did not necessitate political organization. For the development of village governments we must look to a later period, when seignorial management and a more efficient monarchy tended to create them.[2]

As to the borough, any one familiar with the Anglo-Saxon Chronicle and the royal dooms could not fail to perceive how admirably they seemed to justify Keutgen's doctrine of the *Burgfriede*. In his account Stubbs had overlooked the fact that in the tenth century boroughs are not described as gradually evolving, but as being created. In the eye of the law the borough is a very definite thing — a royal institution endowed with official attributes. Maitland therefore adopted Keutgen's idea that the *Burg* or borough was a military foundation, either an old Roman fortress again turned to practical use or a new structure raised against the Danes. With the growth of the English kingdom, many of these boroughs became important administrative centres, but they did not govern themselves. Their reeves, courts, markets, and mints were all royal. Their walls were royal walls, the maintenance and defense of which fell upon the landholders of the surrounding shires.

Furthermore, said Maitland, this military obligation toward the shire borough helps to explain a peculiar feature of Domesday: viz., that the borough, instead of being described as land of the king or land of a baron, is normally given separate treatment at the head of the county survey. It is really no man's land, for within it are grouped holdings of many persons. A large proportion of its inhabitants and houses are said to be attached to outlying manors; and this 'tenurial heterogeneity,' Maitland contended, was a vestige of early arrangements for garrisoning the borough. The thegns of the shire, in order more easily to perform their owed service, came to keep houses and retainers within the walls. By the eleventh century, however, this original military constitution was virtually obsolete. Mercantile interests, as traders settled under the

---

[1] F. W. Maitland, 'The Origin of the Borough,' *E.H.R.*, xi (1896), 13 ff.; *Domesday Book and Beyond* (Cambridge, 1897), pp. 172 ff. Cf. Keutgen's review of Below, *E.H.R.*, viii (1893), 550 ff.

[2] *Domesday Book and Beyond*, pp. 147 ff., 340 ff.

protection of the borough's special peace, tended to become dominant. Already in Domesday a new definition is emerging: under the influence of the French *bourg*, the Latin *burgus* is beginning to mean something that is not primarily a fortress. The older concept of the borough as a royal governmental institution henceforth tends to disappear.[1]

This historical reconstruction of Maitland's — one of the most brilliant ever accomplished by that scholar — has hardly received due appreciation. Few historians accepted it without reserve, and not all who did so quite appreciated the implications of the new doctrine.[2] Most critics, including Vinogradoff, Tait, and Petit-Dutaillis, continued to prefer the older theory of Stubbs and Below — that the borough was essentially a town which had grown out of a village; that it was originally fortified as a trading centre, not that it became a trading centre after being fortified.[3] They produced no new evidence; nor did they demand any. Being unconvinced by Maitland's argument, they merely held to an earlier opinion. Even Vinogradoff's well known defense of the self-governing township was largely a reaffirmation of faith, in which deductive reasoning was invoked to make up for the lack of contemporary sources.[4]

No doubt this failure of Maitland's thesis to bring conviction was in large measure due to his invention of the garrison theory to explain the tenurial heterogeneity of the Domesday borough. For what was actually of relative insignificance almost at once became the centre of the controversy. Ballard's distortions and exaggerations only made the matter worse. And in the effort to refute them, as able a student of the early town as Mary Bateson was led into much profitless speculation, during which the really important issue of the borough's original character was forgotten.[5] Admirable work, it is true, continued to be done on the Norman borough. Charters and customals were analyzed; special topics

---

[1] Maitland thus followed Keutgen as to the origin of the borough, but did not, with him, try to reconcile that idea with Below's *Landgemeinde* theory. Furthermore, since one of his cardinal principles was not to read into a primitive record the notions of a later and much more complex civilization, he did not take for granted that the tenth-century borough was like a twelfth-century borough. Although apparently unacquainted with Rietschel's work, he really agreed with that author in deriving *Stadtfriede* from *Burgfriede* under a rapidly advancing mercantile influence. He was, of course, familiar only with Pirenne's earlier articles (*Domesday Book and Beyond*, pp. 173, 196, notes).

[2] See below, pp. 64, n. 5, 74 ff.

[3] P. Vinogradoff, *The Growth of the Manor* (London, 1905), p. 262, n. 27, and *English Society in the Eleventh Century* (Oxford, 1908), pp. 398 ff.; J. Tait, in *E.H.R.*, xii (1897), 776; Petit-Dutaillis, *Studies*, p. 75.

[4] *Growth of the Manor*, pp. 185 ff.: his argument to justify the use of late evidence is much the same as Below's (above, p. 5, n. 4).

[5] See below, pp. 81 ff.

were exhaustively treated.[1]   But since the publication of *Domesday Book and Beyond*, surprisingly little has been written on the Anglo-Saxon borough and its connection with the chartered town of the twelfth century.[2]   Hence the occasion for the present essay.

That the importance of this subject to the student of English society is almost equalled by its obscurity has been generally recognized; but to one who returns to the problem of the borough after extensive reading on the Continental town the obscurity must seem less impenetrable.   The conclusions of Pirenne and Rietschel, independently arrived at for their respective countries, immediately suggest application to England.   Their theory of urban development is a flexible theory; it is not restricted to one people or to one region.   Furthermore, it postulates a method of approach recommended alike by common sense and by correct principles of historical criticism.

As Carl Becker is fond of warning us, it is futile for the historian to attempt detachment from the world in which he lives; he can explain the past only in terms of the present.   Consequently, we must at the outset

[1] This literature will receive detailed consideration in subsequent chapters.   In the present connection it is sufficient to remark that three authors have especially contributed to our understanding of the mercantile borough: Charles Gross, in his *Gild Merchant;* Mary Bateson, in her notes on the 'Laws of Breteuil,' *E.H.R.*, xv–xvi (1900–01); and James Tait, in his series of articles that is still continuing, *E.H.R.*, xlii–xlvi (1927–32).   In general, the economic historians have added little to the elucidation of the subject.   W. J. Ashley, in his *Introduction to English Economic History and Theory*. Pt. i (10th impression, London, 1919), pp. 68 ff., devoted only a few sentences to the beginning of town life in England.   In 1896 he expressed decided skepticism as to Pirenne's thesis; but this was somewhat moderated three years later, and much of the evidence that he demanded has since been produced.   See *Surveys Historic and Economic* (London, 1900), pp. 162 ff., 238 ff.   W. Cunningham, following current interpretation of the Anglo-Saxon Chronicle, attributed the foundation of the English towns primarily to Danish influence: *The Growth of English Industry and Commerce*, i (3rd ed., Cambridge, 1896), 92 ff.   And the same idea, though somewhat more cautiously advanced, continues to appear in E. Lipson, *The Economic History of England*, i (5th ed., London, 1929), 163 ff.   Even the *Englische Wirtschaftsgeschichte* of Georg Brodnitz (Jena, 1918), which might be expected to apply more recent doctrines concerning the German *Burg*, treats the old boroughs of the tenth century and the new boroughs of the twelfth century as essentially homogeneous.

[2] For general criticism and comment, see (in addition to Petit-Dutaillis, *Studies*, ch. viii) J. Tait, 'The Study of Early Municipal History in England,' *Proceedings of the British Academy*, x (1921–23), 201 ff.   Special mention should also be made of H. W. C. Davis's remarkable paper, 'The English Borough,' in the *Quarterly Review*, ccviii (1908), 54 ff.   Although purporting to be merely a review of Mary Bateson's work on the subject, this article really sketched the whole history of the borough from the Roman to the Plantagenet age — a brief but admirably conceived synthesis which makes us regret that Davis never followed it up with research of his own.   In many respects he expressed opinions that coincide with those developed in the succeeding pages.   He portrayed the early borough as essentially military and agrarian, the twelfth-century borough as essentially mercantile; and thus was necessarily led to suggest a transitional stage dominated by the growth of commerce.   For the elaboration of this thesis, however, the materials supplied by Mary Bateson proved quite misleading.   Her insistence on commercial activity as the controlling element in the tenth-century borough threw his entire picture out of perspective, and the correction could not be made without a re-examination of the sources that Davis himself never attempted.

be careful of our definitions.   So far as the present study is concerned, we cannot take the word town with the meaning of any human settlement and hope to arrive at intelligible conclusions with regard to the mediaeval borough.   'Town' is, of course, derived from the Anglo-Saxon *tun*, which we normally translate rather as 'village.'[1]   Consciously or unconsciously, we base our usage in economics: an agricultural settlement we call a village; a larger settlement, where trade is the principal occupation, we call a town.   Which of the two was the original borough?   Or, if it was neither, precisely what was it?   These questions cannot be answered without a thorough investigation of the pertinent sources.   And if any one is inclined to condemn such an inquiry as tedious pursuit of the obvious, perusal of the literature outlined above should convince him that what he considers obvious has not seemed so to many great scholars.

Ultimately, however, good history, like good science, depends on verification.   The proponents of the mercantile settlement theory claim for it no validity as a mere proposition in logic.   Its great success on the Continent has been won as a working hypothesis that has seemed most in accord with the facts.   If its antagonists have yielded, they have done so through pressure of sound evidence.   And in the course of controversy the triumphant argument has itself been considerably amended and strengthened.[2]   As has been seen from the foregoing analysis, the doctrine of Pirenne and Rietschel tends to embrace all the really constructive criticism of Below and Keutgen.   The theory of the latter, though it does not, as he thought, explain the evolution of towns, remains a valid commentary on the tenth-century fortresses called *Burgen*, an illuminating study of a phase of legal history common to many regions.   As to the *Landgemeinde* theory, Below attributed to a commercial revival all features of the mediaeval town except the communal germ at the heart of it, but by his own admission, that reservation has lost much of its significance.   For when we discover that a town could develop equally well with or without a rural community as a nucleus, how can we avoid the

---

[1] Cf. the French *ville*, from *villa*.

[2] Much of the controversy that has raged over the origin of mediaeval towns resolves itself into a matter of definition.   Facile identification of *Burg* and *Stadt*, of *château* and *ville*, of market and mercantile settlement, has led to an appalling mass of confused historical writing.   Sombart (*Das Moderne Kapitalismus*, 2nd ed., I, 124 ff.) rightly insisted upon the fundamental distinction, for economic history, of village and town; but his own definition of the latter (p. 128) remained vague enough to embrace many kinds of settlements, and so to provoke further dispute.   Tenth-century military posts or centres of administration and official residence, though towns by Sombart's definition, might be very different from the typical town of the thirteenth century.   In expounding a theory of urban origins, the historian should not draw conclusions regarding one sort of settlement, whether or not called a town, from data presented in connection with quite another sort.   See above, p. 13, n. 2.

conclusion that the presence or absence of the village was a matter of quite secondary importance?

The extent to which the ideas of Pirenne and Rietschel have been confirmed by recent work on individual towns will be seen in the following chapter. The total effect comes as a surprise even to one familiar with the more general discussions of origins. In the light of such modern investigation fresh significance has been given to many a well known institution. And in addition a new and fascinating subject of historical research has made its appearance — the topographical study of urban development. Archaeology has been brought to supplement the meagre evidence of written sources; and with this new approach to an old subject, the town is seen to have been more sharply differentiated from other mediaeval settlements than was once suspected.[1]

Many points requiring further elucidation yet remain. Some of them will be subsequently referred to. But the applicability to England of truths already demonstrated for the Continent is indisputably a question deserving careful attention. The time has gone by when the English borough can be considered essentially an Anglo-Saxon, or even a Germanic, institution.

[1] See the essay of Seeliger, above, p. 13, n. 1, together with the examples given below, pp. 23 ff. Particularly in Germany the adoption of Rietschel's view has led to the intensive study of mediaeval town-planning and the growth of lively controversies over the application of principles thereby determined. The extent of this literature may be appreciated by examining the articles cited below, p. 33, n. 4. In this connection it should be noted that, as early as 1891, Pirenne had used a plan of Bruges to illustrate the difference between the *castrum* and the *suburbium* described by Galbert (above, p. 11, n. 1). For a recent and sympathetic review of the mercantile settlement theory in comparison with other explanations of urban development in mediaeval Europe, see J. W. Thompson, *Economic and Social History of the Middle Ages* (New York, 1928), ch. III.

II

URBAN LIBERTIES ON THE CONTINENT

1. Urban Development in Northwestern Europe

IN THE preceding chapter an effort has been made to summarize leading explanations for the growth of towns in mediaeval Europe. The result, it is hoped, has been to show that the history of the English borough is not a subject unto itself, but one which must be studied as part of a broader investigation. To understand urban liberties in England is impossible without some knowledge of urban liberties on the Continent. And thanks to the researches outlined above, the task of providing an introductory sketch of this sort is by no means formidable. Much of the work has, indeed, already been done — and done most admirably — in M. Pirenne's little book on the towns of the Middle Ages. No substitute for his synthesis is here intended; but it may be of advantage, by supplementing generalization with a few concrete examples, to provide definite materials for comparison with the English charters and customals.

This purpose of illustrating developments common to Britain and the Continent must, in the first place, govern the selection of examples. Since the student of English municipal institutions is primarily interested in the northwest of Europe, little attention need be given to problems peculiar to Mediterranean countries. The choice of towns, furthermore, is naturally limited to those whose early history, through easily available materials, is most fully known.

The ensuing discussion makes no pretension to being based on exhaustive research, but in so far as documents are cited, they have been independently analyzed and compared. In the field of archaeological investigation, to go beyond the work of the few scholars who have appreciated its importance has of course been impossible, and the lack of more complete information, particularly on the growth of French cities, has been keenly felt. Nevertheless, the mass of evidence produced by intensive study of local topography is already considerable, and from it may be drawn conclusions of prime significance for the historian of mediaeval England.

In the following pages it is therefore proposed first to consider such data as we have for the earliest period of urban growth, and then to examine prominent grants of liberties. The latter may be taken up

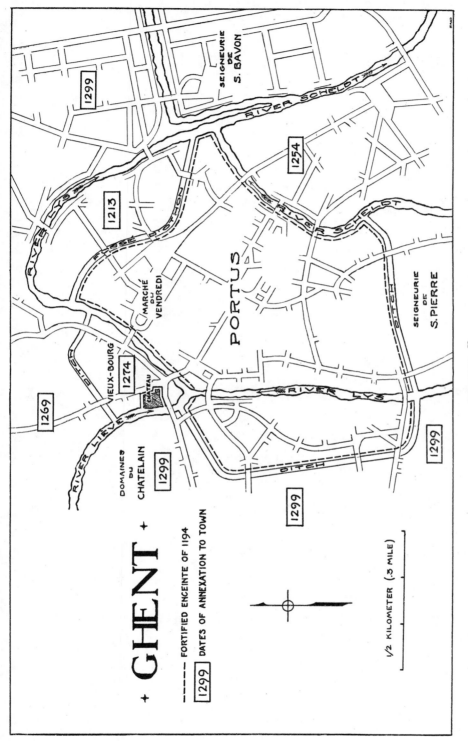

GHENT

‑‑‑‑ FORTIFIED ENCEINTE OF 1194

1299 DATES OF ANNEXATION TO TOWN

½ KILOMETER (.3 MILE)

PLATE I.

without regard to political or linguistic frontiers, for the rise of the mediaeval town was controlled neither by the traditions of peoples nor by the acts of rudimentary states. Moreover, distinctions based upon Roman foundation, princely fortification, ecclesiastical administration, and the like may, for reasons seen above, be regarded as of secondary importance. By affiliation of their charters, the towns of mediaeval Europe are found to constitute more or less distinct families, but such relationship rarely explains matters of more than local interest. The really significant lines of demarcation are those chronologically separating the towns according to their stages of progress. It is this method of classification that is here adopted; for it stresses evolutionary factors, and the topic in hand is the development of urban liberty during a formative period.

Flanders offers a definite starting-point for our investigation. There, as early as the tenth century, trading settlements had arisen alongside many of the count's castles, and the study of local topography conclusively proves that they were nuclei for the great towns of the later period. At the confluence of the Lève and the Lys, for example, the count had fortified a small area as a centre of defense against the Northmen and as administrative headquarters for the surrounding district. This was the original *castrum Gandense*, or burg of Ghent; but long before the year 1000 there had arisen across the river to the south a flourishing commercial quarter called by contemporaries the *portus*. This was the new burg, which, by the end of the twelfth century had grown to be many times the size of the old, and was itself surrounded by strong fortifications. Then, within another hundred years, the outlying feudal and monastic estates had in turn yielded to the encroaching bourgeoisie. Another wide belt of territory had been annexed, and a new ring of fortifications constructed. Even the old burg, now completely surrounded, was incorporated, and its defenses, except for the tower that still stands, were demolished.[1]

Thus emerged the town of Ghent, and in the meantime other Flemish communities had had similar development. Bruges, Arras, Saint-Omer, Lille, and Douai appeared on sites that had never before known urban settlement. In these new centres of trade and industry population grew with unprecedented rapidity. Swamp and meadow were covered with wharves and factories. Country lanes became city streets. Field and orchard were cut into building plots. What amounted to an economic

---

[1] G. Des Marez, *Propriété Foncière*, pp. 183 ff. See Plate I, based on the plan of Des Marez, facing p. 300. A rough estimate shows the Vieux-Bourg to have enclosed less than twenty-five acres; the fortified town of 1191 about two hundred acres. Cf. Pirenne's plan of Bruges in his edition of Galbert de Bruges, p. xlii.

revolution took place, and inevitably this revolution affected social conditions, legal status, and political organization. Most of our evidence with regard to such changes comes from the later charters, but on one point we already obtain definite information: an exceptional tenure was evolved to meet the demands of an exceptional situation. The bourgeois came to hold his land as freely as he held his chattels. In place of the dues and obligations of the peasant he paid only a cash rent; nor was he liable for any feudal service. When, as occurred before 1125 in certain favored localities, his rents were cancelled, he was left with a purely allodial holding; but in any case the tenure of the bourgeois set him apart as the member of a privileged community.[1]

While the commercial revival was thus creating towns *de novo* in Flanders, it was also bringing renewed life to the old Roman cities of the Rhine and Danube valleys. In some, where wide areas had originally been included and increase of population was relatively slow, the ancient fortifications continued to suffice for centuries. So at Mainz the influx of new residents, as late as 1200, seems to have resulted merely in the building over of intramural lands that earlier had reverted to vineyard and arable.[2] But on the whole it was more usual for the trading quarter to grow up outside the old *enceinte*. At Cologne, for example, the *Rheinvorstadt*, with its wharves, shops, merchants' homes, and new market, arose between the river and the original city, the walls of which, before 1000, had been extended on either flank. Early in the twelfth century three other extensive suburbs were enclosed, practically doubling the size of the town. And by 1200 an entirely new wall had been erected to include all the older districts and much besides.[3] To explain these facts we have Cologne's recognized position as the foremost trading centre on the Rhine. Imperial edicts forbade that goods from west, east, or north should be carried past the city. Cologne measures were made the official German standard. By 1100 the merchants of Cologne had become famous throughout northern Europe, where they were rivalled only by those of Flanders; organized in a powerful gild, they constituted the heart of a highly privileged community.[4]

Among the other ancient cities of Germany there was none that ap-

[1] Des Marez, pp. 6 ff., 61 ff.; Pirenne, *Villes du Moyen Age*, chs. III, VI, and works there cited. See above, p. 12.

[2] Rietschel, *Die Civitas auf Deutschem Boden*, p. 63; Gerlach, *Entstehungszeit der Städtebefestigungen*, p. 41.

[3] The fundamental work for the topographical study of Cologne is H. Keussen, *Topographie der Stadt Köln im Mittelalter* (Bonn, 1910), admirably continued and developed by R. Koebner, *Die Anfänge des Gemeinwesens der Stadt Köln* (Bonn, 1922). See Plate II, based on Keussen, frontispiece.

[4] Koebner, pp. 185 ff.

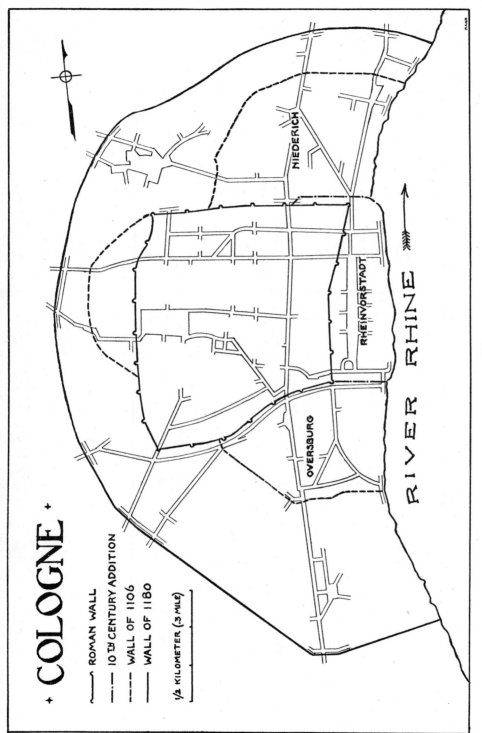

⁺ COLOGNE ⁺

ROMAN WALL
10ᵀᴴ CENTURY ADDITION
WALL OF 1106
WALL OF 1180

½ KILOMETER (.3 MILE)

NIEDERICH

RHEINVORSTADT

OVERSBURG

RIVER RHINE

PLATE II.

proached Cologne in size and prosperity during the twelfth century, but many seem to have developed in the same way. At Constance, for example, the episcopal *civitas* of the tenth century — an extension of the Roman *castrum* — enclosed about ten acres. But this was not the nucleus of the mediaeval town, which grew rather from the annexed trading quarter, or *forum*. By the end of the eleventh century the latter had come to include some eighty acres and its inhabitants enjoyed a special law that was already well known. Within another two hundred years it had spread over a total of 216 acres and, as an entirely new system of walls was built, the ancient *Bischofsburg* disappeared from view.[1]

Meanwhile, to the eastward of the Rhine, mercantile settlements had also developed alongside various royal and ecclesiastical fortresses. As early as 965, according to a grant to the local church, a group of Jews and other traders were living at Magdeburg, and ten years later such *mercatores* received a formal grant of privileges from Otto I. By 1038 the law of the merchants of Magdeburg was famous enough to be given to those of Quedlinburg.[2] And by that time, too, similar colonies had arisen at Merseburg, Naumburg, Halberstadt, Bremen, and Goslar. These communities, and many others which soon appeared in central Germany, have all been carefully studied. In each case the extent of the original settlement is well known and its direct connection with the twelfth-century town has been clearly demonstrated.[3]

In France, unfortunately, the wealth of material that exists for topographical study of the mediaeval city has lain practically untouched. Even the best monographs of the older generation failed to appreciate

---

[1] K. Beyerle and A. Maurer, *Konstanzer Häuserbuch* (Heidelberg, 1908), ii, 26 ff., 158 ff., 183 ff. This second volume, by K. Beyerle, is a model, not only of sumptuous book-making, but of sound historical research — the first detailed study of mediaeval urban topography according to the principles of Rietschel, 'der gründlichste Kenner der älteren deutschen Stadtgeschichte' (p. 163). See below, p. 33.

[2] F. Keutgen, *Urkunden zur Städtischen Verfassungsgeschichte* (Berlin, 1901), pp. 43, 47.

[3] Rietschel, *Markt und Stadt*, pp. 50 ff.; Koehne, in *Historische Zeitschrift*, cxxxiii, 14; Gerlach, *op. cit.*, pp. 57 ff., 61 ff. And see particularly Gerlach's interesting series of plans, which, though crude, admirably serve to illustrate the developments described in the text. Gerlach, as remarked above (p. 12), corrected Rietschel's statements in many respects. For one thing, he pointed out that it is wrong to suppose that there were no mercantile settlements inside the walls of the ancient cities and *Burgen*. The expansion of each place depended on its own peculiar topography. What was true of a tiny *castellum* like Constance or Basel would not apply to a huge *civitas* like Trier. For the same reason we should not expect exactly uniform development among the royal and episcopal fortifications. One of the *Burgen* of Henry the Fowler, Bodfeld, seems to have enclosed only about one acre; but, among the more important fortresses, Magdeburg was probably typical in size. There the first wall, built about the cathedral and the old market, contained an area 400 x 275 meters, i.e., some 27 acres. By the early eleventh century, however, Magdeburg had so increased as to require a new *enceinte*, about five times the size of the old (Gerlach, *op. cit.*, pp. 36, 38, 62, and plan, p. 78). On the persistence of markets and mints in Roman cities, see Rietschel, *op. cit.*, ch. i.

the importance of archaeological evidence for the problem of urban expansion.   Nevertheless, it is well known that in general the cities of Gaul underwent the same mutations as those of Germany.   By the tenth and eleventh centuries we hear of many new commercial settlements, usually outside the Roman walls.   We know that many of these revived French cities rapidly outgrew their ancient defenses.[1]   And in the case of the most famous of all, we have a brilliant study that makes up for the neglect of many authors.

Louis Halphen has graphically shown how Paris in the ninth century was virtually restricted to the original *cité*, the small island defended by Roman walls.   Thither fled for refuge what was left of a population that had once extended far over the southern bank of the Seine.   That now became as desolate as the one to the north, where great marshes reached to the heights of Montmartre.   But by the eleventh century a change was perceptible: a commercial settlement, centering in a new market, had grown up on the right bank and had been surrounded by a palisade and a ditch.   The churches that owned the swampy shore abandoned pasturage for the real-estate business.   Their lands were drained, cut into plots, and sold to bourgeois.   To the *cité* was thus added the *ville*.   And to these two the rising university brought the Latin Quarter, with the growth of which prosperity returned to the left bank.   Henceforth the great monastic establishments of that region were rapidly encroached on by an urban population.   Nevertheless, when Philip Augustus authorized his great new wall, little was enclosed to the south.   The bulk of Paris lay north of what remained 'the city' only by courtesy.[2]

With these instances before us, the history of many another town seems quite intelligible, although its topographical development may never have been adequately treated.   Thus at Cambrai in the tenth century we hear of a small *Bischofsburg* with a stockaded faubourg outside.   By 1070 the latter had grown prosperous enough to be walled with stone, and it was from this quarter that famous disturbances arose within the next few

---

[1] Pirenne, *Villes du Moyen Age*, chs. III, VI; P. Rolland, 'Une Étape de la Vie Communale de Tournai,' *Revue Historique de Droit Français et Étranger*, 1925, 411 ff.   Cf. the article of F. Beyerle, cited above, p. 13, n. 2.   It is characteristic of such older studies as W. Reinecke, *Geschichte der Stadt Cambrai* (Marburg, 1896), and L. H. Labande, *Histoire de Beauvais et de ses Institutions Communales* (Paris, 1890), that they were not accompanied by charts to make clear the topographical development of the cities.   Nor have later historians made good the defect.   For the southern cities even good monographs of the old type are generally lacking.   But for one instance of a commercial *faubourg* outside Roman walls, see C. Bémont, 'Les Institutions Municipales de Bordeaux au Moyen Age,' *Revue Historique*, CXXIII (1916), pp. 1 ff., and cf. the plates in C. Jullian, *Histoire de Bordeaux* (Bordeaux, 1895), pp. 87, 140.   An excellent basis for further research on the mediaeval French cities is provided by A. Blanchet, *Les Enceintes Romaines de la Gaule* (Paris, 1907).

[2] L. Halphen, *Paris sous les Premiers Capétiens* (Paris, 1909), pp. 5 ff.   The text is accompanied by splendid plans in a separate atlas.

years. The ecclesiastical chronicler tells how in 1076 the populace, led by well-to-do merchants, rose in revolt and swore a commune, and how this first insurrection was quickly put down by the bishop. Later, however, another conspiracy was more successful; the townsmen forced the issuance of a communal charter, which was quashed only when, in 1106, the emperor intervened on the side of the church. Many more years passed and much more trouble ensued before the city obtained definite recognition of its liberties.[1]

These sources introduce us, for the first time in a northern country, to the urban commune — the subject of many well known essays, to which some attention has been given in the preceding pages.[2] The familiar arguments of the distinguished authors need not again detain us. It will be sufficient to say that, if we wish to understand the nature of the commune during the formative period, we must forget the juristic definitions of a later age and determine what the word meant to contemporaries. Nor is the task a formidable one. The relevant materials are plentiful, and on the whole they give us clear information. Like the other famous term *universitas*, the Latin equivalent of the English 'commune' bore two sets of interpretations: one general and the other specific. On the one hand, *communa, communia,* and *communio* were often interchangeable with *communitas*. On the other hand, from the eleventh century onward, the same words were increasingly given the special meaning, more or less sinister, of a sworn association. As applied to the Peace of God, such usage was of course without evil implication, but when employed by clerical annalists to refer to combinations against authority, *communa* and its variants became synonymous with *coniuratio* or *conspiratio;* and this was especially true in the case of such insurrections as occurred at Cambrai.[3]

Following the example set in that city, uprisings broke out in many towns of Picardy, including Saint-Quentin, Amiens, Laon, and Beauvais. And wherever it is heard of during this early period, the commune appears as the product of opposition.[4] Originally it was not a set of fran-

---

[1] Reinecke, *op. cit.,* pp. 72, 82, 100 ff.

[2] Above, pp. 14 ff., Appendix I.

[3] The passages are too familiar to need detailed citation. Examples of all the usages mentioned are given by Du Cange, and the most important of the sources on the northern French commune are quoted by K. Hegel, *Städte und Gilden der Germanischen Völker im Mittelalter* (Leipzig, 1891), II, 30 ff.

[4] See particularly the lucid exposition by Pirenne in *C.M.H.,* VI, 518 ff. The same truth seems to hold good for the urban *coniurationes* of Italy, which began in the first half of the eleventh century: C. W. Previté-Orton, in *C.M.H.,* V, ch. V, and authorities there cited. In Germany, with the possible exception of the *coniuratio pro libertate* at Cologne in 1112 (see below, p. 42), a successful revolutionary commune is not heard of in the twelfth century. The towns there were still too weak

chises, but a means of obtaining them. Failing to secure desired reforms by peaceful agitation, the townsmen at some favorable opportunity inaugurated a revolutionary movement to resist oppression. By solemn oath each member swore mutual aid in the common cause, obedience to the elected leaders, and vengeance against all enemies.[1] Sometimes the revolts failed and sometimes they succeeded. In the latter case the concessions which formed the basis of the new régime were generally set down in a formal charter and the communal organization became more or less permanent. To Guibert de Nogent and writers of his class the chief object of such infamous conspiracies was to free serfs and rob the church of its revenues; but the triumphant commune usually resulted in much more than the emancipation of the rebellious bourgeois. Against such implacable hostility as ecclesiastical lords often displayed, half-way measures were of no avail. The insurrectionaries secured autonomy or nothing.

Accordingly, by the later twelfth century, the word commune had acquired still another meaning, that of a self-governing town; and as such many a commune was created out-of-hand by a foundation charter. But even in this respect there was no uniformity. Scores of towns secured the widest of municipal privileges through the liberality, indifference, or powerlessness of their rulers, and in them the sworn association, if it existed at all, played a minor rôle.[2] Not infrequently towns that from the outset had come to be styled communes enjoyed less political authority than others which had never borne the name.[3] Nor can any valid distinction between the two groups be drawn on the basis of theoretic tenure. As has been seen, the definition of commune by Giry and Luchaire had only the slightest basis in fact, and its application has resulted in much confusion. For so long as the rise of the French towns is regarded as primarily a 'communal revolution,' and this is interpreted in terms of legalistic feudalism, more fundamental aspects of social development are inevitably obscured. Historically the communes constituted no distinct group apart from other towns. Rightly to classify the

---

to force more than meagre concessions from the great bishops, who were normally supported by the emperors: F. Knöpp, *Die Stellung Friedrichs II und seiner Beiden Söhne zu den Deutschen Städten* (Berlin, 1928), pp. 1 ff.

[1] See the charters cited below, pp. 37 ff.

[2] In the south of France most of the cities were controlled by lay princes, who generally favored, or at least did not resist, the progress of the bourgeoisie. The great 'consulates' of that region normally did not arise from revolutionary communes: Viollet, 'Les Communes Françaises,' *Mémoires de l'Académie des Inscriptions*, xxxvi, 401; E. C. Lodge, in *C.M.H.*, v, 640; J. A. Brutails, *Essai sur la Condition des Populations Rurales du Roussillon au Moyen Age* (Paris, 1891), p. 260.

[3] This fact was admitted by Luchaire; see Appendix I, below, p. 218.

municipalities of mediaeval Europe, we must ignore accidental titles and examine actual privileges.

2. Elementary Liberties

In this undertaking what might seem the logical point of departure would be the liberties of the oldest communities, but such procedure is hindered by the paucity of our written evidence. Until municipal charters come to abound, we have only the vague statements of chroniclers, eked out by a few incidental references in official documents. And even municipal charters were likely to specify matters of exceptional usage or recent concession, rather than the mass of long established custom that every one took for granted. The older and more prosperous the community, the less would be the demand for written guarantees. Some of the greatest towns on the Continent flourished for centuries with no charters at all. Consequently, if we wish to obtain a statement of fundamental urban liberties, such as the more ancient towns claimed by prescription, we must turn to the charter of a *ville neuve*.

For instance, we have the famous grant by Louis VI to Lorris, establishing privileges that were later extended to scores of little communities throughout the royal demesne and adjacent regions.[1] First of all, says the king, the man who elects to reside at Lorris is to pay only six *deniers* for his house and *arpent* of land. If he lives there peaceably for a year and a day, he is henceforth free and cannot be claimed by a previous master. He is to be quit of all *taille* and forced exactions; of all military service, save for one day within the immediate vicinity; of all watching service and *corvées*, except that those men who own horses and carts have to carry the king's wine once a year to Orleans. Whenever he pleases, the man of Lorris can sell his possessions and go elsewhere. He cannot be tried outside the town, and there only according to specified rules of procedure. Fines and punishments are strictly limited. No one shall be molested while coming to or going from the market of Lorris, unless he has committed some offense on the same day. Various restrictions of tolls, customs, and other dues are established. Purveyance is prohibited. There is to be no obligatory granting of credit, except that the king and queen are to be given two weeks' time to pay for their food.

The features of this charter are too familiar to need detailed comment. Lorris was a very small town, with distinctly second-rate liberties. It had no self-government; all political powers were reserved to the king and

[1] M. Prou, *Les Coutumes de Lorris et leur Propagation aux XIIe et XIIIe Siècles* (Paris, 1884). It is a striking tribute to Prou's scholarship that his little book, written nearly half a century ago, may still be taken as authoritative in practically every detail. The loss of such a master is keenly felt by all students of mediaeval life and institutions.

his ministers. And yet the privileged condition of its inhabitants was clearly marked. By contrast with the average peasant the man of Lorris was a very superior person.[1] Whatever he earned above specified obligations known in advance was his own. He was economically and legally free. He was far removed from the arbitrary régime of domanial exploitation. His tenure and status were typically bourgeois. For although the charter of Lorris contemplated the possibility of agricultural pursuits, its chief concern was clearly the encouragement of a trading population. The normal holding was not a field, but a building plot. The privileges of the residents were essentially such as were everywhere demanded as a minimum by commercial settlers. It was for this reason that the customs of Lorris proved so remarkably popular during the ensuing centuries.

A very similar set of customs, but with some details more sharply drawn, was that given to Verneuil by Henry I of Normandy and England.[2] As reported by his grandson, the liberties of Verneuil provide that each burgess shall receive three acres of land and a garden, for which, no matter how many houses he puts up, he shall pay twelve *deniers* yearly, and so enjoy the privilege of buying and selling within the town. As entrance money he further pays six *deniers* to the royal *prévôt* and one to the latter's assistant. He is also responsible for the annual sum of four *deniers* toward upkeep of the watch, but all further expense of walls, gates and bridges is to be borne by the king. Unless the king personally commands the army, the burgess owes no *chevauchée*. He may not be ordered on errands or other royal business save for the king's own service. Nothing is said of the royal *taille*, which we know from other sources was regularly paid by non-nobles everywhere in the duchy, but forced credit is prohibited, even for the benefit of the king himself.

During the first three years, furthermore, the men of Verneuil are to be quit of all customs throughout Henry's dominions, and from certain specified customs permanently. The king reserves tolls on livestock, wine, salt, grain, fish, leather, cloth, etc., but guarantees to each resident free-

---

[1] So far as legal status was concerned, the bourgeois closely resembled the *hôte*, or agricultural colonist. In fact, there could have been very little difference, except possibly for the wall, between a specially enfranchised village like Torfou and a small town like Lorris: A. Luchaire, *Louis VI le Gros* (Paris, 1890), p. 341; C. Stephenson, in *Revue Belge de Philologie et d'Histoire*, v, 820 ff.; Halphen, *L'Essor de l'Europe*, pp. 91 ff.

[2] *Ordonnances des Rois de France* (Paris, 1723 ff.), iv, 638; appended to a grant of the liberties of Verneuil by Henry II to Pontorson. In the document Verneuil is called *castellum* — showing that occasionally *château* was employed, like *Burg* in Germany or *bastide* in southern France, to mean a fortified town. The commoner usage in Normandy, however, was *bourg*. See R. Génestal, *La Tenure en Bourgage* (Paris, 1900), pp. 209, 225 ff.; H. Legras, *Le Bourgage de Caen* (Paris, 1911), pp. 39 ff.; above, pp. 11–12.

dom from custom for whatever he personally needs as clothing, food, or drink. The milling and baking industries, like those of brewing and wine-making, are open to private enterprise on payment of specified dues and submission to certain regulations. Like other political powers, justice remains in the king's hands, being administered by his *prévôt;* but all burgesses are guaranteed protection in the royal court and, except when pleas are carried to the king in person, trials are to be held in the town. Lawful procedure is carefully safeguarded. Elaborate articles limit the fines and punishments that can be inflicted in certain cases, prescribe methods for the collection of debts, restrict appeals to combat, and make provision for the dozen other judicial matters considered important by an urban population.

Thanks to its greater detail, this description of the liberties of Verneuil brings into clear relief the policy of the grantor. Henry I obviously desired to see a thriving town adjoining his castle. To encourage immigration, rent was placed at a nominal figure and the advantages of burgage tenure promised all comers. The land itself would thus bring Henry very little, for the benefit of unearned increment would go, not to him, but to the men who held of him at a fixed rate. And since ordinary seignorial exploitation was renounced from the outset, it is clear that the proceeds which the king hoped to obtain were chiefly indirect revenues arising from trade—tolls in the local market, customs on imports, dues from crafts, and the like. Besides, increase of population would result in greater profits of justice, enhanced taxes, and opportunities for the sale of additional privileges.

Plenty of other examples could be cited from northern France, but let us rather turn to one from the Midi. It appears that chronic trouble had existed for a long time between the abbot of Saint-Théodard and the men of Montauriol, the *bourg* that had grown up on the Tarn alongside the abbey walls. As a consequence, Alphonse, count of Toulouse, offered a section of his own land immediately adjoining the *bourg* as a new site for settlement. This he named Montauban, and to assure the satisfaction of the transferred population, issued to them in 1144 a formal charter of liberties.[1] To secure the advantage of having the town under his own jurisdiction, Alphonse was thus willing, not only to grant what the abbey had stubbornly refused, but also to compensate the latter by the cession of additional territory.

As to the liberties established, they are remarkably like those of Verneuil. Every settler is guaranteed freedom from claims of outside lords. Rent for a building plot is fixed at twelve *deniers*, and only small pay-

---

[1] Devals Aîné, *Histoire de Montauban* (Montauban, 1855), I, 407.

ments are reserved for recognition of alienation. The count also is to
receive specified customs from imported wheat, salt, and wine; tolls from
the sale of livestock, hides, and leather; and regular sums from all butch-
ers, bakers, millers, smiths, and cordwainers. The count may summon
the residents for military service at his pleasure, but has no power of
requisitioning supplies; when he visits the town he is to pay for all necessities. He also retains control of justice, but except for the most serious
crimes, can take only restricted fines. Finally, although the government
of the town rests with the count, he shows himself anxious from the outset
to secure the co-operation and aid of his bourgeois. The latter are to
build a bridge over the river, and when it has been completed, the count
is to determine its customs by consultation with six townsmen of the
better sort.

Thus began the famous town of Montauban, which flourished exceedingly and by the end of the century was being administered by elected
capitouls.[1] The count's decision had been amply justified. And inevitably, as the success of a few such experiments became known, the example
proved contagious. Liberties that had shown themselves attractive in
one place were extended to scores of others. To the eyes of the ambitious
prince every village on a good highroad or waterway became a potential
metropolis, and new sites were constantly opened for settlement. By the
middle of the thirteenth century a veritable craze for urban development
had spread to every corner of France. The country became dotted with
little towns or would-be towns, all of which were planned after very much
the same pattern. What is true for the northern *villes neuves* applies
equally well to the southern *bastides*, as the most cursory examination of
their charters will prove.[2] They differed in no essential respect from the
communities already studied. Nor did the motives of the founders vary.
Underlying the competition was business enterprise only slightly tinged
with altruism. For unquestionably the original source of inspiration
was the new wealth that reviving commerce brought to the fortunate
lords of the oldest mercantile centres.

In Germany clear evidence of such a policy comes from a remarkably
early period. In 1075 the abbot of Reichenau, in deliberate imitation of
the Rhine cities, tried to turn his village of Allensbach into a trading

---

[1] *Ibid.*, p. 415; customs confirmed by the count in 1195. It seems altogether probable that the ten
capitouls of Montauban originated as a group of leading bourgeois who represented the community
in organizing the new town and making the necessary guarantees to the count. It was presumably
such a group who financed the undertaking and who would recoup themselves by pre-emption on
real estate and business opportunities. This question has recently occasioned much discussion
among German scholars; see below, p. 33, n. 4.

[2] Enumerated and analyzed in M. A. Curie Seimbres, *Essai sur les Villes Fondées dans le Sud-Ouest
de la France aux XIIIe et XIVe Siècles sous le Nom Générique de Bastides* (Toulouse, 1880).

town. Taking advantage of an imperial act that his predecessors had neglected to use, he now proclaimed a *forum* and decreed that the villeins of Allensbach should have the power of engaging in trade, so that they and their heirs might be merchants and enjoy the law of the merchants of Constance and Basel, being henceforth liable only for the services rendered by the latter to their respective bishops.[1] But this somewhat naïve promulgation had no effect. · Allensbach remained exactly what it had been — a simple village. Nor was a similar experiment at Radolfzell by a later abbot much more successful.[2] *Ius fori* was established according to the usages of Constance, with free tenure of land *in allodio;* but no dense population appeared. Radolfzell was not large enough to fortify until the later thirteenth century.

It was thus left for Conrad of Zähringen to achieve the first great success in urban colonization beyond the Rhine; for as a result of his efforts, the town of Freiburg im Breisgau recently celebrated the eight-hundredth anniversary of its foundation. It was on waste land adjoining one of his castles that in 1120 Conrad set up a *forum*, having called together and organized under oath, he says, distinguished traders from the neighboring regions.[3] Each of them is to have a plot measuring 50 by 100 feet and is to pay only one *solidus* as annual rent. The duke guarantees peace and protection to all settlers. They are to be subject only to the law of merchants, particularly the law enjoyed by the merchants of Cologne. Specifically, they are to hold their lands by hereditary right, with the privilege of free sale and devise. They are to be exempt from all forced entertainment, from all tolls throughout the duke's dominions, and from all *taille* or aid, except only for a lawful military expedition. They are to share in the free use of pasture, forest, and river. The duke will appoint no *Vogt* or priest save such as his merchants shall elect.[4] Finally,

---

[1] Keutgen, *Urkunden*, p. 61; Rietschel, *Markt und Stadt*, p. 144.

[2] Keutgen, *Urkunden*, p. 62; Rietschel, *Markt und Stadt*, p. 110; K. Beyerle, 'Das Radolfzeller Marktrecht,' *Schriften des Vereins für Geschichte des Bodensees*, xxx (1901), 3 ff.

[3] Keutgen, *Urkunden*, p. 117; but see the revisions of the text made by F. Beyerle, *Untersuchungen zur Geschichte des Älteren Stadtrechts von Freiburg im Breisgau* (Heidelberg, 1910), pp. 75 ff. Beyerle gives the best comment on the articles of the charter; but cf. G. von Below, *Deutsche Städtegründungen im Mittelalter mit Besonderem Hinblick auf Freiburg im Breisgau* (Freiburg im Breisgau, 1920).

[4] Since the *advocatus* of this document corresponds to the *villicus* of the charters based on it, the passage would seem to mean that the town could elect its own chief magistrate — a most extraordinary privilege for this period. But we also find associated in the government from an early time a group of *coniuratores fori*. This phrase in the original charter refers merely to the *mercatores* who have sworn the liberties of the *forum* (cf. *iurati* as often used to designate the citizens of the commune). The twenty-four *coniuratores* of the additions to the *Stradtrecht* are thus the ordinary group of selectmen, who sooner or later emerge in so many mediaeval towns. Beyerle argues that these twenty-four, who came to be called consuls in the thirteenth century, must have originated as a body of *Unternehmer* who joined Conrad in founding the town. This theory may at once be recognized as

it is provided that the latter shall swear, along with the ducal *minis-teriales*, to preserve and defend the foregoing settlement. And the duke pledges himself to the same engagement by a solemn handclasp.

Because of the fact that so many of the great German towns were later creations of the same sort, the example set by Freiburg is of peculiar significance. From the outset the mercantile character of the establishment was definitely recognized. It began as a *forum* settled by *merca-tores;* for the term *burgenses* came into use only at a later time — presumably after some sort of fortifications had been erected. Nevertheless, the special privilege of the inhabitants did not depend on such technicalities. It dated from the earliest ducal proclamation. The very name of the place advertised it as a free town, and the freedom of its inhabitants lay in their exemption from the ordinary law of the countryside and their subjection to the exceptional law of trading communities.

The origin of German *Stadtrecht* is thus as obvious as its basic similarity to bourgeois custom throughout France. Examination of additional charters would make this fundamental point no clearer; so we may leave the *villes neuves* and see how, while they were being founded, municipal institutions had developed in the older towns.

3. Advanced Liberties

In Flanders the accident of a disputed succession to the countship in 1127 gave the towns what seem to have been their first elaborate charters. Most of these documents were subsequently lost, but we are fortunate in having both original copies of William Clito's grant to Saint-Omer, which thus stands as our most important source for the early municipal history of the county.[1] On the petition of his burgesses, says the would-be count, he confirms their laws and customs. The commune which they have sworn is to remain unchallenged, and all citizens, as his own men, are guaranteed peace and justice according to the right judgment of their *échevins*. And the latter shall enjoy whatever liberty is best enjoyed by *échevins* throughout the land of Flanders. As established under Count Charles, all trials are to be held within the town — in three specified cases before the clergy, in others before the count's *prévôt*. Moreover,

---

founded in probability, but it should not be made too arbitrary. We may admit that the affairs of the community had from the outset been directed by an influential group without committing ourselves to the belief that it had always contained just twenty-four men. Whatever the explanation, it should fit the towns of other countries as well as of Germany; cf. Montauban (above, p. 32) and Ipswich (below, p. 175). On this question see also F. Rörig, *Hansische Beiträge zur Deutschen Wirtschaftsgeschichte* (Breslau, 1928), especially chs I, II, VIII; K. Frölich, in *Zeitschrift des Vereins für Lübeckische Geschichte und Alterumskunde*, XXII (1925), pp. 381 ff.; Koebner, *Köln*, pp. 523 ff.; W. Gerlach, in *Historische Vierteljahrschrift*, XIX (1919–20), 331 ff.

[1] A. Giry, *Histoire de la Ville de Saint-Omer* (Paris, 1877). p. 371.

all suits arising in any *forum* of Flanders are to be settled by the *échevins* without recourse to combat. Should any outsider injure a man of Saint-Omer and, on summons by the *châtelain*, refuse justice within three days, the burgesses may avenge their brother with impunity. They may destroy the culprit's house or slay him; and if they take him, he shall pay for the wrong — *oculum pro oculo, dentem pro dente, caput pro capite.*

Furthermore, William confirms the burgesses' ancient pasture rights and their ancient exemption from military service, except to defend the county of Flanders. They are to be free of *chevage* and *avouéries;* of unjust exactions by the castle garrison; and, 'like the freer burgesses of Flanders,' of all *scot* and *taille*.[1] Members of the gild are exempted from various tolls and the count promises to secure them, if he can, similar liberty in Normandy, England, and Boulogne. Lastly, in compensation for the damage which they have suffered, and in aid of their gild, William gives the townsmen his mint of Saint-Omer, worth annually thirty *livres*. This concession, it is true, was relinquished when Thierry secured the county in the following year, but at that time the burgesses were allowed to farm their own tolls at a rent of one hundred *sous*.[2]

If now we compare this charter with that, for example, of Lorris, they are seen to have some common features. Restriction of military service, abolition of *taille*, promises of protection, and the like are found in both. But the charter of Saint-Omer contains no explicit guarantee of personal liberty or of free urban tenure at a fixed rent. It passes in silence, as being too well established to need confirmation, such elementary features of bourgeois status as were of primary importance for the new town. On the other hand, the men of the older community are shown in possession of three great privileges utterly lacked by those of Lorris: they have a sworn commune; they have a gild merchant; and they have their own board of *échevins*.

So far as the first of these matters is concerned, it would seem to have been neither ancient nor fundamental. There is no evidence for believing that the sworn association had been commonly resorted to by the Flemish towns against their count; while there are many indications that the latter had from the outset favored urban development. The 'commune' of Saint-Omer would therefore appear to have been a product of the recent disturbances — a step taken, under threat of civil war and foreign intervention, to defend the local liberties.[3] In the gild merchant, on the

---

[1] See C. Stephenson, 'The Origin and Nature of the *Taille*,' *Revue Belge de Philologie et d'Histoire*, v (1926), 844.

[2] Giry, *op. cit.*, p. 376.

[3] Pirenne, 'La Question des Jurés dans les Villes Flamandes,' *Revue Belge de Philologie et d'Histoire*, v (1926), 417. See also Appendix I, below, p. 215.

other hand, we undoubtedly encounter an ancient organization, one that had grown up with the community. Essentially a union of prominent merchants, the gild was mainly concerned with matters of business, but was naturally able and willing also to advance the interests of the town at large.[1] In the campaign for social and political privilege we may suspect that gildsmen had always been prominent. At any rate, that was plainly the situation in the early twelfth century.

Our oldest extant gild-ordinances, which by remarkable coincidence also come from Saint-Omer, show the association still voluntary about 1100.[2] The local trader did not have to join the gild; but if he did, he secured increased protection and improved opportunities for profit. Regular meetings were held under elected officers in the gild-hall — some for business, others primarily convivial. Formal wine-drinkings, from which no member might absent himself without good excuse, were paid for by special dues. And whatever was left over, according to the ordinances, was to be devoted to charity or to improve the streets and walls of the town. This same intimate connection between gild and municipality, it should be noted, is emphasized by the charter of 1127, which grants the count's mint to the burgesses for the benefit of their gild. And the other provision, granting freedom from certain tolls to members of the gild, indicates how an association, originally private and voluntary, tended to become an official body endowed with monopolistic franchises.[3]

As to the nature of the first urban constitutions in Flanders, the charter of Saint-Omer again gives us invaluable information. It guarantees to the citizens justice according to the judgment of their *échevins* — the magistrates who, sooner or later, are found at the head of municipal governments throughout the county. Since the ninth century men called *scabini* had been attached to ordinary courts of justice in a large section of the Carolingian Empire. Installed under royal officials, they constituted permanent boards of judgment-finders, and as such had become part of the regular judicial machinery in countless *seigneuries*. In Flanders, specifically, they were earlier connected with territorial courts that met in the count's castles.[4]

So long as the old military burg was not distinguished from the later mercantile burg, it was thus natural to believe that municipal *échevins*

---

[1] Pirenne, *Villes du Moyen Age*, pp. 164 ff.; and in *Revue Historique*, LVII (1895), pp. 82 ff.; H. Van der Linden, *Les Gildes Marchandes dans les Pays-Bas au Moyen Age* (Ghent, 1890).

[2] G. Espinas and H. Pirenne, 'Les Coutumes de la Gilde Marchande de Saint-Omer,' *Le Moyen Age*, XIV (1901), 189 ff.

[3] See also Thierry's grant to the burgesses of Saint-Omer of the land on which the gild hall stands, to be used for trade and as headquarters of the municipal government — Giry, *op. cit.*, p. 378.

[4] Pirenne, 'Les Villes Flamandes avant le XIIe Siècle,' *Annales de l'Est et du Nord*, I (1905), 31 ff.; M. Blommaert, *Les Châtelains de Flandre* (Ghent, 1915), pp. 23, 40, 65, 200, 228.

could be traced back into the Carolingian age.[1] But M. Pirenne has
shown that separate *échevinages* for the towns were new in the twelfth
century; that the office appeared only when the greater trading communities had been set apart from the ordinary territorial system and
placed under their own elected magistrates. The latter, normally twelve
in number, constituted a commission to govern the town, combining in
their hands all political functions — judicial, financial, and executive.[2]
On this essentially simple basis was eventually erected the more elaborate
organization of the thirteenth and succeeding centuries. And underlying
this constitutional evolution was no set of juristic principles. It was
controlled, not by tradition, but by actual needs and practical experimentation.

Turning next to the great episcopal towns, we are again handicapped
by lack of detailed sources for the formative period. The history of the
first commune, that of Cambrai, is known in outline, but its earliest extant charter is that of the year 1184. Among earlier examples perhaps
the best is the grant to Beauvais, which was issued by Louis VI to end
long continued trouble between the bishop and his bourgeois.[3] According to this act, all inhabitants of the city, on whosesoever land they reside,
are, under penalty of body and property, to swear the commune, obliging
themselves to aid each other in all just ways and to obey the decisions
of their constituted authorities. The latter are the peers of the commune
and are to be put on oath not to exile or to harm any one through love
or hate, but to render right judgment. Should any man who has sworn
the commune suffer an injury, the culprit is, if possible, to be brought to
trial before the peers. But if he takes refuge with some protector, the
commune shall try to obtain satisfaction from the latter. Finally, on
failure of that attempt, all men of the commune shall join in gaining re-
venge from the body and possessions of the accused or of his defenders.
Similarly, and by the same means, justice is assured to any outside merchant who comes to Beauvais. Careful provisions are to be taken for the
exclusion of the commune's enemies from the city and for the punishment
of any who may negotiate with them or give them credit. Other articles

[1] Under the influence of the famous *Landgemeinde* theory, L. Vanderkindere extended this idea to
derive the municipal magistracies of the Middle Ages from those of primitive rural communes;
Bulletin de l'Académie Royale de Belgique, Classe des Lettres, 3e Série, XLII (1905), 749 ff.; *Annales
de l'Est et du Nord*, I (1905), 321 ff. But the great Flemish towns had as magistrates only *échevins*,
rather than *jurés;* and the latter seem to have originated as revolutionary leaders in the communes
of Picardy. See the article of Pirenne cited above, p. 35., n. 3.

[2] Pirenne, *op. cit.*, and *Villes du Moyen Age*, pp. 179 ff. The *échevinage* of Arras appears entirely
bourgeois as early as 1111.

[3] Labande, *Beauvais*, p. 267; A. Giry, *Documents sur les Rélations de la Royauté avec les Villes en
France de 1180 à 1314* (Paris, 1885), p. 6.

of the charter deal with the collection of debts, protection of the citizens'
food, measures of cloth, regulation of mills, and the restricted carrying
services still owed the bishop.

At Beauvais we thus find a municipality based upon revolutionary
organization.[1]   The chief concern of the sworn association was to secure
life and property to its members.   Officials were elected, courts were set
up, and legal procedure specified; but eventually the power of enforcement resolved itself into private war.   Immersed in a feudal world, the
aspiring bourgeois, through lack of other resources, had been forced to
adopt feudal remedies.   It was indeed the beginning of a new régime
when the king of France sanctioned their organization and guaranteed
them protection.   To what extent seignorial rights in the town were lost
to the bishop and other holders is not stated, but the implication is that
little of them remained.   It is noteworthy that when the charter of
Beauvais was later used as the model for that of Soissons, a more backward community, articles were added to preserve at least certain remnants of manorial control over individual citizens.[2]

In this connection a useful comparison may be made with the famous
Institutio Pacis proclaimed by Louis VI at Laon in 1128.[3]   There, where
the quashing of an earlier commune had been followed by chronic disorder, the king compromised by arranging a new settlement of the
episcopal claims and re-establishing the municipality under a euphemistic
title.   The city is recognized as an asylum of peace and security for all,
whether free or unfree; but serfs of the local nobles and churches are not

[1] From the generalizations stated above it should not be imagined that revolutionary communes
were never launched against laymen, or that all ecclesiastics were hostile to the urban movement.
Saint-Quentin seems to have been organized very much like Beauvais, and its customs reflect distinct antagonism against the count: A. Giry, *Étude sur les Origines de la Commune de Saint-
Quentin* (Saint-Quentin, 1887), pp. 68 ff.   There is good reason to believe that the liberties of Liége
were developed by episcopal favor and were used as the model for those of Huy in the latter eleventh
century; see G. Kurth, 'Les Origines de la Commune de Liége,' *Bulletin de l'Institut Archéologique
Liégeois*, xxxv (1905), 229 ff.

[2] Above, p. 15.   The Soissons charter may also be consulted in H. F. Delaborde, *Recueil des Actes
de Philippe-Auguste* (Paris, 1916), i, 46.   In his elaborate work on the customs of Soissons, Bourgin
(p. 95) admits that they were to some extent borrowed from Beauvais, but in general treats that fact
as of slight importance.   If, however, we wish to appreciate the true force of a charter, we must
examine it with relation to the community for which it was originally issued; for the laxity of mediaeval clerks in adapting old grants to new purposes is notorious.   Comparison shows that the commune of Soissons, as a form of municipal organization, was taken over *en bloc* from the greater city,
and that articles were added to preserve seignorial control over bourgeois marriages, to specify payment of *chevage* by *capitales homines*, etc.   On the basis of the Soissons charter and similar documents
of a later age it would consequently seem quite unwarranted to conclude that the 'communal revolution' was essentially the product of agrarian society.   For further criticism of this idea see Espinas
in *Le Moyen Age*, xxii (1909), 324 ff.

[3] *Ordonnances*, xi, 185.   See C. Stephenson, in *Revue Belge de Philologie et d'Histoire*, v, 845 ff., and
literature there cited.

to be admitted. To his previous lord the immigrant renders merely *chevage* and as a citizen of Laon is to enjoy freedom of marriage, except within the *familiae* of the clerks and knights who have sworn the peace. *Mainmorte* is abolished and rules for inheritance are specified. The episcopal *taille* is restricted to the payment, on the part of those who owe it, of four *deniers* three times a year. The superior jurisdiction of the bishop is recognized, but on failure of his justice, and in certain other cases, the mayor and *jurés* have the power to assess penalties and enforce the custom of the city. Any one who refuses to submit to their authority incurs the law of retaliation — *caput pro capite, membrum pro membro*.

Although certain marks of a conservative policy are evident in this Laon charter, its general effect was certainly to favor the town. The serfs of local lords were excluded, but all others were guaranteed immunity. *Mainmorte* and *formariage* disappeared, and *taille* was reduced to a fixed payment for certain individuals. *Chevage* might still be taken by the lord of an immigrant if he could get it. Seignorial rights thus attenuated could not long survive. In every thriving urban community the same tendency was manifest. Despite every reactionary coup and every attempted compromise, the old system of domanial subjection and personal service was doomed. Born of an agrarian society, it was incompatible with the demands of a new commercial life.

Nor was this all. The charters of Beauvais, of Laon, and of many other episcopal towns show the bishop still legally possessed of extensive governmental functions. Opposed to him was the new and somewhat turbulent authority of the commune, headed by its sworn men. Between the two no division of power was likely to be permanent, and in the contest for supremacy the might of public opinion proved a decisive factor. No matter how legal they were, unenforceable rights would be subject to constant popular encroachment. In many towns of Picardy we have evidence that the *échevins* remained episcopal judges for some time after communal revolts had set up *jurés* to rival them, but that, by the later twelfth century, they also had become municipal magistrates. By the time that Philip Augustus took over Saint-Quentin, Amiens, Péronne, and Tournai, the *échevins* of these communes were elected by the *jurés*. And the same custom seems to have prevailed at Cambrai, Noyon, Corbie, and other places.[1]

Municipal constitutions in Picardy thus varied somewhat from those in Flanders, but such local peculiarities were really of secondary importance. Eventually the administration of the typical large town in northwestern

[1] Pirenne, article cited above, p. 35, n. 3; Giry, *Saint-Quentin*, pp. 28 ff.; Viollet, *op. cit.*, p. 414.

Europe, no matter how its original freedom had been won, rested with a single group of men, who commonly named one or more of their own number as presiding officers and chose all subordinates. Whether called *échevins*, *pairs*, or *jurés*, and whether or not headed by a mayor, they constituted the magistracy. Furthermore, this original municipal government was essentially aristocratic, being installed and controlled by the class of well-to-do citizens. In Flanders these same citizens regularly constituted also a gild merchant, which had come to monopolize trading rights in the town; but if such organizations generally existed in the Picard communes, they have left slight traces. For a clearer instance we must look to Rouen.

It is not till 1149 that we obtain any definite information regarding the institutions of the Norman capital. In that year the young duke, Henry Plantagenet, gave the city its first extant charter.[1] Each man of Rouen, he says, is to hold as on the day when King Henry, his grandfather, died; and all evil customs introduced since then are to be removed *pro consilio civium*. Offices are to be restored as then enjoyed. General amnesty is proclaimed concerning all debts, pleas, acts, and words before the recognition of his father Geoffrey by the city; so that those who have fled the commune may be free to return. The duke guarantees to his burgesses all their possessions, and confirms their ancient liberties.

The men of Rouen are exempt from all *taille* and arbitrary seizure of property. They are not to be forced to entertain any one save by command of the city's marshal. None of them may be appointed sheriff or other official without his consent and, as granted by Henry I, none is to be made to guard prisoners, in jail or elsewhere. Except for ducal pleas at two stated places, citizens may be tried only in Rouen, and numerous promises are made with regard to judicial procedure. Other articles restrict tolls and define various mercantile privileges. No merchant travelling by the Seine, unless he be a citizen of Rouen, may sail past the city. No ship, saving one annually at Cherbourg, may be equipped for a voyage to Ireland except at Rouen, and every ship from Ireland, on passing Cape La Hague, must come to Rouen for unloading. Members of the gild merchant of Rouen are quit of all custom at London and are there to have exclusive use of the port of Dowgate, as they have had since the days of Edward the Confessor.[2]

The existence of the Rouen gild is thus carried far back into the eleventh century and linked up with our first mention of Norman merchants

---

[1] E. Berger, *Recueil des Actes de Henri II Roi d'Angleterre et Duc de Normandie concernant les Provinces Françaises et les Affaires de France*, i (Paris, 1916), 18.

[2] W. Page, *London: Its Origin and Early Development* (London, 1929), pp. 133, 137.

in London under Aethelred.[1]   Would that we might have other information about this association and its connection with the beginnings of urban life! But on that score we have little besides the record before us. From other sources we may be certain that free bourgeois status and tenure had come to be well recognized in eleventh-century Normandy, and such institutions must have flourished pre-eminently in the great emporium of Rouen.[2]   That some privileges of the city had been formally confirmed by Henry I is also sure, but whether they included features of self-government remains doubtful.   What we know of that king's favorable attitude toward urban progress makes us suspect that they did.[3]   And if the famous *Etablissements* date from the years 1160–70, the constitutional organization which they describe must in part have been considerably older.   Contrary to the opinion of Giry, neither the commune nor its government looks like the out-and-out creation of Henry II.   Instead of a military establishment,[4] the municipality of Rouen seems, like those of Flanders, to have been a gradual development in which an ancient and powerful gild merchant played a dominating rôle.   As at Saint-Omer, the commune appears as a more incidental formation — the product of the civil war under Stephen.[5]

This interpretation is further supported by known facts regarding scores of other important towns.   Throughout the Midi urban evolution was generally peaceable and the sworn association practically non-existent.   The great cities of Provence, Languedoc, Guienne, and Gascony emerge in the early twelfth century with their consular governments already perfected.   Concerning them the chroniclers report no dramatic events and the fact that so few of them received charters during the formative period is itself evidence of an untroubled history.   But no matter how it was reached, the final result is certain: by 1150 the foremost towns of the South had secured, not only such fundamental liberties as were being granted to new settlements like Montauban, but also autonomous administration under elected consuls — magistrates exactly corresponding to the *echevins* and *jurés* of the North.[6]

---

[1] See below, p. 72.

[2] See the works of Généstal and Legras, above, p. 30, n. 2.

[3] See below, p. 181.

[4] See Appendix I, below, p. 216.

[5] H. Prentout, *Études sur Quelques Points d'Histoire de Normandie*, Nouvelle Série, (Caen, 1929). Giry (see Appendix I) argued that the commune of Rouen was granted by Henry II after 1173; that the *communio* referred to in his first charter was not the technical *communa*, but the *communitas* of citizens.   Prentout (p. 19), however, has shown that Giry was wrong in this supposition and that the commune must have antedated Henry II.

[6] Pirenne, *Villes du Moyen Age*, p. 179; Viollet, *op. cit.*, p. 412.   An admirable example is provided by the charter to the men of Saint-Antonin-en-Rouergue from their *vicomte* (c. 1144): A. Teulet, *Layettes du Trésor des Chartes* (Paris, 1863), I, 55.   The document begins with the usual guarantees

In Germany, as noted above, the leading town at the opening of the twelfth century was unquestionably Cologne, whose citizens were already in possession of the elementary bourgeois privileges and to some extent united in a powerful gild. A first revolt against the bishop in 1074 had passed without permanent benefit, but in 1112 a *coniuratio pro libertate* seems to have resulted in further advance. At least it was about this time that a parochial organization appeared under *Bürgermeister* (*magistri civium*), who took charge of various municipal functions, administrative and judicial. Meanwhile the episcopal government through *Burggraf, Vogt,* and *Schöffen* had begun to weaken. Little by little bourgeois control was established, until by the following century a full-fledged urban constitution, with a chief *Bürgermeister* and a council , had come into existence. And all this was accomplished, so far as we know, without the issuance of a single charter.[1]

In political development, as in material prosperity, other German towns lagged behind Cologne. Cities like Mainz, Speier, and Worms first gained general exemption from ordinary seignorial obligations under Frederick I;[2] and self-government, of course, came even later. The twelfth-century customal of Strasbourg, for example, shows the bishop still in control of the city administration, naming mayors and *scabini* from his own *familia*. The commercial class remained separated from the rest of the population by special privilege. But within another hundred years such distinction had broken down. The city as a whole constituted a bourgeois community, governing itself under twelve elected consuls.[3] And this organization, much the same as had earlier developed in France, reappeared in countless other German communities, old and new.[4]

It is not, however, the purpose of this chapter to carry a review of municipal institutions beyond the formative period. By the thirteenth century the standards had been set; the models had been formed. The num-

---

of free tenure and testamentary succession, abolition of restrictions on marriage, exemption from forced exactions and purveyance, limitation of fines, determination of judicial procedure, etc. Then it specifies that twelve *probi homines* shall be elected *ad consulatum et consulendum communitatem ville*, who shall be put on oath to govern the town faithfully. The twelve, chosen from twelve different houses, shall hold for one year only and then name another twelve; but before retiring they shall render accounts for the past year. And it is the consuls who swear in a chief officer, the *baiulus*, to render true justice and perform all duties honestly while he holds the *administracionem vel bailiviam ville*. It should be noted that here as elsewhere the 'consulate' was merely the office of 'consulting' the welfare of the town, not a peculiar form of urban constitution.

[1] Koebner, *Köln*, pp. 308 ff., 485 ff., 538 ff.

[2] Keutgen, *Urkunden*, pp. 14, 17; Knöpp, *loc. cit.*

[3] Keutgen, *Urkunden*, pp. 93, 102; C. Hegel, *Verfassungsgeschichte von Mainz im Mittelalter* (Leipzig, 1882); C. Koehne, *Der Ursprung der Stadtverfassung in Worms, Speier und Mainz,* (Breslau 1890); Koebner, *Köln*, pp. 523 ff.

[4] See the authorities cited above, p. 33, n. 4.

ber of privileged towns was enormously increased, but they merely repeated or extended systems long since proved by experience. Of the great towns that had served as pioneering centres in the Northwest a representative group has been briefly examined above. To enlarge the list would not be difficult, but from the point of view here adopted there would be no advantage in attempting a complete catalogue. Sufficient material has been presented to warrant elementary generalization.

4. CONCLUSIONS

As has been remarked by many scholars, towns appeared earliest and developed most richly in the regions where the main trade routes intersected. And the importance in this respect of the great river valleys is too well known to need reiteration. Furthermore, it may easily be perceived that places situated towards the mouths of rivers, where ships would normally first unload, tended to have the advantage. The Low Countries, Normandy, Picardy, and the Rhine valley constituted a belt of territory obviously defined by commercial relationship; and there urban liberties grew rapidly in the eleventh century, to receive formal recognition in the early twelfth. By the same time highly privileged towns had appeared in the extreme south of France, but the intermediate region — that of the upper river valleys — remained more backward. Reims received its definitive grant in 1182, from the same archbishop who founded the immensely successful *ville neuve*, Beaumont-en-Argonne.[1] The communes of eastern Champagne, Burgundy, and adjoining fiefs hardly antedated the thirteenth century.[2] Even Paris and Orleans were as yet only second-rate towns. And the interior of Germany was similarly a hundred years or so behind the more progressive parts of France.

Thus it is evident that in the long run the desires of individual rulers had little to do with the growth of towns. Nevertheless, the hostile prince was in position to hinder movements that he could not crush; the sympathetic one to guide forces that he could not create. The intensely conservative spirit of many ecclesiastical lords in the twelfth century brought them into conflict with the rising bourgeoisie and eventually ruined their authority. In this respect the statesmanship of temporal princes averaged higher. Throughout the records just examined it is a count of Flanders or of Toulouse, a duke of Normandy or of Zähringen, who shows deeper wisdom than most bishops and abbots. The German emperors, during the twelfth century, played but an insignificant part in the fortunes of their towns; for although their opportunities were un-

---

[1] Varin, *Archives Administratives de la Ville de Reims* (*Collection des Documents Inédits*), I, 391; E. T. Bonvallot, *Le Tiers État d'après la Charte de Beaumont en Argonne* (Paris, 1884).

[2] C. Stephenson, *op. cit.*, below, p. 44, n. 2.

doubtedly limited, such as they had were hardly made use of.[1]   On the other hand, the greatness of Louis VI was nowhere better exemplified than in his policy toward the bourgeoisie.   His intervention resulted in the confirmation of no less than ten communes on ecclesiastical domains within his direct jurisdiction.[2]   True, Louis did not endow Paris or Orleans with self-government, but we cannot doubt that they enjoyed bourgeois liberties, and we have no evidence that local opinion demanded more.[3]   That the king was not inexorable on the subject is proved by his establishment of the commune at Mante, the royal station farthest down the Seine.[4]   Moreover, it was he who issued the widely copied charter of Lorris — enough in itself to make his name illustrious.   He created the *novum forum* at Étampes and conferred elementary privileges upon Compiègne.[5]   His son and grandson merely continued work already well begun.

The share of the king in furthering urban liberty in France is worth emphasizing, not only because it is an interesting subject in itself, but also because it well illustrates the character of the authority that made all such development legally possible.   The town was not founded through the personal emancipation of a servile community; rather it was a settlement living under a special law guaranteed by some holder of regalian powers.   Whether issued by king or vassal, the charter of liberties created a territorial immunity, within which all seignorial rights were subordinated to the will of the grantor.   Bourgeois status was his gift, to be attained on completion of the lawful term of residence.   Thus serfdom ceased to exist in the town save by specified exception, and all in-

---

[1] Knöpp, *loc. cit*

[2] Luchaire, *Louis VI le Gros*, p. cxciii.   Voicing a reaction against the eulogies of earlier historians, Luchaire in his numerous writings was inclined to minimize the rôle of Louis VI as patron of the communes.   It is true that the king was not always consistent, but our information regarding his motives is very incomplete, and the net result of his reign was certainly to bring under his direct control a large number of flourishing towns.   If we had the financial accounts of his reign, we should probably find the origin of the handsome income drawn from the bourgeoisie by his successors.   See C. Stephenson, 'Les Aides des Villes Françaises aux XIIᵉ et XIIIᵉ Siècles,' *Le Moyen Age*, xxiv (1922), 308 ff.

[3] It was not till after the death of Louis VI that troubles connected with an alleged commune broke out at Orléans; see E. Bimbenet, *Histoire de la Ville d'Orléans* (Orleans, 1884–87), ii, 63.

[4] *Ordonnances*, xi, 197.   Comparative study tends to show that Mante was a typical urban foundation at the foot of a castle; there is no reason to believe that it was any more of a military colony than other towns of the time.   Luchaire's conviction in this respect was based on Giry's mistaken interpretation of the Norman charters (see Appendix I).   After the model of Mante a commune was also granted by Louis VI to Dreux; and by his successors to Bruyère, Chevrières, Chaumont, Pontoise, Poissy, and Les Andelys: E. Lefèvre, *Documents Historiques sur le Comté et la Ville de Dreux* (Chartres, 1859), p. 46, n. 2; C. Stephenson, *op. cit.*, p. 281.

[5] M. Prou, 'Une Ville-Marché au XIIᵉ Siècle,' *Mélanges d'Histoire Offerts à Henri Pirenne*, ii, 379 ff.; J. Tardif, *Monuments Historiques* (Paris, 1866), p. 222.

habitants became normally responsible only for stated service owed to the sovereign lord. The obligations of the bourgeois were thus neither arbitrary nor personal; they were the common burdens of a privileged community. He was essentially a citizen rather than a subject.[1]

It is only through such interpretation that the true nature of urban liberties may be appreciated, but the legal aspect is not the only one to be considered. The fundamental similarity throughout wide regions of the privileges granted was dictated, not by juristic, but by practical necessity. The provisions of the charters reflected the demands of the population which they were designed to attract. So, in spite of many local peculiarities, the bourgeois programme may be readily summarized. First of all, the town-dweller sought and obtained the guarantee of personal freedom — the right to come and go as he pleased, to engage in any trade that suited him, to marry and to give his children in marriage without some lord's costly permission. In the second place, he always required free tenure for his goods and lands — liberty to alienate or bequeath them when and how he would, liability for only a fixed cash rent, and consequent exemption from *mainmorte* and other manorial charges upon property. Practically universal also was the close restriction of the more distinctly political powers of the lord. Arbitrary *taille*, military service, and *corvée* were abolished. Rights to purveyance, entertainment, and credit were rigidly defined. In order to protect the town's special law, trials were restricted to the local courts. Fines and other penalties were limited to suit the gravity of offenses. Special procedure in civil cases — particularly such as would arise from business pursuits — was prescribed. Seignorial monopolies were generally abandoned. Many customs duties were forgiven. Trade was encouraged and protected.

These were the elementary urban liberties. Where they were proclaimed, and where settlers came to enjoy them, a town sprang up. But normally increase of population and wealth led to further demands. Bourgeois, already skilled in administration through the experience of business enterprise or gild, desired also to manage their own affairs in the political sphere, and many lords were quick to see that such an ambition, if properly controlled, was by no means incompatible with their own interests. Thus, except when the hostility of the prince led to violent insurrection, autonomy came to the towns rather through gradual evolution than through abrupt innovation; the effect of their charters was merely to confirm or develop existing practices.

The precise extent of bourgeois governmental rights at one particular

[1] C. Stephenson, 'Taxation and Representation in the Middle Ages,' *Haskins Anniversary Essays in Mediaeval History* (Boston, 1929), p. 304.

moment is therefore hard to determine. Ultimate control of municipal magistrates, supreme judicial authority, powers of taxation, and military command regularly remained with the lord or his suzerain. In the delimitation neither of these functions nor of those devolving upon local officials was there any uniformity. But in spite of minor variations, early municipal administrations tended to follow one simple plan. As M. Pirenne has well said, a group of selectmen were installed to do whatever needed doing.[1] The title varied from region to region, but the office was essentially the same. Everywhere the chosen magistrates, by themselves or through appointees, administered justice; collected tolls; held charge of walls, gates, bridges, streets, and other public works; laid taxes; and saw to the payment of the lord's dues. At first no specifically municipal buildings existed. Assemblies of the citizens were held in the open air; smaller courts and meetings commonly in a gild-hall. It was left for a later age to produce *hôtels de ville*, belfries, and elaborate official paraphernalia. For a primitive town primitive methods sufficed.

In the study of urban development throughout western Europe, accordingly, a useful distinction can be drawn between towns of elementary and towns of advanced liberties. The latter, endowed with political rights, may be called communes; but it must be remembered that such usage is a matter of present-day convenience, and not of historical accuracy. During the Middle Ages by no means all great urban centres were so designated, and when the term was used, it did not always have the same technical meaning. As a group, the communes were marked by no peculiarly feudal character. They enjoyed the status of vassal no more than other self-governing towns. The sworn association was an interesting phenomenon, but its significance was local and temporary.[2]

Indeed, the fact of basic importance was the social change, of which all political manifestation in the town was merely one consequence. Communes might be quashed. Governmental immunities might be cancelled. But the substance of bourgeois liberty has proved indestructible. Created by forces beyond the control of the state, it has persisted, and until sapped by some revolution comparable to that which produced it, will persist.

[1] *Villes du Moyen Age*, p. 180.
[2] Above, pp. 14 ff.; and see Appendix I.

III

THE ANGLO-SAXON BOROUGH

1. THE *CEASTER*

TO THE student of English municipal institutions it is a fact of obvious significance that the history of Britain parallels that of the Continent during the Middle Ages. In the one region as in the other a period of Roman dominion is followed by one of barbarization, which in turn yields to a new epoch of social and political reconstruction. Century for century the same general conditions prevail on both sides of the Channel. The fifth sees the collapse of the Roman imperial administration and the permanent occupation of the provinces by northern peoples, whose wars fill the annals of the next four hundred years. In the ninth come fresh barbarian inroads and further relapse into disorder. But in Britain, as in Gaul and Germany, necessities of defense eventually produce new political groupings. Princes like the duke of Saxony, the count of Paris, the marquis of Flanders, and the king of Wessex rise to power by fighting the invader. And their military reorganization has an important bearing upon the history of the towns.

For the whole northwest of Europe the crucial event is the Viking war. The age preceding is dominated by imperial tradition; it is an age of decline — a barbarian period in which the survival of Roman institutions is the matter of paramount interest. The age following, on the other hand, is one of innovation; state and society are reformed, and their reformation is founded on actuality. Thus the beginnings of the modern European political structure are to be sought in the tenth, rather than in any earlier century. And within that structure neither the English borough nor its counterpart on the Continent appears in the least exceptional. Its history is not one of unbroken continuity since ancient times. Two generations of scholars have failed to discover even the slightest evidence of Roman municipalities in Saxon England. And yet, every one knows that something of the old urban system did persist. Just what it was must be determined; for to understand the true character of the barbarians' reconstruction, we must be certain of the materials at their disposal.

Haverfield, whose work on Roman Britain set new standards of thoroughness and accuracy in that much belabored field, gives a list of towns

that may well serve to introduce the present inquiry.¹ In point of size
and prosperity, Londinium was easily the greatest city of the province.
Next came the *coloniae* of Eburacum, Lindum, Camulodunum, and Glevum, together with Verulamium, which ranked as a *municipium*. There
were at least a dozen cantonal capitals, reaching as far west as Isca Dum-
nomorum and Viroconium, and north to Isurium. And for every one of
such great centres there must have been two or three lesser towns, many
of them important enough to be walled. Lastly, beyond the civilian
settlements of the southeast, a string of military outposts extended from
the mountainous peninsulas of the west coast to the great wall on the
north. These were of all sizes, varying from large *castra* of massive stone
construction to *castella* of a few acres each, where the principal defenses
were only earthen ramparts. With the crash of the imperial government
and the advent of barbarian conquerors, what became of this far-flung
organization?

To some degree the modern map gives an answer. The first five of the
cities mentioned are now represented by London, York, Lincoln, Colchester, and Gloucester; but the sixth has been dead for a thousand years.²
Of Haverfield's cantonal capitals barely one-half reappear as urban centres; the others are illustrious only as venerable landmarks, of slight interest to any but historians and antiquaries. Among the lesser places,
Bath, Dover, and Rochester are the ancient Aquae Solis, Dubrae, and
Durobrivae; but these towns are exceptions. Of their one-time peers
even the sites are often unknown. And if one military camp, Deva, underlies a flourishing borough, Chester, most of the rest have lain vacant
since the withdrawal of the legions.

A number of Roman cities did, however, survive the Saxon conquest;
and as a first step toward the determination of what this survival implied,
let us consider the elementary question of names. The prominence of the
suffix *-chester* among towns of Roman descent is very familiar, and there
can be no doubt that the usage was virtually as old as the Saxon occupation. According to Bede, the vernacular for *civitas* was *caestir*. The
English, he reports, say *Hrofaescaestrae* for *civitas Dorubrevis; Vintan-
caestir* for *civitas Venta; Legacaestir* for *civitas Legionum*. A *civitas* is
called *Tunnacaestir* after the priest Tunna. *Kaelcacaestir* he translates
civitas Calcaria.³ So in the land-books Canterbury appears as *civitas*

---

¹ F. H. Haverfield, *The Romanization of Roman Britain* (Oxford, 1923), pp. 57 ff.; also in the *En-
cyclopaedia Britannica* (11th ed.), ɪᴠ, 584 ff.; and in *C.M.H.*, ɪ, ch. ɪɪɪ. R. G. Collingwood, *The
Archaeology of Roman Britain* (London, 1930), chs ɪɪɪ, ᴠɪ; G. Macdonald, *Roman Britain, 1914–28*
(London, 1931), pp. 73 ff.

² The mediaeval town of St Albans, of course, grew up adjoining the abbey, not on the site of the
ancient city.

Dorovernis or *Dornwarana ceaster;* Worcester as *Weogorna civitas, castrum Weogernensis, Wegrinancaestir,* or *Weogerna cestre*.[1]   In the Anglo-Saxon Chronicle we find *Bapanceaster* (Bath), *Cisseceaster* (Chichester), *Colneceaster* (Colchester), *Cyrenceaster* (Cirencester), *Dorcesceaster* (Dorchester), *Eoferwicceaster* (York), *Heastingceaster* (Hastings), *Legraceaster* (Leicester), *Memeceaster* (Manchester), etc.[2]

The conclusion from this array of names leaps to the eye.   To the Saxons generally, the original distinction between *civitas* and *castrum*, i.e., between a city and a fortified camp, was lost.   All places with Roman walls, irrespective of size, population, or past history were alike *ceastra*.[3] The mere history of an ancient word constitutes a powerful argument against the idea that urban life survived the tragic fifth century.   But it would be rash to press this conclusion too rigorously.   There is much additional evidence, and it teaches us to be wary of absolute generalizations concerning Roman towns in Saxon Britain.   They did not, assuredly, all suffer precisely the same fate.

On the Continent episcopal organization was commonly centered in the *civitas*, and a similar tendency is apparent in early England.   There, it is true, the bishops lacked the great immunities of their brethren in Gaul and Germany, but at least some of them had Roman cities for their capitals.   Pope Gregory's original proposal was to have two metropolitans, one at London and one at York; and it was only when the former city proved inhospitable that Canterbury was substituted.   A bishop for the Northumbrians was, however, installed at York and eventually one for the East Saxons at London.   Meanwhile Kent received a second see at Rochester, and Wessex its first at Dorchester,[4] subsequently transferred to Winchester.   These were all in some fashion Roman cities; the Continental tradition did not break down until ecclesiastical organization was extended to all the Saxon kingdoms.   Out of seventeen episcopal sees established by the later eighth century ten centered in mere country villages without the slenderest title to urban rank — a situation that remained to attract the reforming zeal of the Norman Conqueror.[5]

The established policy of the church in the ancient imperial lands thus proved impossible of complete application in Britain.   By the time that

---

[3] Bede, *Historia Ecclesiastica Gentis Anglorum*, ed. C. Plummer (Oxford, 1896), I, 84, 85, 140, 250, 253.   Cf. I, 215: 'castellum Cantuariorum quod dicitur Hrofescaestir.' Also *Verlamacaestir* (I, 21), *Ythancaestir* (I, 173), *Reptacaestir* (I, 9), *Tiouulfingacaestir* (I, 117), etc.   Cf. examples cited, p. 50, n. 3.

[1] *C.D.*, 27, 109, 188, 260, etc.; 32, 82, 91, 290, etc.

[2] *A.S.C.*, see index to vol. I. Cf. W. H. Stevenson, in his edition of Asser (Oxford, 1904), pp. 231–32.

[3] H. W. C. Davis, in *Quarterly Review*, CCVIII (1908), 62.

[4] Dorchester on the Thame, Oxfordshire.

[5] G. Hill, *English Dioceses* (London, 1900), especially his list, p. 153; A. Ballard, *The English Borough in the Twelfth Century* (Cambridge, 1914), p. 72.

Christianity came to be reintroduced, the province was so thoroughly barbarized that most of it had to be treated like heathen Germany. Throughout the interior the Roman *civitas*, except as an unstable memory, had utterly perished. Nevertheless, the location of the first English sees would seem to indicate that the cities of the coast had preserved some remnants of their ancient renown. And this impression is confirmed by other evidence. Traditionally at least, Canterbury, London, York, and Winchester were all royal residences, and the earliest mints were placed in these same cities, as well as in Lincoln, Gloucester, Exeter, and Bath.[1] With the exception of Oxford, the only places where kings are known to have put moneyers before the tenth century were of Roman foundation.

From this period, furthermore, we have a considerable series of charters that concern Rochester and Canterbury. Kings and other persons grant to the local churches lands described as lying in or near the Kentish cities, and in identifying such properties frequent mention is made of walls, gates, streets, and, occasionally, of a market place.[2] Neither Canterbury nor Rochester, obviously, had ever been entirely abandoned; they continued to include at least some inhabitants, some of the ancient structural features, and possibly some vestiges of imperial administration. Of a trading population the records contain no hint. On the other hand, the size of the plots granted and their appropriation to the use of churches make us suspect that the civic territory was not thickly built over. *Mansiones* reckoned in *iugera* are found inside and outside the walls. Normally a house in the city does not appear as a self-contained unit, but is combined with arable, marsh, woodland, and meadow elsewhere in the shire.[3] What little evidence the land-books provide tends to indicate a *civitas* that was principally a shell of masonry, where true urban life had long since vanished and agriculture dominated all classes.

[1] *Catalogue of English Coins in the British Museum*, Anglo-Saxon Series (London, 1887–93), i, 10, 39, 41, 67, 73, 134, 204; ii, xvii ff. See the review of the latter volume by F. York Powell, *E.H.R.*, xi (1896), 759 ff.; and Ballard, *op. cit.*, pp. 43 ff.

[2] *C.D.*, 1, 27, 113, 155, 230, 241, 1041, etc. See especially 109: Dunweald *minister* grants to the church of St Peter and St Paul 'villam unam . . . quae iam ad Quenegatum urbis Dorovernis in foro posita est.' Cf. W. de Gray Birch, *Cartularium Saxonicum* (London, 1885–93), no. 248: grant by Offa of lands in Kent and a *vicum* 'in aquilone parte venalis loci.'

[3] For example, at Canterbury: *C.D.*, 188 (804), 'aliquantulam terrae partem in civitate Dorobernia ad necessitatis refugium, hoc est vi iugera'; 196 (811), 'duas possessiunculas et tertiam dimediam, id est in nostra loquella ðridda half haga', et prata duo ad eas prius et modo pertinentia in orientale parte Sture fluminis sita'; 217 (823), land 'intra moenia urbis Doroverni' 60 x 30 ft., with 30 *iugera* to the north of the city; 1041 (832), 'in Dorobernia civitate etiam unam villam' to which belong five *iugera*, two meadows, and commons of forest; 241 (839), 'unam villam intra civitatem Doroverniae et ad illis pertinentia xxiiii iugeras tamen in duabus locis in Dorovernia civitatis intua muros civitatis x iugera cum viculis praedictis et in aquilone praedictae civitatis xiiii iugera.' And at Rochester: 113 (765), 'terram intra castelli moenia . . . unum viculum cum duobus iugeribus

Apart from Canterbury and Rochester, very few cities are even mentioned in the early Saxon charters. Gloucester and Worcester appear as the sites of famous churches. The West Saxon kings date a few of their acts at the *villa regalis* of Dorchester.[1] We hear of lands at Bath, but they probably lay outside the ancient walls; for the utter desolation of that ancient city is attested, not only by the famous poem, but by modern archaeological research.[2] Nothing is heard of York and Lincoln. We have no grants of land in London before the days of Alfred,[3] and the fact that the streets of the mediaeval city ran athwart the foundations of many Roman buildings clearly indicates that much of its area had lain unoccupied for a long time.[4] Probably, as at Cologne, the population in Saxon times was not sufficient to fill the wide space within the walls, and a belt of waste extended to the north of a shrivelled settlement along the river.[5]

There is, however, enough evidence to warrant the belief—which would be natural enough in any case—that London was never wholly deserted. In the eighth century Bede describes the metropolis of the East Saxons as an 'emporium for many peoples, coming by land and by sea.'[6] And that the port remained the centre of some maritime traffic is also indicated by royal charters allowing certain ecclesiastics to import cargoes free of the local tolls.[7] But such bits of information are far surpassed in positive value by a doom of Hlothere and Eadric. If, they declare, a Kentishman buys cattle (*feoh*) in London, he must do so under the witness of the king's *wicgerefa* or of several other trustworthy men. Then, should his title be subsequently challenged, he must, if possible, bring to the king's hall (*sele*) in London the man who sold him the cattle. Or, in the absence of that person, he must substantiate his purchase by pro-

---

adiacentem plateae'; 145 (789), 'aliquam particulam terrae iuris mei, id est, quasi unius et semis iugeri in civitate Hrofi'; 276 (855), 'unam villam quod nos Saxonice *an haga* dicimus in meridie castelli Hrobi,' and ten *iugera* belonging to it outside with meadow, and marsh; 285 (860–6), 80 acres and 'unum viculum dimidium civitatis Hrobi,' with a marsh belonging thereto.

[1] Gloucester, *C.D.*, 186 (804); Worcester, *C.D.*, 32, 82, 91, 290 (691–864); Dorchester (Dorsetshire), *C.D.*, 232, 236, 1059, 1061 (833–68).

[2] Haverfield, in *V.H.C. Somerset*, I, 224 ff.

[3] The earliest is the well known charter of 898 (*C.D.*, 1074), by which the king grants two *iugera* in the newly restored city to the archbishop of Canterbury and the bishop of Worcester. The document is particularly interesting because it shows the continued existence of the wall parallel to the Thames, with *navium staciones* attached to properties inside the fortifications.

[4] *V.H.C. London*, I, 80 ff.; W. Page, *London: Its Origin and Early Development* (London, 1929), p. 31.

[5] Above, p. 24; Koebner, *Köln*, pp. 60 ff.; and see Plate II.

[6] Bede (ed. Plummer), I, 85: 'quorum metropolis Lundonia civitas est . . . et ipsa multorum emporium populorum terra marique venientium.'

[7] *C.D.*, 78, 95 (734–61); Page, *London*, p. 34.

ducing the king's *wicgerefa* or such other men as had witnessed the trans-
action.[1]

The significance of this Kentish record is that it foreshadows the more
famous enactments of Edward and Aethelstan.[2]   Together with the evidence regarding mints, it demonstrates a connection, tenuous but sure,
between the Roman city and the administrative borough of the tenth
century.   But what was true of such outstanding centres as London,
York, Lincoln, Canterbury, and Winchester by no means held for the
rest of the ancient *civitates*.   The one salient feature common to all of
them was the wall.[3]   That, in the opinion of the countryside, made the
ceaster.   The presence of a market, of a cathedral church, of a royal
residence, of a trading population, or of any population at all, was entirely secondary.   We should naturally suppose that many cities were
continuously used by the Saxons as fortresses, but direct confirmation of
such an inference is entirely lacking.   It is only with the coming of the
Danes that the *burh* suddenly attains prominence in the records.

2. The *Burh*

Introduction of the word that eventually became 'borough' immediately confronts us with a problem of correct historical terminology.   It
has been the habit of most historians to treat borough and town as equivalent terms.   This identification has been natural, because it is one sanctioned by centuries of usage; but to be strictly accurate, language must
be interpreted according to contemporary authority.   We are not justified in making a word have a certain meaning in the tenth century merely
because it had that meaning two hundred years later.   And in this particular case there is especial danger of reading a whole series of modern
ideas into an age which knew them not.   By imagining Saxon England
dotted with boroughs in the ultimate sense of the word, we also imagine
the economic, social, and legal institutions to make them possible.   It
will be safer not to make presuppositions, but, while rendering *burh* as
'borough,' to deduce from the sources only what they plainly imply.

As already remarked, the first great clarification of this subject was
made by Maitland[4]. But another very significant advance for our understanding of the primitive borough has resulted from the combined efforts of J. H. Round, W. H. St John Hope, and Mrs Ella Armitage.[5]
By proving the motte-and-bailey type of fortress a Norman innovation,

---

[1] *G.*, I, 11; and notes, III, 22.

[2] Below, pp. 65 ff.; *H.E.L.*, I, 59.

[3] See the brief but admirable summary of this whole question in Petit-Dutaillis, *Studies*, pp. 72–74.

[4] Above, pp. 17 ff.

[5] J. H. Round, 'English Castles,' *Quarterly Review*, CLXXIX (1894), 27 ff.; 'The Castles of the Conquest,' *Archaeologia*, LVIII (1902), 332 ff.   W. H. St John Hope, 'English Fortresses and Castles of

they first made it possible to draw an intelligible conclusion with regard to the Anglo-Saxon *burh* as a military structure—to conceive it as a primitive form of stronghold which, together with the old army and the old warfare, was rendered obsolete by the great events of 1066. Mrs Armitage in particular, by combining analysis of the Chronicle with the results of archaeological investigation, has brought out many facts of great significance for the inquiry here pursued. But in her effort to make a sharp distinction between the borough and the castle, Mrs Armitage, as Round pointed out, made various generalizations that hardly followed from the evidence presented.[1] Those regarding the origin and nature of the 'private' castle[2] may here be passed over as irrelevant; those regarding the origin and nature of the *burh* cannot be.

After concluding that the 'main idea of the borough' was a 'place of refuge for the whole countryside,' Mrs Armitage adds that it was much more—'a town, a place where people were to live permanently and do their daily work,' 'a fostering seat for trade and manufactures.' Alfred and his children performed a noble and far-seeing work, not only in 'saving the kernel of the British Empire,' but also in 'laying the sure foundations of its future progress in the arts and habits of civilized life.'[3] It is this constant attribution to the primitive borough of traits found in the later borough that necessitates one more review of a very familiar story.

We have seen that the Saxon invaders of Britain adopted the Latin *castrum* as their ordinary name for the walled city, but at the same time they kept the Germanic *burh* with the same meaning that it had on the Continent.[4] In the earliest dooms the word is found only in the sense of a defensible dwelling house, and this usage undoubtedly accounts for a

---

the Tenth and Eleventh Centuries,' *Archaeological Journal*, LX (1903), 72 ff. Ella S. Armitage, *Early Norman Castles of the British Isles* (London, 1913).

[1] *E.H.R.*, XXVII (1912), 544 ff.: 'The deliberate founding of "fortified towns" is an unproved hypothesis; what the *burh* seems to have meant, under these rulers (Edward and his sister), was a fortified enclosure, which may sometimes have been intended only, like those on the Roman wall, for an armed camp.' At the time when I published my short paper in *A.H.R.*, XXXIII (1926), pp. 10 ff., I had not read this criticism of Round's; or I should, of course, have referred to his anticipation of the point that I tried to make in this same connection.

[2] By the 'private castle' Mrs Armitage presumably meant the feudal castle. Whether or not William's castles were entrusted to vassals, he unquestionably regarded them as his own. The situation was the same in France, except that the actual holder of royal authority was likely to be a prince rather than the king himself. In a great fief like Flanders the castle was no more private than it was in England. In some of her interesting chapters Mrs Armitage has endeavored to sketch the origin of the feudal castle, but the subject is one that can be explained only by showing when and how the motte-and-bailey type of fortresss was evolved from the older *Fluchtburg*. The Norman Conquest produced an abrupt change in castle-building for the same reasons as it did so in all other military matters. See above, pp. 11–12; below, pp. 155 ff.

[3] Armitage, p. 29.

[4] Above, p. 9.

large number of ancient place names.   The scores of villages with names
ending in -*bury* were not themselves boroughs; rather they were so called
after the home of some local potentate.[1]   The term *burh*, however, might
also be applied to a greater fortified area, an entrenched camp or a walled
city.   Thus *burh* is occasionally the equivalent of *ceaster*.   One Kentish
city becomes Rochester and the other Canterbury.   In the Chronicle
London is a *wick* or a *bury*, but never a *chester*.[2]   The land-books call
the inhabitants of a *civitas* either *urbani* or *burhwaru*.[3]   And numerous
examples of such usage can be gleaned from other Anglo-Saxon literature.[4]

In general, we may conclude, the Saxons saw a *burh* in any fortified
enclosure, but those of Roman origin were by preference *ceastra*.   The
burga of popular speech were generally mere homesteads protected by
some sort of fence.   Before the ninth century the sources describe only
one new construction on a larger scale.   Bede tells of Bamborough, the
urbs regia built by the Northumbrian king and named after a certain
queen Bebba, and how it was miraculously saved from destruction by
Aidan.[5]   The heathen Penda, having failed to take the place by storm,
collected wood and thatch from the nearby villages and resorted to fire.
But the saint saw the flame and smoke above the city walls and his
prayers were efficacious.   The wall, obviously, was nothing more than
an earthen rampart surmounted by a stockage—or Penda's threat would
not have been so terrible.

Thus preserved, Bamborough remained a great Northumbrian stronghold long after York and the surrounding territory had been lost to the
Danes.   From there the last of the old line ruled as high reeves of Bamborough until their principality was absorbed into the rising kingdom of
England.[6]   What then was the actual character of the great *urbs* described by Bede?   His classical language should not mislead us.   As Mrs
Armitage has pointed out, the Saxon Bamborough occupied the rocky
promontory where the Normans later built their castle.   Its total
area is only four and three-quarters acres.   The mediaeval borough
arose below, where the fierce Penda had found only peasant cottages.
Mrs Armitage, in her anxiety to prove that the early Bamborough was
not a castle, imagines an urban population driven out by the Normans

---

[1] Maitland, *Domesday Book and Beyond*, p. 183; W. H. Stevenson, in *E.H.R.*, xii (1897), 491;
Liebermann, under *Burg* (*G.*, ii, 330).

[2] *A.S.C.*, index to vol. i.

[3] *C.D.*, 259 (845), *in media urbanorum pratorum;* 282 (859), *prata on burgwara medum.*   For other
examples, see H. M. Chadwick, *Studies on Anglo-Saxon Institutions* (Cambridge, 1905), pp. 249 ff.

[4] Liebermann, under *Stadt*, 1 (*G.*, ii, 659).

[5] Bede (ed. Plummer), i, 138, 159; Armitage, p. 11.

[6] Chadwick, *op. cit.*, pp. 185, 232, 259; W. J. Corbett, in *C.M.H.*, iii, 351.

and thus founding a new town.[1] But such an assumption is quite unnecessary. We may surely admit that the Norman castle was quite different from the ancient *burh* and still believe that both were essentially fortresses. An area of less than five acres on top of a nearly inaccessible rock is admirable for a stronghold, but hardly convenient for a trading settlement.

Coming now to the richer account of borough-building in the Chronicle, we are relieved of any necessity for giving the story in full by three admirable studies already published. Besides the book of Mrs Armitage, we have Hope's excellent article on 'English Fortresses and Castles in the Tenth and Eleventh Centuries' and a brilliant chapter by Corbett in the *Cambridge Mediaeval History*.[2] The former, being written to support Round's theory of castle-building as against that of Clark, has much in common with Mrs Armitage's more elaborate work, but differs from it by picturing the original borough as essentially military. Corbett's essay, adopting the structural concept of the borough thus established, makes it a central feature both in the conflict of Dane and Saxon and in the political reconstruction that ensued. And in this latter respect, as we all must, he has followed the illuminating suggestions of H. M. Chadwick.[3]

From all this discussion and rediscussion of the Chronicle the fact clearly emerges that in the second half of the ninth century both combatants extensively employed fortifications of two main sorts: Roman constructions, which were normally of stone, and new constructions, which were normally of earth and wood. The ancient stronghold, of course, still appears as a *ceaster*, but it can also be called a fastness (*faesten*), a work (*geweorc*), or a *burh*. And the recent structure may be described in any of these ways except as a *ceaster*. Thus Alfred pursues the Danes to Exeter, but cannot get at them after they have entered the fastness.[4] The royal army besieges the Danes in Chester, but they are unassailable in the work.[5] During the siege of Rochester the Danes surround themselves with a *faesten*, which is referred to as a *geweorc* when they abandon it.[6] The Danes build a *geweorc* at Tempsford, but when it is taken by Edward, it is called a *burh*.[7] While wintering at Nottingham the Danes are besieged in the *geweorc*, and henceforth Nottingham

---

[1] Armitage, *loc. cit.*

[2] See above, p. 52, n. 5; p. 54, n. 6.

[3] Chadwick, *op. cit.*, ch. vi.

[4] *A.S.C.*, ii, 64 (877). In the article just cited Hope quotes the more important of the following passages.

[5] *A.S.C.*, ii, 72 (894).

[6] *A.S.C.*, ii, 66 (885).

[7] *A.S.C.*, ii, 82 (921).

appears as a *burh*.[1]   It is true that these works and fastnesses often appear as temporary entrenchments, but can we be sure that the *burh* was always more than that?   To answer this question, we must try to tabulate the statistics supplied by the Chronicle.

Alfred's famous *geweorc* at Athelney never reappears in the records after the year of its construction.   Nor are the two similar works that he wrought against the Danes on the Lea ever heard of again.[2]   Mrs Armitage has listed eleven Danish fortifications called *geweorc* or *faesten*.[3] One of them, as we have seen, was at Nottingham, where a famous borough is soon discovered.   A second of them appears at Bridgnorth, where Aethelflaed is later said to have built a *burh*.   A third, that at Tempsford, is actually called a *burh*, but neither it nor the eight others amount to anything in later years.   Besides these Mrs Armitage notes thirteen places where the Danes are reported to have wintered.[4]   Four were Roman cities and three were islands.   Of the rest three do not appear as boroughs in the following two centuries, but three (Torksey, Thetford, and Cambridge) do.   And the last two, like Nottingham, contain traces of what would seem to be the original embankments.[5]   Furthermore, the Chronicle clearly describes as Danish boroughs York, Lincoln, Leicester, Derby, Huntingdon, Northampton, Bedford, and Stamford.[6]   In the first three places the Danes merely took over Roman defenses; in the other five they apparently raised new works.

In the same way the Chronicle indicates the following Roman cities as boroughs under Alfred and his children: Winchester, Exeter, Canterbury, Rochester, Chichester, and Gloucester.[7]   We are told in 886 of the repair of London and in 907 of the renovation of Chester, which a few years before is described as a desolated city (*weastre ceastre*).[8]   So too we hear of the repair and renovation of Colchester,[9] and we can imagine that something of the same sort occurred at Worcester,[10] Towcester,[11] and Man-

---

[1] *A.S.C.*, II, 59 (868), 84 (922); called *arx* by Asser (ed. Stevenson), pp. 25, 230.

[2] *A.S.C.*, II, 64 (878), 73 (896).

[3] Armitage, p. 48. Cf. the *arces* of Asser, pp. 28, 43, 234, 239, 262.

[4] *Ibid.*, pp. 49–54.

[5] *Ibid.*, pp. 44, 55; below, pp. 58, 197, 200.   There is a chance that the Danes made use of a Roman work at Cambridge.   Bede (ed. Plummer, I, 244–45) refers to a *civitatula desolata* which the English called *Grantacaestir*.   See below, p. 200 n. 3.

[6] Hope, *op. cit.*, pp. 78–82; see the passages cited below, pp. 60 ff.

[7] *A.S.C.*, II, 56 (851), 58 (860), 64 (877), 66 (885), 72 (895), 79 (915).   This list can, of course, be supplemented from the Burghal Hidage, below, pp. 61 ff.; and see Appendix II.

[8] *A.S.C.*, II, 67 (886), 77 (907); above, p. 55, n. 5.   Cf. below, p. 60.

[9] *A.S.C.*, II, 83 (921).

[10] See the famous charter for the bishop of Worcester, in which Aethelred and Aethelflaed declare that they have wrought the *burh* at Worcester 'eallum ðaem folc to geborge': *C.D.*, 1075, translation in B. Thorpe, *Diplomatarium Anglicum Aevi Saxonici* (London, 1865), p. 136.   Maitland,

chester.[1] And except for the last two, all of these places remain as boroughs in Domesday. Meanwhile, in addition to boroughs made from old Roman *castra*, and those taken from the Danes, Edward and his sister build their famous series of new boroughs. The total of such constructions is twenty-three, of which not more than one-third stand in any subsequent list of boroughs.[2]

To make accurate estimates from such haphazard statistics is out of the question. We may be perfectly certain that both English and Danes built many boroughs of which the Chronicle says nothing; but such as they are, the figures noted above lead to certain interesting conclusions. Of the Roman fortifications mentioned as boroughs belonging to both sides, three-fourths continue to hold such rank during the next two centuries. Of the new constructions, on the other hand, but slightly more than one-third are equally prominent. And the mortality among places called *burh* is just as great as among those called *geweorc* or *faesten*. There is no basis for the supposition that originally one was any more of a town than the other. Such Danish camps as those at Appledore, Benfleet, Milton, Shoebury, and Tempsford were plainly intended for temporary occupancy. But how did they differ from the *burh* of Huntingdon, which was built and abandoned within a year?[3] And even if we omit those boroughs of Edward and his sister that remain unidentified, we still know of Witham, Eddisbury, Thelwall, Kirkby, Bakewell, Runcorn, and Wyng, which seem to have been of use only during the period of the war.[4] Of the two boroughs constructed at Buckingham in four weeks,[5] which was intended to be more than a fortress? Why did Edward also build two boroughs at Hertford?[6] And why, having taken the

---

Domesday Book and Beyond, p. 194; Stenton, in *V.H.C. Worcester*, IV, 376; Armitage, p. 31. No one has discovered any traces of Roman walls at Worcester, but the Saxon name would imply that the city had in some way been fortified.

[11] *A.S.C.*, II, 81–83 (921). The chronicler tells us that Edward 'timbered' the *burh* at Towcester and later surrounded it with a stone wall. But the site to-day reveals what looks like a Roman camp, with an earthen embankment enclosing about thirty-five acres: Haverfield, in *V.H.C. Northampton*, I, 184; Armitage, p. 41.

[1] *A.S.C.*, II, 84; Armitage, p. 46. The Norman borough was a later growth adjoining the castle.

[2] This does not include any of the reconstructions mentioned above, nor any of the conquered Danish works; but does include the two boroughs at Buckingham and at Hertford and the second boroughs added at Bedford, Nottingham, and Stamford (see immediately below). The list should not of course, be considered at all complete. Shrewsbury is not on it, unless disguised as *Scergeat* (Armitage, p. 33); and Hereford, which is not mentioned, appears as an English borough in 915 (*A.S.C.*, II, 79). For details on all these boroughs, see Armitage, ch. III.

[3] *A.S.C.*, II, 82 (921).

[4] Armitage, pp. 35–47; on *Wigangamere*, Corbett, in *C.M.H.*, III, 364. This leaves as unidentified *Bremesbyrig*, *Cledemuthan*, *Scergeat*, and *Weardbyrig*. Cf. Round, in *E.H.R.*, XXVII (1912), 546.

[5] *A.S.C.*, II, 80 (915).

[6] *A.S.C.*, II, 78 (913).

Danish boroughs of Bedford, Nottingham, and Stamford, did he in each case add a second across the river?[1]

The answer has been given by Hope: these were military positions designed to close the great waterways to the Danes. Wherever possible the king made use of some previously existing stronghold, but in many cases military necessity forced him to make his own boroughs.[2] And we know quite well what they were like. A considerable area was enclosed with a ditch, an earthen rampart, and a stockade, normally cut by four gates. The enclosure, according to the nature of the terrain, might be either rectangular or oval, as were those of the Danes and those of the Romans before them.[3] Unlike the later castle of the Normans, this borough did not include a separately fortified mound and tower, but if a hill was available, it was naturally taken advantage of. As to extent, Round long ago stressed the important consideration: the borough was not the fortress of a feudal conqueror with a small band of professional retainers; rather it was a fortified camp for the whole fighting population of the countryside — in time of need a defense and refuge for all the people.[4] The borough, consequently, was on the average considerably larger than the later castle, but we should not exaggerate its size. Witham and Eddisbury remain as they were constructed by Edward and Aethelflaed. The former, within its outermost wall contains slightly more than 26 acres, but only 9½ inside the inner wall; Eddisbury is not much bigger than the smaller of these enclosures.[5] The original boroughs of Nottingham, Cambridge, Thetford, and Maldon seem to have been respectively of 39, 28, 24, and 22 acres—an average of about one-fourth the area of the ordinary Roman *civitas* in Britain.[6]

Taken together, these facts make a remarkably clear story. The boroughs mentioned in the Chronicle had only one common feature—their all-important military character. Otherwise they varied greatly. Many were Roman structures, of which some had been long inhabited, some not. Others were entirely new erections, either Danish or Saxon, part of which enclosed pre-existing settlements and part only waste land.[7] A con-

---

[1] *A.S.C.*, II, 81 (919), 83 (922), 84 (924).

[2] Hope, pp. 81–82; cf. Corbett's map in *C.M.H.*, III (no. 36).

[3] F. H. Haverfield, *Ancient Town-Planning* (Oxford, 1913); Collingwood, *Archaeology of Roman Britain*, pp. 93–94; Armitage, chs III–IV. Before ascribing too much to the conscious copying of models, it should be remembered that enclosures can only be made with square corners or rounded, and that the defenders would normally want a gate on each side with streets to connect them.

[4] In *Archaeologia*, LVIII (1902), p. 334.

[5] Armitage, pp. 35, 39.

[6] *Ibid.*, pp. 41, 44, 55; below, pp. 187 ff.

[7] Except for the *ceastra*, most of the Midland boroughs are not heard of until the time of the Danish wars. But Tamworth had been a favorite residence of the Mercian kings, for many of their acts were issued there (*C.D.*, 194, 203, 206, 245, 250, etc.); Hereford had been a bishopric since the

siderable number of these works, both old and new, continue to be prominent in the records of subsequent centuries, but a large proportion drop completely out of sight. The relative permanence of some boroughs was due, not so much to the intentions of either Dane or Saxon, as to the accidents of later history. The percentage of survivals among the boroughs of Roman origin resulted, not merely from the greater solidity of their masonry walls, but from their advantageous location for governmental or commercial purposes. And who, in the midst of a war for life or death, could foretell the future in these respects of the fortifications that his campaigns necessitated?

In the face of these facts, it would seem impossible to attribute to Alfred and his illustrious children any conscious policy of town-founding; though, like their contemporaries in Germany and Flanders, they were great burg-builders.[1] Indeed, the similarity of the method employed by these princes throughout widely separated regions is most striking, and tends to discredit the argument that any one person or any one people can be especially accredited with its invention. Nor should it be forgotten that the castle was at first only the same thing under a French name. By the time of the Norman Conquest the castle had become distinctly feudal, with an altered form to suit its altered purpose; but originally it too had been rather a centre of popular defense than one of seignorial domination.

If a model was needed by the English, it could readily be found in the Roman *castrum*, with the military advantages of which they must have been familiar from an early time. The case of Bamborough by itself disposes of the idea that the *burh* was a Danish importation. In their homeland the Vikings had no such institutions; their military architecture was obviously learned in foreign countries, where in so many ways they proved to be apt pupils. And although to a certain extent they early combined trading with freebooting, and although commercial routes and flourishing towns eventually grew up in the wake of their conquering bands, it is quite incredible that from the outset they followed a consistent plan of urban development. Whether in England, in Ireland, or elsewhere, their strongholds were built mainly as a means of subduing

---

seventh century (above, p. 49, n. 5); and the names of various other places which appear as boroughs in the tenth century can be found in earlier charters or ecclesiastical records. We cannot be sure that such vills as Tamworth and Southampton had no fortifications until the reigns of Alfred and Edward; it is unlikely that Bamborough was the only such construction of the previous period. Nevertheless, it is quite impossible to believe that either Danes or Saxons refused to erect earthworks save only about a pre-existing settlement, in the case of a Roman structure, certainly, the presence or absence of a resident population did not matter. It is such considerations as these which prove the futility of making the borough from the outset a legal concept.

[1] Above, pp. 11 ff., 23 ff.

and holding the lands that they coveted.[1]   In connection with their
work of military and political organization it seems probable that the
Danes had much to teach their Saxon opponents, but such matters can
be more logically treated as introducing a secondary stage of borough
evolution.

3. The Burghal District

In the preceding pages we have examined the evidence of the Anglo-
Saxon Chronicle with regard to the beginnings of individual boroughs.
But the same source, rather by implication than by direct statement, also
supplies much information concerning a general system of administration
centering in boroughs the names of which are not always given.   The
first hint that we obtain of such an arrangement comes from the famous
year 894.   When Wessex is threatened by two Danish forces, Alfred
places himself between them and is joined by various bands, both from
his *fyrd* and from the boroughs; for, the chronicler explains, the king
divided his force in two: one half to take the field and the other to stay at
home and hold the boroughs.   Later, in the same year, we are told of
three West Saxon expeditions.   While Alfred with one army goes west
to the relief of Exeter, a second joins the *burhwaru* of London in an attack on the Danish work at Benfleet, which is taken by storm.   At the
same time the men who have remained 'at home in the works' gather
from 'every borough east of the Parret' and throughout a considerable
region extending north to the Severn valley, where they eventually break
the Danish fortress at Buttington and win a great victory.[2]

Thus a far-reaching system of boroughs, with regularly constituted
garrisons, appears already established under Alfred, and in later entries
we hear more of it.   In 912 Edward takes possession of London and Ox-

---

[1] The great authority on this question is of course J. C. H. R. Steenstrup, *Normannerne* (Copen-
hagen, 1876–82), whose portrayal of the Danish genius for town-founding has been quoted by Mrs
Armitage and many other writers.   Like all historians of his time, Steenstrup made no effort to
distinguish between the terms borough and town.   But his sources were the same as those before us,
and the thing that he described (IV, 40 ff.) was essentially a fortress, serving as a centre of dominion
for a warrior class.   The Danish boroughs in Ireland — such as Dublin, Limerick, and Waterford —
were, he pointed out, military colonies supported by the native peasantry of the surrounding regions.
The boroughs of the English Danelaw, he argued, were somewhat differently placed, because there
the countryside was largely resettled by an agricultural population from the homeland — a difference
which may be admitted without presupposing urban settlements in either island.   We may also
grant that the Vikings were to some extent traders as well as fighters; but so too, we should remember,
were the early Germans, the American Indians, and primitive peoples generally.

[2] *A.S.C.*, II, 70–72 (894).   The well known tale of how Alfred divided his *fyrd* is not particularly
clear as it stands in the Chronicle; but the identity of the force that stayed at home with the men who
held the boroughs (ðe þa burga heoldon) would seem proved by the later reference to the thegns who
were then at home in the works (þe ða aet ham waeron aet þam geweorcum).

ford with all the lands that belong to them (*eallum þam landum þe
ðaerto hyrdon*). In 915 a Danish army lands and is met by the men of
Hereford, Gloucester, and the nearest boroughs. In 921 Tempsford is
taken by men from the nearest boroughs, and a similar force from Kent,
Surrey, and Essex captures Colchester.[1] Edward's dominions thus seem
to have been divided into military districts with boroughs for their
centres, within each of which the man power was organized to permit the
raising of necessary crops, the defense of the locality, and occasional
offensive operations.[2]

A burghal system is likewise found operative within the Danelaw. In
915 Edward is joined by almost all the chief men belonging to Bedford
(*þa yldestan menn þe to Bedaforda hyrdon*) and by many belonging to
Northampton. In 917 Aethelflaed acquires the borough of Derby with
'all belonging to it'; and in the next year the borough of Leicester and
'most of the army belonging to it.' In 919 Edward gains the borough of
Bedford and most of the *burhwaru* join him. In 921 the armies belonging to Northampton and to Cambridge submit to him, as do the peasants
about Huntingdon, after he has occupied the borough abandoned by the
Danes.[3] The conquest of the Midlands is thus pictured as the taking
over of a series of strongholds — among them the famous Five Boroughs — together with their attached territories and appurtenant population, both military and agricultural. Throughout the entire story the
conflict surges in and about boroughs.

To supplement the vague implications of the Chronicle, particularly as
to the organization of Wessex, we are fortunate in having from the early
years of Edward's reign what appears to be an official record dealing
with this very matter. The Burghal Hidage, as pointed out by Maitland,
is a list of thirty-odd boroughs, beginning at the eastern Sussex boundary,
continuing westward along the coast to Cornwall, then turning to the
northern shore of Devon, passing south of Mercia to the Thames at Oxford, and ending in Surrey. Kent and London are thus omitted in the
document as it stands, but Buckingham is included; and Essex, Worcester,
and Warwick are added as a postscript. So far as it goes, therefore, the
territorial system here portrayed is exactly that which the Chronicle takes
for granted, and we are further given the precious information that the
districting among the boroughs was based on hidage. After each name
is given a sum of hides, and by combining the items it is possible to dis-

---

[1] *A.S.C.*, II, 78 (912), 79 (915), 82 (921).

[2] See *A.S.C.*, II, 73 (896): how Alfred, after the repulse of the Londoners by the Danes on the Lea,
encamped near the borough so that 'they' (apparently the *burhwaru*) could reap their corn.

[3] *A.S.C.*, II, 80 (915, 917), 81 (918, 919), 83 (921).

cern an arbitrary assessment in even hundreds applied to the West Saxon shires and annexed kingdoms.[1]

On the basis of a text which is manifestly corrupt, and which implies boundaries more or less unknown to us, it is impossible to be altogether precise in our deductions. Nevertheless, by examining the Burghal Hidage in relation to the data of the sources that precede and follow it, we are inevitably led to certain general conclusions. The system of burghal districts, combined with a method of military assessment by hidation, seems to have been new under Alfred, to have been a product of the Danish war. In Wessex the construction of most boroughs was apparently subsequent to the division of the kingdom into shires, as well as to the organization of local courts, whether or not called hundreds.[2] The historical relationship of these administrative units to one another remains obscure, but it is decidedly significant that south of the Thames the burghal districts were comparatively short-lived; Domesday takes no account of them. By that time, indeed, one-third of the places listed in the Burghal Hidage are no longer reputed boroughs at all.[3]

North of the Thames, on the other hand, political geography continued to be founded on the borough. A glance at the map shows that throughout this region, with the exception of East Anglia, the counties are essentially burghal districts. They always have been burghal districts. They are not called shires until the eleventh century, and the County Hidage, which comes from that same period, shows two out of a possible three cases of coincidence with the Burghal Hidage.[4] The application of a new name — and it was as yet a vague one — obviously produced no real change in the institution. We thus gain the impression that in those regions where the burghal district, as the result of war-time need, was superimposed upon an older territorial system, it proved only temporary; but that in those regions where all earlier organization had been erased,

---

[1] Birch, *Cartularium*, no. 579; Maitland, *Domesday Book and Beyond*, pp. 502 ff.; Chadwick, *Studies*, pp. 205 ff.; Corbett, in *C.M.H.*, III, 357 ff.

[2] See below, pp. 106 ff., 116; also Corbett, in *Transactions of the Royal Historical Society*, 2nd Series, XIV (1900), 187 ff., and in *C.M.H.*, II, 544, 550 ff. The origin of the hundred, fortunately, is a problem that need not detain us.

[3] If we exclude the postscript and count both Pilton and Barnstaple, we obtain a list of thirty-one places, of which twenty-one are recorded as boroughs in Domesday. But by that time many of the latter were nearing extinction; only a dozen or so were important enough to secure charters in the twelfth century. Furthermore, Domesday adds various shadowy boroughs like Bruton, Calne, Frome, and Milbourne, which had not appeared in the Burghal Hidage, and which subsequently amount to little. The general impression thus given is of a shifting organization that had become largely obsolete by the later eleventh century. See Appendix II.

[4] Maitland, *Domesday Book and Beyond*, p. 505: Oxford, 2,400 — 2,400; Worcester, 1,200 — 1,200; Warwick, 2,404 (?should be 2,400)—1,200. In the last case we obviously have a fifty percent reduction. For further details see Chadwick, *Studies*, pp. 205 ff.

the burghal district has survived practically unaltered.[1] To whom should credit be given for this reconstruction?

From the evidence of the Chronicle, it is clear that the Danes organized at least some of their conquests about boroughs, but the system of hidation seems rather to have been the work of the Saxon conqueror. Throughout the Midlands we find a remarkably symmetrical plan of assessment, with the territorial hundred containing a hundred hides, persisting for centuries — and it was not Danish.[2] Furthermore, we find only four of the famous Five Boroughs with shires named for them. And even if we allow the Danes Cambridgeshire, we can hardly allow them Huntingdonshire.[3] Altogether, the sources tend to indicate that, although the Danes used the borough as a stronghold from which to dominate the rural neighborhood, the adaptation of the system to serve as the basis of a permanent civil administration was English. Did not, in fact, the victory of the West Saxon kings result from this very superiority of their organization?

However that may be, the burghal district appears prominently, not only in the Chronicle and the Burghal Hidage, but also in the dooms of the early tenth-century kings. Thus, when Aethelstan commands the reeve of every borough to see that tithes are paid from all royal property,[4] he obviously intends his order to be comprehensive; he implies that for the management of his revenue the kingdom consists of burghal districts. They also appear in connection with the administration of justice. Edward proclaims that, under certain circumstances, a man is to be provided with six oath-helpers from the same *geburhscipe* in which he lives.[5] Aethelstan ordains that any one who thrice fails to attend the court is to be liable for the king's *oferhyrnesse*, and should he refuse to pay this fine, 'all the chief (*yldestan*) men who belong to the borough (*to þaere byrig hiron*) shall ride upon him and take all that he has, and place him under surety.'[6]

[1] See below, pp. 68 ff.

[2] Corbett, in *C.M.H.*, III, 336; Chadwick, *Studies*, pp. 223 ff.; below, pp. 97 ff. Review of the evidence thus tends to corroborate the suggestions of Corbett and Chadwick in every major detail. It is only their attribution to the Danes of a *territorial* system of administration that seems to me somewhat doubtful. To justify such a conclusion, the evidence from the Continent must also be taken into account. There is, however, no need of pressing the point here, for it has slight bearing on the main problem under discussion.

[3] Above, p. 57, n. 3.

[4] I Aethelstan, preamble (*G.*, I, 146).

[5] I Edward, 1 (*G.*, I, 138). In vol. I Liebermann translated *geburhscipe* (*geburscipa*) as *Ortschaft*, but in vol. III, 94, changed to *Gerichtsbezirk mit städtischem Mittelpunkt;* see below, p. 67. Corbett, (in *C.M.H.*, III, 402, n. 1) takes the alternative meaning based on *gebur*, peasant, and cites a tenth-century charter referring to 'three villages adjoining Oxford' as *geburlandes*. But perhaps we may consider them as 'borough-lands.'

[6] II Aethelstan, 20 (*G.*, I, 160).

These provisions seem to imply that some permanent judicial organization already exists in the borough — a territorial tribunal to hear exceptional cases and enforce justice throughout the burghal district.[1] The ordinary court, and the only one specifically mentioned in the early dooms, is the *folcgemot*. It is held every four weeks by the reeve in charge of a small rural territory, which as yet bears no distinctive name, but is vaguely referred to as the reeve's *manung*.[2] Here Aethelstan establishes a body of official witnesses to serve in all suits, and here may be attested such small purchases as need not be made before the portreeve in the borough.[3] But without stopping for further comment on these matters, let us turn to the remarkable document styled *Iudicia Civitatis Lundonie*.[4]

'This,' we are told, 'is the ordinance which the bishops and reeves who belong to London borough (*to Lundenbyrig hyra ð*) have agreed upon.' Is it not at once apparent that we have to do with a burghal district about London, which includes lesser territories under reeves and at least parts of several episcopal sees?[5] But if there is any doubt of the meaning, it is dispelled by what follows. After repeating Aethelstan's recent enactments concerning cattle-thieves, the ordinance proceeds to describe the association (*fri ðgild*) that has been erected to help in enforcing them. Offenders are to be rigorously pursued. No quest is to be abandoned either on the north or on the south *mearc* — obviously the two sides of the Thames — before every gildsman with a horse has ridden out. The man who owns no horse is to keep at work until his lord returns. And if any group of kinsmen shall protect a thief and prove strong

---

[1] Liebermann (*G.*, III, 105) took this doom to refer only to the ordinary monthly court, but Maitland (*Domesday Book and Beyond*, p. 185) understood it as referring to the shire-moot. Chadwick (*Studies*, p. 220) suggested that it was rather the court of the burghal district that was meant, but confused the issue by invoking Maitland's 'garrison theory.' My own explanation attempts to avoid these complications (below, pp. 68 ff.). Cf. Aethelred's charter granting to the bishop of Worcester one-half of all his local revenue *ge landfeoh, ge fihtewite, ge stale, ge woh ceapung, ge burhwealles sceatinge, ge aelc þaera wonessa þe to aenigre bote gebyrie* — clauses which certainly imply a court in the borough with jurisdiction over breaches of market law and other matters (above, p. 56, n. 10).

[2] II Edward, 8 (*G.*, I, 144).

[3] II Aethelstan, 12; V Aethelstan, 1 (*G.*, I, 156, 168). See below, p. 65, n. 3.

[4] VI Aethelstan (*G.*, I, 173 ff.). See Gross, *Gild Merchant*, I, 178 ff.; Chadwick, *Studies*, p. 220, n. 2; Corbett, in *C.M.H.*, III. 367; F. M. Stenton, *Norman London* (Historical Association Leaflet, no. 38: London, 1915), p. 2. For reasons stated below, it is impossible for me to see in this document evidence that in the tenth century the 'principal merchants of London' were taking steps to organize the court that later became known as the husting (Page, *London*, p. 217).

[5] Liebermann, applying Maitland's 'garrison theory,' translated *to Lundenbyrig hyra ð* as *zu London[s Gerichtsbezirk durch ihre Hintersassen] zugehören;* explained in *G.*, III, 121. Mr F. L. Attenborough, *The Laws of the Earliest English Kings* (Cambridge, 1922), p. 215, understands the doom to refer to a burghal district.

enough to defy the gild, then the reeve in whose district (*monung*) they are shall call out its full strength and shall further send for aid from the reeves on both sides adjoining. Likewise, when a trail is followed from one such district (*scyr*) into another, there shall be the fullest co-operation of the reeves concerned, who under penalty are to forward the pursuit with their respective forces (*gerefscypas*).[1]

Whether this London *friðgild* was one of a series established throughout the kingdom we have no way of telling. We may, however, be sure that the life therein depicted was entirely typical of tenth-century England. A rudimentary government, depending for its efficacy upon methods which we associate with frontier conditions, a thoroughly agrarian society, dominated by a clearly marked aristocracy — these are the salient institutions revealed by our record. Of a mercantile population there is not the slightest hint. People are classified as *eorlisce* and *ceorlisce*, as men with horses and without horses, as riders and workers. The only forms of property that are expected to be stolen, and for which compensation can be claimed, are horses, oxen, cows, pigs, sheep, and slaves. From this *civitas Lundonie* it is a far cry to urban London.

Nevertheless, we know that by this time organized trade did exist in the boroughs, and it has been generally thought to have ushered in a new epoch in their history. To examine that idea we must leave the later fortunes of the burghal district and turn back to other evidence on the borough as an administrative centre.

4. The *Port*

It is surely a significant fact that, within Liebermann's great collection, the official borough makes its formal appearance in the dooms of Edward the Elder, the king whose reign saw the drawing up of the Burghal Hidage and the reorganization of the Midlands. Edward orders that no one shall trade except in a *port*, and with the witness of the portreeve or other trustworthy man.[2] By itself this enactment would be decidedly obscure, but our understanding of it is fortunately aided by the decrees of his successor. Aethelstan first repeats Edward's doom, and then amends it by providing that transactions involving less than 20*d*., the price of a cow, may be lawfully conducted elsewhere.[3] He also forbids the coining of money outside a *port*, and allots thirty-seven moneyers to twelve specified places (Canterbury, Rochester, London, Winchester, Lewes, Hastings, Chichester, Southampton, Wareham, Dorchester, Exeter,

---

[1] Liebermann (*loc. cit.*) interpreted the *scir* of this passage to be the county, and so translated *gerefa* as *Grafschaftsvogt*. Mr Attenborough rightly doubts this identification.

[2] I Edward, 1 (*G.*, i, 138).

[3] II Aethelstan, 12–13 (*G.*, i, 156–8); see above, p. 64. In VI Aethelstan, 6 (*G.*, i, 176), compensation for an ox is defined as 30*d*., for a cow 20*d*.

Shaftesbury), and adds that there shall be one moneyer in each of the other boroughs (*burgum*).[1]

Within certain limits, therefore, we may conclude that in these documents *port* and *burh* are synonymous terms.[2] The borough is still a fortress, because Aethelstan commands that each *burh* be repaired within a fortnight after Rogation days;[3] but not every fortified position, ancient or recent, is a *port*. The last clause of Aethelstan's doom on the mints obviously means that a moneyer is to exist in each other such borough as he has already mentioned, that is to say, in each other *port*. The twelve named are all in the south; in the rest of the kingdom, Aethelstan seems to imply, the mint shall be placed in the official district borough — the shire borough, as it comes to be called.

The word *burh* has thus acquired a technical meaning. In royal documents it does not refer to a mere defensible dwelling, nor to such a temporary camp as the Chronicle often calls *geweorc*. The borough of the dooms may have originated as a purely military work of that kind, but it has since received other attributes. It is a specially authorized and protected fortress, permanently maintained by the inhabitants of the surrounding district. It includes an official market and an official mint. It seems to be the meeting place of a court superior to the *folcgemot* of the ordinary reeve. A borough which has thus been made a governmental centre ranks as a *port* and is under the control of a royal officer called a portreeve.[4]

Now although this word *port* first attains prominence in the records of the tenth century, its derivation is well known. It is the Latin *portus*, which had continued throughout the earlier age to mean, not merely a seaport, but any regularly constituted trading centre.[5] Like *castrum*, it seems to have come into Anglo-Saxon directly from spoken Latin, and so must likewise have borne some relation to an actually surviving Roman institution. Examples of its use before the tenth century seem to be lacking but that the word was more than a mere literary invention is amply proved by its constant reappearance in the English vernacular of later centuries.[6] What, then, had the term come to imply before its adoption into the official vocabulary?

---

[1] II Aethelstan, 14 (*G.*, I, 158).

[2] As has, of course, been pointed out by Maitland, Liebermann, and other scholars.

[3] II Aethelstan, 13 (*G.*, I, 156).

[4] Maitland, *Domesday Book and Beyond*, pp. 193 ff.; Chadwick, *Studies*, pp. 228 ff.; Liebermann, under *Stadt*, 13–15 (*G.*, II, 661–2); W. A. Morris, *The Mediaeval Sheriff* (Manchester, 1927), pp. 6 ff.

[5] Pirenne, as cited above, pp. 11–12.

[6] Maitland, *op. cit.*, 196, n. 1; Liebermann, under *Stadt*, 1 (*G.*, II, 659); T. N. Toller, *Supplement to Bosworth's Dictionary of the Anglo-Saxon Language* (Oxford, 1921), under *Port*. For later usage see below, pp. 95, n. 4, 177, n. 2, 193, 199; Corbett, in *C.M.H.*, v, 537.

In the dooms two features are emphasized as especially characteristic of the *port*, the market and the mint. Neither was a creation of the tenth century, for both had continued to exist in the Roman cities taken over by the Saxons. Long before mints were established elsewhere in England, money had been coined in the ancient *ceastra*, and in these same places had been located the earliest official markets of which we have any certain knowledge. As early as the seventh century London is found under a wickreeve, whose headquarters are in a royal hall and who is specially commissioned to authenticate purchases.[1] Not merely as a fortress, but also as a *port*, the model for the tenth-century borough was plainly the *civitas*.[2]

This, however, does not mean that Edward and Aethelstan were in any real sense the restorers of British industry and urban life. The West Saxon kings, like their Frankish contemporaries, minted only pennies, and they were used only for the simplest of transactions. The only important trade contemplated by the dooms is in cattle and slaves.[3] Of the commerce that had once streamed along the British roads and waterways, the merest trickle persisted into the period with which we are dealing. The mints and markets of Aethelstan are but faintly reminiscent of the Roman originals. All that we know of tenth-century England leads us to believe that it was more thoroughly agrarian even than Gaul or Germany. And if the Scandinavian connection was eventually to stimulate a commercial awakening, it had not as yet had time to produce perceptible results. The age of town-founding still lay far in the future.

The impossibility of attributing an urban character to the early borough is admirably illustrated by Liebermann's translation of the dooms. If any one was competent to undertake the task, it was assuredly that eminent scholar; but even his learning did not avail to find an acceptable substitute for the word borough. *Port* and *burh* he normally read as *Stadt*, but in the passage where the *burh* is ordered to be kept in repair he placed *Burg*, and in the following section concerning mints compromised with *Burg-Städte*.[4] The *burh* of the preamble to I Aethelstan Liebermann originally translated as *Stadt*, but in his third volume he substituted *Gericht* (*Amtsprengel*) because he had decided that others besides *Stadt-*

---

[1] Above, p. 51; cf. p. 25, n. 3.

[2] It would therefore seem impossible altogether to agree with Corbett (*C.M.H.*, iii, 362) and the many other writers who have detected the beginnings of a new urban epoch in the dooms of Edward and Aethelstan.

[3] Liebermann, under *Handel, Münze* (*G.*, ii, 492, 591); Chadwick, *Studies*, chs. i–ii; Pirenne, *Villes du Moyen Age*, pp. 37 ff.

[4] Above, pp. 65, notes 2, 3; 66, notes 1, 3.

vögte must be referred to.[1]   This alteration he justified by a dual interpretation of *burh* already set forth in his glossary, but that was necessitated only by his presupposition that the borough was normally a town.[2]
So too he altered his reading of *byrig* in II Aethelstan from *Gerichtsstadt*
to *Gerichtstätte*.[3]   And the description of the London *friðgild* caused him
even greater trouble.[4]   Fortunately, the English language permits us to
leave the original word to be explained by its own context; so, without stopping for further discussion at this point, we may proceed to examine the dooms of the subsequent period.

Apart possibly from certain administrative changes, Edgar's enactments reveal the borough system continuing as before.   He issues detailed instructions for the holding of the hundred, and commands that
the borough court meet three times and the shire court twice a year.[5]
The first of these courts could have been new in nothing but name; it was
the ancient *folcgemot*, which Edward had ordered to be held monthly.
Under Edmund it suddenly appears as the hundred — a designation obviously connected with a system of assessment by hidage, which will
come up for further discussion below.[6]   But what of the other two
courts?   If any tribunal superior to the hundred had existed earlier, it
should, according to the evidence already cited, have been the borough
court; but now we hear also of a shire court.

In attempting to understand this rather cryptic provision of Edgar,
it should be noted that, although their times of meeting are not identical,
the borough court and the shire court resemble each other in being widely
separated from the frequently called hundred court, and in requiring the
attendance of the ealdorman and the bishop.   The only intelligible explanation is that both were superior courts with jurisdiction over broad
districts.   Perhaps the borough court differed from the shire court in
name rather than in fundamental character, and perhaps the dual system
of nomenclature reflected a dual system of actual administration.
South of the Thames the unit was the large shire, which included a number of boroughs; north of the Thames the smaller burghal district.[7]

---

[1] *G.*, I, 147; III, 97.   See Attenborough, *Laws*, p. 206.

[2] *G.*, II, 28.

[3] *G.*, I, 161; III, 104.

[4] Above, p. 64, n. 5.

[5] I Edgar, III Edgar, 5 (*G.*, I, 192, 202).

[6] III Edmund, 2 (*G.*, I, 190).   See Liebermann, under *Hundred* (*G.*, II, 518); Chadwick, *Studies*,
pp. 239 ff.; Corbett, in *C.M.H.*, III, 366 ff.; below, pp. 97 ff.; above, p. 62, n. 2.

[7] This is the most natural interpretation of the doom, although Liebermann expressed doubt as to
whether attendance of bishop and ealdorman was required at both courts (*G.*, III, 136).   See the
remarks of Miss A. J. Robertson, *The Laws of the Kings of England from Edmund to Henry I* (Cambridge, 1925), p. 305; and on the general problem involved, the authorities cited above, p. 64.

This duality is indicated in other ways. Edgar declares that in every borough and in every shire he maintains the rights held by his father.[1] Furthermore, when establishing permanent witnesses for markets, he separates the boroughs into two categories: those which are to have a commission of thirty-six, and smaller boroughs which, like hundreds, are normally to have twelve.[2] Are not hereby the boroughs that still stand over districts contrasted with those that have been incorporated in shires? As will be seen below, Domesday affords convincing evidence that a local court of frequent session was commonly associated with the borough, and that it was called the hundred simply because it was the court of a territorial hundred which, large or small, included the borough.[3] Since these hundreds, if not actually older, were created along with the burghal districts, Edgar's dooms must have referred to them as well as to the rest. No separate decree was needed for borough hundreds.

If this reading of the sources is correct, we are forced to conclude that the judicial organization of the tenth-century borough was territorial rather than urban; that in itself the borough had no separate court at all, and that its prominence in the dooms was due to the fact that it was the centre of the most important administrative district. This prominence continues into the eleventh century. Aethelred declares that every vouching to warranty and every ordeal must take place in the king's borough.[4] Canute decrees that 'the various boroughs shall have one law of purgation,' and that, while compurgators for the ordinary oath may be taken from three hundreds, those for the triple oath shall be selected 'from as wide a territory as belongs to the borough.'[5] How can these dooms be understood unless it be supposed that a court of superior jurisdiction, whatever its name, was established in each of the greater boroughs? The fact that at this same time the burghal districts of the Mid-

---

[1] IV Edgar, 2a (*G.*, I, 208).

[2] IV Edgar, 3–5 (*G.*, I, 210).

[3] Below, pp. 111 ff.

[4] III Aethelred, 6 (*G.*, I, 230). The provision is incorporated in a series of dooms dealing with Danish districts, and may not have applied to the southern shires (see Liebermann's notes, *G.*, III, 156 ff.). It is preceded by articles concerning breach of the king's peace: that in one borough court (*burhgaþinðe*) being held six times as serious as one in the wapentake, but only half as serious as one in the court of the Five Boroughs. And the following enactment orders that, to clear a suspect of theft, a man must go to the triple ordeal after depositing 8*l.* as security, half with the lord concerned (*landrica*) and half with the king's reeve in the *port*. The borough court here referred to is plainly the court of a wide district, and it meets in a *port*.

[5] II Canute, 22, 34 (*G.*, I, 324, 336). The interpretation of the passages would seem to follow from those discussed in the previous note. Liebermann (*G.*, III, 205) had his usual difficulty in translating these dooms.

lands regularly came to be called shires seems not to have affected the actual organization of the government.[1]

The borough court of the dooms has been a constant source of trouble for investigators who have tried to identify it with the borough court of the twelfth century. The two were totally different. The old borough court was in no way whatsoever a municipal institution.[2] It bore its name, not because it was made up of burgesses, but because it was installed in a borough which was the administrative centre of a district. There is no reason for supposing that such a court, whether called *burhgemot* or not, met in every borough. And if, at the same time, a court of frequent session was associated with the borough, it was properly the court of the hundred rather than the court of the borough; it was peculiar to the borough only in so far as the latter dominated its rural environment.

In general, therefore, the testimony of the early sources tends to corroborate the view, originally advanced by Maitland, that the Anglo-Saxon borough was essentially a military institution. Point for point its history is paralleled by that of the burg in Flanders and Germany. In these countries, too, scholars for a long time were misled by the name into identifying the early stronghold with the later commercial town and were consequently forced to attribute to tenth-century princes a conscious policy of urban development. But on the Continent this idea has been abandoned by leading historians for at least a quarter of a century.[3] When Maitland wrote, the attack on the accepted doctrine was just beginning; he could not realize how utterly that doctrine lacked the support of substantial evidence. Nevertheless, with characteristic acumen he hesitated to follow his contemporaries in always thinking of the borough as an urban centre. He did not take for granted that the borough had necessarily developed out of a village community, and he refused to accept either market or mint as implying a permanent mercantile population.[4]

Maitland's thesis is fundamentally sound. It is not dependent on what has come to be called his 'garrison theory.'[5] His reinterpretation of the dooms and the Chronicle remains a brilliant and lasting contribution to our knowledge of the borough. But Maitland's interest lay primarily

---

[1] II Canute, 18 (*G.*, i, 320) repeats III Edgar, 5. On the disappearance of the borough court from the later law-books, see below, p. 111, n. 3.

[2] Cf. Liebermann, under *Gericht*, 12 (*G.*, ii, 451): 'Das Angelsächsische Stadtgericht . . . beruht nicht auf municipaler Selbständigkeit, ist kein Organ einer Bürgergemeinde, speist nicht eine Stadtkasse und wird abgehalten vom königlichen Beamten . . .'

[3] Above, pp. 9 ff., 12.

[4] *Domesday Book and Beyond*, pp. 195–96.

[5] See above, pp. 18 ff.; below, pp. 81 ff.

in the history of law, and historians of law seem always to be fascinated by legal continuity. The present essay takes no exception to such a viewpoint; but it does seek to emphasize a phase of the problem that Maitland scarcely touched — the social transformation of the borough. If considerable space has been devoted to the primitive *burh*, the object has been primarily to show what it was not, to indicate that the urban character of the borough in the twelfth century was presumably a recent acquisition. The essential beginnings of town life are not to be found in a military fortification, a special royal peace, a peculiarity of territorial organization, or even an official market place; but rather in the new grouping of population induced by commercial revival.

Concerning this latter phenomenon in Britain, as on the Continent, there has been no great conflict of opinion. It first definitely manifests itself in the eleventh century. The early dooms give not the slightest indication of a town-dwelling merchant class. The only professional traders mentioned are wanderers, who seem to be regarded as dangerous characters.[1] But from the time of Edgar on we encounter various bits of evidence that point to an increase of maritime trade. We have the famous story of the man who, with his own capital, fares thrice across the sea and becomes of thegn-right worthy.[2] There is Bishop Aelfric's quaint description of the merchant who tells the inquisitive schoolboy how he imports precious metals, gems, fine cloth, perfumes, drugs, ebony, glass, wine, and oil.[3] The chroniclers add a few vague and rhetorical statements.[4] But the first royal dooms to contemplate commercial dealings that transcend a local cattle market are those of Aethelred.

For one thing, Aethelred devotes much more attention than any of his predecessors to the matter of coinage. He makes detailed provision for the detection and punishment of counterfeiters and of merchants and other persons who connive at the circulation of bad money.[5] He continues, though unfortunately in vague terms, Edgar's regulation of

---

[1] Hlothere and Eadric, 15; Alfred, 34 (*G.*, ɪ, 11, 69). See Liebermann, under *Handel*, 14 (*G.*, ɪɪ, 493); Gross, *Gild Merchant*, ɪ, 3, n. 2.

[2] *G.*, ɪ, 458.

[3] T. Wright and R. P. Wülker, *Anglo-Saxon and Old English Vocabularies* (2nd ed., London, 1884), ɪ, 96.

[4] The most definite is the statement in the *Vita Oswaldi* concerning York, below, p. 189, n. 3.

[5] III Aethelred, 16; IV Aethelred, 5–9 (*G.*, ɪ, 232–6). The man in charge of all matters concerning coinage, weights and measures, the market, the court, etc. remains the portreeve. Aethelred continues the practice of maintaining mints only in boroughs, reducing the number of moneyers to three for *omni summo portu* and one for every other *port*. But the rule must have been changed or relaxed in the eleventh century, for eventually coins are minted in many places that seem never to have been boroughs. See the authorities cited above, p. 50; Liebermann, under *Münze*, *Münzfälschung* (*G.*, ɪɪ, 591–92).

weights and measures.[1]   He treats with the Danes to secure, among other ends, protection of trading ships and their cargoes.[2]   But in this connection the most significant act of Aethelred's reign is his famous ordinance concerning tolls at London.[3]   Here we learn of merchants from the Netherlands, northern France, and Germany, who bring to England lumber, fish, blubber, cloth, gloves, pepper, wine, and vinegar, and who thence take wool, livestock, and grease.   We hear vaguely of special privileges held by certain groups of these traders, among whom are distinguished the men of Rouen, who within a half-century, if not earlier, have organized their famous gild.[4]   Under the general name of *Flandrenses* we can hardly be wrong in detecting such merchants as have formed the *portus* at Ghent, the *suburbium* at Bruges, and similar settlements elsewhere in the county.[5]   And the men of the emperor, who are said to enjoy the same laws as the English but without any right of pre-emption over the Londoners (*burhmanni*), are in all probability inhabitants of the great *Rheinvorstadt* at Cologne.[6]   As yet we obtain no definite information concerning analogous development at London, but there can be no doubt that by this time the city is well launched on a career that leads away from the life pictured in Aethelstan's *Iudicia* and towards the metropolitan society of to-day.

Having thus abruptly afforded a glimpse of the new mercantile activity that was already transforming the cities of Europe, the dooms revert to their ancient course and so come to a prosaic end.   For further details we must turn to the great treasury of fact known as Domesday Book.

---

[1] III Edgar, 8 (*G.*, i, 204).   The original standard was that of Winchester, amended *c.* 1000 to be that of London and Winchester.   See Liebermann, under *Gewicht*, 8 (*G.*, ii, 473).

[2] II Aethelred, 2 (*G.*, i, 222).

[3] IV Aethelred (*G.*, i, 232; Ballard, *Domesday Boroughs*, p. 116).

[4] Above, p. 40.

[5] Above, p. 23.

[6] Above, p. 24.

IV

THE DOMESDAY BOROUGH

1. DOMESDAY TERMINOLOGY

IN THE preceding chapter a re-examination of the most important Anglo-Saxon records led to the conclusion that, in the time of the Danish war, the borough was primarily a fortress. Whether of Roman or of more recent construction, it then served an essentially military purpose, being used as a base for territorial conquest, as well as for refuge and defense. Subsequently, as the English kingdom came into existence, many boroughs were made centres of administrative districts. Such boroughs, placed in charge of royal portreeves, were organized as permanent strongholds; they were the meeting-places of superior courts; and they contained mints and markets. Whatever the precedents that had earlier been set for the official borough, or *port*, of the tenth century — and some of them seem to have been Roman — it was not possessed of the traits that we consider distinctively urban. Like the contemporary burg on the Continent, it was dominated by agrarian, rather than by mercantile interests. Of the social and political privilege that came to characterize the borough of the Norman period, the sources hitherto examined present no trace.

Inevitably, therefore, we are led to the tentative decision that the outstanding burghal features of the subsequent age were themselves the product of that age. But there is more evidence to be taken into account. Archaeological research has brought out facts of signal importance in this connection, and a wealth of information rewards the careful study of Domesday Book. The topographical expansion of the borough must be postponed for separate treatment in a final chapter; at present it is rather the testimony of the great survey that commands our attention — a mass of detail so difficult of comprehension that an extensive controversial literature has already grown up about it. This literature cannot be avoided by any discussion that aims to explain the nature of the Domesday borough. Many troublesome questions must be dealt with at length merely to demonstrate their relative unimportance. Thus, it is hoped, a clearer understanding of essentials may eventually be gained, and a better approach made to the chief problem under consideration — the true origin of town life in England.

For the guiding principles of Domesday interpretation we are indebted to J. H. Round.[1] In the course of his fundamental studies that scholar incidentally brought out many truths with regard to the boroughs, and in subsequent publications he added much important criticism on special topics that will receive due attention below. But in the latter respect his discussion, like that of all interested students, was given new orientation by Maitland, whose *Domesday Book and Beyond* began a new epoch in the study of the early English towns.[2]

A striking feature of Maitland's work, and one pre-eminently displayed in connection with the boroughs, was his feeling for historical evolution. But his talent in this direction, unfortunately, was not shared by his ardent disciple, Ballard. The latter, in his little volume on the Domesday boroughs, collected and combined with the utmost care all the passages in the record that he considered relevant.[3] Wherever the text said *burgus* or *burgenses*, there and there alone Ballard saw a borough — a town, whose inhabitants were burgesses in the sense that they were members of a privileged community. For to him the borough was a static concept. Although he meticulously enumerated and classified the boroughs of various ages, he seems never to have suspected that realities might have changed while the names remained the same. Our initial task, accordingly, will be the re-examination of his tables.

From the statistics at our disposal we may form three outstanding lists of boroughs: those of the tenth century, drawn principally from the Anglo-Saxon Chronicle and the Burghal Hidage; those of the eleventh century, drawn from Domesday; and those of the twelfth century, drawn from the early municipal charters. Using the first two sources mentioned, we secure for our introductory list about seventy-five names; but by adding places known to have contained mints in the tenth century or to have formed part of the tenth-century territorial system, we may bring up the total to slightly over a hundred.[4] Of this number about seventy boroughs continue to be so ranked in Domesday; the rest fail to maintain their position. But Domesday reports over thirty other boroughs presumably of more recent creation, thus bringing the second list to the same length as the first.[5] For the third we may take Ballard's enumeration of 114 boroughs obtaining charters before the death of King John, about

---

[1] 'Danegeld and the Finance of Domesday,' in P. E. Dove, *Domesday Studies* (London, 1888–91), I, 77 ff.; *Feudal England* (London, 1895), Part I.

[2] See above, pp. 17 ff.

[3] A. Ballard, *The Domesday Boroughs* (Oxford, 1904); supplemented by *The English Borough in the Twelfth Century* (Cambridge, 1914).

[4] See above, pp. 55 ff., 61 ff., 65 ff.; also Appendix II.

[5] Ballard, *Domesday Boroughs*, pp. 9–10.

one-half of which were new foundations.[1]   In all, the second and third lists have about sixty names in common; the first and third about forty-five.

It is thus obvious that between the tenth and thirteenth centuries burghal status was by no means a constant.   While one group of boroughs was being born, another group was dying off.   And if any clue to the changing standards exists, it should be found in Domesday Book.   The subjoined table includes the names of seventy-eight boroughs described in Domesday as antedating the Norman Conquest, and most of them had enjoyed such rank for well over a century.[2]   They are a varied lot.   Some are large and some small; some have many inhabitants and some very few; some return a handsome income and some practically nothing.   The test for the classification is plainly neither size nor population nor general prosperity; a place is called a borough if it has already borne the name a long time.   The clerks try to apply a standard based on ancient usage, and in many cases it seems to have proved an uncertain guide.

This list, however, does not exhaust the localities that are called *burgi* in Domesday.   We read that at Norwich, Nottingham, and Northampton new boroughs have been established since the Norman Conquest, and that they have been settled mainly by Frenchmen, colonies of whom are also reported living at Hereford, Shrewsbury, Southampton, Wallingford, and York.[3]   Again, Domesday describes the same sort of thing in connection with certain of the feudal castles built by the invaders.   'Henry de Ferrers,' says the survey of Staffordshire, 'has the castle of Tutbury.   In the borough about the castle are 42 men living only by their trading, and they render together with the market 4*l*. 10*s*.'[4]   Similar foundations appear at Wigmore, Castle Clifford, Quatford, Rhuddlan, Penwortham, Okehampton, Berkhampstead, and Arundel.[5]   At St Alban's the abbot has 46 burgesses worth 11*l*. 14*s*. a year from toll and other dues.[6]   The abbot of Fécamp has a new borough in his manor of Ramsley and one at Steyning that is not very old.[7]   Nor do the king's boroughs of Reading and Sudbury appear in the more ancient lists.[8]

---

[1] *B.B.C.*, I, 26 ff.

[2] Appendix II.

[3] Respectively, *D.B.*, II, 118; I, 280, 219, 179, 252, 52, 56, 298.   A few Frenchmen are also reported to hold *masurae* at Cambridge, and we hear obscurely of *terrae Anglorum*, as if there were also *terrae Francorum;* but the latter do not appear (*D.B.*, I, 189).   For further details on these French settlements, see below, pp. 98, 189, 196 ff.

[4] *D.B.*, I, 248[b]: 'Henricus de Ferreres habet castellum de Toteberie.   In burgo circa castellum sunt XLII homines de mercato suo tantum viventes et reddunt cum foro IIII lib. et x sol.'

[5] Respectively, *D.B.*, I, 183[b], 183, 254, 269, 270, 105[b], 136[b], 23.

[6] *D.B.*, I, 135[b].

[7] *D.B.*, I, 17.   The new borough was probably Rye (Ballard, *Domesday Boroughs*, p. 9, n. 1).   On Steyning, see below, p. 92.

[8] *D.B.*, I, 58; II, 286[b].   See below, pp. 86, 115 ff.; Appendix II.

At Clare, Louth, Bradford, and Pershore groups of new settlers called *burgenses* are found in close connection with a market.[1]   At Ashwell there is a borough with only 14 burgesses and 9 cottars, but in toll and other customs it renders 49*s.* 4*d.*[2]   Eye *T.R.E.* was held by Edric; now by the king.   Then there were 60 villeins, bordars, and serfs; now only 36, but there is a *mercatus* in which dwell 25 *burgenses.*[3]   Such burgesses as these are evidently traders.   It is plain from dozens of entries, however, that the mere presence of a market by no means implies permanent residents;[4] and when the latter are encountered, they are not always called *burgenses.* At Berkeley we hear of a *forum*, in which are living 17 men who pay rent.[5] At Cheshunt 10 merchants render 10*s. de consuetudine.*[6]   The nucleus of Abingdon appears as 10 merchants living before the gate of the church and rendering 40*d.*;[7] of Bury St Edmund's as the craftsmen and others who serve the abbey.[8]   In Windsor there are 69 rent-paying houses and 26 that are quit; but it is not called a borough.[9]

From these data it is at once evident that we must beware of premature generalizations about Domesday boroughs.   As Round demonstrated in

[1] *D.B.*, ii, 389b; i, 345, 67b, 174b.

[2] *D.B.*, i, 135–135b.

[3] *D.B.*, ii, 319b.   The near agreement of the figures suggests that some of the villeins at Eye had been turned into burgesses, but no such conclusion is warranted by comparative study of the other entries.   Probably it is only a case of coincidence.

[4] Ballard, *Domesday Boroughs*, p. 98.   On the whole, the Domesday evidence tends clearly to support the distinction brought out above with regard to the Continent (pp. 10 ff., 32 ff.): that a mere market (whether called *mercatus* or *forum*) is not to be seen as the nucleus of a town, but only the mercantile settlement.   Historically, the term bourgeois (*burgenses*) arose from the practice of fortifying the quarters where they settled; but socially, it could have made little difference whether they lived inside ramparts or not.   The open *forum* could be turned into a *burgus* very quickly. Ballard's chapter on these newer settlements is quite satisfactory, although some of the 'boroughs' that he recognized may be only the result of a scribe's omission of a place name, showing where attached burgesses were actually resident (see below, p. 82, n. 1).   It is, however, to Mary Bateson that we are chiefly indebted for proving the character and importance of the early seignorial boroughs (see below, pp. 120 ff.)

[5] *D.B.*, i, 163 (*Berchelai*): 'Ibi unum forum in quo manent xvii homines et reddunt censum in firma.'

[6] *D.B.*, i, 137 (*Cestrehunt*).

[7] *D.B.*, i, 58b (*Bertune*): 'In domino sunt iii carucae et lxiiii villani et xxxvi bordarii cum xxxiiii carucis et x mercatores ante portam aecclesiae manentes reddunt xl den.'   Cf. Round, in *V.H.C. Berkshire*, i, 313: 'the typical town that rises at the abbey gate.'

[8] *D.B.*, ii, 372.   Domesday describes 'the vill where lies buried St Edmund, glorious king and martyr,' as having had *T.R.E.* a population of 215 households, not counting 95 bordars.   But recently, the survey says, it has grown to include much land that was earlier under cultivation; so that now no less than 342 houses stand on what had been arable fields.   This was much more of a town than many of the tiny settlements which Domesday calls *burgi*.   Perhaps it had not yet received the fortification required for a borough; but more likely the clerk happened to omit the words that Ballard thought so important.   In any case, the burgesses of St Edmund's are recognized by royal charter within fifteen years of the inquest (below, p. 127).

[9] *D.B.*, i, 56b.   See Round, in *V.H.C. Berkshire*, i, 313.   The borough of Windsor arose beside the new Norman castle.

so many connections, the practice of eleventh-century scribes was entirely at variance with the modern technical use of terms. Identical things are frequently given different names in Domesday, and behind the same word are often hid things that to us would appear quite distinct. In particular, we should hesitate to equate our concept of town with the Domesday *burgus*. We cannot from the outset be sure that all places so called in the survey were actually towns, as contrasted with the many that were not so called. And will any one really familiar with the social history of the Middle Ages take for granted that the Domesday *burgensis* was fundamentally the same as the thirteenth-century burgess? Fortunately, we do not have to be satisfied with mere suppositions of that sort; comparative analysis of the entries permits the drawing of quite reliable conclusions.

In the first place, it should be noted that *civitas* appears in the record as a local variant of *burgus*. By tradition, certain ancient foundations are known as *civitates*, but they are also *burgi;* the latter appellation may almost always be substituted for the other without doing violence to the context.[1] And occasionally *urbs*, *portus*, or *villa* is likewise employed without technical significance in place of the commoner *burgus*. Secondly, careful study of the pertinent entries quickly proves that, when Domesday locates properties as being inside or outside the borough, it means inside or outside the walls.[2] Primarily, therefore, the *burgus* or *civitas* was a walled enclosure; whether it was always something more than that can only be decided by determining the meaning of *burgensis*. This, as any one will discover who runs through a few of the Domesday descriptions, is no easy task; but without at once trying to solve all the problems that present themselves in this connection, we may throw together a collection of typical entries and then see if they at all agree in defining the term *burgenses* — which, in the meantime, may be rendered 'burgesses' without presupposing anything with regard to them.

The burgesses of Exeter, or some of them, 'have outside the city 12

---

[1] The only passage that I have encountered where this may not be done is one for Gloucester (*D.B.*, I, 162), *in burgo civitatis*. On the *civitates* of Domesday, see particularly Maitland, *Domesday Book and Beyond*, p. 183, and *H.E.L.*, I, 634; Round, in *V.H.C. Essex*, I, 414. An early essay of Round's in the *Antiquary*, v (1882), 245 ff., argued that the *civitas* of Colchester was the *burgus* plus the surrounding territory; but this wide district is unmistakably referred to by Domesday as the hundred (see below, pp. 105, 112–13).

[2] At Colchester (*D.B.*, II, 104) properties *in burgo* are contrasted with those *extra muros*. At Stafford (*D.B.*, I, 246) Earl Roger has 3 *mansiones quae iacent ad halam*, and also 31 *intra murum*. The description of Hereford (*D.B.*, I, 179) says that the same customs were observed by the *habitantes in civitate* and those *extra murum manentes*. That of Lincoln (*D.B.*, I, 336) uses *extra murum* as a variant for *extra civitatem*. Cf. *D.B.*, I, 9b: 'In hundret et in civitate Cantuariensi habet Adam filius Huberti de episcopo IIII domos et II foris civitatem quae reddunt VIII den.'

carucates which render no custom except to that city.'[1]	At Lidford there
are 28 burgesses inside the borough and 48 outside.	'Among them all
they render to the king 60*s*. by weight, and they have 2 carucates out-
side the borough.'	At Barnstaple there are 40 burgesses inside and 9 out-
side; at Totnes 95 inside and 15, *terram laborantes*, outside.[2]	At Malmes-
bury the abbot holds 4½ houses 'and outside the borough 9 cottars who
geld with the burgesses.'[3]	In two of the *ferlingi* at Huntingdon there are
116 burgesses rendering all royal customs and geld, and 'under them are
100 bordars who help them in the payment of geld.'	In the other two
ferlingi are '140 burgesses minus half a house' rendering all customs and
geld, and they have 20 haws for which they pay all customs.	To the
borough 'belong' 280 acres of arable, from which the king gets two-thirds
of the income and the earl one-third, and which is leased and cultivated
by burgesses.[4]

In the time of King Edward the burgesses of Steyning 'worked *ad
curiam* like villeins.'[5]	Eight burgesses of Tamworth pertaining to Dray-
ton 'work there like the other villeins.'[6]	The church of St Juliana has
certain land worked by two burgesses with two plough teams.[7]	At Buck-
ingham there is land for 8 teams, but 5½ work it — 2 in demesne and 3½
in the hands of villeins.	There are 26 burgesses, 11 bordars, and 2 serfs.[8]

[1] *D.B.*, I, 100: 'Burgenses Exonie urbis habent extra civitatem terram XII carucarum quae nullam consuetudinem reddunt nisi ad ipsam civitatem.'	See below, pp. 90–91, 103–04.

[2] *D.B.*, I, 108[b].

[3] *D.B.*, I, 64[b]: 'Abbas Malmesberie habet IIII masuras et dimidiam, et foris burgum IX coscez qui geldant cum burgensibus.'	Cf. the hundred bordars *cum hortulis suis* outside Warwick (*D.B.*, I, 238, *Cotes*).

[4] *D.B.*, I, 203: 'In burgo Huntedone sunt IIII ferlingi.	In duobus ferlingis T.R.E. fuerunt et sunt modo CXVI burgenses consuetudines omnes et geldum regis reddentes, et sub eis sunt C bordarii qui adiuvant eos ad persolutionem geldi. . . .	In aliis duobus ferlingis fuerunt et sunt CXL burgenses dimidia domus minus ad omnes consuetudines et ad geldum regis, et isti habent quater XX hagas pro quibus dabant et dant omnes consuetudines. . . .	Ad hunc burgum iacent II carucatae et XL acrae terrae et X acrae prati unde partiuntur censum rex II partes et comes terciam.	Hanc terram colunt burgenses et locant per ministros regis et comitis.'	The Huntington description is one of the most obscurely phrased in all Domesday.	The second sentence here quoted obviously does not mean that the 140 burgesses live in only 20 houses, for as elsewhere *burgensis* is equated with *domus* (see below, p. 82).	The *hagae* of this passage correspond to the *bordarii* above — subordinate men, for whose dwellings superior men pay the royal *consuetudines*.	It will be noted that the only appurtenant lands mentioned are the king's, but presumably the burgesses also held some of their own.	The acres and carucates of these entries are generally fiscal units, rather than actually measured fields (below, pp. 97 ff.).

[5] *D.B.*, I, 17: 'ad curiam operabantur sicut villani T.R.E.'

[6] *D.B.*, I, 246[b] (*Draitone*): 'VIII burgenses in Tamworde huic manerio pertinentes et ibi operantur sicut alii villani.'	See below, p. 92.

[7] *D.B.*, I, 253; below, p. 105.

[8] *D.B.*, I, 143: 'Bochingheham cum Bortone pro una hida se defendebat T.R.E. et modo similiter facit.	Terra est VIII carucarum.	In dominio sunt II et villani habent III carucas et dimidiam et adhuc II et dimidia possunt fieri.	Ibi sunt XXVI burgenses et XI bordarii et II servi.'

In the borough of Nottingham there were *T. R. E.* 173 burgesses and 19 villeins. Outside the borough are 6 carucates which geld with it, and they were divided among 38 burgesses. Now *burgenses* have 6 carucates and 20 bordars and 14 teams. At Derby 41 burgesses out of 243 held 12 carucates with 12 teams *T. R. E.* Now there are 100 burgesses and 40 other lesser burgesses.[1] In Kent the archbishop's cook used to hold the 'little borough named Seasalter.' Now a certain Blize holds it of the monks. 'In demesne is one team, and there are 48 bordars with one team.' There are also a church, 8 fishponds worth 25*s.*, and woods for 10 pigs.[2]

Lastly, we have some remarkable entries for the East Anglian boroughs. Of the 276 burgesses listed by name at Colchester, 152 hold 1296 acres of arable, but some properties render no custom except what the burgesses pay on their heads.[3] In the borough of Ipswich were 808 burgesses *T. R. E.;* now there are only 110 rendering custom and 100 poor burgesses who pay to the king's geld only a penny each on their heads. On adjoining lands we hear of freemen and villeins and of *homines bordarii* who have no land of their own, but live on that of others. Of his burgesses in Ipswich; Richard, son of Earl Gilbert, has only commendation from the 12 who live on their own lands, but *sac* and *soc* over 4 others, one of whom is a serf.[4] In and about Thetford we also hear of serfs and bordars, some of whom pay scot only on their heads; and of 943 burgesses, 36 of whom were so subject to the king that they could not seek other lords without his license. The others could, but the king kept all custom from them except heriot.[5] At Norwich there were 1,320 burgesses; now there are 665, together with 480 bordars who render no custom because of poverty.[6] At Dunwich there were 120 burgesses; now there are 232, and also 178 poor men.[7]

---

[1] *D.B.*, I, 280; below, pp. 92, 196 ff.

[2] *D.B.*, I, 5.

[3] *D.B.*, II, 104, 106[b]: 'Modo non reddunt consuetudinem nisi de suis capitibus.' The figures are those of Round, in *Antiquary*, VI (1882), 5. Cf. *V.H.C. Essex*, I, 414 ff.

[4] *D.B.*, II, 290, 393.

[5] *D.B.*, II, 118[b], 173.

[6] *D.B.*, II, 116.

[7] *D.B.*, II, 311[b]. The inferiority of Little Domesday is clearly seen from its description of the boroughs. The statistics that it records in this connection are so chaotic that few positive conclusions can be drawn from them. The most complete account is that of Colchester and, as Round remarks (*loc. cit.*), 'the whole effect produced is that of a landowning community, with scarcely any trace of a landless, trading element.' Elsewhere we are not so fortunate. The figures on population at Thetford are intelligible enough (*T.R.E.* 943 burgesses, now 720 and 224 vacant houses), but the Ipswich entry leaves 270 burgesses not accounted for, and in that for Norwich the discrepancy is greater (below, p. 198, n. 1). Furthermore, the reports concerning the lands of the burgesses are quite incredible. If 152 burgesses out of 276 at Colchester held 1,296 acres, why should only 21 out

These, of course, are but a few of the many passages that deal with the subject in Domesday, but it is impossible to glance through them without becoming convinced that *burgensis* is not a technical word in the survey and that it bears no reference to legal status.   For how can we distinguish the *burgenses minores* of Derby or the *pauperes burgenses* of Colchester and Ipswich from the *bordarii* of Nottingham, Norwich, Thetford, and Huntingdon; or these from the cottars of Malmesbury and the burgesses beyond the walls of Totnes?   Burgesses might hold arable or not; might have plough teams or not.   They might work like villeins; might they not be villeins?   It would be rash to say that the *villani* of the first Buckingham entry were not the *burgenses* of the second.   If a serf could be a burgess at Ipswich, we can hardly be certain that all the other burgesses listed in Domesday were freemen.   If the bordars of Seasalter were not also burgesses, there were none in the borough.[1]

Nevertheless, these random statistics are not meaningless.   Whenever the survey attempts to classify *burgenses*, a line is drawn between men who have lands and those who do not.   We may by no means be sure that none of those mentioned were engaged in trade or industry; but such matters were apparently not considered of major interest.   Taxable property was primarily real estate, rather than cash or merchandise.   The large number of bordars reported to be 'under' certain burgesses would indicate that the latter were landed proprietors whose fields were cultivated by poorer men.   And this supposition is borne out by the fact that these upper-class burgesses are frequently described as of thegnly or near-thegnly rank.[2]   There may have been exceptions, but the chief source of wealth in most old boroughs was evidently the soil.[3]

Such *burgi* as those described above seem, therefore, to have lacked a clear-cut social character; their inhabitants were not burgesses in the

of 720 at Thetford hold 6 carucates and 60 acres?   Can we believe that 808 burgesses at Ipswich had only 40 acres, or that 1,320 at Norwich had only 80?   Indeed, we are told that in the latter borough one burgess named Edstan had 18 acres of arable and 12 of meadow, and we know that only a few Norwich burgesses had 80 acres in Humbleyard Hundred (below, p. 90).   Such results must have been due either to incomplete returns or to faulty compilation.   Dunwich was clearly a thriving settlement of fisherman (M. Bateson, in *E.H.R.*, xx, 151) and Yarmouth, we might suppose, was the same sort of place.   But what was Maldon?   Domesday tells us that 15 out of 180 burgesses held 81 acres and that the rest had only their houses in the borough (*D.B.*, II, 5b).   Since the survey casually refers to a ship furnished the king by the burgesses (*D.B.*, II, 48), we should naturally imagine a maritime town.   But how did these landless burgesses differ from the *bordarii* mentioned elsewhere?   The project of making an accurate comparison of these boroughs is rendered hopeless by the jumbled records before us.

[1] For other references to villeins and bordars in boroughs, see Ballard, *Domesday Boroughs*, pp. 69 ff.   Serfs are also mentioned at Chester (*D.B.*, I, 263).   On the peasantry in general, Maitland, *Domesday Book and Beyond*, pp. 26 ff.; Vinogradoff, *English Society*, pp. 431 ff.

[2] See below, pp. 91 ff.

[3] Maitland, *Domesday Book and Beyond*, p. 196.

later sense of that word. In Domesday *burgensis* is a vague term, denoting a 'man of the borough,' preferably a landowner. Lesser men, according to the whim of the clerk, were sometimes called *burgenses*, sometimes not. To press these deductions further entails many complications. Tenure, always a difficult subject, is especially puzzling in Domesday, which indistinctly combines vestiges of an older system with Norman innovations. Still, if certain fundamentals are kept in mind, it is not impossible to obtain a reasonably clear idea of how borough properties were held both *T.R.E.* and *T.R.W.* And in this inquiry we should begin, not with the tenure of the burgess, but with that of the baron.

2. Lords and Lands

The fact that the land of the borough was normally divided among a large number of great lords was first emphasized by Maitland, who made 'tenurial heterogeneity' the basis of his well known garrison theory.[1] Since royal boroughs had been built against the Danes, he argued, the thegns of the shire had been obliged to keep troops there for the sake of national defense. Thus had arisen the attachment of borough haws to nearby rural properties, which, outliving its original purpose, remained to be attested by Domesday. To this thesis Ballard offered a considerable amendment. Developing a suggestion of Maitland's into a rigid scheme of interpretation, he applied the peculiar custom of 'mural mansions' at Oxford to all the more important boroughs. The duty of wall-repair that rested with the landholders of the shire had, he said, been shifted by them to retainers kept for that end in the borough. So the characteristically 'composite' structure of the 'county-town' was the consequence of the tenth-century *burh-bot* system.[2]

Neither Maitland's nor Ballard's presentation of the garrison theory has elicited much enthusiasm among students of English history. Practically all commentators have expressed a skeptical attitude and sought to find other explanations for the Domesday passages in question. Mr Tait, doubting the validity of any single formula, suggested that the attachment of burgesses to rural manors might have resulted from the immigration of peasants to a town.[3] Mary Bateson, on the other hand, interpreted the evidence as mainly referring to 'out-burgesses' — men who, though legally members of the urban community, were actually resident on manors.[4] Yet, as Ballard rightly insisted, Domesday in this con-

---

[1] See above, pp. 17 ff.

[2] *Domesday Boroughs*, ch. II; below, pp. 101–02.

[3] *E.H.R.*, XII (1897), 775.

[4] *E.H.R.*, XX (1905), 148. Although Mary Bateson's suggestion has been generally supported by other critics (e.g., Davis, in *Quarterly Review*, CCVIII, 60; Petit-Dutaillis, *Studies*, pp. 81 ff.), it is con-

nection generally uses *mansiones, masurae, domus, hagae,* and *burgenses* as synonymous terms.[1] And if it is properties rather than persons that were appurtenant to manors, both of the preceding arguments fall to the ground. Round's suggestion, so far as it goes, seems happier: that the owners of rural estates found it advantageous to have men in the boroughs for business reasons, as at Droitwich to secure a supply of salt.[2] But this idea is hardly applicable in more than a few instances. ·

On the negative side the critics' objections have been many and weighty. Well summarized by M. Petit-Dutaillis,[3] they need no further recapitulation. Ballard's thesis has been proved to rest upon wholly inadequate data, and though Maitland's original contention is decidedly preferable, even that can hardly be called probable. For while we may heartily approve his central doctrine concerning the origin of the borough, and even accept the garrison as a vital part of its early constitution, we do not therefore need to support his explanation of tenurial heterogeneity. Indeed, if we re-examine that mooted question, perhaps it will be found not to deserve the prominence that it has hitherto enjoyed.

First of all, there should be no misapprehension concerning the meaning of 'appurtenance' in Domesday. As is quite well known, the inquest of 1086 primarily dealt with the evaluation of properties in terms of annual income, and with a view to reassessment of taxation. In the eyes of the commissioners the normal unit of seignorial exploitation was the

---

fronted by what to my mind are two fatal objections. Aside from the matter of Domesday interpretation indicated below, there is a more fundamental consideration. M. Bateson's argument presupposes a system of burgess privilege based on mercantile life such as is not found in England before the twelfth century. Nor do we have any evidence of 'out-burgesses' on the Continent until a much later period than the one under discussion. The idea that the tenth-century *burh* was a mercantile town led her, as it seems to me, to misinterpret the significance of borough custom and to undervalue her own discoveries with regard to burgage tenure (see below, pp. 148 ff.; and cf. the criticism of Davis's article, above, p. 19, n. 2). For all his devotion to *Domesday Book and Beyond,* Ballard seems never to have appreciated the implications of Maitland's view in this connection.

[1] *Domesday Boroughs,* p. 13; in *E.H.R.,* xxi (1906), 704; *English Borough,* pp. 66–67. Cf. Hemmeon, *Burgage Tenure in Mediaeval England* (Cambridge, Mass., 1914), p. 162. M. Bateson's reply (*E.H.R.,* xxi, 709 ff.) rightly emphasized the weakness in many respects of Ballard's classification, but made no effort to refute the argument here stated. Her own doctrine of 'unattached' burgesses, for reasons given in the previous note, to me is unconvincing. See particularly the examples of Domesday usage cited above, p. 78, n. 4, and below, pp. 189 ff.

[2] In *V.H.C. Hereford,* i, 297; *Worcester,* i, 268; *Surrey,* i, 286. In the last of these chapters Round brought out another point which deserves greater prominence than has been given it, that houses in the borough were desirable merely for residential purposes. There is good reason for believing that many Anglo-Saxon thegns lived in boroughs because they were centres of royal government and thus of society. But, unfortunately, we have little direct evidence of such a practice (see below, pp. 90 ff.; above, p. 13, n. 2). As M. Bateson pointed out, Dunwich appears in Domesday as a fishing settlement; but it should be noted that neither Dunwich nor Droitwich bear the usual marks of an ancient borough (above, p. 74; below, pp. 86, 115; Appendix II).

[3] Petit-Dutaillis, *Studies,* pp. 78 ff.

manor, which, under the prevalent system of finance, was farmed out to the reeve who administered it. Thus any source of revenue paid into a manor was said to belong to (*pertinere*) or to lie in (*adiacere*) that manor. And Domesday is filled with complaints of income lost to estates without proportionate decrease in the charges placed upon them.[1]

Now, as every student of Domesday knows, the final compilation described the lands of each county as comprised either in royal or in baronial manors. Considerable difficulty was naturally encountered in fitting the returns of the local juries into such an arbitrary plan, and the result was often a vague and confused record. Hundreds, except for the purpose of mere geographical reference, were commonly reported to be appurtenant to the manors with which their proceeds were farmed.[2] Occasionally this was also true of a royal borough,[3] but more generally the latter, being farmed as a separate unit and yet constituting something more than a manor, lay outside the normal organization. And it was perhaps this consideration, more than anything else, that led the Domesday compilers regularly to give the borough, along with other extraordinary odds and ends, an exceptional position in the book.

Maitland contended that the borough was normally placed at the head of the county survey, or 'above the line,' because its tenurial heterogeneity made it 'no man's land'; but he was forced to admit so many exceptions as to vitiate the argument.[4] Besides, tenurial heterogeneity really has no bearing on the case; for a town in the Middle Ages was regularly said to be on the demesne of the man who enjoyed direct jurisdiction over it, without regard to the ownership of the soil. And enough examples of similar usage exist in Domesday and other records of the English king-

---

[1] Vinogradoff, *English Society*, pp. 305 ff.; Ballard, *The Domesday Inquest* (London, 1906), ch. VIII, and in *E.H.R.*, XXI, 700. On the farm system in general, C. Stephenson, 'The *Firma Unius Noctis* and the Customs of the Hundred,' *E.H.R.*, XXXIX (1924), 162 ff. Dozens of examples could be cited, but one must suffice. *D.B.*, I, 219[b] (*Gretone, Corbei, Dodintone*): 'Plurima desunt huic manerio quae T.R.E., appendebant ibi, tam in silva et ferrariis quam et aliis reditibus. . . . Multa desunt huic manerio quae T.R.E. ibi adiacebant in silva et ferariis et aliis causis. . . . Multa desunt ei pertinentia ad firmam in silvis et aliis causis.'

[2] Maitland, *Domesday Book and Beyond*, p. 92; Vinogradoff, *English Society*, p. 323; Morris, *The Mediaeval English Sheriff*, p. 31.

[3] Notably the Somerset boroughs: Langport (to Somerton), Axbridge (to Cheddar), Ilchester and Milbourne Port (to Milbourne), Bath (to Easton) (*D.B.*, I, 86–87). Cf. the Wiltshire boroughs of Calne, Bedwyn, Warminster, and Devizes (*D.B.*, I, 64[b], 65); but it is not certain that all the burgesses here recorded were actually resident on the lands with which they were valued. The same distinction reappears in connection with mediatized boroughs: e.g., Romney (*D.B.*, I, 4, *Aldintone*), Hythe (*D.B.*, I, 4[b], *Salteode*), and Taunton, apparently attached to the manor of Taunton (*D.B.*, I, 87[b]). On the other hand, the boroughs of Pevensey, Chichester, and Lewes, which were evidently farmed as individual units, precede respectively the holdings of the count of Mortain, of Count Roger, and of William de Warenne (*D.B.*, I, 20[b], 23, 26). See Ballard, *Domesday Boroughs*, pp. 7, 77.

[4] See Round, in *V.H.C. Somerset*, I, 122.

dom to prove that the idea was quite familiar there.[1]   Ballard's suggestion that the Domesday location of the great boroughs was based upon possession of the earl's third penny lacks the support of clear evidence and fails to account for such prominent cases as Hereford and Shrewsbury.[2]   No exact formula can be made to explain all the anomalies of Domesday in this respect, but the general arrangement of the perfected volume certainly tends to show that royal properties and rights that did not fit into the usual manorial organization were set 'above the line.'   All the Midland boroughs were so placed and were evidently farmed individually.[3]   And though hardly consistent in its treatment of the southern counties, the survey is not altogether capricious.   As a rule, the lesser boroughs are recorded as being attached to manors and are there described; the larger ones stand alone.[4]   At any rate, the question, thus regarded, becomes a matter of clerical practice rather than of legal necessity, and therefore one that hardly deserves protracted argument.

Whatever its basis, this system of recording took care of the king's revenues logically enough, but it failed to provide satisfactorily for all of those drawn by barons.   As a result, such items were listed in a very haphazard fashion, being noted sometimes under the borough and sometimes under the manors to which they were attached.[5]   No complete catalogue is made of them, for the frequent duplications were undoubtedly equalled by omissions, and in many places the account is hopelessly obscure.   Little profit accrues from a statistical table made out of such material.   It is rather the general features of the system that demand our attention.

When Domesday describes a house or burgess as appurtenant to a manor, just what does it mean?   Merely, it would seem, that the rent from the former was paid into the latter and was farmed along with it.[6]

---

[1] C. Stephenson, 'Taxation and Representation in the Middle Ages,' *Haskins Anniversary Essays in Mediaeval History* (Boston, 1929), p. 304.   Cf. *D.B.*, I, 179; 'Modo habet rex civitatem Hereford in dominio.'   Ipswich is described under the heading: 'Hoc custodit Rogerus Bigot in manu regis' (*D.B.*, II, 290).

[2] Ballard, *Domesday Boroughs*, p. 43; *English Borough*, p. 38.   Ballard's table (*ibid.*, p. 83) shows that he took the matter of the third penny for granted in about half of his instances.

[3] Warwick was no exception, for, as Round showed (*V.H.C. Warwick*, I, 291), it was only the earl's third penny that was attached to *Cotes* (*D.B.*, I, 238).

[4] Why Barnstaple, Lidford, and Guildford (*D.B.*, I, 30, 100) are entered under *Terra Regis* does not appear, but perhaps there were manorial connections not brought out in the survey.   See below, p. 114.

[5] Ballard, *Domesday Boroughs*, pp. 11 ff.

[6] *D.B.*, II, 63 (*Turruc*): 'et VII domus sunt Londoniae que iacent huic manerio et in hac firma.' *D.B.*, II, 76[b] (*Haingheham*): 'Tunc valebat XIII lib.; modo XX.   Huic manerio iacent XV burgenses in Sudberia et appreciantur in illis XX lib.'   Cf. *D.B.*, I, 154 (Oxford): 'Iernio habet unam mansionem reddentem VI den. pertinentem ad Hamtone.   Filius Manasse habet unam mansionem reddentem IIII den. ad Blecesdone.'   In Little Domesday *ad nullam firmam pertinentes* means 'independent of any

The fact that baronial properties in a borough were regularly attached to estates of the same shire led Maitland and Ballard to find particular significance in the practice. But, as a matter of fact, the basis of the connection was geographical rather than political, for it disregarded county lines whenever the borough lay close to one of them. Indeed, the neat maps made by Ballard to prove his theory of 'contributory properties' prove nothing of the kind; they simply show that, as we should expect, one land could be conveniently administered in conjunction with another only when both lay in the same neighborhood.[1]

Nor is there any reason for supposing the system universal. Many borough houses must have been unattached to manors because they were owned by lords who had no other property in the vicinity.[2] How their rents were collected is a matter of conjecture, for Domesday is silent on the subject. There was, however, nothing to prevent a man who possessed both lands and jurisdiction in a borough from giving them a manorial organization of their own. Within another century private sokes had become exceptional in the boroughs and had to be protected by royal intervention, but in 1086 they were still usual.[3] Like the other arrangements just considered, they were not the product of governmental ordinance, but usages that had grown up to suit the needs of seignorial administration.

Considered from this point of view, the borough's tenurial heterogene-

---

manorial organization' (Vinogradoff, *English Society*, pp. 330, 377). Just as burgesses might be wrongfully attached to a manor (see below, n. 2), so they might be subtracted from one (*D.B.*, i, 7–9, *Aiglessa, Ledesdune, Hov, Celca*). Ballard of course recognized these facts (*Domesday Boroughs*, pp. 16–17; in *E.H.R.*, xxi, 700), but to him the manorial connection itself seemed to demand explanation of an abstruse sort.

[1] This idea was in part suggested by Mr Tait (*E.H.R.*, xii, 775). The fact that borough properties were often distributed among manors lying outside the shire has been emphasized by all critics of the garrison theory and was of course admitted by Ballard; see his maps of Chichester, Lewes, and Wallingford (*Domesday Boroughs*, pp. 14, 28). Cf. Vinogradoff, *English Society*, pp. 307–8; 'the measure of an economic organization, of an estate, is after all only its capacity of being ruled from one centre.'

[2] Note the case of the house at Guildford (*D.B.*, i, 30), which the burgesses say does not belong to any manor (*non adiacet alicui manerio*), but has been unjustly annexed to his property by the bishop of Bayeux. Cf. *D.B.*, i, 11: 'Isdem Hugo tenet in Dovere unum molinum qui reddit xlviii ferlingels de frumento et non pertinet ulli manerio.'

[3] *D.B.*, i, 158: 'Isdem Robertus habet xlii domus hospitatas in Oxeneford tam intra murum quam extra . . . et xxx acras prati iuxta murum et molinum x sol. Totum valet iii lib. et pro i manerio tenet cum beneficio S. Petri.' *D.B.*, i, 336 (Lincoln): 'Tochi filius Outi habuit in civitate xxx mansiones praeter suam hallam et ii aecclesias et dimidiam, et suam hallam habuit quietam ab omni consuetudine. . . .' The lands of the archbishop at York, which lay in the district outside the city, were *ad firmam aule suae* (*D.B.*, i, 298). This *aula* was undoubtedly the same as the *curia archiepiscopi*, mentioned above as lying in the archbishop's shire in the city (see below, p. 191). Cf. the *curia* or *aula* of Hamo the steward at Colchester (*D.B.*, ii, 106), On the later sokes, see below, pp. 131 ff.

ity loses the significance that Maitland attributed to it and becomes a matter for more commonplace explanation.   Why, in fact, should the dispersal of borough lands be made so much of a mystery?   That result could readily have been produced by ordinary grant and regrant.   There is every reason for believing that the kings never owned all the soil in the ancient Roman cities, and from the seventh century on they are to be seen alienating what they had.[1]   The later boroughs must from the outset have enclosed land belonging to many individuals, and they could naturally dispose of it like other real property.[2]   Its increasing desirability for residence or business pursuits would lead to its rapid subdivision and sale.   Nor is it apparent, as Ballard confidently asserted, that the attachment of borough haws to rural estates exactly coincided with, or was necessitated by, the new era of fortification.[3]   Occasionally in the tenth century the charter to a thegn mentions land in a borough as appurtenant to a manor; but for every grant with such a provision there are many without.[4]   Instead of the systematic practice demanded by the doctrine of Maitland and Ballard, the land-books reveal an arrangement so haphazard as to appear accidental.

It is also significant that the same phenomenon is encountered in new and old boroughs alike.   Ballard included under the unfortunate name of 'quasi-county boroughs' Rhuddlan, Reading, Twineham, Bristol, Grantham, Sudbury, Dunwich, Yarmouth, Hythe, and Romney because of their 'composite' structure.[5]   On second thought he dropped the first three, as being rather 'subdivided simple boroughs,' but left the others.[6]   It is clear, however, from his own tables that the following five were each shared by two properties, and the last two were not very 'composite.'   Furthermore, Ballard recognized most of them as 'intra-hundredal' and as having few if any marks of antiquity.   Some of them, in fact, look like boroughs created no earlier than the eleventh century.[7]   But a much clearer case is afforded by Arundel.

---

[1] Above, pp. 50 ff.

[2] See above, p. 58; also the grant of a haw at Worcester by the bishop in 904 (*C.D.*, 339).

[3] *Domesday Boroughs*, p. 107.   Ballard cited two charters dated 811 and 838 (*C.D.*, 196, 239), by which haws in Canterbury and Rochester are respectively granted in connection with lands in Kent; but he quite gratuitously assumed that they must have been issued, like the well known charter of 804 (*C.D.*, 188), to provide places of refuge.

[4] The charters mentioning haws attached to manors are listed by Ballard.   Most grants of land do not describe the appurtenances in detail.   Among those that do, but which include no borough properties are *C.D.*, 454, 543, 556, 1077, 1134, 1159, 1163, 1169, 1171, 1188, 1203, 1218, 1247, 1253 (900–969).   The 'change in the forms of conveyance,' which Ballard thought so significant, would seem to imply, if anything, only the growth of manorial organization.

[5] *Domesday Boroughs*, pp. 9–10.

[6] *English Borough*, p. 84, notes.   The quotation is from *Domesday Boroughs*, p. 9.

[7] See below, p. 115, and Appendix II.

There a *burgus* and *portus aquae* are described by Domesday under the rubric *Castrum Harundel* — the castle built by Roger Montgomery where before had stood little besides a mill. How many burgesses he has in demesne the record does not state, but seven of his vassals have seventeen.[1] Perhaps, as at Rhuddlan, the borough was founded as a sort of joint enterprise.[2] So too at Castle Clifford four Norman tenants of Ralph de Toëni are reported to be holding twenty-three carucates *in castellaria*, and they have in demesne sixteen burgesses.[3] The French borough of Norwich, Domesday tells us, has been made on land which the earl for that purpose ceded to the king, to be held in common by the two. But by 1086 land in it has been secured by eight other barons, who have amongst them thirty-three burgesses.[4]

Indeed, in what mediaeval town did the title to all the land remain with a single person? Alienation of urban property, and even its attachment to rural estates, was by no means unknown on the Continent.[5] Why should such practices in a particular region and at a particular time be set aside as distinctly remarkable? And there is another fact that should not be forgotten: the tenurial heterogeneity of the borough is prominent in Domesday only as the consequence of a clerical practice. While the record divided the vill into its constituent properties and scattered them among the tenants-in-chief, it described the borough as a whole. But in any compilation that reproduces the information as originally returned, the composite character of the lesser unit clearly appears, and many a rural vill is shown to have been a patchwork of seignorial holdings.[6] In other words, even the older borough was normal rather than exceptional in its tenurial pattern; the feature that served to distinguish it from the ordinary village was not a method of private land-holding, but political organization.

---

[1] *D.B.*, I, 23; Round, in *Archaeologia*, LVIII (1902), 332. In spite of Mrs Armitage's statement (*Norman Castles*, p. 98), Arundel is not in the Burghal Hidage.

[2] *D.B.*, I, 269: 'Robertus de Roelent tenet de Hugone comite medietatem eiusdem castelli et burgi. ... In ipso manerio Roelend est factum noviter castellum similiter Roelent appellatum. Ibi est novum burgum et in eo XVIII burgenses inter comitem et Robertum. ...' See below, pp. 93, 122.

[3] *D.B.*, I, 183.

[4] *D.B.*, II, 118.

[5] See the authorities cited above, pp. 9, 24.

[6] Maitland, *Domesday Book and Beyond*, pp. 22, 131 ff. This fact is of course obscured by the Domesday arrangement of properties but clearly emerges from such a document as the *Inquisitio Comitatus Cantabrigiensis*. See, for example, Hamilton's edition (London, 1876), pp. 35, 64: Badburgh with seven hides and five tenants-in-chief, Melrede with ten hides and six tenants-in-chief. Cf. C. S. Taylor, *An Analysis of the Domesday Survey of Gloucestershire* (Bristol and Gloucestershire Archaeological Society, 1889), pp. 268, 284: Shipton, five manors; Ampney, eight manors. In the Domesday survey of Dorsetshire *Wintreburne* appears as a manorial heading no less than thirty times.

Lastly, in this connection, may be noted what relation the question just considered bears to the subject of burgage tenure. After the Norman Conquest borough lands, like all others, were considered as being either *terra regis* or *terra baronum*. The haw possessed by a baron, lay or ecclesiastical, was said to be part of his fief.[1] It was held by feudal tenure — whether by knight service, free alms, or some other variety depended on the terms of the contract. This arrangement persisted; nobles continued to hold lands in the boroughs, and not by burgage tenure, because they were not burgesses. But the Saxon predecessors of these same barons, according to Domesday, were often *burgenses*.[2] Whether they may be said to have enjoyed a system of burgage tenure can be determined only by further investigation.

3. Burgage Tenure

In the twelfth century burgage tenure appears as the characteristic system by which a burgess holds urban land, a system universal among boroughs and peculiar to them.[3] It was a heritable tenure by fixed money rent, normally in return for all service. Unlike feudal tenure, it bore no obligation for feudal service; unlike villein tenure, it involved neither agricultural labor nor manorial dues; unlike free socage, it carried complete liberty of alienation. Thanks to Hemmeon's excellent description, we know exactly what burgage tenure was like in the later age.[4] But when and how had it been evolved?

This problem was incidentally treated by Mary Bateson in her splendid article on the 'Laws of Breteuil.' In one particular respect, she thought, the concept of borough came to be modified as a result of the new Norman foundations: the old royal borough had not been characterized by a uniform system of landholding, which, on the other hand, did exist in the seignorial boroughs. The term burgage was assuredly not Saxon, and she was inclined to believe that the tenure was at least in large part a French importation.[5]

For such a theory Hemmeon voiced utter contempt. Although, he asserted, burgage tenure is not to be encountered under that name in Anglo-

---

[1] *D.B.*, I, 143 (Buckingham): 'Willelmus de Castellon de feudo episcopi Baiocensis habet II burgenses qui fuerunt homines Lewini comitis. . . . De feudo Alberici comitis I burgensem reddentem regi II den.' *D.B.*, I, 64ᵇ (Malmesbury): 'De feudo episcopi Baiocensis est ibi dimidia masura vasta.' *D.B.*, I, 246 (Stafford): 'Isdem Robertus habet de feudo suo XLI mansiones.' *D.B.*, I, 336–336ᵇ (Lincoln): 'Domum de qua abbas de Burg ut dictum est non dedit geldum ipsam clamat Normannus Crassus de fevo regis.' Cf. H. W. C. Davis, *Regesta Regum Anglo-Normannorum* (Oxford, 1913), nos. 221, 230.

[2] See in particular the entries for Hertford, York, and Colchester (*D.B.*, I, 132, 298; II, 106).

[3] See below, pp. 138 ff.

[4] Hemmeon, *Burgage Tenure in Mediaeval England*, chs I–III.

[5] *E.H.R.*, XVI (1901), 344.

Saxon England, the institution was not new in 1066. Landgable was the ordinary name for burgage rent in the time of the Plantagenets and earlier. Where we find *landgablum* in Domesday, there is burgage tenure. The boroughs owed their uniform tenurial pattern, not to the influence of a foreign law, but to their own primeval custom. For in this respect the mediaeval towns, whether of England, France, or Germany, were islands in a feudal ocean, 'relics of a submerged and ante-feudal continent.'[1] Thus, although Hemmeon approved of the 'elaborate and scholarly account' of Des Marez, the lengthy arguments of that writer and of Génestal on the problem of origins he pushed aside as 'profitless ploughing of desert sands.'[2] Presumably Hemmeon believed the Maurer-Below theory too well established to require argument; at any rate, though without referring to it, he accepted its major postulates.[3] On it he built for himself what amounted to a highly speculative doctrine concerning the origin of burgage tenure, and so was led to make cynical remarks about Mary Bateson's conclusions. Verification of his own thesis really demanded analysis of the whole Saxon institutional system. Instead of making an effort in that direction, he was content with citing a few passages in Domesday. Let us see if they bear out his interpretation.

It is quite true that in the twelfth century the word landgable regularly denoted a burgage rent. Had it always had the same meaning? We have only to turn to the *Rectitudines Singularum Personarum* to be convinced that it had not. The *geneat*, says that famous document, pays *landgafol* and grass-swine yearly. He rides and carries, drives loads, works to support his lord, reaps, mows, hews deer hedge, etc. He keeps head-ward and horse-ward and goes on errands far and near wherever he is directed.[4] Finding, then, *landgablum* a common charge of *burgenses* in Domesday, should we conclude that it was a burgage rent, or that they were *geneatas*? Surely, in attempting to answer such a question, we must do more than indicate a familiar name: we must try to get at the essential character of the thing. To mark burgage tenure, landgable must be a heritable money rent in return for all service. The correct solution to our problem can be given only after careful scrutiny of all pertinent sections of the survey.

We have already seen that the *burgenses* of Domesday constituted no

---

[1] Hemmeon, pp. 3, 64 ff., 162.

[2] *Ibid.*, pp. 7–9, 172 ff. Hemmeon's appendix on urban tenure in Germany does not refer to Rietschel's work.

[3] Above, pp. 4 ff.

[4] *G.*, I, 445; translation adapted from Maitland, *Domesday Book and Beyond*, p. 328. For comparison of the *geneat* and the *radcniht*, see *ibid.*, pp. 56–57, 307–09; Vinogradoff, *English Society*, pp. 69 ff.; Corbett, in *C.M.H.*, III, 402–4. And see below, pp. 91 ff.

well defined class, but that many of them were evidently landed proprietors. And if we extend our observations a little, it becomes apparent that the holdings of such burgesses were not always restricted to the borough. Among the lands held in chief of the king in Bedfordshire is listed the *terra burgensium de Bedeford*, and they are Anglo-Saxon possessors who have survived the Conquest.[1] Of the same sort are evidently the two burgesses of Norwich who are reported to hold 12 acres in two vills of Norfolk,[2] and the other burgesses who have 80 acres in Humbleyard Hundred with 14 bordars and a plough team. The latter, indeed, would seem to be some of those burgesses who, as Domesday tells us, have been driven from Norwich by poverty and oppression.[3] Having estates in the county, did they not take refuge on them? In any case, these holdings are, of course, not burgages; the tenures here indicated, however different in detail, are alike in being thoroughly agrarian.

Nor can we be certain that all properties held by burgesses in or near boroughs were necessarily of a different character. In this connection we may examine a famous passage in the description of Canterbury — a complaint against Odo of Bayeux, whom Domesday so often pictures as an accomplished robber. The bishop, it is here alleged, had seized as part of his fief, and had later subinfeudated, various lands which by right belonged to burgesses of Canterbury. These included 45 houses outside the city, from which the said burgesses had enjoyed *gablum*, but over which the king had held *sac* and *soc;* and also 80 acres which had been held *in allodia* by burgesses.[4] This has often been cited as an example of

---

[1] *D.B.*, I, 218: 'In Bideham tenet Osgarus de Bedeford I virgatam terrae de rege. . . . Ipse qui nunc tenet tenuit T.R.E. et potuit dare cui voluit. . . . In eadem villa tenet Ulmarus burgensis de rege II partes unius virgatae. . . . Istemet tenuit T.R.E. et potuit dare cui voluit.' See Round, in *V.H.C. Bedford*, I, 204.

[2] *D.B.*, II, 114: 'In Framingeham et in Treussa tenent duo burgenses Norwici XII acras terrae. Semper valuerunt II sol.'

[3] *D.B.*, II, 118: 'Terra burgensium. In hundret de Humiliat semper LXXX acrae et XIIII bordarii et I caruca et III acrae prati et valent XIII sol. et IIII den.' On the previous page (117ᵇ) we hear of six burgesses who had fled the borough to live *in Humilgar Hundret*. Cf. *D.B.*, I, 127ᵇ (*Fuleham*): certain burgesses of London share with certain Frenchmen 23 hides *de terra villanorum*, having under them 31 villeins and bordars. *D.B.*, I, 142: 'In Herford Hundredo. . . . Petrus quidam burgensis tenet II hidas de rege in Dodesdone.' *D.B.*, I, 376: 'Clamores in Westreding. . . . Terram quam Gozelinus filius Lamberti clamat in Carletone super Normannum Crassum invadiaverunt III burgenses Lincoliae Gudret et Lewinus et Siwinus de Agemund T.R.E.'

[4] *D.B.*, I, 2. But a clearer version is given by the *Inquisition of St Augustine's* (ed. A. Ballard in *British Academy Records of Social and Economic History*, IV, pt. II), p. 10: 'Item demonstrant burgenses civitatis XLV mansiones terre unde habebant LIII sol. de gablo T.R.E., et ipse rex habebat inde sacam et socam (*D.B.*: 'de quibus ipsi habebant gablum et consuetudinem; rex autem habebat sacam et socam'). Haec omnia nunc tenet Ranulfus de Columbeles et Vitalis de Canterbire de feudo episcopi Baiocensis, sed illi non cognoscunt nisi de XXVI. Adhuc tenet idem Ranulfus V agros terre cum una ecclesia que pertinent ad monasterium S. Augustini. Item dicunt burgenses quod idem Ranulfus tenet quater viginti agros de allodiis eorum, et ipse dicit se eos tenere de episcopo Baiocensi. Adhuc

communal ownership, but it surely is not.[1] The *burgenses* concerned
were no privileged community laying claim to corporate holdings, but
a number of landed proprietors resident in the city. Through the local
court they asserted the loss of at least two kinds of property: fields held
by hereditary right and houses granted to other persons at money rents.
If burgage tenure appears in the record at all, it is not the tenure of the
burgesses in question, but of the men who hold haws of them. It should,
however, be noted that in Domesday *gablum* is merely an occasional substitute for *census*, rent that might be paid for arable or mills, as well as
for urban property.[2] Unless it is so affirmed in the survey, we cannot be
sure that payment of *gablum* dispensed with other obligations.

In amplification of this statement an illuminating comparison can be
made of the customs at Hereford and Shrewsbury.[3] At the former borough, says Domesday, there were resident inside and outside the walls
103 men. Each of them was free to sell his holding and to leave, but
only after paying the king's reeve one-third of the proceeds. Furthermore, if any one was prevented by poverty from performing his service,
the reeve confiscated his house and gave it to a more substantial person.
What this service was appears from the subsequent description of customs, helped out by certain additional information from Shrewsbury.
First of all, the burgess paid landgable, but besides that was responsible
for various special dues and even for labor at certain times of the year.
The better sort of men, those possessing horses and full complements of
land (*integrae masurae*), rendered riding and hunting services; others
only performed guard duty within the borough. At the death of an upper-class burgess the king received as heriot his horse and arms; from one
of the lower class 10s.[4] And at least at Shrewsbury widows and girls paid

---

idem Ranulfus tenet XXXIII agros terre quos burgenses semper habuerunt in gilda eorum de donis
omnium regum.' The *allodarii* appear below (p. 31) as holders of *sac* and *soc* and their lands as liable
for payment of relief on their death. On the probable meaning of the last sentence in the entry
quoted, see below, p. 119. Cf. *D.B.*, I, 9ᵇ (*Latintone*): 'Has terras T.R.E. tenuerunt burgenses
Cantuariae et usque ad episcopum Baiocensem qui ab eis cepit.' *Inq. St Aug.*, p. 14 (*Ratingdune*):
'Hoc dimidium solinum clamant burgenses civitatis sicut aliam supradictam terram.'

[1] Comparison of many Domesday entries tends to verify Maitland's opinion (*Domesday Book and
Beyond*, p. 201). The same conclusion had already been expressed by Round (*Antiquary*, VI, 98).
Ballard (*Domesday Boroughs*, pp. 87–89) was still inclined to see collective ownership in the passage.
See below, p. 111.

[2] *D.B.*, I, 9 (*Tunestelle*): 'De istis solins quos Hugo de Port habet tenuit Oswardus v ad gablum....'
D.B., I, 12ᵇ (*Levesham*): 'Ibi III servi et XI molini cum gablo rusticorum VIII lib. et XII sol. reddentes.'
Inq. St Aug., p. 6: *gablum* from mills. See Liebermann, under *Abgabe* (*G.*, II, 264).

[3] *D.B.*, I, 179, 252; Round, in *V.H.C. Hereford*, I, 296 ff.; Tait, in *V.H.C. Shropshire*, I, 295; Maitland, *Domesday Book and Beyond*, p. 199.

[4] The heriot of the riding burgess was that of the lesser thegn in II Canute, 70–71 (*G.*, I, 356). Cf.
D.B., I, 181 (*Arcenefelde*): 'Si liber homo ibi moritur, rex habet caballum eius cum armis. De villano
cum moritur habet rex I bovem.' Throughout the counties of Derby and Nottingham the lesser

for permission to marry.   In spite of a distinctly uniform apportionment of landgable, there was as yet, we may be sure, no burgage tenure in the English quarters of these boroughs.   The social system is that of the *Rectitudines* rather than that of the municipal customals.

Again, we find particularly interesting reports from Nottingham and Derby.[1]   With its usual disregard for precise terminology, Domesday speaks of *burgenses, villani, bordarii, equites,* and *mercatores;* and although some figures are given, they cannot be fitted into a statistical table. Nevertheless, it is not hard to distinguish an agrarian aristocracy, holding most of the land and having it worked by poorer men — an aristocracy of *cnihtas,* riding-men, who are liable for the heriot of a lesser thegn.   Furthermore, it is perfectly apparent that at Nottingham this ancient order has begun to give way.   Many houses that formerly held *equites* are now in the hands of *mercatores.*   And forty-eight of them pay 36*s.* rent, an average of 9*d.* each.[2]   It is certain that the older type of burgesses rendered *opera* as well as landgable.[3]   Did the newer ones do so?   We may well suspect that Domesday notes the change of occupancy just because they did not.

As at Shrewsbury and Nottingham, we hear of landgable in many of the other old boroughs, but also not infrequently of renders in kind,[4] and sometimes of agricultural services.   The burgesses of Cambridge, like those of Hereford, seem to have owed occasional labor on the king's outlying estates.[5]   Eight burgesses of Tamworth are reported to work like other villeins on the royal manor of Drayton.   Before the Norman Conquest the burgesses of Steyning worked *ad curiam* like villeins.   And we encounter similar villein-burgesses at Droitwich, Gloucester, and Ches-

---

thegn paid heriot to the sheriff, *ubicunque maneat in burgo vel extra* (*D.B.,* I, 280[b]).   Similar customs prevailed in Yorkshire, except that the burgesses of York paid no heriot (*D.B.,* I, 298[b]): 'Burgenses autem Eborace civitatis non dant relevationem.'   At Thetford heriot went with the right of commendation; at Stamford it did not (*D.B.,* I, 336[b]; II, 118[b]).   Heriot was paid by the lawmen at Stamford and Cambridge (*D.B.,* I, 189, 336[b]) and presumably elsewhere.   See Maitland, *Domesday Book and Beyond,* p. 73; Liebermann, under *Heergewäte* (*G.,* II, 501); below, p. 111, n. 4.   On riding burgesses in the tenth-century borough, see above, pp. 63 ff.

[1] *D.B.,* I, 280; above, p. 79, and below, p. 196.   See Stenton, in *V.H.C. Nottingham,* I, 236, and *The First Century of English Feudalism* (Oxford, 1932), pp. 132 ff.; Maitland, *Domesday Book and Beyond,* p. 191; Gross, *Gild Merchant,* pp. 181 ff.

[2] 'Willelmus Pevrel habet XLVIII domus mercatorum reddentes XXXVI sol. et XII domus equitum et VIII bordarios.   Radulfus de Burun habet XIII domus equitum; in una harum manet unus mercator.'

[3] We hear of *census* both from houses and arable, and of *opera burgensium* at Nottingham.

[4] Ballard, *Domesday Boroughs,* pp. 77 ff.

[5] *D.B.,* I, 189: 'Burgenses T.R.E. accomodabant vicecomiti carrucas suas ter in anno; modo novem vicibus exiguntur.   Nec averas nec currus T.R.E. inveniebant, quae modo faciunt per consuetudinem impositam.'   Cf. Hereford (*D.B.,* I, 179): 'III diebus in Augusto secabat ad Maurdine et una die ad fenum congregandum erat ubi vicecomes volebat.'

ter.[1] In such boroughs we may therefore be certain that, although *gablum* was perhaps the usual return from a tenement, it was not universal; nor did its payment regularly acquit the burgess of other seignorial obligations. What in these respects was the situation in the new borough?

As would be expected, Domesday gives no consistent treatment to the communities of French settlers. Some are accorded a few random lines of description, while others receive nothing beyond casual mention. But practically all are reported in Domesday to be enjoying a privileged position. The houses now occupied by French burgesses at Shrewsbury and York are listed immediately after the waste properties, obviously because they do not render geld and the other ancient customs.[2] From Wallingford comes the same kind of report, except that some figures are given us: twenty-two houses of Frenchmen render 6s. 5d., which amounts to just $3\frac{1}{2}d.$ each, or less than half the average *gablum* of the older tenements.[3] In the new borough of Norwich each burgess pays only a penny rent besides his forfeitures.[4] In Southampton the sixty-five French and thirty-one English settlers since the Conquest pay only 4l. 6d. *de omnibus consuetudinibus* — which would seem to indicate a uniform rent in return for all service.[5] Of the French colonists at Hereford the only liberty reported in Domesday is the one shared with the burgesses of Rhuddlan, i.e., the limitation of their forfeitures, except for the three royal pleas, to 12d.[6]

---

[1] Above, p. 78. *D.B.*, I, 176ᵇ (*Wicelbold*): 'XIII burgenses in Wich secantes II diebus in Augusto et Marcio et servientes curiae.' *D.B.*, I, 163 (*Teodechesberie*): 'Hi radchenistres arabant et herciabant ad curiam domini. In Gloucestre erant VIII burgenses reddentes v sol. et IIII den. et servientes ad curiam.' Agricultural labor could, of course, be profitably exacted from burgesses only in connection with lands which lay very near the borough. In some of these cases, where the service was owed the king, the record is not clear as to whether the obligation was borne by all burgesses or only by royal tenants. But from the point of view here taken, it does not matter; such a custom was incompatible with the burgess status of the twelfth century.

[2] We hear of the French colony at Shrewsbury only through the famous complaint of the English burgesses, that they are still rated for the same geld, although 51 houses have been destroyed for the castle, 50 others are waste, and 43 French burgesses hold houses that paid geld *T.R.E.*, while the earl has given to the new abbey 39 burgesses who once gelded with the rest (*D.B.*, I, 252; below, p. 104). For the Frenchmen of York, see below, pp. 189–90.

[3] *D.B.*, I, 56. King Edward had 276 haws rendering 11l. *de gablo*, plus royal service with horses or by water. Now all customs are as before; but eight haws have been destroyed for the castle and six others pay nothing as the result of special grant. 'De super plus sunt XXII masurae francigenae reddentes VI sol. et v den.' Although the entry is more obscurely stated, the purport seems to be the same as the one for Shrewsbury.

[4] *D.B.*, II, 118: 'ex annua consuetudine reddebat unusquisque I den. preter forisfacturas.' Penny burgage rents are later found prevalent in the East Anglian boroughs (Hemmeon, *Burgage Tenure*, pp. 67 ff.).

[5] *D.B.*, I, 52: 'Postquam rex Willelmus venit in Angliam, sunt hospitati in Hantone LXV francigene et XXXI angligene. Hi inter se omnes reddunt IIII lib. et VI den. de omnibus consuetudinibus.' The arithmetic of this whole passage is very bad, and the addition of the sixpence looks like a mistake.

[6] *D.B.*, I, 179: 'Francigene vero burgenses habent quietas pro XII den. omnes forisfacturas preter tres supradictas.' Cf. Rhuddlan (*D.B.*, I, 269): 'Ipsis burgensibus annuerunt leges et consuetudines

There is, however, every probability that the law of Breteuil, by which they were distinguished from the native inhabitants, already included burgage tenure.[1]

On review of the evidence, therefore, Mary Bateson's major contention appears entirely justified. It is true that, as pointed out by Hemmeon and Ballard, she attributed to the law of Breteuil various customs that were common to the towns of western Europe. The foreign influence exerted upon the boroughs after the Conquest was French rather than Norman. But the fact remains that the tenurial system which came to characterize the English burgess community is earliest encountered in the great commercial towns of the Continent, and in England first definitely appears where French trading colonies had been established. This is not to say that burgage tenure was wholly a foreign importation. We may be certain that it did not prevail throughout those of the old boroughs which, as late as 1086, were still dominated by agriculture; but in the greater seaports, where commerce had developed long before the Norman Conquest, the situation may well have been different.

As we have seen, the use of the term *gablum* in Domesday is no sure indication of burgage tenure; nor does the size of the payment provide any reliable clue as to its nature. In newly founded towns it was customary for the lord, in order to attract settlers, to place only a nominal charge on the land itself. The same procedure might be followed for the sake of developing a particular quarter within or near some older centre.[2] In either case the practice involved the conscious action of a great landlord and resulted in uniformity of payments throughout a whole district. In Domesday the clearest instance of such a foundation is the French borough of Norwich, where the penny rent remained characteristic of the community; but further evidence of a uniform standard of payment comes from some of the other new settlements. Along the Welsh border the shilling burgage was the rule later, and it presumably existed from the outset in the Bretollian colonies of Rhuddlan and Hereford. And elsewhere, when we are given the figures, French burgesses seem to be living under a uniform financial arrangement.[3]

At York we hear of French settlers, but neither their rents nor those

---

quae sunt in Hereford et in Bretuill, scilicet quod per totum annum de aliqua forisfactura non dabunt nisi XII den. praeter homicidium et furtum et heinfar praecogitata.' See Mary Bateson, in *E.H.R.*, XV (1900), 302 ff., 754 ff.

[1] See below, pp. 120 ff.

[2] Above, pp. 29 ff.

[3] Hemmeon, *Burgage Tenure*, pp. 170 ff. In addition to the passages quoted on the previous page, see below, p. 196.

of their neighbors are recorded.[1]   At Lincoln we are told of houses that paid penny landgables *T.R.E.*, but we have no assurance that the rate was common to the whole city.[2]   Indeed, we may be quite certain that in the bulk of the old boroughs there was no absolute uniformity of rents. The sums paid as *gablum* to the king or to his thegns are often recorded in Domesday, and occasionally groups of tenants appear in the old boroughs with rents following a regular pattern — one which seems to indicate that at some time a considerable estate had been cut into uniform *mansiones*.[3]   The prevalence of such a system in a frontier post like Hereford makes us suspect an artificial arrangement dating from the very creation of the borough.[4]   But speculation of that sort is rather futile. As a whole, the pertinent statistics of Domesday utterly defy organization under any rational plan.[5]   One who attempted to trace the origins of burgage tenure by tabulating rents would be quickly lost in a welter of meaningless figures.   And that project would not only be hopeless; it would also be based on a misconception of the problem.

To decide the true nature of a tenure, we should know more than the

---

[1] *D.B.*, I, 298.   The 400 houses at York that Hemmeon cites (p. 161) as rendering, the better ones a penny each and the rest less, are called *non hospitatae* — a phrase which he omits.   These houses are considered partly waste, as contrasted with the 391 *mansiones hospitatae* and the 40 so waste that they render nothing (see below, p. 189).

[2] *D.B.*, I, 336: 'Tochi filius Outi habuit in civitate xxx mansiones praeter suam hallam et II aecclesias et dimidiam, et suam hallam habuit quietam ob omni consuetudine; et super alias xxx mansiones habuit locationem et praeter hoc de unaquaque unum denarium, idest landgable. . . .   Hanc aulam tenet Goisfridus Alselin et suus nepos Radulfus.   Remigius episcopus tenet supradictas xxx mansiones in aecclesia S. Mariae, ita quod Goisfridus Alselin nichil inde habet, neque scangium neque aliam redditionem.'   This is a troublesome passage; because, if *locatio* is given its ordinary meaning, we have one man getting two kinds of rents from the same property (see Ballard, *Domesday Boroughs*, p. 72).   The word, however, is plainly used as the equivalent of *scangium* in the following passage, and so may be understood as an alienation fee paid on change of tenants.   These houses of Tochi may all have belonged to one development; another house that he held, and which paid a penny for landgable, was outside the wall.   At any rate, we must remember that there were over a thousand other houses at Lincoln, concerning which our record supplies no details.

[3] For example, we are told (*D.B.*, I, 64[b]) that the king's 51 houses at Malmesbury each rendered 10*d. de gablo*.   At Huntingdon the 30 haws held by St Benedict of Ramsey likewise paid 10*d.* each; as apparently did those destroyed for the castle (*D.B.*, I, 203).   Cf. Southampton (*D.B.*, I, 52), where two men are said to have rendered since the time of King Edward 12*d.* each; 27 men 8*d.* each; and 50 men 6*d.* each.

[4] *D.B.*, I, 179.   Each *integra masura* paid 7½*d.*   But see *D.B.*, I, 181[b]: 'In Hereford Port T.R.E. habuit Walterus episcopus c masuras II minus.   Qui manebant in eis reddebant c sol. VI sol. minus.' Cf. Shrewsbury (*D.B.*, I, 252), where 252 *domus* rendered 7*l.* 16*s.* 8*d. de gablo* — a little over 7*d.* each.   It is interesting to note that in these boroughs we can be absolutely certain that uniform landgable did not imply burgage tenure (above, pp. 91 ff.).

[5] In particular see Northampton (*D.B.*, I, 219). where we find such statistics as the following: 23 houses 29*s.* 4*d.*; 1 — 16*d.*; 2 — 32*d.*; 1 — 4*d.*; 8 — 9*s.* 4*d.*; 32 — 28*s.* 8*d.*; 2 — 16*d.*; 4 — 64*d.*; 4 — 4*s.*; 1 — 16*d.*; 21 — 10*s.*, etc.   At Gloucester (*D.B.*, I, 162) we similarly find one *mansio* at 51*d.*, one at 26*d.*, one at 41*d.*, one at 14*d.*, one at 12*d.*, etc.   For other examples, see Hemmeon, pp. 160–161; and on the landgables of the *Liber Winton.*, p. 65.

size of the rents paid. Under the custom of the later town, land could be held at much more than a nominal figure and still be burgage; but land held for a slight cash payment plus heriot, merchet, boon-works, riding service, restrictions on alienation, and the like, would not be.[1] It cannot be too strongly emphasized that the tenurial liberty of mediaeval townsmen lay not so much in the uniformity of their rents, as in the uniformity of the accompanying privilege.[2] Careful study of the problem shows that burgage tenure was inseparable from burgess status, and this could not emerge except in a free borough community. To what extent such a development is indicated in Domesday must therefore be the next point for consideration.

4. Borough Assessment

In attempting to study boroughs and burgesses from the data of Domesday, we must remember that the commissioners of William cared nothing for the problems that interest us. Their object was not to distinguish social classes or to define institutions, but to record sources of income. The nature and previous history of the source were relatively insignificant matters; the important considerations were whether or not it belonged to the king, and whether or not it was paying what it should. Lands, houses, churches, mills, fish ponds, markets, animals, and men — all are alike property in Domesday, for they all produce revenue. Intangible rights of possession, lordship, jurisdiction, and government are indiscriminately thrown together as *consuetudines*[3] — things that can be bought, infeudated, or stolen. The borough itself is a mere bundle of such perquisites. The men connected with it are either receivers of *consuetudines* or payers of *consuetudines*, and each group is subdivided according to what is got or given.

Thus, among the proprietors beside the king, we discover men entitled to *gablum* only and men also enjoying other rights in the borough. *Burgenses* are classified according to three main distinctions: whether they pay rent to the king or to a baron; whether they contribute to the king's geld or not; and whether they are under royal soke or outside it. In all these respects Domesday supplies a considerable array of figures, but tabulation of statistics on the size and wealth of the boroughs before and after the Norman Conquest must be combined with the data of other sources still to be examined. Attention for the present may be concen-

---

[1] This is well brought out by the latest work on the subject — E. W. W. Veale, *Burgage Tenure in Mediaeval Bristol*, published as the introduction to vol. II of the *Bristol Record Society's Publications* (Bristol, 1931), p. 31.

[2] See above, pp. 24 ff., 45 ff.

[3] On 'the great vague term *consuetudo*,' see Maitland, *Domesday Book and Beyond*, pp. 67 ff., 76 ff.; Vinogradoff, *English Society*, pp. 383 ff.; Ballard, *Domesday Boroughs*, pp. 62 ff.

trated on a simpler problem — the financial and political organization of the borough in relation to the surrounding country.

Within the system of fiscal and military assessment Round long ago proved that, at the time of the Norman Conquest, the boroughs as a class had received no separate treatment. They were still rated in the primitive fiscal units devised for the country at large, and although they varied greatly amongst themselves, in general their variations were common to the respective counties in which they lay. In those regions where the five-hide unit prevailed it was shared by the boroughs. But in Nottingham, Leicester, Lincoln, York, and the other Danish boroughs, as in the adjoining shires, men counted rather by sixes and twelves, and land was rated in carucates. Likewise, the marked peculiarities of East Anglian assessment showed themselves both in vill and in borough.[1] Nor did the complication end here, for the amount of service rendered at a given evaluation also varied from place to place.

Thus, Stamford is said to have defended itself for 150 carucates *in exercitu et in navigio et in danegeld;*[2] Bedford for 50 hides *in expeditione et in navibus.*[3] For many boroughs only the hidage is given — Cambridge and Shrewsbury 100 hides each, Huntingdon and Chester 50 each, Bath 20, Worcester 15, Hertford 10, Yarmouth 5, Buckingham 1, and Fordwich $\frac{1}{4}$.[4] Elsewhere equivalent information is supplied indirectly. According to a custom that seems to have been widespread, a royal military summons produced one soldier from every five hides; so it was presumably on an assessment of 100 hides that Oxford was responsible for 20 men in the royal host, or for 20*l.* as the equivalent.[5] Warwick served as 50 hides, sending 10 men to the army; but for *sea-fyrd* provided four boatswains or 4*l.*[6] Similarly, Leicester furnished 12 men, or in case of a naval expedition, dispatched 4 horses to London.[7]

---

[1] Round, *Feudal England*, pp. 44–103. Round's suggestions have since been followed by many writers in books and articles too numerous to specify; but see particularly the introductions to the pertinent Domesday surveys in the Victoria County Histories.

[2] *D.B.*, I, 336ᵇ. According to Domesday, the borough was rated at 12½ hundreds; but as used in this context, the Danish 'hundred' was a fixed unit of 12 carucates (Round, *Feudal England*, p. 73). This peculiar method of assessment was presumably employed also in the other Danish boroughs of Lincoln, York, Leicester, Nottingham, and Derby; though it is not specifically mentioned (see below, n. 7).

[3] *D.B.*, I, 209. The borough, like the ancient royal demesne in the shire, 'had never been hidated'; that is to say, it had never gelded (Round, in *V.H.C. Bedford*, I, 194; below, p. 99).

[4] Ballard, *Domesday Boroughs*, p. 65.

[5] *D.B.*, I, 154.

[6] *D.B.*, I, 238.

[7] *D.B.*, I, 230. If we accept Round's view (*Feudal England*, p. 71) that the Danish six-carucate unit corresponded to the five-hide unit elsewhere, Leicester's 12 men would imply an assessment of 72 carucates. Mr Stenton (in *V.H.C. Nottingham*, I, 236) has expressed the opinion that Nottingham was rated at 6 carucates. But the 6 carucates recorded by Domesday constituted the fiscal

In several of these instances it will be noticed that money could be furnished instead of troops, and from many other entries in the survey it appears that such funds went to the support of the king's mercenaries — the house-carls who had formed a professional standing-guard in England since the reign of Canute, and who, it has been suggested with great plausibility, were garrisoned in the leading boroughs.[1] 'When the king went on a campaign either by sea or by land,' says the description of Malmesbury, 'he had from this borough either 20*s.* for feeding his *buze-carli* or he took with him one man as from an honor of five hides.'[2] At Lewes, 'if the king sent his men to guard the sea in his own absence, 20*s.* was collected from all the inhabitants, no matter on whose land they resided, and this sum was given to the men who kept arms in the ships.'[3] In Colchester it was customary to collect 6*d.* from each house and the proceeds could be devoted either to an expedition or *ad victum soldariorum regis.*[4] At York a house in the city was equated with a carucate in the district outside and all were alike responsible for the 'three works.'[5]

None of these four instances, it will be noted, mentions any tax beyond that taken in place of military service — an arrangement that reappears in the Dorset boroughs. Shaftesbury was assessed at 20 hides, Dorchester and Wareham at 10 each, and Bridport at 5; but their service to the

---

assessment of certain appurtenant lands only, not of the whole borough. Cf. the 12 carucates at Derby and the 84 at York (*D.B.*, I, 280, 298). In this latter connection Domesday makes one of its most cryptic remarks: 'each of these carucates gelded for as much as a house in the city and was in the three works with the citizens.' If the statement is taken to mean that each *mansio* was rated at a carucate, we obtain an impossible total for the whole district of nearly 2,000 carucates (see Appendix III and below, p. 99). And yet it is plain from the subjoined details that these 84 carucates, like the others listed elsewhere, were fiscal units. Mr Farrar (*V.H.C. York*, II, 133 ff.) considers the shires of the city as each equivalent to 12 carucates (the hundred of account at Lincoln and Stamford). On this basis, the original rating of the city, at seven shires, would be 84 carucates; and 168 for the whole wapentake (if that is what the district was called). This at least is a reasonable result, compared with the hidage of the other boroughs, or the apportionment of the borough aids under Henry I (see Appendix V). In any case, we are brought to the conclusion that the verb *geldare* of this passage does not refer to assessment of the regular Danegeld, but, like its occasional substitute *scottare* (below, p. 181, n. 2) refers to a repartition of public burdens within the assessment district, viz., the three works (*fyrd*, *brig-bot*, and *burh-bot*). This interpretation agrees well with what we know of Shrewsbury, where the complaint of the English burgesses clearly implies a repartition of the tax within the geldable area, i.e., the hundred of Shrewsbury (see above, p. 93, n. 2; below, pp. 104, 111 ff.).

[1] Vinogradoff, *English Society*, p. 21. Cf. *D.B.*, I, 56 (Wallingford): 'Rex Edwardus habuit xv acras in quibus manebant huscarles.' On the house-carls see also Stenton, *The First Century of English Feudalism*, pp. 119 ff.

[2] *D.B.*, I, 64ᵇ: 'Quando rex ibat in expeditionem vel terra vel mari, habebat de hoc burgo aut xx sol. ad pascendos suos buzecarlos aut unum hominem ducebat secum pro honore v hidarum.'

[3] *D.B.*, I, 26: 'Si rex ad mare custodiendum sine se mittere suos voluisset, de omnibus hominibus, cuiuscunque terra fuisset, colligebant xx sol. et hos habebant qui in navibus arma custodiebant.'

[4] *D.B.*, II, 107. The entry is given in the present tense, but the reference to *soldarii* clearly indicates a custom *T.R.E.* See Round, in *V.H.C. Essex*, I, 422.

[5] Above, p. 97, n. 7.

king, except for the renders of provisions styled *firma noctis*, was restricted to payments for the king's house-carls at the rate of one mark per ten hides.[1] This same scheme prevailed also in Devonshire, where the boroughs enjoyed even lower assessments — five hides for Exeter and the same figure for Barnstaple, Lidford, and Totnes together.[2] And to the description of these boroughs is coupled the famous remark that they gelded only when London, York, and Winchester gelded — which has generally been taken to imply some sort of communal bargaining.[3] But if, as seems likely, the Devon boroughs were of an old agrarian type; and if, as is certain, the lesser ones failed to attain true urban rank in the following century, such an interpretation of the entry appears incredible. Indeed, a review of the evidence affords a much simpler explanation.

In many regions the ancient demesne of the crown is found exempt from the ordinary geld, though not necessarily so from *fyrd*.[4] The custom of the countryside was then shared by the nearby boroughs, for their payments to the house-carls may be taken as a commutation of military liability, rendered convenient through the local residence of such troops. But whatever may be made of that suggestion, Domesday clearly shows that Edward's tax was an occasional one, and that the three great cities had essentially the same obligation as Exeter.[5] The Domesday comment, as

---

[1] *D.B.*, I, 75: 'In Dorecestre T.R.E. erant CLXXII domus. Hae pro omni servitio regis se defendebant et geldabant pro x hidis, scilicet ad opus huscarlium unam markam argenti, exceptis consuetudinibus quae pertinent ad firmam noctis.' Bridport, Wareham, and Shaftesbury are given similar entries. As Round demonstrated (*Feudal England*, p. 114), the Dorset boroughs, like those of Somerset and Wiltshire, were combined with manors of the royal demesne for the payment of the ancient food rent called *firma noctis*. Aside from this, says Domesday, their only responsibility was for the stated commutations of *fyrd*. Thus, although they 'gelded' on a hidage basis, they shared the frequent exemption of ancient demesne from the regular Danegeld (see Round, in *V.H.C. Somerset*, I, 394; *Hampshire*, I, 401). Miss Demarest has argued from these same passages that the *firma* was an ancient tax assessed on a hidage basis, but I cannot see that the text warrants her interpretation (*E.H.R.*, XXXIX, 161 ff.; below, p. 101).

[2] *D.B.*, I, 100: 'Haec civitas T.R.E. non geldabat nisi quando Londonia et Eboracum et Wintonia geldabant, et hoc erat dimidia marka argenti ad opus militum. Quando expeditio ibat per terram aut per mare, serviebat haec civitas quantum v hidae terrae. Barnestapla vero et Lideford et Totenais serviebant quantum ipsa civitas.' The same information is given by the *Liber Exoniensis* (*D.B.*, Add., p. 80), except that it substitutes *ad soldarios* for *ad opus militum*. Cf. *D.B.*, I, 108[b] (Totnes): 'Hoc burgum non geldat nisi quando Exonia geldat, et tunc reddit XL den. pro geldo. Si expeditio vadit vel per terram vel per mare, inter Totenais et Barnestaple et Lideford tantum reddunt servitii quantum Exonia reddit.' See Round, *Feudal England*, pp. 431 ff.

[3] By myself, as well as by others, until closer reading of Domesday made me skeptical of the usual interpretation (*E.H.R.*, XXXIV, 466–67).

[4] See above, n. 1; also p. 97, n. 3.

[5] On York see above, p. 97, n. 7. Geld at London does not appear in the survey at all, and for Winchester we have only one reference. *D.B.*, I, 44 (*Bolende*): 'Ipsa abbatia tenet in civitate Wintonia XXXI masuras de quibus habet omnes consuetudines quietas excepto geldo regis. A quo etiam geldo est quieta propria domus abbatissae.' But this geld was presumably a payment *ad soldarios*, as in the adjacent shires.

thus read, means only that certain boroughs were exempt from all but extraordinary taxation on a low assessment, and the mystery that has hung about the passage is dispelled.

Furthermore, may we not detect behind this small entry the protest of a local jury against the unprecedented exactions of the Conqueror? The groans of the chroniclers in this connection are famous and are confirmed by the evidence of Domesday and other records. Whatever it had been before, the Danegeld under William became an annual tax and so remained under his sons.[1] No exception was made in favor of the boroughs. Domesday indicates that on the whole they continued to pay according to their old ratings;[2] but although individual payments were usually no heavier, the total of their contributions over a period of twenty years was enormously increased. Moreover, in at least some of the boroughs a new exaction on a hidage basis was added to the older geld.

This was the *monetagium*, a foreign impost introduced in England by the Conqueror. Under the general practice of the age, the king or holder of regalian right could change the coinage at pleasure. And though he was supposed to do so only to maintain the standard of issue, the practice degenerated into a means of enhancing the returns from the local mints. Such procedure not only caused the users of coin great inconvenience, but forced them to pay for the reminting of their silver. Out of this situation grew the tax called *monetagium*, a sort of seignorial blackmail levied in return for the guarantee that during a given period the coinage would not be demonetized.[3] In his coronation charter Henry I promises to abolish the *monetagium commune quod capiebatur per civitates et comitatus quod non fuit tempore regis Eadwardi.*[4]

In Domesday the exaction appears at Lincoln as *geldum regis de monedagio* and at Huntingdon as the *geldum monete* which William established in the borough.[5] Since the latter innovation is said to have altered the

---

[1] Round, in *Domesday Studies*, I, 80 ff.

[2] For example *D.B.*, I, 143 (Buckingham): 'Pro una hida se defendit T.R.E. et modo similiter facit.' *D.B.*, I, 209 (Bedford): 'T.R.E. pro dimidio hundret se defendebat et modo facit.' The language of many other entries implies a similar retention of the old customs; for exceptions, see below, p. 101 n. 1.

[3] The exaction is a familiar one on the Continent; see Du Cange, under *Monetagium*; Liebermann, under *Münzänderung* (*G.*, II, 590); A. J. Robertson, *Laws*, p. 371.

[4] *G.*, I, 522.

[5] *D.B.*, I, 336ᵇ: 'Aluredus nepos Turoldi habet III toftes de terra Sybi quam rex sibi dedit, in quibus habet omnes consuetudines praeter geldum regis de monedagio.' *D.B.*, I, 203: 'Huntedunburg defendebat se ad geldum regis pro quarta parte de Hyrstingestan hundret pro L hidis, sed modo non geldat ita in illo hundret postquam rex Willelmus geldum monete posuit in burgo.' Mr Stenton (in *V.H.C. Huntingdon*, I, 320) reads *geldum monete* as 'money geld' — an anticipation of the later *auxilium burgi*. But the weight of the evidence is opposed to the idea that William established any such system as that found under Henry I (see below, pp. 160) ff.

fiscal connection of the borough with Hurstington hundred, where it had gelded for fifty hides, circumstances of the same sort may have produced the similar changes in hundredal relationship reported by other documents at Northampton and Bath.[1] Furthermore, the existence of this tax may serve to explain the mysterious statement that 'the burgesses of Colchester and Maldon render 20*l. pro moneta*,'[2] and the otherwise inexplicable increase in the dues *de moneta* at Thetford, Lincoln, Gloucester, and Nottingham.[3] The common interpretation has been that, at least in some of these cases, the burgesses were farming the mint, but it is more likely that the entries refer to the *monetagium*.[4]

Finally, in connection with hidage assessments, we may glance at two other matters which to a certain degree affect the boroughs. The view has been advanced by Miss Demarest that the food render frequently called *firma noctis* also appears in Domesday disguised as *denarii de hundret, geldum carucatarum terrae, census,* or *consuetudo regis,* and that it represents an ancient tax assessed on the hide both within and without boroughs.[5] Such an argument constantly demands the drawing of the most extraordinary meanings from the most ordinary remarks in the survey and thus runs counter to many of the interpretations adopted above. But, since it has no bearing upon the major issue of urban development, the question of the *firma noctis* may here be passed over without more detailed consideration.[6]

The *burh-bot* theory of Ballard, on the other hand, is distinctly relevant to the present study, and the slight attention accorded it here is due to the

[1] On Northampton see Round, *Feudal England*, p. 156. The *Inquisitio Geldi* (*D.B.*, Add., p. 18) reports 95 hides for the hundred of Bath, excluding 20 hides for the borough. Following the statement of the *firma burgi*, the *Liber Exon.* (*D.B.*, Add., p. 106) concludes: 'Exceptis his LX lib. et marca auri quas supradiximus reddunt burgenses C sol. de moneta.' Cf. *D.B.*, I, 132: 'Burgum Hertforde pro X hidis se defendebat T.R.E. et modo non facit.

[2] *D.B.*, II, 107ᵇ: 'Et praeter hoc reddunt burgenses de Colecestra et de Melduna XX lib. pro moneta et hoc constituit Waleramus et advocant regem ad turtorem quod condonavit illis X lib., et tamen Walchelinus episcopus querit ab illis XL lib.'

[3] *D.B.*, I, 162, 280, 336; II, 118: Gloucester, 20*l.*; Nottingham, 10*l.*; Lincoln, 75*l.*; Thetford, 40*l.* At Ipswich, however, it is the moneyers who are said to owe 20*l.* a year (*D.B.*, II, 290).

[4] Ballard (*Domesday Boroughs*, p. 76) was certain that the mint was farmed by the burgesses at Colchester and Maldon; Round (in *V.C.H. Essex*, I, 419–22) was more cautious. Neither noted the fact that the setting of a joint farm for the two boroughs would have been a most remarkable arrangement. Ballard's list of payments connected with mints (p. 77) is useful, but his classification cannot be trusted.

[5] *E.H.R.*, XXXIII (1918), 62 ff.; XXXV (1920), 78 ff.; XXXVIII (1923), 161 ff.; XLII (1927), 161 ff.

[6] According to Miss Demarest's most recent article, reference to this peculiar tribute is found in the *consuetudo* owed by all burgesses, royal and baronial, at Colchester, Ipswich, Norwich, Gloucester, and Hereford; in the *geltum regis* at Ipswich; in the two marks of silver owed by the *regii burgenses* of Colchester; in the penny rents paid by settlers in the new borough of Norwich (above, p. 93, n. 4); and in the customs claimed by burgesses of Canterbury from their properties beyond the walls (above, p. 90, n. 4).

fact that it is already quite discredited.[1]   The main points involved are
these.   The dooms and the land-books show that the obligation to keep
the borough walls in repair had anciently fallen on the landholders of the
surrounding territory.   Domesday refers to the matter three times.   At
Chester it was the custom for each hide within the county, on summons
from the reeve, to send one man to rebuild the bridge or the walls of the
city.[2]   At York 84 carucates beyond the walls were 'in the king's three
works with the citizens.'[3]   At Oxford *T.R.E.* there were 721 geld-paying
houses and 292 called *mansiones murales* because, in return for wall-repair, they were quit of all royal custom except *fyrd*.[4]   On the basis of
this last instance Ballard constructed his case, arguing that all the 'composite' boroughs were so because the thegns of the shire had put retainers
there to keep up the walls.

A theory based on the custom of Chester, however, is intrinsically as
probable as Ballard's, and what is known of such practices in general
would lead us to suppose that ordinarily the obligation for wall-work was
not rectricted to a few *mansiones*.   The York entry shows the liability
common to the whole assessment district.   It is rather the Oxford custom
that appears exceptional.   How and when certain houses had there come
to be freed from geld and burdened with a special duty of fortification
is a matter of conjecture.   But surely the 'mural mansions' were not distinguished from the rest because they were 'contributed' by thegns of the
shire.   Was it not rather because they were located along the ancient
borough rampart?[5]   In any case, the arrangement was undoubtedly military and royal; it carries no suspicion of communal action.

[1] Above, pp. 81 ff.

[2] *D.B.*, I, 262ᵇ.

[3] Above, p. 97, n. 7.

[4] *D.B.*, I, 154.   The addition of the *mansiones murales* is my own.   It includes all houses enumerated in the second column, for that is obviously a continuation of the same list, which begins with
the great tenants and ends with the little ones.   It is true that the Domesday scribe did not separately
identify each of these latter *mansiones* as being mural, but the compilation is as consistent as most in
the survey.   Furthermore, it is plain that if the returns included a list of ordinary householders, it
was omitted from the final book, which records only the exceptional properties that were quit of
consuetudines.   Ballard (*Domesday Boroughs*, p. 33), of course, preferred to reject most of the
Domesday list, for he was then able to claim identification, in some fashion or other, of 27 out of 34
householders.   But if we add the other enumerated tenants, his total is only 27 (or less) out of 99!
And these figures leave out of account the 721 other houses, the holders of which are not recorded.
Can we believe that none of them belonged to thegns of Oxfordshire?   And yet, with over two-
thirds of the evidence missing, Ballard could blithely conclude: 'It is therefore perfectly clear that all
the houses contributed by the landlords of the county were charged with the repair of the walls of
Oxford.'

[5] Though the fact was not noticed by Ballard, official records afford clear evidence that the obligation of wall-repair still lay with certain properties in Oxford as late as the thirteenth century.   A
writ of 17 April 1227 ordered the bailiffs of Oxford to distrain 'omnes illos qui tenentur claudere
villam Oxonie quod sine dilacione claudant quantum ad singulos eorum pertinet de villa predicta

We thus fail to find, throughout this whole group of services based on hidage, a clear example of urban privilege. Within another century the distinction between borough and country became fundamental in all fiscal matters. Neither in 1066 nor in 1086 can we detect any such differentiation. On the contrary, the two are included under one general plan of administration. Irregularities exist in large number, but they do not serve to distinguish boroughs from villages. If the payment of a special geld to the house-carls was peculiar to the boroughs — and that is by no means certain — the peculiarity can be most easily explained as a consequence of the borough's ancient military character.[1] The assessment of houses at York was hardly significant of urban growth, for the normal unit of property in all the boroughs was the *mansio*.[2] And when we hear of a poll-tax in East Anglia, it is not restricted to a burgess class.[3] From the evidence examined, the only reasonable conclusion is that the eleventh-century borough, for purposes of taxation and military service, was undifferentiated from rural England. Both were embraced under a system that had grown out of a thoroughly agrarian society. To discover a new tax peculiar to towns, we have to wait for the Pipe Rolls.[4]

This conclusion, furthermore, receives strong support from another set of facts, which now demand consideration. It has already been noted that Domesday frequently describes burgesses or houses beyond the walls with the same obligations as those within. At Lincoln and Stamford certain outlying properties geld with the burgesses.[5] At York 85 carucates outside the city 'are in the three works with the citizens.'[6] Certain lands at Leicester, Huntington, Nottingham, and Derby are without the borough but 'belong to it.'[7] At Exeter *burgenses* have outside the city

---

claudere': *Rotuli Litterarum Clausarum* (Record Commission, 1833–34), II, 181. And on the following 10 August the injunction was repeated with regard to the prior of St Frideswyde's, the master of the Hospitallers of St John, and twenty-seven other persons mentioned by name (*ibid.*, II, 196). The commutation of this obligation was known as *muragium*, and is referred to in writs at least twice (*Close Rolls, 1234–37*, p. 204; *1247–51*, p. 480). Cf. A. Wood, *Survey of the Antiquities of the City of Oxford*, ed. A. Clark (Oxford Historical Society, 1889), I, 240. In the later thirteenth century references to this ancient arrangement drop out of the rolls and the duty of fortification, as in other boroughs, appears common to all burgesses. Was not this the consequence of the erection of a new and enlarged wall? See below, p. 204, n. 2.

[1] Above, p. 98.

[2] Above, p. 97, n. 7. Cf. especially Hereford (above, p. 91), but in almost every borough Domesday distinguishes houses that geld or render custom from those that do not.

[3] Above, p. 79, notes 3–5.

[4] Below, pp. 160 ff.

[5] *D.B.*, I, 336: 'In campis Lincoliae extra civitatem sunt XII carucatae terrae et dimidia, praeter carucatam episcopi civitatis' — described in detail below. Cf. the close of the Stamford entry (336[b]).

[6] Above, p. 97, n. 7.

[7] *D.B.*, I, 230 (Leicester): 'Extra burgum habet ipsa (Judita comitissa) VI carucatas terrae pertinentes ad burgum.' On the other boroughs, above, pp. 78–79.

12 carucates that render custom only to that city, and in the same way *burgenses* of Canterbury have 33 acres *ad gildam suam*.[1]

The rich variety of expression displayed in these passages should not be allowed to obscure their essential sameness of meaning. They do not indicate a relationship based on ownership, communal or individual; but one involving assessment to geld or other royal service. They all illustrate one general truth, that the area thus assessed was not wholly enclosed by the wall. In most instances, unfortunately, the information given us is of the vaguest, but the 84 outlying carucates at York are described as being *in circuitu civitatis* and in eleven vills mentioned by name. And when they are located on the map, they are found to constitute a considerable district to the north and east of the borough proper.[2] This territory is given no name in the regular survey of York, but a duplicate entry gives us a further hint as to its identity. At the end of the volume the carucage of the county is summarized wapentake by wapentake under the three ridings of Yorkshire, and there the region labelled *in geldo civitatis* is found preceding the wapentakes of Westriding.[3] If York was not officially a wapentake, it was clearly the equivalent of one.

What then, in the English shires, was this geld district which was of the borough but not in it? Its name is writ large in Domesday. It was the hundred. For example, let us turn to Shrewsbury. The city, says Domesday, gelded *T.R.E.* for 100 hides. Of these St Almund had 2; St Juliana $\frac{1}{2}$; St Milburga 1; St Cedd 1$\frac{1}{2}$; St Mary $\frac{1}{4}$; the bishop of Chester 1; Edith 3, which are now held by Ralph de Mortemer.[4] The entry does not say so, but these 9$\frac{1}{4}$ hides lay outside the city. For if we look in the next column, we find the bishop of Chester recorded as holding the manor of Meole *in hundredo civitatis;* and in the same hundred 1$\frac{1}{2}$ hides at Shelton, which the church of St Cedd holds of him. Under the rubric of Shrewsbury Hundred, St Milburga holds a hide at Sutton, and St Mary a virgate at Meole, a manor of Ralph de Mortemer, assessed at 3 hides.[5] The church of St Juliana holds half a hide and there has two teams and

---

[1] Above, p. 90, n. 4. Either the burgesses (as at Colchester) assert that the lands should geld with the city, or (more probably, as at Huntingdon) certain burgesses lay claim to particular lands which earlier had contributed to their individual quotas. In any case, the entry bears no reference to a gild. Cf. the 32 houses and the mill held by *clerici civitatis ad gildam* (*Inq. St Aug.*, pp. xxii, 15). In the case of this latter passage the *Domesday Monachorum* (f. 4) provides still another version: 'tenent clerici S. Gregorii ad eorum ecclesiam.' Of this very interesting survey Ballard reproduced only occasional portions. Thanks to the kindness of Miss Neilson, who is preparing an edition for the *V.H.C. Kent*, I have been able to consult the entire MS.

[2] See Mr Farrar's map in *V.H.C. York*, II, 136.

[3] *D.B.*, I, 379.

[4] *D.B.*, I, 252.

[5] *D.B.*, I, 252[b].

two burgesses, *in hac terra laborantes*. The church of St Almund has 2 hides 'of the 100 hides which are computed in the geld of the city.'[1] And the roll is complete. The hundred of Shrewsbury, including the borough and various outlying vills, was assessed at an even hundred hides.

Exactly the same phenomenon recurs in the survey of Cheshire, except that the assessment of Chester is only fifty hides. The two hides said to lie outside the city but to geld with it are found listed in three vills under the rubric of Chester Hundred.[2] Such a district in other shires is frequently called a half-hundred. There are several in Bedfordshire, where the borough of Bedford is itself rated at fifty hides.[3] But the clearest evidence of the arrangement is in East Anglia. Domesday officially designates Norwich, Colchester, and Thetford as hundreds; Ipswich and Maldon as half-hundreds.[4] And the description regularly begins with the outlying vills and follows with the borough proper. Cambridge similarly is said to defend itself as a hundred, and we know that it was the centre of a rural district upon which other hundreds impinged.[5] We hear of the 'hundred of the vill of Winchcombe'; so Gloucester was presumably a hundred too.[6] And by analagous reasoning we may classify Oxford as a hundred and Warwick as a half-hundred.[7] Hereford, Wallingford, and Stafford were probably organized under the same plan.

In all these cases the terminology reflects a system of arbitrary assessment by which the territorial hundred is presumed to include a hundred hides, but there are many irregularities and exceptions. The Danish boroughs of Leicester, Nottingham, Derby, Stamford, and Lincoln (with Torksey) were presumably, like York, the centres of wapentakes assessed in multiples of the six-carucate unit.[8] Huntingdon, though

---

[1] *D.B.*, I, 253. The capricious way in which these hides are recorded is worth noting, because it illustrates the doubtful value of the hundredal rubrics in Domesday. To argue from them alone is always hazardous.

[2] *D.B.*, I, 262ᵇ; J. Tait, *The Domesday Survey of Cheshire* (Chetham Society, N.S., LXXV, 1916), p. 38, and map opp. p. 258.

[3] *D.B.*, I, 209, 211, 215, etc. On this, and what immediately follows, see Corbett, in *Transactions of the Royal Historical Society*, 2nd Series, XIV (1900), 215 ff.

[4] *D.B.*, II, 5ᵇ, 104, 116, 118, 290.

[5] *D.B.*, I, 189; Maitland, *Township and Borough*, p. 41; cf. the map in Hamilton, *Inquisitio Comitatus Cantabrigiensis*. Ballard was familiar with some of the facts, but constantly misunderstood their significance (*Domesday Boroughs*, p. 65; *English Boroughs*, 37, 71). His final verdict on the subject attributed the exclusion of the Saxon boroughs from the rural hundreds to the 'superstition of the invaders and their consequent avoidance of the old Roman towns and the extramural territories on which their dead were buried'!

[6] *D.B.*, I, 162ᵇ: 'Postea reddebat xx lib. cum toto hundredo eiusdem villae . . . Modo adiunctis III hundredis reddit XXVIII lib. de xx in ora.' In this connection Domesday gives no hint concerning Gloucester. On Bristol, see below, pp. 204, n. 1.

[7] See above, 97.

[8] Above, p. 97, n. 7.

rated at fifty hides, is said to have gelded with the (double) hundred of Hurstingston.[1] Worcester constituted fifteen hides in Fishborough Hundred; Northampton twenty-five hides in Spelhoe Hundred.[2] Hertford defended itself for ten hides, but Domesday reports a Hertford Hundred containing, with the borough, about a hundred hides.[3] Buckingham defended itself for only one hide, and we hear of no Buckingham Hundred.[4]

The south of England shows even greater diversity. There are hundreds of Canterbury, Rochester, Fordwich, Sandwich, and Pevensey, which are apparently geld areas, though not of a hundred hides each.[5] On the other hand, Romney and Hythe, like Guildford and Southwark, lie in hundreds that are named after rural manors.[6] Exeter seems to be organized as a separate hundred, and we may guess that Winchester is also.[7] There is a hundred of Bath and a hundred of Dorchester. But most of the boroughs within ancient Wessex appear to be attached to royal manors, with the hundreds centering in the latter rather than in the former.[8]

To make a wholly symmetrical picture from such disparate materials is obviously impossible. Nevertheless, comparison of the borough descriptions tends to bring out certain truths that fit smoothly into the results of recent Domesday criticism. Throughout the regions conquered

[1] Above, p. 100, n. 5; Round, *Feudal England*, p. 58.

[2] *D.B.*, I, 175^b; Round, *Feudal England*, pp. 61, 156.

[3] *D.B.*, I, 132, 133, 136^b.

[4] *D.B.*, I, 143.

[5] For Canterbury Hundred, *D.B.*, I, 5, 9^b; *Inq. St Aug.*, p. 11; *D. Mon.*, f. 6 (above, p. 77, n. 2; 104, n. 1). For Rochester Hundred, *D.B.*, I, 5^b, 8^b; *D. Mon.*, f. 9. Fordwich is described as lying in Fordwich Hundred (*D.B.*, I, 12). Sandwich 'lies in its own hundred' (*D.B.*, I, 3) — an equivalent expression, as may be seen by comparing the following entries: (*D. Mon.*, f. 7) 'Ipsum Cert est hundret'; (*D. Mon.*, f. 9) 'Hoc idem manerium (Brunlege) est hundred'; (*Inq. St Aug.*, p. 18) 'Prestune manerium S. Augustini est in se ipso hundredo'; rubricated in *D.B.*, I, 5, 5^b, 12^b, under the hundreds of *Cert*, *Bronlei*, and *Prestetune*. The *D. Mon.* (f. 7) tells us that Seasalter 'is in no hundred,' and we are left to guess the meaning without further assistance. No information in this connection is given for Dover and the ancient *ceaster* of Hastings (see above, p. 49) is not described at all; probably each headed its own hundred. Likewise, since there was a Pevensey Hundred, (*D.B.*, I, 22), we should expect hundreds of Chichester and Lewes (above, p. 83, n. 3). Steyning Hundred was presumably named for the vill, rather than the borough, which has every appearance of being a new creation (*D.B.*, I, 17, 28, 29). The evidence is incomplete and unreliable, but it seems to indicate that a borough was no more of a hundred to itself than was a vill for which a hundred was named; and that only the oldest boroughs enjoyed even such distinction.

[6] *D.B.*, I, 4, 4^b, 30, 32. See below, p. 114. The *D. Mon.* (f. 7) records Saltwood and Hythe *in hundred de Heda;* but this looks like a scribal error for the *Hen Hund*' of *D.B.*

[7] Domesday gives no hundredal rubrics, but Exeter clearly appears as the centre of an assessment district (above, pp. 77–78). There is, of course, no description of Winchester in the survey.

[8] Domesday indicates no hundreds for Dorset, Somerset, and Wiltshire, but the list is supplied by the *Inquisitio Geldi* (*D.B.*, Add., pp. 1 ff.). There (p. 24) Dorchester Hundred appears as the only one of Dorset named for a borough. In Somerset (p. 58), along with the hundred of Bath, we find a hundred of Taunton; but was it not, like the hundreds of Calne and Cricklade in Wiltshire (pp. 2, 7, 13), named for the vill rather than the borough? See above, p. 83.

and organized by the West Saxons in the tenth century there emerges with surprising distinctness a system of arbitrary assessment centering in the hundred or wapentake, which is commonly rated as a hundred hides or the equivalent in Danish units. The borough, with a certain surrounding territory, constitutes one of these districts and is assessed precisely like the others. In the regions earlier attached to Wessex the system of rural organization and assessment loses some of its neatness; it appears less arbitrary, as if resulting from the adaptation of older practices, rather than the imposition of a uniform plan. And in Wessex proper the outlines become so indistinct that the existence of any regular system may well be denied.

It is, however, very significant that in this older kingdom the boroughs that most definitely appear at the head of hundreds were of Roman foundation. What we seem to discern is a territorial organization that developed before most of the West Saxon boroughs existed, and before any uniform scheme of hidation had been perfected. Later, as the building of boroughs and the creation of assessment units were carried out together in the recovered Danelaw, the two were from the outset nicely coordinated. And throughout all this political construction the dominant considerations were from the first military. The hide was a *fyrd* unit long before Danegeld was collected; the borough was a fortress long before it was anything more.[1]

If the borough's hundredal organization were only a matter of assessment for royal service, review of the complicated details cited above would hardly be demanded in the present connection. They could be dismissed with the remark that they belonged to an obsolescent system which had no bearing upon urban growth in the eleventh century. But, another matter is involved. The hundred was not only a geld district; it was also a judicial organization. In studying the development of municipal institutions we cannot avoid the problem of the borough court — which, in turn, involves the whole system of privilege in the early borough.

5. BURGESS PRIVILEGE

As remarked above, one of the most prominent features of the borough descriptions in Domesday is the enumeration of properties from which the king does not receive full revenue. Except in the case of a completely mediatized borough, it may be said that the king regularly received geld and military service from all burgesses.[2] Only infrequently are even

---

[1] See above, pp. 61 ff.

[2] This fact is brought out by innumerable passages in the borough descriptions. See particularly the language of the entries cited above, pp. 97 ff.; also Ballard, *Domesday Boroughs*, p. 67.

great ecclesiastics reported to be holding borough lands exempt from all customs.[1]   On the other hand, both lay and clerical possessors of haws are noted in many boroughs as enjoying *sac* and *soc*.[2]   And together with the forfeitures which such liberty seems to have carried with it, powerful men were often entitled, by virtue either of personal lordship or of territorial immunity, to a portion of the royal tolls and other dues.[3]   Continuing after the Norman Conquest, this system of special privilege was not only confirmed by feudal grant, but was considerably extended by usurpation. One constantly recurring complaint in Domesday is that barons have been withholding service which *T.R.E.* their haws always rendered.

All this is quite familiar.   What deserves somewhat greater emphasis is the fact that in such cases the Saxon landlords had often been *burgenses*, and that occasionally such persons are reported to be still maintaining their position in 1086.[4]   At Warwick there are nineteen burgesses 'with *sac* and *soc* and all customs, and so they held them in the time of King Edward.'[5]   And whenever the details are given us, the lawmen and moneyers seem in the same way to have belonged to a local aristocracy.[6]

---

[1] At York the archbishop had all royal *consuetudines* in his shire (*D.B.*, I, 298), but ordinarily it is only an occasional hall or a few houses that appear entirely quit of geld and service (Ballard, *Domesday Boroughs*, p. 69).

[2] Good examples of men holding *sac* and *soc* and all customs except geld are found in Guildford, Huntingdon, Stafford, York, and Lincoln (*D.B.*, I, 30, 203, 246, 298, 336).   The entries for Southward, Guildford, and Wallingford (*D.B.*, I, 30, 32, 56ᵇ) show that the essence of the privilege called *sac* and *soc* lay in the right to collect the forfeitures that were incurred by certain persons or by persons in certain houses.   Whatever the origin of the custom, it appears as a mere financial perquisite, to be claimed from the local court or royal official.   See Maitland, *Domesday Book and Beyond*, pp. 98 ff.; Ballard, *Domesday Boroughs*, pp. 48 ff., 58 ff., 82 ff.   On many points in this connection Ballard's discussion is rather confused.

[3] Holders of toll are mentioned at Huntingdon and Lincoln (*D.B.*, I, 203, 336), and at Canterbury a detailed account of such a privilege is given (*D.B.*, I, 3; *Inq. St Aug.*, pp. 7–8).   Cf. the York document of 1080 (*Yorkshire Archaeological Journal*, XVIII, 412 ff.; below, p. 190, n. 2), which recognizes the archbishop's right to levy toll on all men transacting business in his shire, whether or not they have first entered the king's shire; and, vice versa, a similar right on the part of the king in his shire. In the East Anglian boroughs, as in the shires, commendation appears prominently (e.g., Norwich and Ipswich, *D.B.*, II, 116, 392ᵇ), and it sometimes entitled the holder to heriot (above, pp. 79, 91, n. 4).

[4] Above, pp. 90–91.

[5] *D.B.*, I, 238: (following a list of baronial holdings) 'praeter has supradictas masuras, sunt in ipso burgo XIX burgenses qui habent XIX masuras cum saca et soca et omnibus consuetudinibus, et ita habebant T.R.E.'

[6] Below, p. 111, n. 4; Ballard, *Domesday Boroughs*, pp. 51 ff.   At Lincoln (*D.B.*, I, 336) Domesday reports the names of the twelve lawmen who were holders of *sac* and *soc* T.R.E.   There are still the same number and they continue to have the same privilege.   Four of the lawmen have been succeeded by their sons, but the fact that two Norman barons are named among the twelve makes us imagine that the office was attached to certain properties, rather than to certain families.   At Stamford (336ᵇ) there were likewise twelve lawmen 'qui habebant infra domus suas sacam et socam et super homines suos, praeter geld et heriete et forisfacturam corporum suorum de XL oris argenti et praeter latronem.'   They still enjoy the same rights; but now there are only nine who have 'under them' 51½ houses.   Domesday also mentions four *iudices* at York (298), who held extraordinary

Such holders of *sac* and *soc*, it is plain, enjoyed no special status as burgesses; their privilege was precisely that of many thegns throughout the countryside. Whether the man held land in or out of a borough, and whether or not styled *burgensis*, his tenure remained the same. The differentiation of a country-dwelling nobility from a town-dwelling bourgeoisie was wholly foreign to the Anglo-Saxon system, and had hardly emerged even in 1086.

Accordingly, most of the local customs reported in the survey may be passed over very quickly, for they deal rather with peculiarities of royal or baronial income than with municipal franchises. Such were the seignorial perquisites vaguely comprised under *sac* and *soc*, the heriots, marriage dues, riding and carrying services, boon-works, and other *corvées* not infrequently referred to.[1] Interesting as they may be to the legal historian, the details mean little to one attempting to trace the development of towns. The only significant fact in connection with this whole category of obligations is that the eleventh-century burgess was not quit of them.

Scarcely more urban in character were the tolls described by Domesday as being collected in many boroughs. From ancient times the king had charged for the right to transact business in his official markets, and this revenue formed one of the principal items in the borough's farm. In England as on the Continent, however, the right to establish markets had been liberally granted out, and Domesday reports dozens of rural *mercatus* that differed from the others only in point of size and prominence.[2] The only borough tolls that Domesday sees fit to enumerate are on horses, oxen, and slaves.[3] Of much greater significance for the history of the towns was the trade by sea, concerning which Domesday has a few random entries. We learn some interesting facts about merchants at Chester and we are told in remarkable detail about a dispute over tolls at Canterbury,[4]

---

consuetudines by grant of the king; and they seem to be included below (298b) among the holders of *sac* and *soc* and all customs (e.g., *Turgod lag*). At Cambridge (189) there is merely an incidental reference to *harieta lagemannorum*, which was of thegnly amount (see above, p. 91, n. 4). Cf. the moneyers of Hereford (*D.B.*, I, 179).

[1] Above, pp. 91 ff.; Ballard, *Domesday Boroughs*, pp. 80–87. On carrying services (*averae*), such as are referred to at Cambridge (*D.B.*, I, 189), see Round, in *V.H.C. Hertford*, I, 269 ff.

[2] Above, p. 76.

[3] *D.B.*, I, 26 (Lewes). But this is one of the subjects on which Domesday gives almost no information; note that at Pevensey the proceeds of toll have risen from 20*s.* to 80*s.*, and at Dover from 8*l.* to 22*l.* (*D.B.*, I, 2, 20[b]).

[4] *D.B.*, I, 2, 262[b]–263. Cf. the dispute over toll at Southwark (*D.B.*, I, 32); also the other references given by Ballard (*Domesday Boroughs*, pp. 73–74). Toll was of course collected at many points on river and seashore apart from boroughs; for examples see the *clamores* of Lincolnshire, (*D.B.*, I, 375[b]–376).

but neither these nor similar passages elsewhere contain the slightest hint of communal activity.

A rapid survey of the ordinary *consuetudines* of Domesday thus shows that the Anglo-Saxon borough was permeated with special privilege; but it was the privilege of individuals, not that of the community as a whole. In fact, the very existence of such privileges as we have been examining was incompatible with an urban society characterized by uniform tenure and status. Under such conditions, was there any possibility of municipal autonomy? The day has long passed when it was customary to find local self-government prevalent throughout Anglo-Saxon England. As we have seen, the dooms and other contemporary documents may be searched in vain for a borough managing its own affairs. Before detecting one in Domesday, we must be very sure of our proof.

In one of his scholarly essays Mr Tait has recently subjected the *firma burgi* to a thorough re-examination.[1] From his detailed analysis of the Domesday materials it is apparent that the borough in 1066 was still being administered by the old portreeve, who commonly was responsible for its farm. And the only change in the general system made by the Conqueror was the subordination of the reeve to the greatly enhanced authority of the sheriff. Under the altered plan — and it was not universally followed — the *firma burgi* became one item in the *firma comitatus*, to be sublet at the discretion of the sheriff to his own appointee.

Under neither arrangement did the burgesses themselves have any necessary share in the financial administration. Domesday constantly repeats protests of the local juries against the exactions and tyranny of the king's officials, but supplies only one hint of any concession to a demand for burghal autonomy. 'The burgesses of Northampton annually render to the sheriff 30*l*. 10*s*. This belongs to his farm.'[2] If the passage means what it says, the men of that borough had already contracted with the sheriff to farm their own revenues. Such an anticipation of later communal activity would seem highly improbable on the part of most boroughs in 1086. But in view of Northampton's remarkable prosperity, which apparently began with the establishment of the French borough, the tale as thus read is not incredible.[3] For it should be noted that the arrangement implied by the Domesday entry was as new as it was exceptional.

---

[1] J. Tait, 'The *Firma Burgi* and the Commune in England,' *E.H.R.*, XLII (1927), 321 ff.

[2] *D.B.*, I, 219: 'Burgenses de Hantone reddunt vicecomiti per annum xxx lib. et x sol. Hoc pertinet ad firmam ipsius.' The possibility that Bath was self-farming is negatived by what has already been seen in connection with the payment by the burgesses of 100*s*. *de moneta* (above, p. 101, n. 1).

[3] See Appendices IV, VI.

This instance stands alone. The passages that have been held to attest the farming of a mint by the burgesses can be more reasonably interpreted otherwise.[1] And the same can be said of the alleged examples of communal ownership in the borough. References to common pasture do exist, and they imply for the borough as much of a corporate character as for the vill, but no more.[2] The entries dealing with markets, mills, forges, salt-works, and other local enterprises fail to produce evidence of organization beyond that of the ordinary manor. As a unit of seignorial administration the borough was no more distinctively urban than as a unit for geld assessment. What can be said of it as a judicial district?

On the authority of Edgar's famous doom, it has generally been assumed that every borough as such had to have a separate court. But as noted above, there are good reasons for believing that the enactment never had that meaning.[3] It is a remarkable fact that in the whole of Domesday there is no single mention of a borough court under that name. And yet some judicial organization in the borough is everywhere taken for granted. The survey constantly refers to the profits of justice in the borough, to forfeitures incurred by burgesses, and to business that must have been transacted in some local court. Nor is the name of that court a mystery; it was the hundred.

At Chester the *iudices civitatis* had, under heavy penalty, to attend the hundred.[4] And that city, as we have already seen, constituted, with

[1] Above, p. 101.

[2] Of the possible instances of borough property cited by Ballard (*Domesday Boroughs*, p. 87), the Canterbury and Exeter entries have already been disposed of (above, pp. 90–91, 103–04). Against the well known cases of common pasture at Oxford and Cambridge may be set another that is less famous (*D.B.*, II, 339b): 'In hundret de Colenes est quedam pastura communis omnibus hominibus de hundret.' Thus we are left the one passage in the notoriously difficult and occasionally corrupt description of Colchester (*D.B.*, II, 107): 'In commune burgensium IIII XX acrae terrae, et circa murum VIII percae, de quo toto per annum habent burgenses LX sol. ad servicium regis si opus fuerit; sin autem in commune dividunt.' The phrase *in commune burgensum* would naturally be translated 'in the commons of the burgesses,' and so would normally refer to common pasture. It is true that *terra* in Domesday usually means arable, but immediately above the word is used to include pasture. At any rate, the eight perches round the wall, as Round showed (*Antiquary*, VI, 97), included the city ditch and so must have been pasture. Perhaps a portion of the common land had been put under cultivation, to produce an income of 60s. But the most interesting feature of the passage is its clear implication that the burgesses had no common chest. The money had either to be devoted to their common obligation toward the king or divided amongst them.

[3] Above, pp. 68 ff. The fact that the *Leges Henrici Primi*, 7, 4 (*G.*, I, 553) ascribe two annual meetings to the shire court and to the borough court may be taken to indicate, if not an official identification of the two, at least a confusion of them in the mind of the Norman author. Other compilations of the same age refer to the hundred and the county as the only normal jurisdictional units: e.g., *Leis Willelme*, 43; *Leges Edwardi Confessoris*, 22, 5 (*G.*, I, 517, 648). Ballard (*Domesday Boroughs*, pp. 120 ff.) completely misunderstood the subject. See also Liebermann, under *Gericht*, 12 (*G.*, II, 451).

[4] *D.B.*, I, 262b; Tait, *Domesday Survey of Cheshire* (Chetham Society, 1916), p. 32. Since *iudices* reappear at York, there seems to be little doubt that they were the same as the lawmen (*lagemanni*)

certain outlying territory, the hundred of Chester, assessed at fifty hides. Thus when we read that the half-hundred of Ipswich testifies against the claim of Roger the sheriff to certain lands at Ipswich,[1] we gain valuable information. Taken in conjunction with the facts brought out above,[2] this statement means that the court of Ipswich Borough was the court of Ipswich Hundred, the territorial district called half-hundred in Domesday presumably because it had been so rated for the geld. But in the present connection the matter of hidation is important only because it is involved in the greater scheme of political organization.

Time out of mind, the hundred courts had been the real basis of the royal government, constantly employed for the administration of justice, the assessment of taxes and other royal services, and the maintenance of law and order generally. When William I wished to secure information on local matters, he naturally sent his commissioners to the hundreds, where juries were sworn to make answer to his questions. The returns, out of which the great book was eventually constructed, were thus made by the hundreds, and it is their authority that Domesday constantly quotes in all disputed questions.[3] When, therefore, it says that the half-hundred of Ipswich testifies, it is not using an empty formula or reporting mere hearsay; it is summarizing the official verdict of a court. And similar entries occur with great frequency.

A certain burgess owned a mill in Thetford; now Roger Bigot claims it by gift of the king, *sed hundret nescit quomodo*.[4] Colchester is a hundred like Thetford, but it is *burgenses* who are said to claim five hides in Lexden

---

of Lincoln, Stamford, and Cambridge, who were thegnly holders of *sac* and *soc* (above, p. 108, n. 6). They are not referred to in the dooms under that name, but III Aethelred, 3 (*G.*, I, 228), provides that twelve senior thegns in each wapentake shall assist the reeve in administering justice. This enactment, it is true, was presumably drawn for the more exclusively Danish districts, but in all likelihood represented a policy applied in all hundreds. At any rate, the *iudices* of Chester sat in the hundred and Chester was no Danish borough. The pertinent evidence thus points, not to a purely Scandinavian institution of territorial princes (as pictured, for example, by Mr Allen Mawer, *C.M.H.*, III, 333), but to a group of doomsmen set up as part of the regular machinery in the hundred. See Maitland, *Domesday Book and Beyond*, p. 211; Liebermann, under *Lagamen*, (*G.*, II, 565); Ballard, *Domesday Boroughs*, pp. 51 ff. As the hundred was called wapentake in Danish regions, so the doomsmen were called lawmen. But was not the office essentially the same as that of the Frankish *scabini*? On the *scabini* or *iudices* in the Flemish burgs, see above, p. 36, n. 4; and for later developments, below, p. 182.

[1] *D.B.*, II, 392b: 'Dimidium Hundret de Gepeswiz. In burgo de Gepeswiz tenuit Wisgarus I aecclesiam S. Petri T.R.E. cui pertinebant tunc et modo VI carucatae terrae pro manerio ... Ex supradictis VI carucatis terrae calumpniatur Rogerus vicecomes c acras et v villanos et I molinum ad manerium regis de Branfort, et v villani de eodem manerio testantur ei et offerunt legem qualem quis iudicaverit, sed dimidium hundret de Gepeswiz testantur quod hoc iacebat ad ecclesiam T.R.E. et Wisgarus tenebat et offerunt derationari.'

[2] Above, pp. 104 ff.

[3] Round, *Feudal England*, pp. 51 ff., 118 ff.

[4] *D.B.*, II, 173.

ad consuetudinem et compotum civitatis.[1] Now, as Round demonstrated many years ago, Lexden lay well outside the walls of the borough; the land there belong to the custom of the city because the five hides at which that land was assessed were computed in the hundred of Colchester. In this case it obviously makes no difference whether the record says *burgenses* or *hundret*. And when we find information of the same sort regarding properties in or near other boroughs, we cannot doubt that it was supplied through courts of similar organization.

As we have seen, Domesday reports outlying lands that geld or ought to geld with Canterbury, Exeter, Shrewsbury, Chester, Nottingham, Derby, Lincoln, Stamford, York, etc.[2] Sometimes the statements are full and sometimes they are brief; but they must all have rested on returns from the respective hundreds or wapentakes. In fact, the borough descriptions as a whole were constructed from materials collected in local courts, and so constantly refer to the testimony there taken. Occasionally it is the deposition of one man or of a small group that appears in the record, but more often we are given the decisions of regularly constituted juries. Thus 'Sandwich lies in its own hundred' and the 'men of that borough testify' as to what they consider an exorbitant farm.[3] Cambridge, the centre of a district not included in the ordinary hundreds, 'defends itself for a hundred,' and the burgesses record many complaints against their sheriff Picot.[4] Bedford 'defended itself for a half-hundred *T.R.E.*' in military and naval service, but the land of the vill has never gelded except for one hide, and that unjustly *ut homines dicunt.*[5] Throughout Yorkshire and Lincolnshire the men of the separate wapentakes are reported testifying to many *clamores*, but at York and Lincoln it is the burgesses who are said to declare on oath or to speak.[6] And each of these cities was located in a district that was plainly treated like a wapentake.

For Huntingdonshire, likewise, Domesday reports a long series of *clamores*, and as the result of some clerk's fancy they include certain information that supplements the foregoing description of the borough.

---

[1] *D.B.*, II, 104; see map and discussion by Round, in *Antiquary*, V, 246; VI, 6.

[2] Above, pp. 103 ff.

[3] *D.B.*, I, 3.

[4] *D.B.*, I, 189: 'Reclamant autem super Picotum vicecomitem communem pasturam sibi per eum et ab eo ablatam.'

[5] *D.B.*, I, 209; above, p. 97, n. 3.

[6] *D.B.*, I, 375: 'Clamores quae sunt in Sudtreding Lincoliae et concordia eorum per homines qui iuraverunt . . . Wapentac dicunt . . . homines de Wapentac deratiocinaverunt . . . Wapentac testificatur' etc. *D.B.*, I, 336: 'Super has xxx mansiones habebat rex theloneum et forisfacturam, ut burgenses iuraverunt . . . Burgenses vero omnes Lincoliae dicunt quod iniuste habet.' *D.B.*, I, 298: 'sed burgenses dicunt non eam fuisse quietam T.R.E. . . . sed burgenses dicunt unam ex eis non fuisse comitis.' See above, p. 104.

On the authority of 'the men who have sworn in Huntingdon,' statements are added in connection with four disputed titles. Three of them concern borough properties more or less vaguely referred to earlier; the fourth has to do with five hides in Brockton.[1]　Now this vill is described as lying in the hundred of Hurstingston, with which the borough had gelded for fifty hides.[2]　It appears that the *iuratores* of Huntingdon were speaking for the whole hundred; if so, the borough was incorporated with it for judicial as well as financial administration. Similar conclusions may be drawn with regard to Guildford in Woking Hundred,[3] Southwark in Kingston Hundred,[4] and Sudbury in Thingoe Hundred.[5]　And there can be no doubt that the court of Blithing Hundred was attended by men of Dunwich.[6]

Accordingly, we fail to find that Anglo-Saxon burgesses in any way formed a class apart for the enjoyment of judicial privilege. Like other men throughout the country, they were frequently subject to the soke of greater persons, and occasionally themselves held soke over their own inferiors. If such a right of jurisdiction implied the holding of a private court, residence in a borough was no impediment to its operation. Normally, however, burgesses like other men owed suit to a local popular court, where justice was dispensed in the king's name under the presi-

---

[1] *D.B.*, I, 203, 208: 'Dicunt homines qui iuraverunt in Huntedune. . . .' It is here stated that Count Eustace has unjustly seized a certain church and a certain house; earlier he is alleged wrongfully to have many such properties in his possession. In one place we hear of *terram Hunef et Gos;* in the other of 16 houses held by Gos and Hunef *T.R.E.*

[2] *D.B.*, I, 204 (*Broctune*): 'Eustachius calumniatur v hidas.' See above, pp. 105–06.

[3] *D.B.*, I, 30. The description of Guildford stands under the rubric of Woking Hundred and contains various complaints about baronial seizures of haws in the vill. Concerning one 'the men' (presumably the burgesses, for they are referred to above as *homines*) testify. With regard to the second, however, it is *homines de comitatu* who speak, and they also seem to be quoted as to a third (*dicunt etiam homines qui iuraverunt*). This entry is exceptional in many ways and perhaps we should attribute some of its details to clerical bungling. The men of Woking Hundred testify below (*D.B.*, I, 31).

[4] *D.B.*, I, 32. The entry is given under the rubric of Kingston Hundred in connection with a manor of the bishop of Bayeux, who is said to hold a minster and a hythe at Southwark. His title has been contested in the king's interest by the sheriff. 'The men of the hundred, French and English,' testify as to a suit over the matter that had been blocked by the bishop. 'The men of Southwark' testify that *T.R.E.* no one had the right to collect toll there except the king. 'Ipsi homines de Sudwerche derationati sunt unam hagam et theloneum eius ad firmam de Chingestone. Hanc comes Eustachius tenebat.' This is another obscure description, but it seems to indicate a delegation from Southwark testifying in the court of Kingston Hundred. The men of Southwark apparently also claim as against the bishop a house that should contribute to the farm of Kingston, the royal manor for which the hundred was named. If so, the borough must in some fashion have been embraced within that farm. But it is idle to speculate on such faulty evidence.

[5] *D.B.*, II, 286ᵇ. The vill of Sudbury, in connection with which are reported 55 burgesses, is said to pay 5*s.* geld, being thus rated at 25 hides. And note: 'Ecclesia S. Gregorii de L acris libere terrae, teste hundret.' Cf. Yarmouth (*D.B.*, II, 118ᵇ).

[6] *D.B.*, II, 312; Maitland, *Domesday Book and Beyond*, p. 96.

dency of his representative. And nothing in Domesday would lead us to believe that this court was at all peculiar to the borough; on the other hand, whenever information is given us, it points to the ordinary hundred. In so far as the borough coincided with the hundred, the hundred court was also a borough court; but in no case of which we may be sure was the hundred coterminous with the walled area. Rather it embraced a larger district in which the borough occupied a more or less dominant position.[1]

In this connection Ballard expressed two opinions, neither of them satisfactory. From his study of the later charters, from the Dunwich entry, and from a misreading of a custom at Hereford, he originally concluded that burgesses regularly had to attend hundreds outside their own boroughs. Subsequently, as the result of Mary Bateson's criticism, he abandoned this view and worked out an elaborate classification of boroughs on the basis of their 'hundredality.' Boroughs which Domesday describes at the head of the county survey he listed as 'extra-hundredal'; those described elsewhere, but without hundredal rubrics, he left blank. Some of those placed in hundreds named for their respective boroughs he labelled 'own'; solely where the names of the borough and the hundred were not the same did he apply the term 'intra-hundredal.'[2] But a moment's reflection will show that Domesday's failure to insert a hundredal rubric proves nothing, and that the location of a borough 'above the line' does not prove much.[3] Besides, the actual relationship of a borough to a hundred hardly depended on the mere name of the latter. In order to gain any understanding of that problem, we must discard Ballard's tabulation in its entirety.

On review of the evidence, we may rather distinguish two kinds of hundreds that included boroughs: those named for them and those not named for them. Within the former group are included the burghal hundreds of the Midlands, the North, and East Anglia — where, as al-

---

[1] Cf. Maitland, *Domesday Book and Beyond*, p. 209, n. 6: 'It is very possible that, at least in the earliest time, the moot that was held in the borough had jurisdiction over a territory considerably larger than the walled space, and in this case the urban would hardly differ from the rural hundred. A somewhat new kind of "hundred" might be formed without the introduction of any new idea.' Mr Tait (*Domesday Survey of Cheshire*, p. 32) has expressed the opinion that the hundred court at Chester may have been so called 'because the city with its suburbs formed a separate hundred.'

[2] *Domesday Boroughs*, p. 53; *English Boroughs*, pp. 36 ff.; M. Bateson, in *E.H.R.*, xx (1905), 146; Round, in *V.H.C. Hereford*, i, 299. In his table (*English Borough*, pp. 83–84) Ballard listed Canterbury, Pevensey, Chester, Shrewsbury, Dorchester, Winchcombe, etc. as 'extra-hundredal'; Fordwich, Ipswich, Maldon, Norwich, Rochester, Sandwich, and Thetford as 'own.' Bath, Calne, Cricklade, etc. he left blank. Just what impelled his classification in each of these cases I am unable to determine, for the principles stated on pp. 36–37 are obviously insufficient to explain his practice.

[3] Above, p. 84.

ready noted, these hundreds were often reckoned at a hundred hides each. And with them may be placed such southern hundreds as Canterbury, Rochester, Sandwich, and Pevensey, which were not such neatly constructed fiscal units. Inside the hundreds of the other sort are found, in addition to the newest boroughs, those of Romney, Hythe, Yarmouth, Dunwich, Guildford, Southwark, and also practically all the West Saxon boroughs. The division is very significant. Throughout the region north of the Thames the whole system was obviously artificial, and there it would seem that the hundreds were created after the boroughs had been built. Subsequently, when new boroughs came into existence, they naturally remained in the hundreds where they happened to be; and for this reason we may consider boroughs like Dunwich and Yarmouth to have been younger than Ipswich or Thetford. The same explanation may perhaps hold for Romney and Hythe in contradistinction to Sandwich and Pevensey. And this line of reasoning applies with equal force to the ancient kingdom of Wessex, for there too we may detect hundreds — though perhaps not called by that name — antedating most of the boroughs in that region.[1]

These are fascinating trends of speculation, but to follow them farther would lead us away from the subject in hand. No matter what may have been the relative age of borough and hundred in the different regions of Anglo-Saxon England, the system as we find it in Domesday is practically uniform for all the important places. The borough, without a great expanse of additional territory, is large enough to be constituted as a hundred; it is the dominating settlement within the district. Eventually, expert study of local boundaries may bring out additional facts concerning the character and origin of these burghal hundreds, but at present the evidence is insufficient to warrant precise generalization. From what we can see of it in Domesday, the system appears more rural than urban — an arrangement that attempted to equate centres of official and military life with groups of simple villages. The organization of a hundred about the borough was a recognition of its administrative importance, not of its social peculiarity. And all boroughs were not treated alike. What is said of York and Lincoln, or even of Shrewsbury and Maldon, will not hold for Buckingham, Sudbury, Reading, Guildford, and most of the southwestern boroughs. It is surely a mistake to believe that each of them had a court independent of the ordinary hundreds or, for that matter, any separate court at all. In the eleventh century we are not justified in generalizing about borough institutions as distinct from the ancient territorial system of government. For the first traces

---

[1] Above, pp. 62, 106–07.

of a peculiarly municipal administration of justice we must look to the charters and customals of the later age.

Before burgesses demand a burgess court, they must have a burgess status to defend, a burgess law to enforce. Such conditions we have failed to detect throughout the great majority of old boroughs. In the French boroughs, on the other hand, common burgess privilege seems to have been the rule. The most famous example is the law of Breteuil enjoyed by the new settlements at Rhuddlan and Hereford. But there is strong evidence to show that all the trading colonies founded after 1066 were from the first characterized by a similar franchise. And occasionally, by way of exception, we find evidence of some such development even in an old borough. The description of York contains vague references to a burgess custom, and a chance entry in another connection shows that it included freedom from heriot, which elsewhere was commonly paid by thegns in and out of boroughs.[1]

In the time of King Edward the burgesses of Torksey 'had the same customs as those of Lincoln, and in addition that whoever of them had a house in that vill paid neither toll nor custom on entering or leaving.' The statement is far from clear, but seems to refer to levies on merchandise passing the borough gates.[2] In any case, the privilege was one of a seafaring community, for the succeeding passage says that men of Torksey were accustomed, 'with their ships and other instruments of navigation,' to carry the king's messengers to York, and that the cost of the trip was borne by the sheriff. Furthermore, the record adds, if any burgess wished to depart to some other place, and to sell his house which was in the said vill, he might, if he pleased, do so without the knowledge or license of the reeve.'[3] Unfortunately, Domesday does not see fit to enumerate the customs of the men of Lincoln, the great city to which Torksey was joined for the payment of geld,[4] and we are left to guess that, as at York, some degree of common liberty had there made its appearance even before the Norman Conquest.

In this connection we may re-examine the famous Dover entry:[5]

---

[1] Above, p. 91, n. 4.

[2] *D.B.*, I, 337. Ballard, *Domesday Boroughs*, (p. 74) rightly notes in this connection the London gate that produced 20*s.* a year (*D.B.*, II, 15ᵇ).

[3] The statement of the Lincoln burgesses (*D.B.*, I, 336) that no one could sell his land *extra civitatem nec extra parentes eorum* without the king's grant can hardly be interpreted as a municipal liberty.

[4] Torksey is described as a *suburbium* of Lincoln, apparently for the following reason: 'T.R.E. reddebant Torchesiy et Harduic in Lincolia quintum denarium de geldo civitatis. Ad hanc quintam partem dabat Torchesyg II den. et Harduic tercium.'

[5] *D.B.*, I, 1. The *Inq. St Aug.* gives the following account (p. 23): 'Et quando rex dedit burgensibus illorum sacam et socam, tunc burgenses e contra dederunt regi xx naves', etc. See the remarks of Ballard, *ibid.*, p. xxiii.

Burgenses dederunt xx naves regi una vice in anno ad xv dies et in una quaque navi erant homines xx et unus. Hoc faciebant pro eo quod eis perdonaverat saccam et socam.

Was it all the burgesses or only some of them who owed the king ship service in return for a grant of *sac* and *soc?* And what did the latter phrase imply? Ballard, after comparing this passage with those concerning Guildford, Southwark, and Wallingford, came to the conclusion that King Edward had granted *sac* and *soc* to the burgesses individually rather than collectively.[1] This interpretation, to be sure, is a quite possible rendering of the Latin text, if the reciprocal service is correspondingly read as the contribution of individuals. But that conclusion is flatly contradicted by the well known obligations of Dover and the other Cinque Ports in the following century.[2] And surely we do not have to accept as the sole alternative meaning that 'the whole body of burgesses' had 'jurisdiction over the whole borough.'

Luckily, the description of Dover does not stand alone. King Edward, we are told, had given the men of Sandwich 'their customs' and that borough owed the same service as Dover.[3] The burgesses of Romney, in return for sea service, are said to enjoy all customs and all forfeitures except the three held by the archbishop,[4] and the same arrangement seems to have prevailed at Hythe.[5] Thus we find *consuetudines,* including forfeitures, in these ports equated with *sac* and *soc* at Dover.[6] Using that key, we may decide that the Confessor had granted to the men of Dover, as to those of certain other boroughs, various revenues that he had previously enjoyed there — in particular some of his profits of jus-

---

[1] *Domesday Boroughs*, pp. 50–51; cf. pp. 88–89. The meaning in this connection of Ballard's remarks in *Inq. St Aug.*, p. xxv, is hard to grasp.

[2] See below, pp. 156 ff.

[3] *D.B.*, I, 3; *Inq. St Aug.*, p. 20: 'reddit regi servicium in mari sicut illi de Dovra et homines illius ville antequam rex eis dedisset suas consuetudines reddebant xv lib.' *D. Mon.*, f. 6: 'reddit regi servitium in mare sicut Dovera [qualitate scilicet, non quantitate] et homines illius villae antequam rex eis dedisset suas consuetudines reddebant xv lib.'

[4] *D.B.*, I, 4b, 10b: 'de quibus habet archiepiscopus III forisfacturas, latrocinium, pacem fractam, foristellum. Rex vero habet omne servitium ab eis et ipsi habent omnes consuetudines et alias forisfacturas pro servitio maris, et sunt in manu regis'; 'de eis habet rex omnem servitium et sunt quieti pro servitio maris ab omni consuetudine praeter tribus: latrocinium, pace infracta, et forstel.' *D. Mon.*, f. 7: 'de quibus rex in mare habet servitium ideoque quieti sunt per totam Angliam exceptis tribus forisfactis que habet Rodbertus in Rumene.'

[5] *D.B.*, I, 4b; *D. Mon.*, f. 7: 'Et in burgo de Hede sunt cc et xxv burgenses qui pertinent huic manerio, de quibus non habet Hugo nisi III forisfacta.' Sea service is also mentioned as having been rendered at Fordwich (*Inq. St Aug.*, p. 17). Cf. Maldon, below, p. 158, n. 6.

[6] Cf. *D.B.*, I, 2: 'Per totam civitatem Cantuariae habet rex sacam et socam, excepta terra aecclesiae S. Trinitatis et S. Augustini et Eddevae reginae et Alnod cild et Esber biga et Siret de Cilleham.' *Inq. St Aug.*, p. 9: 'Regina E. et Alnoth cild et Osberrn bigga et Sired de Chileham isti habuerunt in civitate consuetudines suas de suis hominibus.'

tice and presumably geld as well, for none of the Cinque Ports are ever recorded as paying any.[1] In return the men of Dover had bound themselves to furnish the king twenty ships, manned and equipped, for fifteen days' service annually. How the funds were collected and administered Domesday does not state, but the settlement must have implied some sort of communal organization. Since a royal reeve still continued to officiate at Dover, we need suppose only that he turned over to responsible burgesses a sum of money previously rendered to the king.[2] But that the first step toward the formation of a true urban community had been taken before 1066 seems evident. And with this conclusion one further bit of information in Domesday well agrees: at Dover every resident in good standing was free of toll throughout England[3] — the earliest statement that we have of a privilege later guaranteed by so many municipal charters.

We must, of course, recognize the fact that our record is far from complete. If the Domesday compilers had been more generous with their information, we should doubtless find other instances of communal liberty before the Conquest. Nevertheless, the force of the survey as a whole is to make the customs just examined appear, not survivals from antiquity, but innovations foreshadowing a new age. And wherever we find these exceptional arrangements they are intimately associated with seafaring and commerce. The clearest evidence comes from the new French settlements, and next to them from the future Cinque Ports and from other maritime boroughs like York and Lincoln. In such places we obtain glimpses of the new and uniform burgess privilege without which there could be no burgage tenure. But fully to appreciate the significance of this development, we must turn to sources of another category — the town charters of the twelfth century.

[1] Below, pp. 157–58; Appendix IV.

[2] *D.B.*, I, 1: 'Modo appreciatur XL lib. et tamen prepositus inde reddit LIII lib.' The *prepositus regis* is also mentioned as collecting a *communem emendationem* for breach of the king's special peace.

[3] *D.B.*, I, 1: 'Quicunque manens in villa assiduus reddebat regi consuetudinem quietus erat de theloneo per totam Angliam.' *Inq. St Aug.*, p. 24: 'Et omnes burgenses qui ibi manebant non dabant theloneum in tota Anglia.' Cf. the language of the Romney entry, above, p. 118, n. 4.

V

THE BOROUGH COMMUNITY

1. Charters to New Boroughs

AT FIRST glance the Domesday material reviewed above, with its persistent obscurity and meaningless variety, must seem rather bewildering; but after careful analysis its main purport may be stated in remarkably brief scope. In general, the Anglo-Saxon borough was not a community of privileged citizens. Its inhabitants enjoyed no uniform burgess franchise; they held their properties by no system of burgage tenure; they had no self-government. The typical borough of 1066 was essentially what it had been a century earlier — a military and official centre. The men who lived inside the walls remained socially indistinguishable from those who lived outside, being principally members of the agrarian aristocracy or their dependents. Except for the fact that the borough might be administrative headquarters for a larger district, its judicial organization was that of a rural hundred. It was assessed for military and fiscal purposes exactly like the surrounding country. The portreeve was no more of a communal chief than was the sheriff or the hundredman. He presided over the territorial court that met in the borough and collected the royal revenues, including those from the official market. And if in such matters he relied upon the co-operation of local assistants, the latter were a select group of thegns, rather than a municipal council.

By way of exception, we may detect in some of the greater seaports certain indications of communal privilege. But these are unmistakably described as innovations, and are associated with vague hints of mercantile development — a subject regarding which additional facts will be brought out in the concluding chapter. So far as Domesday is concerned, the clearest evidence of a new urban system is found in the French boroughs — deliberately founded commercial settlements, where from the outset we encounter a régime of burgess franchise on a uniform tenurial basis. To appreciate the significance of this contrast, however, we must turn to the sources of the twelfth century.

It was over thirty years ago that Mary Bateson first demonstrated the importance for British social history of the *ville neuve*.[1] Following the clue offered by a casual remark in Domesday, she was able to prove the direct influence of an obscure Norman *bourg* upon urban development

---

[1] 'The Laws of Breteuil,' *E.H.R.*, xv–xvi (1900–01); above, pp. 75 ff., 93 ff.

throughout considerable regions in England, Wales, and Ireland. Norman barons, transferred from the Breton to the Welsh march, built French towns as well as French castles, and alongside their French knights established French traders. Thus the laws of Breteuil became also laws of Hereford, Shrewsbury, Rhuddlan, Bideford, Haverfordwest, and a host of similar foundations. Moreover, seignorial boroughs with no proved relationship to Breteuil often reveal, by the general character of their liberties, that they were actually descended from urban communities beyond the Channel.

This famous thesis, though at once given the wide recognition that it deserved, has not stood unchallenged. It was caustically attacked by Hemmeon for exaggerating the influence in England, not only of Breteuil, but of the French *bourgs* generally.[1] Although, he insisted, minor peculiarities of certain insignificant boroughs could be justly attributed to Norman importation, the substance of municipal custom in England was thoroughly native. But since Hemmeon's confident assertions with regard to burgage tenure have themselves proved somewhat rash,[2] we should naturally hesitate, without careful verification, to accept his other strictures. As a matter of fact, the labor of that inquiry has to some extent been spared us by a thoughtful study of Ballard's — virtually the last that he was able to complete.[3] Taking Mary Bateson's imaginative reconstruction of the 'Bretollian laws,' Ballard first increased her enumeration of possibilities to thirty-four, and then proceeded with methodic thoroughness to analyze and reclassify the documents in which any of the alleged instances occurred.

His conclusion was rather startling. Out of the thirty-four laws he found only three that could, he thought, properly be called Bretollian: the limitation of amercement to 12*d.*, the restriction of military service to one day, and the abolition of the assize *mort d'ancestor* (which Mary Bateson had failed to recognize). But in three cases he was forced by his own tests to accept as Bretollian a six-penny amercement also, and so to prove that after all there was nothing sacred in the figure twelve. The restriction of *ost et chevauchée*, however unusual in England, we at once recognize as a common custom on the Continent, and one no more Bretollian than the shilling rent. And could Ballard suppose that exemption from the possessory assizes existed anywhere before the Norman Conquest? The net result of his research was to demonstrate that there were really no laws of Breteuil at all!

---

[1] *Burgage Tenure in Mediaeval England*, pp. 166 ff.
[2] Above, pp. 88 ff.
[3] 'The Law of Breteuil,' *E.H.R.*, xxx (1915), 646 ff.

The *reductio ad absurdum* of course follows from the premise that the customs which Domesday reports being enjoyed by the Frenchmen of Hereford and Rhuddlan can be reduced to a set of articles originally peculiar to the one locality Breteuil.   Perhaps Ballard did not make just that premise, but in estimating the legal influence that could be rightly attributed to Breteuil, he certainly obscured the problem with which he started.   Domesday says of Rhuddlan that it is a new borough shared between Robert of Rhuddlan and Hugh, earl of Chester, and that 'they gave to those burgesses the laws and customs which are in Hereford and Breteuil.'[1]   No one will suppose that these laws and customs consisted only of the one exemption that Domesday specifies; they must have embraced a whole series of special liberties, such as those which Henry I confirmed at Verneuil and which Henry II extended to Pontorson.[2]   Very likely the Verneuil custom in large part duplicated the Breteuil custom. Why should it be only the essentially different portions of the latter that constituted the foreign *leges* at Hereford?

The point is that the men of these French boroughs were definitely stated to be living under a special law that differentiated them from other men, including English burgesses.   This law was introduced from Normandy between 1066 and 1086, and it was associated with the little *bourg* of Breteuil.   The fact that it was shared then or later with a dozen other communities, French or English, does not affect the question in the slightest.   It certainly ought not to be argued that, because similar customs are eventually found in most boroughs, the system was essentially a native growth; we know too little about the origin of those later customs. Mary Bateson was aware of the fact that the customs of *villes neuves* often resembled each other.   As she pointed out, the important consideration was not the exact amount set for the maximum amercement, but that a maximum was set; not the size of the burgage rent, but that it was one involving a uniform tenure.

Mary Bateson's reasons for designating various liberties Bretollian are not always clear; at times she seems to have been bewildered by an unexpected wealth of evidence.   Perhaps, in the enthusiasm of her discovery, she did exaggerate the rôle of the one *bourg*.   But she unquestionably recognized that the influence exerted on the English boroughs was French rather than Bretollian.   She used the law of Breteuil, really, to introduce an essay on burghal colonization in England, and whatever may be thought of her effort to reconstruct the actual *leges*, that essay stands as a brilliant and lasting work.[3]

[1] Above, p. 93, n. 6.
[2] Above, p. 30.
[3] *E.H.R.*, xvi, 92 ff., 332 ff.   In her *Customary Rents (Oxford Studies in Social and Legal History,*

Ballard, it would appear, never grasped the true significance of Mary Bateson's thesis at all. While making his collection of borough charters,[1] he was led to compare them with similar grants on the Continent — a most praiseworthy undertaking, but one for which he lacked materials as well as scholarly preparation.[2] Detailed analysis of the two groups of documents only convinced him that the differences between them far exceeded the similarities.[3] The British charters he pronounced 'more advanced' than the French because they reflected a stronger royal administration. But is the intrinsic character of a charter determined by the title of the man who granted it? Was Saint-Omer 'less advanced' because Louis VI had no real authority in Flanders? In everything but name the real king of that country was the count. Actually, the peculiarities of English municipal custom that Ballard emphasized were superficial or

---

II), pp. 177 ff., Miss Neilson has shown that the fixed amercement was not 'distinctive in later times exclusively of towns modelled after Breteuil'; that the same principle is found, for example, in a payment known among the Ramsey villages as *fulstingpound*. It may be added that many other bourgeois liberties, such as abolition or restriction of tallage, military service, *corvée*, etc., become increasingly common in rural communities from the thirteenth century on. Personally, I find it hard to believe that these liberties were vestiges of a primitive village custom. Considerable reading of English and Continental cartularies has convinced me that in the tenth century the mass of the population, whether technically free or servile, was subjected to an arbitrary system of seignorial exploitation, and that this system was relaxed, at first for individuals and then for whole communities, under pressure of economic changes in the eleventh and twelfth centuries. Alongside commercial development, agricultural colonization must be recognized as an important factor in effecting a great social transformation. But this is a subject in which our present lack of definite information renders generalization hazardous. See the references given above, p. 30, n. 1; below, p. 164, n. 5.

[1] Ballard's collection (*B.B.C.*, I), although it made easily available a mass of scattered material, remains unsatisfactory. His method of splitting documents and arranging the fragments under analytical titles has no doubt been popular with readers who, like Ballard, have wanted to examine municipal institutions *en bloc*. But the inevitable result of such procedure was to destroy all historical perspective in the volume and to make the task of tracing urban evolution maddeningly difficult. The historian who aims at more than a superficial description must study whole charters and by comparison seek to determine the nature and scope of their contents at particular times. This he cannot do in the *B.B.C.* without running through a maze of cross-references based upon the preconceptions of the editor. For example, if he wishes to use the charter of Tewkesbury, which is otherwise unpublished, he first secures from Ballard (*B.B.C.*, I, cxliv) the following cabbalistic series: II A 2, 7, 9, 12, 15, 16, 18; II B 17, 18; III 3, 10; IV A 4; IV B 5; IV C 4; IV D 4; V A 8; V B 4; VII I (c). Then without the benefit of page references, he must search through the volume until he finds each fragment in its proper section. Often it is convenient to have a compilation of this sort in order to trace the extension of a single privilege; but it cannot take the place of a critical edition of entire documents. In the following notes the *B.B.C* will be cited only in connection with materials which are readily accessible there. See below, pp. 113, n. 5, 147, n. 4.

[2] *B.B.C.*, I, cv ff. While Ballard's selection of French charters was fairly comprehensive, the restriction of his attention to those German charters included in Gengler's *Codex Iuris Municipalis* (which includes only the letters A to D) is hard to justify. But the fundamental defect in his method was that the documents were indiscriminately thrown together without regard to relative age and importance. Ballard's knowledge of historical literature on the towns of the Continent seems to have been very slight.

[3] *E.H.R.*, xxx, 656.

insignificant;[1] the similarities that he ignored were monumental. To be convinced of this truth we have merely to select a few outstanding examples, and in doing so we cannot avoid following where Mary Bateson led.

A well known document reports the 'liberties and free customs of Cardiff and Tewkesbury given and conceded by Robert and William, onetime earls of Gloucester.'[2] These boroughs, as Mary Bateson showed, stand among the foundations of Norman barons along the Welsh frontier; and although their Bretollian character is doubtful, they are quite characteristic of the French group in general. In the first place, as rent for his burgage, each burgess pays 12d. annually *pro omni servicio*. He is not liable for heriot or relief, and he enjoys freedom of marriage. He may in any way alienate his burgage if it has been bought. If it has been inherited, he should consult his heirs before alienating it; if they refuse to buy, he may do with it as he pleases. Freedom of sale and devise also applies to chattels. All trials are restricted to the borough. The burgess owes no manorial suit for fulling or dyeing; he may brew and bake freely, and without any payment of custom; he may own horse mills or hand mills. And finally the charter gives a list of tolls charged in the town.

To multiply details of similar grants would be easy but tiresome, for with slight variation the articles are repeated over and over again. Thus the charter of Swansea from William, earl of Warwick (1153–84), prescribes the same burgage rent, the same exemption from external trials, the same liberty of baking, brewing, etc., but adds the restriction of military service to one day and the limitation of ordinary forfeitures to 12d.[3] That of Haverfordwest from William Marshall, earl of Pembroke (1189–1219), reserves military service to the lord, but includes the law of a year and a day for acquiring property or free burgess status.[4] And the liber-

---

[1] He mentions freedom from toll throughout the kingdom, legalized reprisal for toll unjustly taken, distraint of non-burgesses to force attendance on the borough court, and prohibition of trial by battle. He seems to exaggerate the prevalence of combat in the Continental towns. The French peculiarities noted are principally the sworn commune, the legalization of private war, and the *lex talionis*.

[2] *Cartae et Alia Munimenta quae ad Dominium de Glamorgancia Pertinent* (Cardiff, 1910), I, 94: 'Hec sunt libertates et libere consuetudines de Kerdif et de Theokesburia date et concesse per Robertum et Willelmum comites aliquando Gloucestrie.' Ballard dates the liberties 1147–83, viz., under the second earl (*B.B.C.*, I, xxvii). But the towns must have been founded by Robert, if they did not, as M. Bateson suggested (*E.H.R.*, xv, 516), go back to Robert Fitz-Hamon. The articles are repeated, with various changes, in a fourteenth-century confirmation to Tewkesbury (*B.B.C.*, I, 256) — circumstances which make it impossible to date with any certainty such an addition as that permitting the election of bailiffs and catch-polls (p. 243). There is, however, nothing in the earlier document that may not well have been proclaimed when the boroughs were founded.

[3] *Cart. Glam.*, I, 136.

[4] *B.B.C.*, I, 67, 73, 75, 92, 104; M. Bateson, in *E.H.R.*, xv, 517.

ties of Okehampton, Frodsham, Leek, Bideford, Lostwithiel, Preston, and many other boroughs discussed by Mary Bateson all bear, as she demonstrated, a strong family resemblance.[1] Differences in local custom obviously existed among them, but we are led to suspect that much of the variation is merely the effect of the records from which our information is derived. At least, we may never assert the lack of a particular franchise merely because of its absence in a charter, and the fundamental guarantees of burgage tenure and of free status are universal. But before drawing further conclusions let us broaden the inquiry to include other communities of the same general character.

Among the many charters issued by Henry II is one to the new town of Pembroke.[2] All liberties enjoyed under Henry I are ratified. Tenure of land for a year and a day is to be henceford valid. 'And if any one shall live in the said vill for a year and a day, no matter whence he come and whether he be free or serf, ever after he is to remain my free man.' Inheritance of property is guaranteed on payment of 12*d*. relief. Wardship is restricted to a child's relatives and friends. Military service is reserved, but on condition that the burgess may return within twenty-four hours. Use of the royal forest is permitted without obligation for pannage. Except for royal pleas, no burgess is to be tried in any court but his own hundred. Forfeitures are restricted to 12*d*., and various provisions are made with regard to distress and other judicial matters. All ships coming to Milfordport must offer their goods for sale at Pembroke bridge. All merchants of the county must belong to the Pembroke gild, and so are to secure freedom from toll throughout the king's dominions. And they are to enjoy their right to hold fairs, together with all other good and established customs.

As Mary Bateson suggested,[3] there is a possibility that the liberties of Pembroke were established, not by Henry I, but by the first Norman castellan, a son of the earl of Shrewsbury. The king, however, was quite familiar with such urban foundations, and at Verneuil and other places in Normandy was doing his utmost to extend them.[4] Nor were his efforts restricted to the French side of the Channel. In 1080 Robert of Normandy built a new castle on the Tyne, and below it there soon developed a town that was destined to win great fame and prosperity. If a foundation charter was issued, it has not come down to us; but we have two ver-

[1] Besides the article of M. Bateson, see that of Ballard cited above, p. 121, n. 3.
[2] *Calendar of Patent Rolls, 1377–81*, p. 106.
[3] *E.H.R.*, XVI, 101.
[4] Above, pp. 30–31. This is a fact which M. Bateson somewhat neglected. She seemed inclined to draw a rather sharp distinction between royal and seignorial boroughs. And was it for this reason that she omitted mention of Newcastle?

sions of the liberties granted by Henry I, as determined by inquest under his grandson.[1]

The burgess of Newcastle, asserts the record, may give or sell his land and thence go freely, unless involved in a lawsuit. Should he hold land in burgage for a year and a day, justly and without challenge, no claim against it shall hold good, except in the case of a claimant who has been outside the kingdom or who is an infant.[2] If a peasant comes to the borough and there dwells as a burgess for a year and a day, he shall henceforth remain such, unless originally authorized by his lord to reside only for a fixed term.[3] The son of a burgess, living in his father's home and eating at his father's table, shall enjoy the same liberty as the parent. Within Newcastle, furthermore, there is no merchet or heriot.[4] Pleas involving burgesses must be begun and finished in the borough, unless they are pleas of the crown. The burgess shall not be liable for trial by battle except in a case of treason, but shall defend himself by compurgation.[5] As forfeiture the burgess pays only six ores to the reeve. Burgesses may distrain outsiders either inside the borough or elsewhere, and without official permission, unless the latter persons have come to town for the county court, for military service, or for castle-guard. But no burgess may distrain another burgess without license from the reeve. Every burgess of Newcastle may, if he pleases, bake his own bread, or grind his own grain by hand mill. No one except a burgess may buy merchandise within the neighborhood of the borough, nor may any one buy inside it except from a burgess.[6] All goods brought by water to Newcastle must be sold on land, with the exception of salt and herrings; but a burgess may buy what he will from a ship touching at Tynemouth and wishing

---

[1] *B.B.C.*, I, xxxvii. The more familiar text (A) will be found in *S.C.*, pp. 133–34; the other (B) in the *Percy Chartulary* (Surtees Society, cxvii, 1911), pp. 333 ff. They are headed: (A) 'Hae sunt leges et consuetudines quas burgenses Novi Castelli super Tinam habuerunt tempore Henrici regis Angliae et habere debent'; (B) 'Hec sunt leges et consuetudines quas Henricus rex concessit burgensibus suis de Novo Castro.'

[2] *B.B.C.*, I, 71: (A) 'Si quis terram in burgagio uno anno et una die . . .'; (B) 'Quicumque in burgo terram tenuerit uno anno et una die . . .'

[3] *B.B.C.*, I, 103: (A) 'Si rusticus in burgo veniat manere, et ibi per annum unum et diem sicut burgensis maneat in burgo, ex toto remaneat, nisi prius ab ipso vel domino suo prelocutum sit ad terminum remanere'; (B) 'Si villanus veniat ad burgum manere, et uno anno et una die terram in burgo tenuerit sine prolocutione domini sui vel propria ad aliquem terminum, remaneat in burgo sicut burgensis.'

[4] The documents both add *blodwit*, the old Saxon fine for bloodshed, and *stengesdint*, 'beating with a pole' — perhaps some form of corporal punishment.

[5] *B.B.C.*, I, 132: B gives another version, but both add that a burgess should not fight a villein unless he has first given up his burgage.

[6] *B.B.C.*, I, 168, 211: the documents also forbid the foreigner to buy cloth for dyeing even in the market, or to work or cut it. One adds that he may not cut up fish for sale.

to depart immediately. The document concludes with the official tolls levied in the early twelfth century.

These customs of Newcastle are of extraordinary interest, not only because of their intrinsic importance, but because they were so widely copied. Extended by the king to Alnwick, Hartlepool, and other places in the north of England, they also, through adoption in the Four Burghs (Roxburgh, Stirling, Edinburgh, and Berwick), became the urban standard for Scotland. And under the bishops of Durham the same set of franchises was bestowed upon Durham, Gateshead, Wearmouth, and Norham[1] — the most extensive series of towns founded by an ecclesiastic in England, where as a rule cathedral boroughs had been kept under royal control and the newer monastic boroughs remained backward for centuries.

In this latter respect the outstanding exception was Bury St Edmund's which, as noted above, had grown into a considerable town before 1086.[2] Domesday gives us no hint of borough privilege in the vill, but early under Henry I we hear that the burgesses of St Edmund's are to enjoy freedom from toll in all markets and fairs throughout the king's dominions.[3] And a document of Stephen describes various liberties that are claimed by the burgesses.[4] Every *maisura de burgali terra* pays a penny to the reeve annually. If a burgess there holds land for a year and a day, whether bought or inherited, he is thenceforth guaranteed possession against all adverse claim; and such land he may freely sell, subject only to the preemption of the kin. No burgess can be impleaded outside the borough; he owes no suit to shire or to hundred, but responds only in his own *portmannemot*. And provisions are added with regard to the levying of distress for debt, the maintenance of guards for the gates, and the repair of the ditch. From these fragments it is not hard to guess the nature of the privilege which, with or without a formal charter, had come to be secured by the men of Bury St Edmund's under Henry I.

From the examples cited the only possible conclusion is that the new borough, whether created by king or by baron, by ecclesiastic or by layman, normally enjoyed the same general franchises; and that the urban liberties thus established in England differed in no essential respect from those established on the Continent. Nor is this truth evinced merely by the fact that English charters were occasionally copied from French grants. The resemblance of new boroughs in the British Isles to Lorris,

---

[1] *B.B.C.*, I, 25.

[2] Above, p. 76, n. 8.

[3] *E.H.R.*, XXIV (1909), 425; *B.B.C.*, I, 180. The charter is one of Henry I (1102–3) in favor of the monastery.

[4] *A.H.R.*, II (1897), 689.

Verneuil, Montauban, Freiburg, and other *villes neuves* was no matter of chance borrowing.   When we discover foundations of the same type from Wales to Languedoc and from Scotland to Saxony, we may be sure that they were made in response to a European demand.

Concerning the nature of this demand the English evidence serves wholly to corroborate that from the Continent.   The remarkably early testimony of Domesday is particularly welcome, because it reveals the actual beginnings of many small settlements whose history would otherwise be quite obscure.   And, a little later, we get from Newcastle an especially vivid description of customs which, except for one or two references to peculiarly English institutions, might equally well have applied to many a Continental town. Free hereditary tenure, the law of a year and a day, exemption from manorial obligations, guarantee of trial within the walls, special judicial procedure, limitation of fines, and the assurance to the citizens of a local trade monopoly — all these features are common to the new towns of Europe generally.   And other privileges, not specified at Newcastle but found in the charters of such boroughs as Pembroke, Cardiff, and Swansea, are paralleled in dozens of Continental communities.

These facts are so clearly evident from the sources that there can be no denying them.   Indeed, they have not been disputed except — if he really meant what he said — by Ballard.[1]   When, however, we press the investigation one stage farther and inquire which liberties, if any, were the fundamental ones, we encounter a controversial subject — the essential meaning of the word *burgus* in the twelfth century.   On this question various famous historians have had something to say, and yet something still remains to be said.   For until the basic character of the old borough and its true relationship to the new borough are determined, all proposed solutions must continue to rest on doubtful factors.   Thus we are brought back to a distinction already made familiar by the examination of Domesday Book.

2. Charters to Old Boroughs

As will be more clearly shown in the following chapter, the Pipe Rolls indicate as the leading boroughs of the early twelfth century London, York, Lincoln, Norwich, Northampton, and Winchester.[2]   Of these at least London and Lincoln held quite exceptional privileges from Henry I, but if the latter town received a charter at that time, it has not come down to us.   On the other hand, London's grants from William I and Henry I are extant, and they provide us with much valuable information. The older document confirms the liberties enjoyed under Edward and

---

[1] Above, p. 123.
[2] Below, p. 161.

guarantees hereditary tenure to the burgesses, both French and English.[1] The other exempts the citizens from scot, Danegeld, *murdrum*, trial by battle, forced entertainment, and tolls throughout England; restricts all trials to the city; regulates the holding of the local courts; limits amercements; grants the citizens the farm of London and Middlesex; and permits them to elect their own sheriff and justiciar.[2]

Further testimony to the greatness of the capital is to be seen in the wide extension of its liberties throughout the kingdom. As early as 1156 Henry II confirms the men of Oxford in the possession of all customs as under Henry I, including their gild merchant with a monopoly of trade in the borough, and exemption from all trials outside the borough.[3] As previously, they are also to enjoy the liberties of London, sending thither in case of doubt to obtain the decision of the citizens. At the royal coronation they are to act with the Londoners in the service of the buttery, and they may engage with them in common trade at London and elsewhere. Exeter and Barnstaple receive similar confirmations, but without the addition of other specific articles.[4] Gloucester is to have freedom from toll and all other liberties as under Henry I and as enjoyed by the citizens of London and Winchester.[5]

But more remarkable is the writ of Henry I in favor of Wilton, which runs as follows:[5]

Precipio quod burgenses mei Wiltoniae de gilda mercatoria et de consuetudine mea Wiltoniae habeant omnes quietantias et libertates de theloneo et passagio et omni consuetudine ita bene et plene sicut burgenses mei Londoniae et Wintoniae melius et liberius habeant.

This is plainly the same sort of concession as that made to Gloucester,

---

[1] *G.*, I, 486.

[2] *G.*, I, 524; below, pp. 180 ff.

[3] *S.C.*, p. 198. This charter is especially remarkable for the emphasis with which it confirms the London customs at Oxford. It is not that a few articles are copied from one charter to another; the men of Oxford and of London are said to have all their customs and liberties and laws in common. 'Et si dubitaverint vel contenderint de iudicio aliquo quod facere debeant, de hoc Londonias mittant nuncios suos, et quod Londonienses inde iudicabunt firmum et ratum habeant.' In such matters the London court is obviously the authority consulted, and the enforcement of the Londoners' decisions is guaranteed by decreeing judicial self-sufficiency for the smaller borough. 'Et extra civitatem Oxenforde non placitent de aliquo unde calumniati sunt, sed de quocunque in placito ponentur, se disrationabunt secundum leges et consuetudines civium Londoniarum et non aliter; quia ipsi et cives Londoniarum sunt de una et eadem consuetudine et lege et libertate.' The service of these burgesses at the king's 'festival' should be compared with the 'honors at court' enjoyed by the barons of the Cinque Ports; see below, p. 157.

[4] *B.B.C.*, I, 6, 13: 'Et sciatis eos habere consuetudines Londoniarum et ita testati coram me ipsi barones Londoniarum ita libere et honorifice et iuste sicut unquam melius habuerunt tempore avi mei.' Bedford received the same customs *via* Oxford in 1189.

[5] *B.B.C.*, I, 12.

except that the privilege is to be enjoyed only by members of the gild.
And the reason for the variation would seem to be that the original grant
to Winchester was couched in similar terms. At any rate, the oldest extant charter to that city grants to the citizens in the gild merchant freedom from toll throughout England, and in subsequent documents these
persons appear interchangeably with the *cives Wintonienses*.[1] Indeed,
this same feature recurs in the numerous other charters that confer the
liberties of Winchester upon smaller communities. For example, Chichester obtains from Stephen a confirmation of all its ancient rights both
de burgo and *de gilda mercatoria*, and from Henry II two nearly identical
charters: the first issued for the *cives de Cicestria*, the second for the *cives
de Cicestria qui sunt de gilda mercatoria*.[2]

Thus, to judge from the phraseology of the charters, London and Winchester were the two most prominent towns of England at the accession
of Henry II. But it seems certain that in actual privilege both were exceeded by the relatively insignificant borough of Wallingford. To the
men who helped him to gain his final triumph Henry in 1156 makes a
most remarkable grant.[3] The burgesses are confirmed in the enjoyment
of all free customs held under his predecessors, including their gild merchant with a monopoly of trade throughout the neighborhood and under
the exclusive rule of its aldermen and *ministri*. The king's reeve is specifically forbidden to interfere with the government of the gild and to
levy *scotales*, *gersumae*, or other injurious exactions. Burgesses are to be
tried only in their own *portmoot*, and are there to be protected against all
arbitrary action by the reeve. Their forfeitures are to be fixed by their
fellow burgesses. Furthermore, the men of Wallingford are to be quit of
all gelds, Danegelds, and hidage; of all servile labor; of all work on castles,
walls, ditches, parks, bridges, and roads; of all toll throughout England;
and even of their annual *gablum*, so far as it may be due the king. In fine,
Henry guarantees them any liberty which they can show to have been
enjoyed by their ancestors or by the citizens of Winchester. And Wallingford actually had other liberties beyond those stated in the charter.[4]

Concerning York we have even scantier information. Henry II grants
the citizens the usual confirmation of rights held under his grandfather,
specifying only their gild merchant and hanses in England and Normandy
and their freedom from lestage along the entire seacoast.[5] For North-

---

[1] *S.C.*, 196, 197, 260; Tait, in *E.H.R.*, xlv (1930), 536.

[2] *B.B.C.*, i, 4. Cf. Bath, Ilchester, Andover, etc. (pp. 14, 185); and for Petersfield, see below, pp.
141, 151, 171, 177.

[3] *Calendar of Charter Rolls* (Rolls Series), ii, 68.

[4] See below, p. 169.

[5] *B.B.C.*, i, 6.

ampton no charter is extant before that of Richard in 1189.[1] Norwich, together with the usual ratification of ancient customs, receives merely one assurance: that if anybody during the reign of Stephen has withdrawn himself from the communal obligations, he shall return to his duty; for the king has given exemption to no one.[2] This clause of course refers to the exceptional status generally demanded for their men by ecclesiastical lords — a claim that continues to cause endless disputes, and which by this time can be made good only through special action of the king. The royal letters sanctioning private sokes in many localities all serve to bring out the same truth, that inhabitants of the borough are normally subjected to a uniform law and, unless they have been specifically excepted, must share its burdens as well as its benefits.[3] But perhaps the fullest illustration of this usage is to be found at Lincoln.

Henry II's charter of 1157 confirms the citizens in all liberties, customs, and laws enjoyed under his predecessors, particularly their gild merchant, which as heretofore is to include the merchants, not merely of the city, but of the whole county. And all men who dwell within the four divisions of the city and live through trade shall be *ad geldas et consuetudines et assissas civitatis*, as accustomed in the past. If any one buys land of the burgage of Lincoln and holds it peaceably for a year and a day, no adverse claim shall hold good if the claimant has been within the kingdom during that time. In the same way and with the same qualification, any man who maintains lawful residence in Lincoln for a year and a day shall henceforth freely remain there as the king's citizen.[4] And these provisions are subsequently developed and strengthened by various royal precepts.[5]

---

[1] C. A. Markham and J. C. Cox, *Records of the Borough of Northampton* (Northampton, 1898), I, 25.

[2] *B.B.C.*, I, 8, 108. Norwich, like Northampton and Lincoln, received the liberties of London from Richard (p. 10).

[3] *B.B.C.*, I, 107 ff., 125 ff.

[4] *S.C.*, p. 197: 'Concedo etiam eis quod si aliquis emerit aliquam terram infra civitatem de burgagio Lincolniae et eam tenuerit per annum et unum diem sine calumnia . . . extunc ut in antea bene et in pace teneat eam et sine placito. Confirmo etiam eis quod si aliquis manserit in civitate Lincolniae per annum et unum diem sine calumnia alicuius calumniatoris et dederit consuetudines et cives poterint monstrare per leges et consuetudines civitatis quod calumniator exstiterit in regione Angliae et non calumniatus est eum, extunc ut in antea remaneat in pace in civitate mea Lincolnia sicut civis meus. . . .'

[5] *B.B.C.*, I, 108, 168, 178, 210. These writs (which Ballard classified under four separate heads) provide: (1) that all persons living by trade in Lincoln must share with the citizens all royal gelds and the *assissas civitatis*, as under Henry I; (2) that no foreign merchant may dye cloth or sell it by retail in the city unless he joins the gild and bears all common customs of the town; (3) that all foreign merchants coming to Lincoln, and in particular Norwegians coming to any port of Lincolnshire, must pay the accustomed toll at Lincoln. Cf. the famous writ of Henry I in favor of Cambridge (p. 168): 'Prohibeo ne aliqua navis applicat ad aliquod litus de Cantebrugeseira nisi ad litus de burgo meo de Cantebruge, neque carece onerantur nisi in burgo de Cantebruge, neque aliquis capiat alibi theloneum nisi ibi.'

From the same year we have an equally remarkable grant in favor of
Nottingham.   Henry confirms the ancient customs of the burgesses, but
singles out for particular emphasis their freedom from toll within a wide
area and throughout the length of the Trent.   The men of Nottingham-
shire and Derbyshire are to bring their goods to market on Friday and
Saturday of each week, and no person thus coming is liable for any distress except in connection with the king's farm.   Moreover, no one may
deal in dyed cloth within a circuit of ten leagues about Nottingham, except in the borough.   Under the usual restrictions, tenure of land for a
year and a day establishes a valid title.   'And if any one, whencesoever
he may come, remains in the borough of Nottingham for a year and a day
in time of peace and without adverse claim, thenceforth no one shall have
any right in him except the king. . . .   And whoever resides in the borough,
no matter of whose fief he may be, must render tallages along with the
burgesses and contribute toward the borough's debts.'[1]

To appreciate the force of these grants, they should be compared with
various disputes reported in Continental charters of a somewhat earlier
date.[2]   If the serf of A was admitted as a settler within the immunity of
B and there remained, what rights did A have over his man?   The general
rule, as decided by the courts, was that after the passage of a year and a
day B enjoyed exclusive rights over the settler, and A could claim nothing except what B chose to allow him.   Thus a serf, by establishing legal
residence on specially privileged land, gained actual freedom; for henceforth he was bound merely by the common obligations of the territory
where he resided.   The law of a year and a day became the bulwark of
bourgeois liberty through the application of this same principle.

It is perfectly evident, therefore, that by the middle of the twelfth century free status was one of the advantages accruing to the man who lived
in a borough and placed himself in scot and lot with the burgesses.   If
the custom was established in new boroughs on their foundation it was
because it had already come to be the recognized attribute of boroughs

---

[1] *S.C.*, p. 198: 'Et si aliquis, undecunque sit, in burgo de Notingeham manserit anno uno et die
uno tempore pacis absque calumnia, nullus postea nisi rex in eum ius habebit.   Et quicunque burgensium terram vicini sui emerit et possederit per annum integrum et diem unum absque calumnia
parentum vendentis, si in Anglia fuerint, postea eam quiete possidebit. . . .   Et quicunque in burgo
manserit, cuiuscunque feodi sit, reddere debet simul cum burgensibus talliagia et defectus burgi
adimplere.'   Cf. the Northampton customal of 1190 (*B.B.C.*, I, 104, n. 2): 'Quicunque manserit
sine calumpnia domini sui et ibi fuerit ad focum et locum et scottum et lottum per unum annum et
unum diem debet ibi manere per libertatem burgi.'   Also John's charter to Dunwich (*B.B.C.*, I, 105):
'Si vero aliquis nativus in prefato burgo manserit et terram in eo tenuerit et fuerit in prefata gilda
et hansa et loot et scot cum eisdem burgensibus per unum annum et unum diem, deinceps non possit
repeti a domino suo sed in eodem burgo liber permaneat.'

[2] Above, p. 44; and see C. Stephenson, 'The Origin and Nature of the *Taille*,' *Revue Belge de
Philologie et d'Histoire*, v, 827–51.

in general. By way of exception, the man of a church, although resid-
ing within the walls, might still be regarded as outside the borough. In
that case, he remained serf or sokeman or priest or whatever else he might
be, and he was normally forbidden to engage in trade.[1] The interde-
pendence of the burgess status and the mercantile calling is thus constantly implied and leads in turn to another identification, that the man
in scot and lot with the town is also a member of the gild.

Thus we are introduced to the famous statement of Glanvill:[2]

Item si quis nativus quiete per unum annum et unum diem in aliqua villa pri-
vilegiata manserit, ita quod in eorum communam scilicet gildam tamquam civis
receptus fuerit, eo ipso a vilenagio liberabitur.

By which the learned author obviously intended to say that a serf could
obtain freedom by living unchallenged for a year and a day in a privileged
town, and there being admitted to the burgess community or gild. If
membership in one did not always imply membership in the other, it certainly did in enough cases to warrant such a loosely phrased remark as
Glanvill's.[3] And in any case we are very grateful for any generalization
to supplement the vague and fragmentary evidence of the charters.

The grants just examined — those secured by the six leading boroughs
of the early twelfth century and the related documents — may be taken
as quite representative of the class. For every line of definite information that they happened to include there were pages that they wholly
omitted. Many ancient boroughs, like York and Winchester, received
only general confirmations from Henry II,[4] and for Colchester, Guildford, Hereford, Huntingdon, Stafford, Worcester, Ipswich, and Yarmouth
even that meagre testimony is not forthcoming. On the contrary, two
other boroughs, both of them unquestionably old, for some reason secured
charters that contain most unusual details.

Bristol first emerges from obscurity after the Conquest, but for reasons
to be more fully explained below, there can be no doubt that the borough
was a Saxon work, to which was added a Norman castle after 1066.[5] Under Henry I both were given to Robert Fitz-Hamon, and after him to
Robert, earl of Gloucester, the founder of Cardiff and Tewkesbury.[6]
From Robert, Bristol passed to his son William, and from him, with the

---

[1] Cf. the provision regarding Huntingdon, *B.B.C.*, i, 107. And with the entries quoted for Lincoln and Nottingham may be compared those for Shrewsbury and Stafford (p. 109).

[2] *De Legibus et Consuetudinibus Regni Angliae*, v, 5; ed. G. E. Woodbine (Yale University Press,
1932), p. 87.

[3] See Tait in *E.H.R.*, xlv, 531; and below, pp. 151, 171–172, 176.

[4] *B.B.C.*, i, 4 ff.

[5] Below, pp. 202 ff.

[6] Above, p. 124. For the political history of Bristol, see W. Hunt, *Bristol* (London, 1887), ch. ii.

hand of his daughter, to John of England. Meanwhile the town had already become a famous trading centre. In 1155 Henry II granted the burgesses quittance of toll and all custom throughout his dominions,[1] and in 1171 he issued his well known charter confirming the city of Dublin as a Bristol colony, to be inhabited by the men of that borough and to be held freely and quietly with all the liberties and free customs there enjoyed.[2] But the document does not describe the Bristol privilege in detail; for that information we must turn to John's charter of 1188.[3]

To all burgesses living within the walls, and within certain specified bounds outside, John grants their holdings — in messuages, orchards, and buildings on the water or elsewhere — to be held in free burgage, i.e., *per servitium landgabuli* as rendered within the walls. The burgesses are guaranteed free marriage for themselves and for their sons, daughters, and widows; nor is any personal wardship owed for any of these persons to any lord. The burgesses are exempt from forced hospitality and prise of wine;[4] and they may grind their corn wherever they please. They are quit of the murder fine, of the recognition jury, and of all trial by battle except on appeal for the slaying of a stranger in the town. They shall not be impleaded outside the walls save in connection with tenements that do not pertain to their own hundred, which is to be held weekly. And many clauses are added concerning debt, distress, amercement, and other judicial matters inspired by Henry I's charter to London.[5] No foreigner is to stay in Bristol longer than forty days for the selling of his merchandise, and none may keep a tavern except on a ship. No one but a burgess may sell hides, corn, and wool; or cloth by retail, unless it be at a fair. And John confirms to the men of Bristol quittance of tolls as earlier enjoyed, and all reasonable gilds as held under the earls of Gloucester.

This is a most interesting charter from many points of view. If for no other reason, it would be outstanding through its significance for Dublin and other Irish boroughs.[6] But apart from this consideration, the Bristol

---

[1] N. D. Harding, *Bristol Charters* (Bristol Record Society, 1930), p. 2. The charter is phrased as a new grant; not a confirmation.

[2] *Ibid.*, p. 6. The wording of this document is most remarkable and clearly implies that the Irish city had been colonized by a group of Bristol men. The history of the Danish borough of Dublin and its relation to this crucial event deserves to be carefully studied by some one familiar with the local topography.

[3] *Ibid.*, p. 8.

[4] Comparison with the London charter and similar documents shows this the proper translation of the clause concerning *hospicium*. It can hardly refer to the keeping of a lodging house, as thought by the most recent translator.

[5] For the articles more or less directly copied from the London charter, see *B.B.C.*, I, 82, 87, 135, 144, 147, 150–152, 196. We have no record that Bristol was ever formally given the liberties of London, but the influence of the capital upon John's grant is undeniable.

[6] Dublin's charters from John were essentially reissues of the Bristol charter. For the Irish towns modelled after Dublin, see *B.B.C.*, I, 28 ff., 255.

customs challenge attention because of their own remarkable character. If we strip off the various articles copied from London, the residuum is a set of elementary liberties strikingly reminiscent of those granted to such boroughs as Cardiff and Tewkesbury. Indeed, the resemblance makes us suspect that the liberties of Bristol originated with Robert Fitz-Hamon or his predecessor, possibly influenced the foundation of the Welsh towns, and were later amended by the superimposition of certain borrowings from the capital.[1] However this may be, we have a Saxon borough treated by the Norman invader as if it were a *ville neuve*. And who shall say that in many ways it really was not one?

Somewhat similar information comes from Leicester, one of the Five Boroughs of the Danelaw, which under Henry I is found in the hands of Robert de Beaumont, ancestor of the famous earls of Leicester. Before 1118 this Robert issues a charter confirming his merchants of Leicester in the possession of their gild merchant, as enjoyed since the time of William I — a grant ratified in favor of the burgesses by his son, Robert, earl of Leicester.[2] The same earl also issues another charter conceding to all the burgesses of Leicester and to all who may join their community that, in return for their accustomed rents plus an increment of 8*l.*, they may hold of him *libere et quiete ab omnibus consuetudinibus et ab omnibus rebus pertinentibus hundreto et herieto;* so that they may never be summoned for trial or other matter outside Leicester, but shall respond only in the churchyard court as anciently accustomed.[3]

Whatever the earlier *burgenses* may have been, those of the early twelfth century were plainly *mercatores*. It is they who, already organized in a gild merchant, received the liberties that constituted Leicester a privileged town. These were mainly three: burgage tenure, freedom from heriot, and exemption from outside pleas. Subsequently (*c.* 1254) the rents here referred to, or *gavelpennies*, were bought by the town for an annual payment, and the tenements concerned became virtually allodial property.[4] Meanwhile the community had also prevailed upon the earl to cancel certain dues in place of reaping service, for cows that escaped into his fields, and for the carrying of grain to mills other than his own.[5] By the opening of the thirteenth century Leicester had thus freed itself

---

[1] Above, pp. 124 ff.; below, p. 181.

[2] M. Bateson, *Records of the Borough of Leicester* (Cambridge, 1899), I, 1–3.

[3] *Ibid.*, I, 4.

[4] *Ibid.*, I, 46.

[5] *Ibid.*, I, 8. M. Bateson (p. xxiii) saw in these documents evidence that a manorializing influence had been checked; that 'the ancient burghal element triumphed.' In other words, because Leicester had been some sort of borough for centuries, it must also have been characterized by burgess privilege: an exemption from manorial services in the twelfth century could merely restore a pristine liberty that had somehow been obscured. It is this same general idea that has caused trouble for Mr Tait and other writers (see below, pp. 139 ff.).

from the last remnants of manorial subjection — the culmination of a gradual process of emancipation in which we have every reason to believe that the mercantile class from the outset played a leading part.   For the earlier identity of *burgenses* and *mercatores* is continued by the proved identity in the later period of the gild and the municipal government.[1]

But this consideration at once raises questions of far-reaching significance, to which for the moment no adequate attention can be given.   The object of the foregoing pages has been merely to present a brief summary of the leading charters to boroughs that antedated the Norman Conquest. The account is by no means exhaustive, but it comprises all the more noteworthy enactments and gives a fair representation of the others. And if the resultant effect is far from distinct, that is because such grants were not intended to draw complete pictures.   The liberties of the older towns in England, as on the Continent, rested primarily on prescriptive usage, which the king's formal letters ratified *en bloc*.   In many cases, as we have seen, little definite information is afforded, but occasionally individual privileges were considered important enough to warrant special mention, and this practice often gives us clues toward a better understanding of the urban system.   Eventually some attempt will be made to follow them down.   London and the Cinque Ports will be given separate treatment in another chapter.   And certain matters of special interest will be more fully discussed immediately below.   As a preliminary to further investigation, however, it may be useful to summarize the outstanding features of the materials thus far reviewed.

In the first place, there can be no doubt of the borough community. That was implied by the grant of the charter itself, which conceded special rights to be held in common by the group of men styled burgesses. And although there were exceptions, this borough community normally included all residents within the walls or a prescribed area outside them. Time and again it is stated that all such inhabitants, on whosesoever land they live, must share the general obligations of the town in return for participating in its privileges.

Secondly, we may surely detect within the community of burgesses a dominant mercantile element.   In this respect the emphasis of the charters is unmistakable.   Whenever more than a vague confirmation is given, the outstanding articles regularly have a direct bearing upon commerce. Ships must unload their cargoes in the borough; trade within a certain region is reserved to burgesses; foreign merchants must join their organization and submit to their rules; traders from the borough are freed of customs throughout the king's dominions; fairs and markets receive spe-

---

[1] Bateson, *Records of Leicester*, I, xl ff.; Tait, in *E.H.R.*, XLV, 538 ff.

cial protection; tolls are enumerated. In most localities, furthermore, the gild merchant is singled out for confirmation. Often it is the only privilege to be specifically mentioned, and whenever it appears, it is always marked as an institution of prime importance. Indeed, the language of several charters implies an intimate connection between gild and borough that challenges further study.

A third very prominent feature of the early records is the attention that they give to judicial matters. Burgesses are normally liable for suit only in their own local court, where they are assured of trial according only to their own law.[1] And to judge from the provisions of the charters, that law is of particular benefit to men engaged in business. Wager of battle is ruled out as of obvious disadvantage to the bourgeois. Collection of debts and the enforcement of contracts through distress is specifically authorized, but the lawless seizure of a burgess's chattels scrupulously prevented. Even the limitation of forfeitures, which any man might welcome, would be an especial boon to one whose wealth was notoriously in cash.

The plain language of the charters thus leads us to conclude that in the time of Henry I the borough was a community of men living principally through commerce and enjoying privileged status by virtue of the special law which there obtained. Whatever it had previously been, the borough henceforth appears as a town. To contemporaries, in fact, it mattered little whether the history of the locality could be traced back to King Alfred, to Julius Caesar, or only to Robert Fitz-Hamon; the antiquity of the foundation affected neither material prosperity nor legal capacity. The judicial and mercantile liberties held by inhabitants of old and new boroughs were obviously the same, and these privileges must have carried the same implications. The law of a year and a day is most prominent in grants to new boroughs, but from a diversity of evidence appears to have been common to all. Burgage tenure, as we have seen, is specified in few charters to old boroughs, but there can be no doubt that it was taken for granted in the rest. All our evidence agrees that the system was universal throughout urban settlements.

According to general European practice, a grant of advanced privileges assumed the possession of the more elementary. The same principle holds good in England. Before London could secure such a charter as that of Henry I, it must have come to enjoy customs like, for example,

---

[1] The charters constantly presuppose that the law of the borough is declared by the burgesses, or a select group of them, in the local court. Otherwise there would have been no point in restricting trials to the borough. See above, p. 129, n. 3; *B.B.C.*, I, 113, and following sections. And note the Wallingford article (p. 153): 'Et si aliquo forisfacto vel recto iudicio aliquis eorum forisfactus fuerit, per rectam considerationem burgensium erga prepositum illud emendet.' Cf. below, p. 141–42.

those of Newcastle. Oxford, to receive the liberties of London, must already have shared the social constitution of the capital. The implications of the charters inevitably suggest that old and new boroughs were fundamentally alike. By what line of reasoning has any other view come to be expressed?

3. The Freedom of the Borough

In one of his recent studies Mr Tait has re-examined the *liber burgus* clause in the charters of the twelfth and thirteenth centuries; and thanks to his analysis, the force of that bit of legal phraseology now emerges much more clearly. Mr Tait shows that, although the formula first appears in the reign of John, other expressions had been earlier employed to mean exactly the same. In other words, the underlying concept was virtually as old as the practice of issuing municipal charters and had reference merely to the borough itself. The adjective *liber* was only an adornment; for in the twelfth century all boroughs were free boroughs.[1]

An admirable example of the varying usage found in this connection is afforded by the charters of Wells.[2] Bishop Reginald (1174–80) confirms the grant of his predecessor, that the vill of Wells 'shall be a borough forever.' Every holder of a messuage *nomine burgagii* is to enjoy freedom of residence, of ingress and egress, and of selling, mortgaging, and bequeathing his property, on payment of the due rent of 12*d*. Judicial procedure is defined and the buying of raw hides in the town is restricted to men in scot and lot with the burgesses. Later Bishop Savaric ratifies this charter, but declares the town to be a *liber burgus*. And finally John adds his approval, stating that Wells is to have all the liberties and free customs of a free borough and of free burgesses and all those pertaining to markets and fairs. That in these documents, and in others like them, *burgus* meant something quite definite is evident; but what was it?

According to Gross, the word did not imply any one fundamental attribute; the borough was a variable complex of different liberties.[3] On the other hand, Maitland was convinced by the language of many charters that the establishment of burgage tenure, involving the abolition of manorial customs, alone sufficed to transform a village into a borough.[4]

---

[1] J. Tait, 'Liber Burgus,' in *Essays in Mediaeval History Presented to Thomas Frederick Tout* (Manchester, 1925), pp. 79 ff.; cf. Ballard, *English Borough*, pp. 76 ff.

[2] *B.B.C.*, I, 2, 3, 31.

[3] *Gild Merchant*, I, 5.

[4] *H.E.L.*, I, 640. Maitland's classic account of municipal evolution in England remains the finest synthesis that we have on the subject. In almost every phase of the subject, particularly on the growth of self-government and on the gradual emergence of a corporate character, he will be found in his own matchless way to have sketched the essentials. The one important point that, in my opinion, he failed to appreciate was the revolutionizing effect upon the old borough of its mercantile development. In *Domesday Book and Beyond* (pp. 196 ff.) he came very near expressing the view

In this conclusion Ballard mainly concurred. Burgage tenure was indispensable to the borough; but, he contended, a borough court was equally necessary. And in reply to the obvious comment that separate judicial organization was common to hundreds of simple manors, he cited Maitland's statement that burgage tenure was also to be found in places not called boroughs.[1] As Mr Tait pointed out, however, the cases of burgage tenure on which Ballard's opinion rested were apparent exceptions only. A town might really be a borough though never so styled in the records. Burgage tenure was thus exclusively burghal, while possession of a court was not.[2]

As between the theories of Gross and Maitland, Mr Tait hesitates. Maitland, he feels, was unquestionably right so far as the new borough was concerned, but with regard to the 'great boroughs of immemorial origin' he considers Gross's view to be perhaps preferable.[3] At least, he believes, certain thirteenth-century charters tend to bear out that scholar's contention.[4] Such examples, however, even if they were clearer than they are, could have but slight significance toward interpreting the word *burgus* as used 175 years earlier. Besides, it is hard to see how such a single phrase could have meant one thing for an old borough and another for a new borough, unless the two groups were more sharply distinguished than they have appeared in the preceding pages. And there are other considerations to be taken into account.

Under the system of feudal tenures brought to England by the Nor-

---

here emphasized, but stopped just short of it. So in the *H.E.L.* (and in *Township and Borough*, p. 71) he still suggests that burgage tenure originated through the influence of the borough's tenurial heterogeneity, and he connects with the same feature the establishment of exclusive jurisdiction for the borough court (p. 645). He even finds (p. 648) that the law of a year and a day for the attainment of personal freedom was by origin 'an assertion of royal right,' and so derives burgess liberty from that of the king's ancient demesne. He cites his evidence, but in his interpretation leaves out of account the factor of social change. To do that is, it seems to me, to miss the dominant fact in the urban history of the Middle Ages. See above, p. 71.

[1] *English Borough*, p. 30; *B.B.C.*, i, lxxxix.

[2] *B.B.C.*, ii, xlix ff. In the case of the few apparent exceptions that have ever been cited, it may with excellent logic be said that in the earlier period existence of burgage tenure is itself proof of burghal status. But eventually there was much experimentation in borough-making, and the effort to give some village an urban character might lead to an anomalous situation.

[3] 'Liber Burgus,' pp. 84–89. Mr Tait has placed so many qualifications on his conclusions that to state them briefly but fairly is difficult. It is, however, the old borough that causes the trouble: 'The appearance of the free borough clause in charters granted to existing boroughs, some of which are registered as such in Domesday Book, whether mesne or royal, presents a difficulty on any interpretation of the formula, but it is perhaps less serious if we adopt Gross's view than if the meaning of the term is definitely restricted to the fundamental requisites of a borough.'

[4] The charters cited in this connection (pp. 85–87) were all of Edward I and the alleged interpretation turns on the precise force of clauses introduced by *et quod, ut quod,* and the like — an exceedingly precarious undertaking. On the other hand, the charters (pp. 88–89) that negative such an interpretation are clearer as well as earlier.

mans, the baron could proclaim a borough wherever he chose within his own jurisdiction. This right was inherent in the political authority that he held of the king, and so its exercise could never produce a result other than the king might produce if he chose.[1] A seignorial foundation could therefore differ from a royal foundation only in unessential details. As a matter of practice, the baron might be willing to define customs in ways not popular with the kings, and there were of course privileges that transcended the power of the ordinary vassal to grant. But as has been remarked, the former possibility seems never to have had important consequences, and even the baron's legal disability could be overcome by royal intervention. Moreover, all distinction between seignorial boroughs and the rest was quickly lost as escheat or forfeiture brought the former into the king's hands. And, in the meantime, many old boroughs had been mediatized and so had come to receive their charters from barons.

It is therefore quite impossible to classify urban liberties in England as being either essentially royal or essentially seignorial. Nor can we discover that the Norman kings considered the boroughs which they founded in any way distinct from those which they inherited. If the old boroughs seem to form a class apart, it is because their charters do not ordinarily enumerate the most elementary privileges. But that is not always true; occasionally an old borough in seignorial hands is guaranteed even such rights as burgage tenure and exemption from manorial obligations. These liberties were surely as desirable at Gloucester and Lincoln as at Bristol and Leicester. If they were omitted from the charters of the former boroughs, it was hardly because they were not enjoyed there.

From an examination of the evidence we gain the distinct impression that — as would indeed be quite natural — town populations placed greater trust in the king than in the baronage. We are led to believe that William I, despite the severity of his financial exactions, actively encouraged the development of the bourgeoisie. The Conqueror could hardly have been required to issue municipal charters, even if they had at that time been customary, and under Henry I the men of his boroughs were apparently willing that their liberty should remain a matter of unwritten custom. How extensive and how firmly established that liberty was appears from the confirmations of Henry II. Thus the elaborate provisions of the seignorial charters should not be taken as indicating a peculiar magnanimity on the part of the donors. Settlers who would flock to a town under the mere assurance of royal protection could perhaps be attracted to a baronial colony by only the most formal of guarantees. Although the law of Breteuil and similar promulgations had con-

---

[1] Above, pp. 44–45.

siderable local influence, the standards of urban liberty in England were set by the royal boroughs. And this was true, not only of the king's own towns, but of many that belonged to his vassals.

It has already been remarked that Bristol enjoyed at least some of the London liberties under the earls of Gloucester;[1] and it was their ancestor, Robert Fitz-Hamon, who gave his men of Burford a gild merchant with all customs held by the burgesses of Oxford in theirs.[2] The bishop of Winchester secured from Stephen that his burgesses of Taunton were to enjoy such quittance throughout England of toll, passage, and custom as was enjoyed by the men of London and Winchester.[3] This statement seems to indicate only trading privileges, but when the countess of Gloucester promised all settlers at Petersfield the liberties enjoyed by the citizens of Winchester in their gild merchant, the grant was plainly intended to be more inclusive.[4]

Indeed, charters conferring upon new boroughs the laws of old boroughs are not at all unusual. On its foundation by Ralph, earl of Chester, Coventry was guaranteed tenure in free burgage together with the liberties of Lincoln.[5] The bishop of Norwich, having been authorized by King John to select any English town as a model, proclaimed a free borough at Lynn according to the custom of Oxford.[6] And occasionally we are given greater detail. A charter of 1194, issued by Roger de Lacy, confirms to the burgesses of Pontefract 'their liberty and their free burgage and their tofts' to be held of him in fee at the rent of 12*d*. each.[7] Furthermore, they are to have all the liberties and free customs of Grimsby. As enumerated by the charter, these include free sale of property, guarantee of the title to land if held unchallenged for a year and a day, acquisition of burgess franchise by purchase of a toft or part of one,[8] exemption from all trials outside the borough except for pleas of the crown, assessment of

---

[1] See above, pp. 134–35.

[2] Gross, *Gild Merchant*, II, 28–29. Only a fragment of the original charter remains, but it is all supplied by the confirmation of William, earl of Gloucester. Besides the gild, it guarantess free sale and devise of land and chattels, together with a monopoly of selling wool and hides in the market.

[3] *B.B.C.*, I, 12.

[4] *B.B.C.*, I, 27; see above, p. 130.

[5] *B.B.C.*, I, 27.

[6] *B.B.C.*, I, 32.

[7] *Historical MSS Commission*, Report VIII, 269: 'confirmavi burgensibus meis de Pontefracto et heredibus et successoribus suis libertatem et liberum burgagium et toftos suos tenendos de me et heredibus meis in feudo et hereditate libere et quiete honorifice et integre, reddendo annuatim mihi vel heredibus meis XII denarios pro quolibet tofto integro. . . .'

[8] If a man has several houses on his toft and rents them out, the one who lives in the principal house is to be 'quit and free as a burgess'; the other tenants are to enjoy freedom of buying and selling in the borough on payment of 4*d*. annually to the reeve.

forfeitures by fellow-burgesses, and a considerable number of other judicial and mercantile privileges.[1]

The most noteworthy instance of such practice, however, is found in the charters of Beverley.[2]   The archbishop of York, with the assent of Henry I, grants to the men of that vill 'all the liberties of York, to be enjoyed according to the same law as used by the men of that city.'[3]   In particular, the burgesses of Beverley are to have their *hanshus*, with the same law of liberty as obtains in the *hanshus* of York.   They are to enjoy the rights of free entrance and departure, and are to be exempt from all toll throughout Yorkshire. Furthermore, all toll at Beverley is granted to the burgesses for the annual payment of eighteen marks, except for tolls collected on three stated festivals, when they are reserved to the bishop and chapter. But on such occasions the men of Beverley are to pay nothing.

In ratification of the archbishop's action Henry I then makes the following grant:[4]

Sciatis me concessisse et dedisse et hac mea carta confirmasse hominibus de Beverlaco liberum burgagium secundum liberas leges et consuetudines burgensium de Eboraco et suum gilde mercatorum cum placidis suis et teloneo et cum omnibus liberis consuetudinibus et libertatibus suis in omnibus rebus.

And with these charters may be profitably compared that of Henry II to Hedon:[5]

Sciatis me concessisse Willelmo comite Albem' liberum burgagium in Hedduna sibi et heredibus suis in feudo et hereditate, ita quod burgenses eius Heddune libere et quiete in libero burgagio teneant sicut burgenses mei de Eboraco vel Nichol' (i.e., Lincolnia) melius et liberius et quietius tenent illis consuetudinibus et libertatibus.

As Mr Tait has pointed out, the *liberum burgagium* of the foregoing documents expresses essentially the same idea as the *liber burgus* of later

---

[1] In 1208 Leeds was given a charter with all the liberties of Pontefract, reciting those which Pontefract had received as of Grimsby (*B.B.C.*, I, 29).   Meanwhile, in 1201, Grimsby had secured from John a grant of the liberties of Northampton (p. 10); and since Northampton in 1189 had been given the liberties of London, the charter of Grimsby was copied from that of London.   Mary Bateson (*E.H.R.*, xv, 309) noted the general resemblance between the liberties of Pontefract and those of the French boroughs, but because the former were derived from Grimsby felt it necessary to attribute them to the Danes.   In spite of the fact that Grimsby was a Danish borough, has any one ever been able to show that these enumerated customs were in any way Scandinavian?

[2] Gross, *Gild Merchant*, II, 21; *S.C.*, p. 131; *B.B.C.*, I, 23–24.

[3] 'confirmasse hominibus de Beverlaco omnes libertates eisdem legibus quibus illi de Eboraco habent in sua civitate.'

[4] Archbishop William's confirmation substitutes: 'liberale burgagium villae Beverlaco et burgensibus ibi commorantibus iuxta formam liberalis burgagii Eboraci . . .'

[5] *B.B.C.*, I, 38.

usage.[1] In one Beverley charter, specifically, it is the equivalent of the *libertates* or *liberae consuetudines* (*leges*) of the others. The burgage of Beverley is the sum total of the liberties that make it a borough, and they are to be determined according to the laws of York. In essentials, therefore, the freedom of the two towns must be the same.[2] But York is old and Beverley is new. For that reason is burgage tenure less fundamental in one than in the other? As to the holding of the individual, the Beverley charters say nothing, but that of Hedon is clear and specific. The town is constituted a *liberum burgagium* because the burgesses hold *in libero burgagio*, as do those of York and Lincoln. And similar implications are found in a number of other charters.[3]

Indeed, the history of the words in the twelfth century is otherwise incomprehensible. The borough is a privileged community; the burgess is a privileged member of the community; he and he alone may hold by the privileged tenure of that community. The townsman's plot of land is called *burgagium* because it is inseparable from the *burgagium* that constitutes the free borough. As Mr Tait has suggested, burgage was more than a tenure.[4] It was a social and legal status, a mode of life dependent on membership in a community. A borough could not be established without also establishing burgess franchise and burgage tenure.

In his other deductions it is harder to follow Mr Tait. In the face of the Beverley evidence, how can we distinguish the 'burgality' of a Domesday borough from that of a Norman foundation?[5] Furthermore, why must we conclude that the *liberum burgagium* of the early charters was, like the *liber burgus* of the later ones, 'a variable generic conception'? By broadening the sense of *burgagium* to include more than Hemmeon de-

---

[1] *Op. cit.*, p. 95: 'In the use made of *liberum* (*liberale*) *burgagium* in two of the three Beverley charters, and especially in that of archbishop William, we have a clear anticipation of the *liber burgus* formula which expressed the same idea in concrete form.'

[2] *Ibid.*, p. 96: 'The Beverley town charters show that the privileged status of a great and ancient town like York could be summed up in the same term "free burgage" as was applied to new mesne boroughs, though in the first case no grant to that effect was producible.'

[3] See in particular Bradninch and Whitby (*B.B.C.*, I, 38–39): 'confirmavi burgensibus meis de Bradninch burgariam suam et placias suas sicut illae liberatae sunt et assignatae tenendas et habendas illis et heredibus suis in feodo et iure hereditario . . .'; 'dedisse et concessisse in perpetuum Wytebyam in liberam burgagiam et burgensibus ibidem manentibus libertatem burgagiae et leges liberas liberaque iura . . .' The confirmation of the first charter substitutes *burgagia* for *burgariam*. Cf. Pontefract (above, p. 141, n. 7) and Lincoln (above, p. 131, n. 4). The term *burgarium* appears in Normandy: A. Legras, *Le Bourgage de Caen* (Paris, 1911), App. B, no. 10.

[4] *Op. cit.*, p. 95: 'It is usual to translate *burgagium* in this sense by "burgage tenure," but "borough tenure" would be preferable as avoiding confusion with the derivative use of *burgagium* for the individual burghal tenement and leaving room for a good deal of "liberty" or "law" or "custom" which was not all tenurial, though the free tenement at a money rent was the most fundamental element in the borough.'

[5] Above, p. 139.

scribed as burgage tenure we are not driven to accept Gross's dictum. The concept of the free borough or the free burgage in the twelfth century, as appears from the documents of that age, was not variable, but stable.   Nor is this a mere verbal quibble; it involves the very fundamental question of what the borough then was.

To Gross, as to Stubbs, the borough seemed 'only a more strictly organized form of township' — especially characterized by a 'separate judiciary.'[1]   The borough, as contrasted with the gild merchant, was essentially old; its elemental constitution could not be affected by a mere formula in a Norman charter.   The *liber burgus* clause in official documents was largely a rhetorical adornment that implied the bestowal of certain additional franchises, but no particular one or particular group of them.   Thus Gross sought to refute the view that 'the gild was the all-pervading, life-giving principle of the borough.'   The gild, he insisted, was not the 'fertile germ' to which the town constitution owed its existence.   That was rather the borough court.[2]   Gross's chief concern, obviously, was with his own thesis; his interest in the *liber burgus* formula was at most secondary, and to prove the point at hand he did not find it necessary to make a thorough analysis of all the pertinent sources.   His definition of the borough was merely that of the Maurer-Below school, which was just then coming into its great ascendancy.   There was no reason why Gross should question its accuracy.

Of more recent years, however, confidence in the theory of urban origins favored by Stubbs has been rudely shaken, and it is no longer possible to accept Gross's interpretation of the borough charters without revision. By denying that the word *burgus* had any technical and constant meaning in the twelfth century, scores of documents are deprived of any clear meaning, and Mr Tait has definitely faced that fact.   Nevertheless, his interesting essay, by attempting a compromise between Gross and Maitland, leaves us with very much the same dilemma that perplexed Mary Bateson: how the borough could at the same time be a revolutionary artificial creation and an ancient royal institution.[3]

The only way out of the difficulty, it is here suggested, is to abandon the presupposition on which Gross's definition rested and to regard *burgus* as having acquired a radically new meaning in the course of the Norman period — that of a privileged town.   To express this idea the Latin translation of the Anglo-Saxon *burh* was at first felt inadequate, because the old borough was not a privileged town.   To designate a settlement characterized by uniform free status and free tenure, the French *bourgage*,

[1] Above, p. 16; Gross, *Gild Merchant*, I, xix, 85.

[2] *Ibid.*, I, 86 ff.

[3] *E.H.R.*, XVI, 332 ff.

Latinized as *burgagium*, was preferred.[1] Later the phrase *liber burgus* was generally employed. If boroughs had always been free boroughs, would the adjective have been thought so essential?

These conclusions, it will be noted, not only follow from analysis of the English sources; they fit the known facts concerning the towns of Europe generally. On the Continent we have found bourgeois status uniform over a large region without respect to political frontiers. The French merchants who accompanied the Norman conqueror to England brought foreign custom with them. The boroughs which they settled or helped to settle could have differed in no essential respect from the *bourgs* whence they came. To apply varying standards in such cases is impossible. Urban liberty must have been the same on both sides of the Channel.

The evidence cited above is old, and if the deductions here drawn appear new, it is assuredly not because of their abstruse character. It is rather because of certain ideas that have prevailed with regard to the Anglo-Saxon boroughs. For if they had been from the beginning what they were in the twelfth century, the true test of their burghal status must have been a matter of continuous tradition —and precisely what that implied was extremely hard to prove. But this logical difficulty is at once avoided by accepting the view expressed in the preceding chapters: that the tenth-century borough was not a privileged community; that as late as Domesday neither *burgus* nor *burgensis* was a technical term; that the meaning given to these words in municipal charters must have been the result of a social change that first produced true urban life.[2] By thus regarding the twelfth-century borough as being a comparatively new development, no matter what the site on which it grew, its essential uniformity is readily appreciated.

Yet, even after we have described the Norman borough as a community and sketched the fundamental rights and obligations of its members, we have left vague one very important question. The charter of liberties may have been legally granted to some thousands of citizens, but actually they were by no means of equal responsibility. Who were the men that negotiated for the grant, that defined the needs of the town, that guaranteed rents and services, that constituted the efficient nucleus of the communal organization? The answer commonly given has been based in legal theory, but it is now becoming evident that practical considerations were really paramount.

[1] The earliest use of the word that I have encountered is that (1037–67) cited in Généstal, *La Tenure en Bourgage*, p. 207, n. 1: Richard, count of Evreux, grants to the abbey of Saint-Taurin 'quidquid habat (sic) in burgensibus scilicet in foro et in burgagio suo et in feriis suis.' M. Généstal understands *burgagium* to refer to some sort of payment, but does it not mean rather the burgess community?

[2] Above, pp. 80 ff.

4. Courts and Gilds

In the middle of the nineteenth century the most popular theory for explaining the origin of the English towns was that begun in Germany by Wilda and popularized in France by Thierry.[1] In England this doctrine of municipal evolution from the gild was thought to find especially thorough confirmation from the numerous sources that mentioned such organizations before and after the Norman Conquest. It was stated with the utmost assurance by various authors that the mediaeval borough was identical with the gild merchant, and that the latter was but a modification of the Anglo-Saxon gild.[2] True, Stubbs was somewhat skeptical of this thesis as a whole and threw the weight of his support rather to the view of Georg von Maurer.[3] But considerable prestige still remained with the gild theory until it was exploded by Charles Gross.

To recapitulate the argument of that scholar's well known book is quite unnecessary. He so thoroughly exhausted the sources and so cogently marshalled his evidence that no further attempt has been made to identify gild and borough. Moreover, he decisively proved that between the social gilds of the Saxons and the gilds merchant of the Normans there could have been only the slightest of connections. The mercantile organization of the borough, so far as could be judged from extant records, followed the conquest of 1066 and at least to a large degree resulted from it, through the commercial stimulation which it engendered. According to Gross, however, this development was entirely secondary to the history of the borough itself. For in the latter he saw an ancient community grouped about an ancient court. The centre and well-spring of all municipal institutions was judicial organization.[4] And to the weight of this opinion was added the support, more or less qualified, of Maitland, Ballard, and Mary Bateson.[5]

Great authorities have thus agreed in regarding the continuity of the court from Anglo-Saxon times as the dominating factor in the history of the borough. But if the interpretation of the sources in the preceding pages is sound, our faith in this alleged continuity is inevitably broken. We cannot be sure that every borough had a separate court; or, when courts are referred to in connection with boroughs, that they were all of the same kind. If courts were always given to seignorial boroughs after the Norman Conquest — and that is by no means certain — they were

---

[1] Above, pp. 5, 14.

[2] Gross, *Gild Merchant*, I, 77 ff., 167 ff.

[3] Above, p. 16.

[4] *Gild Merchant*, I, 85.

[5] *H.E.L.*, I, 638 ff.; *B.B.C.*, I, cii–ciii; Ballard, *English Borough*, p. 54; M. Bateson, *Mediaeval England* (New York, 1904), pp. 124 ff.; and see below, p. 148.

assuredly very different from the territorial courts of the king, under which, as we have seen, the older boroughs had been comprehended in a variety of ways. Some of these boroughs, as the heads of districts, occasionally witnessed the meeting of a superior court called *scirgemot* or *burhgemot;* most of them were hundredal in that they each constituted the centre of a hundred named for the borough.[1] But from a hundred court of the ancient type to a municipal court with exclusive jurisdiction over the inhabitants the change was a radical one, whether accomplished by sudden transformation or by gradual transition.

Domesday Book clearly indicates an old judicial system still persisting in 1086.[2] The institution of lawmen with thegnly rank, the common occurrence of personal and territorial sokes, the general absence of features that we should recognize as truly municipal — all bespeak the prevalence of an ancient custom that was the same for borough and open country. When we encounter exceptional practices, such as the limitation of forfeitures at Rhuddlan or the communal enjoyment of *consuetudines* at Dover, they are explicitly marked as innovations. On the Continent liberties of this sort commonly appear in connection with an urban scheme of law and justice, the foundation of which is the practically universal guarantee to bourgeois of trial within their respective towns.[3] In England, with the granting of formal charters, the same phenomenon recurs. Among a variety of lesser provisions, the one great judicial privilege of the burgess is exemption from outside suits. This article, as already observed, is generally found in charters to new boroughs. But as early as the reign of Henry I it stands in the charter to London, as well as in the customs of Newcastle and of Bury St Edmund's. And it is repeated in a score of grants under Henry II.[4]

Like burgage tenure or personal freedom, this judicial franchise everywhere appears as a mark by which the townsman is distinguished from the peasant. It is inconceivable that such liberties did not evolve together and under the same impetus. As a burgess, a man lived under the special law of a borough, and to guarantee his privilege he was normally exempt from trial except in his own court. The latter might bear an old name, be presided over by an official with an ancient title, and go through forms of procedure sanctioned by centuries of tradition; but its spirit was

[1] Above, pp. 68 ff., 111 ff.

[2] Above, pp. 107 ff.

[3] Above, p. 45.

[4] See the long list of excerpts in *B.B.C.*, I, 115–21. It is obvious that the exemption from shires and hundreds, though separately classified by Ballard (pp. 123–124), was a mere variety of this privilege. Normally it was not necessary, for the court of the local hundred usually met in the borough, as did also the shire court in many cases.

new.   Legally it might be the same organ that had spoken for the borough
since the days of Aethelstan or even earlier.   Actually it was a different
institution, for it represented a different borough.

On the subject of borough custom our leading authority has been Mary
Bateson, who was among the first to appreciate the close relationship in
this respect of England to the Continent, and who so eloquently demonstrated the newness of many boroughs.[1]   Nevertheless, while compiling
her volumes for the Selden Society, it was the persistence of archaic usage
in the towns that chiefly fascinated her.   'The primary interest of borough custom, as of all custom, is the glimpse it affords into a remote past.'
But how remote was that past?   According to the editor, the law revealed
by the customals is a mixture of old and new: the old being vestiges of
primitive English and Danish folk-law; the new consisting of reforms consciously made by the later town populations.   Both features were dictated by selfish interests.   'So far as the old folk-law could be used to
give the burgesses additional facilities and franchises against outsiders,
it was adhered to; but when it tended to hamper the burgesses — for instance, in its strict rules for verbal accuracy in pleading — the more advanced of the borough courts were prepared to amend or abolish the old
system'.[2]

From this argument, to which no exception can be taken, it would follow that in the study of borough custom the important consideration is
not its continuity with the past, but its vital relationship to the society
that produced it.   If the old in borough custom outweighed the new, we
should conclude that the burgess class of Norman times was essentially
a survival from the Anglo-Saxon period.   That evidently was Mary Bateson's opinion — one which she shared with the leading authorities of the
day.[3]   But in the light of more recent criticism, is the view tenable?

Turning to Mary Bateson's own analysis of her compilation,[4] we find,
out of a total of 137 pages, 47 devoted to procedure, but of the latter 25
are taken up with attachment and distress.   Of the 137, furthermore, 18
deal with contract, 11 with the organization of the courts, and the rest
with the tenure of land and chattels.   It is a very familiar fact that the
law of the boroughs retained much archaic practice because royal privilege generally isolated them from the operation of the common law.   Part
of this retention was purely accidental, but, as Mary Bateson showed, a
great deal of it was not.   Burgesses naturally preferred compurgation to
trial by battle and objected to such innovations as the assize of *novel dis-*

[1] Above, pp. 120 ff.

[2] *Borough Customs* (Selden Society, 1904, 1906), ii, xv ff.

[3] Above, pp. 18 ff.

[4] *Borough Customs*, ii, xx-clvi.

seisin because they were incompatible with the tenurial franchise of the borough. And many of the other procedural anomalies in the towns were due to conscious amendment rather than to mere habit. The system of debt-collection by distress Mary Bateson recognized as derived, not from the self-help of Germanic antiquity, but rather from practical methods, adopted under royal sanction, of enforcing bargains.[1] Indeed, the whole mass of provisions regarding debt and contract were so obviously based on mercantile necessity that there is no need of elaborating the point.

The articles on judicial organization, as we have just seen, carried on some ancient traditions, but in general were inspired by demands that hardly antedated the twelfth century. In treating the subjects of alienation, inheritance, testamentary succession, rights in land and chattels, wardship, seignorial claims, and the social and proprietary complications of marriage, Mary Bateson detected occasional connections with primitive custom, but that all these matters were ultimately involved in burgage tenure she must have realized. And in the explanation of that fundamental problem it was she who first argued for the essential novelty of the institution.[2] Thus, in spite of the fact that much antiquated custom lingered on in the towns of the thirteenth century, the law enforced by the urban courts was in general no survival of the tenth. The forms were perhaps the forms of the old territorial moots, but the substance was such as they could never have known.[3]

From the viewpoint of the present study, the important consideration is therefore not the descent of the borough court from the more or less doubtful institutions of Danes and Saxons, but the actual group that constituted it. At any time in its history the men who dominated the court were presumably those who dominated the borough. In the early eleventh century they would be the local agrarian aristocracy — lawmen or others of thegnly rank. In the early twelfth century they would still be

---

[1] *Ibid.*, II, xviii.

[2] Above, p. 88.

[3] It is to be hoped that eventually some specialist in early law will give this subject adequate consideration. In the present study the necessity of maintaining balanced treatment, as well as the incompetence of the author, precludes the making of more than a few superficial observations. Most customals, furthermore, date from a period long subsequent to the one with which we are here concerned, and the task of distinguishing the original elements is one to tax the ablest of critics. The problem, however, challenges the attention of any one who examines, with more than a superficial interest, the volumes assembled by Mary Bateson. By trimming off later accretions and by ignoring minor variations, cannot this mass of material be reduced to a few fundamental principles that clearly emerged before the end of the twelfth century? And on analysis will these principles be found new or old? Will they prove to be dominated by Saxon, Danish, Frankish, or other tradition? My own impression is that, in so far as they may reveal a distinctive character, it will defy classification except as urban. But the validity of such a generalization remains to be demonstrated.

the local aristocracy, but no longer agrarian. By this time the thegns had given way to merchants, and that change implied a world of difference. The earlier group did not demand municipal charters. The latter did, and it was they who made the town as we know it.

Herein lies the great significance of the gild merchant for the history of the boroughs. The exaggerations of the older writers were after all founded on one truth, that the town was practically, if not legally, a union of men living through trade. In the light of recent municipal studies the gild has recovered some of its lost prominence. Once more it may be perceived to have had an intimate connection with the beginnings of urban self-government.

Thanks to the work of Gross, who assembled all the pertinent material on the subject, it is singularly easy to summarize what is known of early English gilds. And such a summary may at once be seen to bear out the conclusions already reached with regard to an economic transformation within the borough. The burgesses who under King Edward met for practical or convivial purposes in the gild-halls of London, Winchester, Cambridge, and Exeter were thegns or *cnihtas*, members of the landed aristocracy. With the Norman Conquest their clubs broke up or died a lingering death. Their buildings were converted to other uses. As the twelfth century opened, nothing but occasional use of an antiquated title yet served to commemorate a social order that had utterly passed away.[1]

Meanwhile, the new mercantile organizations had made their appearance. The Burford charters reveal a gild merchant at Oxford going back to the later eleventh century, and those of Beverley one at York under Henry I.[2] The chapman's gild at Canterbury was earlier than 1109.[3] And in Leicester, Lewes, Chichester, Wilton, Winchester, Lincoln, Wallingford, Southampton, and other places the documents indicate gilds dating at least from the early twelfth century.[4] As Gross demonstrated, the gild merchant can be traced back to the generation of the Conqueror, but no earlier; and as he believed, the system was probably an importation

---

[1] Gross, *Gild Merchant*, I, 174 ff. The gild at Dover did not survive the Conquest, as appears definitely from the statement in *D.B.*, I, 1: 'Willelmus filius Gosfridi III (mansuras) in quibus erat gihalla burgensium.' Cf. *Inq. St Aug.*, p. 25: 'Willelmus filius Ganufridi habet unam gidhallam quam burgenses habent perditam. Haec erat elemosina regis et ibi sunt tres domus.' The same was true of the three gilds at Winchester, mentioned in the *Liber Winton*. (*D.B.*, Add., pp. 531, 533, 536; Round, in *V.H.C. Hampshire*, I, 530 ff.). The fate of the London *cnihtengild* is too familiar to need further comment; for that and other examples of Anglo-Saxon gilds see Gross, *loc. cit.* As he suggested, most of the alleged gilds of Domesday disappear on correct interpretation of the passages in question (above, p. 104, n. 1).

[2] Above, p. 142. Cf. the York document of 1080 (below, p. 190, n. 2).

[3] Gross, *Gild Merchant*, II, 37. The members are called *cnihtas* — the one link with the Anglo-Saxon gilds that the documents prove.

[4] *B.B.C.*, I, 6, 12, 202 ff.

from the Continent. The predominance of agriculture in the boroughs till then, the facts known of the Anglo-Saxon gilds, the prior existence of the gild merchant in Flanders, Normandy, and the Rhinelands, the settlement of French traders in many English localities — all tend to disprove any continuity of the institution in Britain across the year 1066.[1]

These conclusions of Gross so logically follow from the evidence, that they may be accepted as definitive. But it is no longer possible to agree so unreservedly with his views as to the relative importance for urban development of court and gild. The former, it appears from re-examination of the sources, can hardly be accredited with the municipal functions that were once attributed to it. And the recent work of Mr Tait forces us to reconsider the whole question of the connection between gild and municipality. The testimony of Glanville, the charters of Winchester and of its affiliated towns, together with various records of Leicester, Oxford, Exeter, and other places, prove beyond a doubt that, as early as the first half of the twelfth century, the gild merchant and the burgess community were practically identified in many localities. And this identification was not, as Gross thought, restricted to purely mercantile affairs.[2]

At a time when the boroughs were still politically subordinated to royal officials, while their courts were yet bound by the traditions of agrarian society, it was the gild merchant which normally provided a means for communal activity, which frequently came to speak for the newly developed town. The system that is found in such communities as Leicester during the thirteenth century was merely the extension of an informal practice that had earlier been widespread. But such considerations lead us beyond the subject of this chapter to another that must now be taken up in detail.

[1] *Gild Merchant*, I, 2 ff.
[2] Tait in *E.H.R.*, XLV, 530 ff.; above, pp. 129 ff.; below, pp. 171, 177.

VI

BOROUGH SELF-GOVERNMENT

1. Borough Services

IN previous chapters we have seen the general nature of the borough as described by Domesday and again as it is revealed in the earliest municipal charters. The two sets of data thus obtained inevitably suggest comparison and contrast, but before that problem can be given adequate consideration, other sources must be taken into account. For the moment, therefore, we may restrict our attention to a simpler matter — the relative size of the boroughs at the time of the Norman Conquest. As remarked above, Domesday is interested, not in men, but in properties. *Burgenses* are generally equated with *domus*, and these with *mansiones* or *masurae*. That is to say, the unit on which the survey concentrates is a plot of land that normally bears one house containing one resident family. In a great many cases, furthermore, the *burgensis* also holds land beyond the walls, which may be worked by tenants who live on it or in the borough. Sometimes these tenants are separately listed and sometimes they are not. Sometimes they are called by one name and sometimes by another. In such particulars the practice of the clerks was never consistent, and if we tabulate their statistics, we cannot expect to secure accurate results.[1]

Nevertheless, Domesday arithmetic has its advantages; it permits us to add men and houses to form a total which may be called *mansiones*. And a list of these totals for the period before and after 1066, taken very generally, leads to useful conclusions.[2] In the first place, it shows how very small the borough of the eleventh century was. The relationship of these figures to actual population must remain a matter of doubt, but if we multiply all by the conventional five, our results will at least be uniform. Such procedure shows York the only borough on the list that could possi-

---

[1] See above, pp. 77 ff., 81.

[2] See Appendix III. Many of the figures in this list are obtained by combining statistics of very doubtful meaning, and even when the totals are supplied by Domesday, it is not always clear what they include. Sometimes we are given reports only for the time of William. Sometimes nothing is recorded except the holdings of the king or of a baron, and it is for some such reason that Dover, Romney, Lewes, Pevensey, Southampton, and other thriving boroughs have to be omitted Furthermore, it must be remembered that London, Winchester, Bristol, and Hastings have no regular descriptions in the survey. It is therefore obvious that the individual rankings here given are of dubious worth, but the validity of the list as a whole is attested by that of the aid-paying boroughs under Henry I (see Appendix V).

bly claim 10,000 inhabitants, and only two others (Norwich and Lincoln) that could have had over 5,000. Three (Oxford, Thetford, Ipswich) appear with *c.* 4,000; one (Gloucester) with *c.* 3,000; seven (Wallingford, Chester, Leicester, Stamford, Cambridge, Colchester, Exeter) with *c.* 2,000; thirteen (Sandwich, Northampton, Wareham, Huntingdon, Canterbury, Shaftesbury, Shrewsbury, Warwick, Derby, Hythe, Torksey, Maldon, Nottingham) with *c.* 1,000; and the remaining twenty boroughs with less. In other words, out of forty-six listed boroughs, forty-three stand below a total of 5,000 inhabitants; thirty-nine below 3,000; and thirty-two below 2,000. In fact, if we include the smallest boroughs on the list, we shall be reckoning in scores rather than in hundreds.[1]

Our table of *mansiones*, in the second place, graphically reveals the material ruin brought to the boroughs by the Norman Conquest. Out of thirty-two cases where comparison is possible between the years 1066 and 1086, our record reports five of increase, one of equality, and twenty-six of decrease. And under this latter head we perceive losses running as high as twenty per cent at Lincoln; thirty per cent at Shaftesbury and York; forty per cent at Shrewsbury, Derby, and Dorchester; fifty per cent at Wareham, Chester, and Oxford; and up to eighty-six per cent at Ipswich. To that extent properties which rendered custom *T.R.E.* are recorded as now utterly destroyed or so waste that they produce no income. The result was effected in a variety of ways. Much of the desolation was that incidental to armed conquest and rebellion; but much was also due to the building of new castles, the endowment of new churches, and the scattering of the old landed aristocracy. The Norman reorganization of the kingdom was not limited to political arrangements. The introduction of a baronage and a bourgeoisie constituted according to a French pattern profoundly affected the economic and social life of the borough. And Domesday proves that to the juries of 1086 the change seemed less a blessing than a calamity.

It should not, however, be forgotten that in the descriptions of the boroughs, as in other respects, the great inquest was primarily concerned with taxation, both actual and potential. The bulk of the borough sta-

---

[1] For examples of the smallest boroughs, see above, pp. 75–76. In this connection it is worth noting that, throughout the richer agricultural counties, Domesday reports dozens of manors possessing fifty to a hundred villein households each. And occasionally much greater ones are encountered. For example, in Kent we find *Middeltune* with 309 villeins, *Aldintone* with 190, *Tarenteford* with 142; in Sussex, *Mellinges* with 219, *Hertinges* with 128, etc. (*D.B.*, i, 2ᵇ, 4, 16, 23). The manor of Steyning includes 178 villeins; the borough of Steyning 123 *masurae* (*D.B.*, i, 17). In the manor of Somerton there are 80 villeins; in the attached borough of Langport 34 burgesses. Under Milbourne manor are reported 70 villeins and only 56 burgesses (*D.B.*, i, 86, 86ᵇ). Similar statistics could be added to fill many pages, but these are sufficient to show that at least two-thirds of the old Domesday boroughs had fewer inhabitants than many rural vills.

tistics that are given us have this in common, that they deal with *consuetudines*. They report income which the king enjoys, which he has given away, or of which he is being despoiled. And it must also be remembered that the returns were made in the assessment district itself, and by the men who were themselves responsible for the *consuetudines*. Every franchise secured by individual or group, every razed building, every vacant property increased the burden on those who had to make up the ancient quotas, and so added force to a plea for reduction.[1] Is it any wonder that waste, usurpation, and poverty loom so large in the borough entries, and that, alongside this tale of accumulated misfortune, the Conqueror's rents and taxes assume monumental proportions?

Mr Tait has recently given us an admirable analysis of burghal finance and administration between the reigns of Edward the Confessor and John.[2] He has shown that, in spite of the shifted importance of earl, sheriff, and portreeve, the *firma burgi* in the twelfth century remained very much what it had been in the eleventh. All that William did in that connection was to stiffen up the old system and enhance its returns. The result plainly appears from Mr Tait's tabulation of the figures. Out of thirty-five cases in which a comparison can be made, at least thirty show an increase of the farm between 1066 and 1086, and in ten it is over one hundred per cent.[3]

To account for these figures various factors must be considered. The Norman administration was unquestionably more efficient than the Anglo-Saxon, and confiscation had brought into the king's hands much that Edward had lacked. Furthermore, the *firma burgi* did not always embrace one constant set of items; what looks like a tremendous increase may have largely resulted from new financial arrangements.[4] Our information is hardly ever complete, and we may not be sure that it is impartial. As remarked above, we may well suspect that 'the men who swore' were more interested in proving poverty than wealth. Growth of a trading population might actually reduce the number of *mansiones* charged with the geld while greatly enlarging the returns from market, harbor, and court. When all this is said, however, the Conqueror cannot be wholly acquitted of extortion. If we compare his *firmae* with those of Henry II, we find almost as many decreases as increases.[5] And yet we

---

[1] Above, pp. 103 ff., 112 ff.

[2] 'The *Firma Burgi* and the Commune in England, 1066–1191,' *E.H.R.*, XLII (1927), 321 ff.

[3] *Ibid.*, p. 360.

[4] Manors and rural hundreds were sometimes farmed along with a borough, and the silence of the records as to such arrangements is no proof that they did not exist.

[5] Dunwich, Lincoln, Northampton, and Norwich afford outstanding examples of a steady increase obviously based on advancing prosperity; but cf. Colchester, Shrewsbury, Hereford, and Wallingford. In the case of the latter two, unless William's farm included extra items not specified in Domesday, the figures are so large as to appear fantastic.

know that in those hundred years most towns enormously advanced in resources. When either Norman or Plantagenet cut down a rent, it must have been impossibly high.

For these reasons it is evident that the *firma burgi* is no good criterion of urban prosperity under William I; and for the later period the statistics become less reliable as well as scantier [1] On the other hand, the Pipe Rolls give us an extraordinarily detailed record of borough taxation, which enables us to draw precise conclusions of far-reaching significance. As remarked above, Domesday shows the ancient system of assessment for geld and *fyrd* still prevalent throughout the boroughs;[2] but by the middle of the twelfth century it has totally disappeared. In the Pipe Roll of 1130 no geld is received from the boroughs, which instead are charged with sums called *auxilia*, and they are not based upon the old rating in hides.[3] London's charter from Henry I frees the city from Danegeld.[4] The *Libertas Londoniensis*, which dates from the reign of Stephen, declares that the citizens owe no service by land or sea except in defense of their own home.[5] Various baronial grants limit the fiscal and military obligations of burgesses in terms exactly corresponding to Continental practice.[6] We have obviously passed from one age to another. The borough is no longer being treated as a mere administrative district, but as a community distinct from the surrounding country.

The principal cause of this alteration in official policy has already been seen. We cannot doubt that in England, as on the Continent, it accompanied the emergence of a peculiarly urban population, conscious of its own interests and powerful enough economically to make its demands heard. But there was another factor that must be recognized as having contributed to the same result — the military revolution produced by the Norman Conquest. Down to 1066 the boroughs retained their ancient character of royal strongholds. Concerning their organization we have no detailed information, but it is impossible to read the Anglo-Saxon Chronicle without becoming convinced that in the eleventh century the boroughs were still of prime importance for all military and naval opera-

---

[1] The practice of including the *firma burgi* in the *firma comitatus* usually prevented separate figures for the first item from being inserted in the rolls, while the growth of communal autonomy greatly affected the system as a whole. The desire of an ambitious borough to get rid of the sheriff and his subordinates might lead to the establishment of an excessive farm. And the limitation of the sum by charter, although the grant might not be in fee, tended to make it more or less a conventional payment.

[2] Above, p. 100.

[3] See below, pp. 160 ff.

[4] See below, pp. 181 ff.

[5] See below, p. 159, n. 3.

[6] See below, p. 159, n. 4.

tions.[1] Not only were the king's mercenaries stationed there, but the *burhwaru* were themselves a warlike lot.   It was no mere coincidence that William had his chief trouble in reducing the boroughs, and that he immediately built castles to subdue them.[2]

Indeed, we may go further and say that the castles were deliberately erected to supplant the boroughs as military centres.   Above Roman wall or Saxon rampart now rose Norman motte and keep; thegn and house-carl gave way to knight and serjeant; *burh-bot* became obsolete and castle-guard was supplied from newly created feudal tenures.   As the greatness of the earl faded, the portreeve tended to become the subordinate of the sheriff; and since the latter was usually a royal constable also, the head-quarters of the local government were shifted from the shire borough to the adjoining castle.   Thus the borough, with its military prominence, lost its political ascendancy and became a home for traders and artisans.

There was, however, one noteworthy exception to this generalization: while feudal tenures could supply a mounted army, they could not supply a fleet.   A duke of Normandy who had become also king of England was constrained by his position to maintain great respect for sea-power.   Established custom in his new dominion already provided the ships that he would constantly need.   Naturally, he preserved such convenient arrangements and developed them into an elaborate organization that long outlived the Middle Ages — the league of the Cinque Ports.   Four of them (Dover, Sandwich, Romney, and Hythe) are proved by Domesday to have promised quotas of ships to Edward the Confessor and in return to have received certain communal privileges, apparently including *sac* and *soc*, quittance of toll throughout England, and exemption from geld. These liberties are confirmed by twelfth-century charters and continue to be enjoyed as the lawful complement of the anciently determined service of ships.[3]   There can be no question that in this case the Norman perpetuated a Saxon institution.   Individually the Cinque Ports, so far as may be proved by contemporary records, have the oldest municipal franchises in the kingdom.

As to the age of the association itself, that remains a more questionable matter.   The first comprehensive charter to the group was that of Edward I, but it was only a confirmation of existing custom, most of which can be traced far back into the twelfth century.[4]   The original Cinque Ports,

---

[1] See especially the entries in *A.S.C.* for the years 994, 1003, 1009, 1013, 1015, 1016.   The boroughs continue to be very prominent in naval affairs under Edward.   On the house-carls, see above, p. 98; on Bristol, below, pp. 202 ff.   Cf. Maitland, *Domesday Book and Beyond*, pp. 190–91.

[2] See *A.S.C.*, under the year 1067; also above, pp. 63 ff., and works there cited.

[3] See above, pp. 118 ff.

[4] M. Burrowes, *Cinque Ports* (London, 1888); Round, *Feudal England*, pp. 552 ff.; Petit-Dutaillis,

as the name signified, were five: Hastings, Dover, Sandwich, Romney, and Hythe. The liberties of the four latter, as just noted, may confidently be ascribed to Edward the Confessor; but by one of its characteristic vagaries Domesday omits all description of the head port, Hastings, and we are left to guess that it must have been similarly privileged.[1] Otherwise, how would the name have originated?

To the five Richard added the 'two ancient towns,' Rye and Winchelsea, providing that they should find two of the twenty ships owed by Hastings, and so share the liberties enjoyed by the barons of Hastings and of the Cinque Ports.[2] But from the confirmations of Henry II we learn that these liberties had existed earlier, and had then been virtually as extensive as they later appear under Edward I.[3] The portsmen were quit of all toll and custom throughout the king's dominions; they were free of shires and hundreds, and outside their own towns could be impleaded only at their common court of Shipway; at Yarmouth they were specially entitled to the use of shore and quay and to joint control with the king's officers of the annual fair;[4] at the king's coronation they held a silk canopy over his head;[5] they were exempted from all gelds, aids, and

---

Studies, pp. 86–87; Ballard, in *E.H.R.*, xxiv (1909), 732, and *B.B.C.*, i, 184, 258; Tait, in *E.H.R.*, xliv (1929), 200. Round justly criticized Burrowes for assuming the Anglo-Saxon origin of the confederacy, but himself went far astray in asserting that it did not antedate the reign of Edward I — for him an astonishing mistake, partially admitted in his *King's Serjeants and Officers of State* (London, 1911), p. 329.

[1] See above, p. 106, n. 5. The precedence of Hastings in the early twelfth century seems clearly indicated by the charters cited below, and by the fact that, like Dover, it originally supplied twenty ships, while Sandwich, Romney, and Hythe supplied only five each. But the decline of Hastings is already attested by Richard's charter to Rye and Winchelsea, whose quota by 1229 is increased from two to fifteen. It is therefore evident that the greatness of Hastings dated rather from the eleventh century than from the subsequent period. See Burrowes, pp. 70 ff., 91.

[2] *Calendar of Charter Rolls*, iii, 219: 'Et si quis versus illos placitare voluerit, non respondeant neque placitent aliter quam barones de Hastinges et de Quinque Portubus placitant, et in tempore Henrici patris nostri placitare solebant.'

[3] Henry II's charter to the barons of Hastings (*ibid.*, iii, 221) grants, in return for their service of twenty ships for fifteen days, all their free customs, with quittance of toll, honors at court, 'strand and den' at Yarmouth, etc. The confirmations of the other four ports are vaguer, but that of Sandwich provides that the citizens shall plead only where they have been accustomed so to do, and the Hythe charter adds *scilicet apud Sippeweiam*. So there can be little doubt that they already enjoyed a common judicial organization through the court at Shipway. Finally, the grant to the men of Lydd and Dengemarsh (*ibid.*, iii, 220) specifies that, in return for the service of one-fifth of a ship along with the men of Romney, they are to be quit of toll and all other customs *sicut homines de Hastingis sunt, et sicut quieti esse debent ex comsuetudine quinque portuum*.

[4] This custom deserves more thorough study than it has thus far received. The account of Burrowes (pp. 166 ff.) is fanciful in the extreme.

[5] The right can be traced back into the twelfth century and was undoubtedly what is referred to in the charters as 'honors at court' (Burrowes, p. 63; Round, *King's Serjeants*, pp. 329 ff.). Cf. London and Oxford, above, p. 129.

tallages.[1] Furthermore, these liberties and their reciprocal obligations were already well enough established to be shared by lesser places.   Long before Richard added Rye and Winchelsea as 'members' of Hastings, Folkstone had been joined with Dover, Lydd and Dengemarsh with Romney, and Sarre with Sandwich.[2] And Pevensey had probably been admitted to the league at an equally early time.[3] The conclusion would therefore seem inevitable that the organization of the Cinque Ports was at least as old as the reign of Henry I.

Beyond that we are left to conjecture.   The sources give us no information as to the government of the ports during the early period.   The constable of Dover castle does not appear as warden of the Cinque Ports until the thirteenth century.[4] So far as we may judge from existing evidence, the basis of the association was its common privilege in return for common service.   Both of these features seem to have antedated the Conquest of 1066; and yet we must probably attribute to the Norman genius the perfection of the confederacy.   It first definitely emerges in the twelfth century and from the outset bears a French name.   But more to the point is the design of the establishment, so neatly fitted into the military organization of the kingdom — an adaptation and improvement of native institutions altogether characteristic of a statesman like William the Conqueror or Henry I.[5]

Compared with the Cinque Ports, even such a great city as London remained quite undistinguished.   Indeed, the king's towns generally lacked all written guarantees in connection with their liabilities for military or naval service.[6] By Henry II's assize, burgesses were to be sworn to arms

---

[1] Exemption from tallage is specified in the later charters, and the Pipe Rolls show the Cinque Ports free likewise of the earlier gelds and *auxilia;* see Appendix IV.

[2] *B.B.C.*, i, 180, 183; above, p. 157, n. 2.

[3] See John's charter to the barons of Pevensey, which takes for granted their association with the Cinque Ports (*Calendar of Charter Rolls*, iii, 220).

[4] S. P. H. Statham, *History of the Castle, Town, and Port of Dover* (London, 1899), p. 298.   But it would seem likely that, with or without the title, the office was older.

[5] Nothing like the league of the Cinque Ports is to be found on the Continent.   The rural communes of Picardy, thought by Round to be a possible source of inspiration, were mere groups of villages modelled after the *Institutio Pacis* of Laon (above, p. 38) and were all much later than the English organization.   In the Norman kingdom of Sicily some of the towns furnished ships, but were not combined in any sort of league: W. Cohn, *Die Geschichte der Sizilischen Flotte under der Regierung Rogers I und Rogers II* (Breslau, 1910), pp. 79 ff.   The history of the Cinque Ports, particularly their institutional and topographical development, stands in great need of investigation.   The dissertation of M. Benoist-Lucy, *Les Cinq-Ports* (Paris, 1911), is only a superficial sketch of well known facts.

[6] The absence of such provisions is strikingly shown in *B.B.C.*, i, 89–90.   Aside from the Cinque Ports, the only apparent exception was Maldon.   A charter of Henry II is known to us from an inspeximus of Edward I (*Calendar of Charter Rolls*, ii, 351), which confirms the burgesses in their exemption from toll, scutage, tallage, and all 'forinsec service' in return for the one ship which they

in the same fashion as other freemen.[1] The king claimed and enforced the right to muster into his militia men from town and country alike. And in the same way he might commandeer ships and sailors for the protection of the coast. Such operations, however, were local in their scope and could be justified as measures of defense. For offensive campaigns on land only feudal contingents were brought from a distance, and for naval expeditions the fleet of the Cinque Ports normally sufficed. It was not till the later thirteenth century that more ambitious projects, together with notable changes in warfare, made the boroughs' liability for service an issue of any importance.[2]

There can, however, be no doubt of the townsmen's attitude, even during the earlier period. The assertion in the *Libertas Londoniensis* proves at least that a claim to exemption was set up by the Londoners.[3] And along the Welsh border, where feudal warfare was as chronic as in France, grants to the towns occasionally included the same military immunities that were usual on the Continent.[4] The general absence from English municipal charters of clauses restricting the burgesses' service testifies, not to their indifference on the subject, but to the peaceful conditions that prevailed throughout the Norman kingdom. There bourgeois were fortunate in enjoying conditions which their cousins across the Channel might long for in vain. And the king's interest was better served by collecting heavy taxes from the towns than by burdening them with unpopular levies. Thus we are again confronted by the fact that the relations

---

are bound to equip for the king annually. But boroughs were never liable for scutage and Henry II's tax was not called tallage in 1171, when this charter is supposed to have been issued (see below, p. 164). Furthermore, the Pipe Rolls prove that Maldon was taxed like the other boroughs in the later reign of Henry II, although it had not paid the earlier *auxilia* in place of Danegeld (see Appendix IV). These articles, together with many other suspicious features in the charter, make it impossible to accept as authentic. On the other hand, Domesday obscurely refers to the fact that in 1086 the burgesses of Maldon were liable to find a horse for the king's army and a ship for his fleet (*D.B.*, II, 48), and an isolated writ of Henry III in 1229 (*Close Rolls 1227–31*, p. 253) summons from Maldon *navem quam nobis invenire tenemini*. Is it possible that the entry in Domesday inspired a forgery, which in turn led to Henry III's precept? Henry II's alleged charter was certainly accepted in good faith by Edward I. Perhaps a more thorough search of the thirteenth-century records will throw more light on the subject. But for the present inquiry the matter is of minor significance.

[1] *S.C.*, p. 183: 'Item omnes burgenses et tota communa liberorum hominum habeant wambais et capellet ferri et lanceam.'

[2] The main facts are set forth in *E.H.R.*, XXXIV (1919), 460–66. The remaining portions of this article I wish to be regarded as entirely superseded.

[3] *G.*, I, 675: 'Cives vero Lundonie non faciunt bellum, nec ire debent in expeditione navali vel terrestri, quia liberi et quieti sunt ab omni exercitu. Servare debent civitatem sicut refugium et propugnaculum regni; omnes enim ibi refugium et egressum habent.' London received no formal grant to this effect until the early years of Edward III: *Munimenta Gildhallae Londoniensis* (Rolls Series, 1859–62), I, 146, 160, 168.

[4] *B.B.C.*, I, 89; above, pp. 121, 124 ff.

of borough and crown are best understood through examining fiscal obligations.

2. Borough Taxation

The Pipe Roll of 1130 shows the Danegeld superseded in the boroughs by round sums called *auxilia*.[1] With regard to the connection between these two exactions nothing is directly stated, but study of the record brings out a few relevant facts. Various entries of arrears prove that not only the geld but also the aids had been levied for three consecutive years, and at least in some cases the boroughs had been paying uniform amounts.[2] This information is supplemented by the rolls of Henry II, who, as is well known, took two Danegelds: the first in the second year and the other in the eighth year of his reign. In connection with both of them the boroughs paid *auxilia*, which for the most part were identical with those taken by Henry I — and this in spite of the fact that during intervening years they were taxed at a much higher rate.[3] It is therefore evident that at some time after 1086 a system of fixed aids from the boroughs had been substituted for the antiquated geld, and the nature of the change would seem to imply deliberate reform.

As author of the innovation the evidence points toward Henry I, during whose reign so many important changes affecting the towns first make their appearance. However this may be, the policy that inspired the reformer is plain. Liability for geld on the part of the boroughs is shown by Domesday to have been cumbered with all sorts of peculiar arrangements. Methods of assessment varied from place to place, and in many localities the tax was bound up with responsibility for military and naval service.[4] To increase the complication came the establishment of French colonies quit of all ancient exactions, and the growth of a mercantile population which no doubt clamored for similar exemption.[5] About the time of Henry I, as we have seen, institutional irregularities in the boroughs were somehow ironed out; burgesses generally came to hold by burgage

---

[1] Above, p. 155. This, of course, has long been familiar. The *auxilia* from the rolls of 1130 and 1156 were tabulated by Maitland as an introduction to his discussion of the borough (*Domesday Book and Beyond*, p. 175). Before that Stubbs had expressed the opinion (*Const. Hist.*, i, 412) that the aids were fixed annual payments accompanying the geld; and he merely followed Madox, *History and Antiquities of the Exchequer of England* (2nd ed., London, 1769), i, 601. None of these authors however, made clear the relation of this impost to the later tallage.

[2] See Wallingford, Colchester, and Tamworth in Appendix IV.

[3] In 8 Henry II the sums are usually recorded without special designation, as being merely 'from' such and such a place. But occasionally they are called *auxilia*, and the contribution of Worcester is styled *donum*. In spite of numerous variations, the remarkable constancy of the figures is too obvious to require comment.

[4] See above, pp. 97 ff.

[5] See above, p. 93.

tenure and to enjoy uniform status.[1] Obligations for service were made the same for all. And it was quite in line with this simplification that the old Danegeld should give way to a graded series of payments that bore the more agreeable name of aid, and to which all citizens might be made to contribute.[2]

However this may be, the king, by the change, secured a larger income than he had enjoyed under the old system,[3] and the urban population got recognition of its separate identity and its peculiarity of custom. Under Henry I twenty-six names stand on the list besides the small anonymous boroughs of Dorset and Wiltshire, and the rolls of Henry II, being more complete, add another half-dozen. Of these original aid-paying boroughs all had been mentioned in Domesday and most were important enough to receive charters in the course of the twelfth century. But the Dorset boroughs disappear from the list under Henry II, and all those of Wiltshire except Calne, which is relatively insignificant. Wallingford is also dropped after being pardoned, because of poverty, all sums due for the years 1128–30. The Cinque Ports, for reasons already noted, paid no aids; nor did such newer towns as Dunwich, Carlisle, and Newcastle-on-Tyne. And of course nothing is heard of important boroughs like Bristol and Leicester because they were in baronial hands.

As to the amounts raised, they vary from London's 120*l.* to the 20*s.* of Calne. Winchester ranks second and is followed in order by Lincoln, York, and Norwich. Canterbury, Oxford, Exeter, and Colchester are tied for sixth place; Gloucester, Worcester, and Wallingford for seventh. Then come Cambridge, Nottingham, Northampton, and the field. Toward the bottom we find some weak candidates for burghal standing, but, taken as a whole, it is a sound list. On it are the leading royal towns of the early twelfth century arranged in what must have been approximately their relative order of wealth. To guess the basis on which the assessment was made is a hazardous undertaking, but one or two hints are supplied by the records. It is known that, to supplement the inadequate geld from the shires, the king, by negotiation with the county courts, secured additional contributions, which appear in the rolls as *dona*, *auxilia*, or *assisae*. These sums were made up by apportionment among

---

[1] See above, pp. 136 ff.

[2] London's 120*l.* is styled the city's geld in the *hidagium* of Middlesex (Round, *Commune of London*, p. 257), but this would seem to be due merely to lax usage in an unofficial survey.

[3] For example, at 2*s.* on the hide Cambridge would have paid 10*l.*, Oxford the same, Huntingdon 5*l.*, Northampton 50*s.*, and Worcester 30*s.* As *auxilia* these boroughs paid respectively 12*l.*, 20*l.*, 8*l.*, 10*l.*, and 15*l.* According to Domesday, Exeter was liable only for a half-mark on 5 hides, and the Dorset boroughs were assessed at the same rate on 45. Under the new system they rendered respectively 20*l.* and 15*l.*

the local landholders, for not infrequently individual shares were remitted by royal favor.[1]   In all probability the same procedure was originally followed in dealing with the boroughs, but since their aids were normally constant, assessment would tend to become permanent and certain lands would become burdened with certain amounts.

Thus, by the accession of Henry II, the traditional system was already outworn; the *auxilia* had gone the way of the ancient geld.   In the roll of 1156 the aids of Guildford, Hertford, Oxford, Winchcombe, Southwark, Shrewsbury, and Lincoln are reported to be partly waste, and at the last three of these places *dona* are recorded in addition to the accustomed payments.   Even when the original obligation was met in full, the king apparently felt that many communities were being undertaxed, and they were induced to contribute supplements.   Thus Canterbury, Gloucester, Worcester, Derby, and York were each charged with a *donum* as well as the *auxilium*, and Ipswich with an *assisa*.   And Cambridge, Hereford, and Stafford each paid two *auxilia*.[2]   The names obviously are of no significance; whichever was employed, the Plantagenet was launching a new tax on the bourgeoisie.

This fact clearly emerges from the rolls of 1158–61, during which years Henry's fiscal experimentation was continuous.   Scutages, aids, or 'gifts' were taken from military tenants, great ecclesiastics, moneyers, and Jews, as well as from the counties and boroughs.[3]   In the fourth year only four northern towns were taxed, but they paid 817*m.*   In the fifth year *dona* totalling well over 4,000*m.* were exacted from thirty-four boroughs.   And in spite of the fact that they had just met a stiff demand, seven of the western boroughs gave nearly 140*m.* more in the following year.[4]   Again

---

[1] R. L. Poole, *The Exchequer in the Twelfth Century* (Oxford, 1912), p. 48; C. H. Haskins, in *E.H.R.*, xxvii (1912), 101.   In *P.R. 31 H. I* the aids of the boroughs are treated exactly like those of the counties and the Danegelds: small portions of them are regularly credited to the sheriff as being pardoned by the king to certain persons.   Many of these 'pardons' look like appropriations of individual payments on a fixed assessment to recipients specified in advance.   Others, however, would seem to be actual remissions of the tax; see in particular the entries for Colchester (p. 138).

[2] See columns four and five in Appendix IV, with the notes.   Since the roll is defective and poorly constructed, it is possible that in a few cases the payment of arrears gives the impression of a double assessment.   But this explanation will not apply to most of the entries.   Henry was clearly supplementing an inflexible system of *auxilia* by additional exactions.

[3] On these and the succeeding levies, see Round, *Feudal England*, pp. 276 ff.; J. F. Baldwin, *The Scutage and Knight Service in England* (Chicago, 1897), ch. ii; J. H. Ramsay, *The Angevin Empire* (London, 1903), pp. 251 ff.; *B.B.C.*, i, lxxix ff.   With the exception of the last, these accounts treat the *auxilia* of the towns only incidentally; and Ballard's discussion of the tax barely raises the question of its general nature.   The statistics cited, especially those in Ramsay, show that the tallage was by all odds the most profitable of Henry II's imposts.

[4] The general levy of 1159 was made for the Toulouse campaign, but it was preceded and followed by considerable fighting in Wales, and the latter was presumably the occasion for the *dona* of 1160. All the sums collected from the boroughs in these years are listed in Appendix IV.

in the seventh year a general levy was made, in which thirty-six boroughs contributed over 2,800m.[1] When it is remembered that only about 700m. were got from about thirty places under the old Danegeld aids, the advantage of the newer system is obvious.

In Henry's eighth year, as we have seen, the Danegeld and accompanying *auxilia* of his grandfather make their last appearance in the rolls. They were no longer needed; for by this time the tax usually called scutage and that which is eventually called tallage had become regularly established. Again the names are of small moment. The first impost bore upon the feudal class, being levied at so much on the knight's fee. The latter was taken primarily from the middle class, and was limited only by the ability of each community to pay. Since the usual occasion for royal taxation was war, both were frequently collected at the same time; but that was not always the case. In such matters the king consulted his own convenience, and his taxes were not exclusively military.[2]

The imposition on the towns continued to be distinctly heavy, but it was only an occasional one. After 1162 Henry made but five general levies of the sort: one every three or four years until 1167, and then a last one after a lapse of ten. Of these the first came in the eleventh year, when over 1,700m. were received as *auxilia* from thirty-seven places. The westernmost boroughs, however, paid nothing, perhaps because, being near the scene of the war, they furnished troops instead. On the other hand, in Northumberland and Yorkshire the list of aid-paying localities was extended to include at least half a dozen names that had never appeared on it before — some of them mere villages.[3] And three years later this tendency was carried to its logical outcome when the *auxilium ad filiam maritandam* was collected. On that occasion and regularly thereafter the tax was assessed, not merely on the boroughs, but throughout all demesnes, escheats, and wardships.[4]

By 1166, accordingly, the tallage has emerged in everything but name.

[1] This exaction (completely recorded in Appendix IV) accompanied a scutage taken from the tenants-in-chief.

[2] Without counting the aids of 1160–61, Henry levied three further scutages — in his eleventh, eighteenth, and thirty-third years. But taxes were taken from the towns in the eleventh, nineteenth, twentieth, twenty-third, and thirty-third years.

[3] Besides Scarborough, which is included in Appendix IV, the roll reports small sums from Knaresborough and Boroughbridge in Yorkshire; and from Bamburgh, Rothbury, Sadberge, and Newburn in Northumberland. One or two other additions to the list will be noticed, including Wilton and Salisbury.

[4] The rolls record as paying the aid many little boroughs or places that had at one time been so called, such as Buckingham, Cirencester, Axminster, Shaftesbury, Lidford, Braunton, St Edward's, etc.; but their contributions are equalled by those of many ordinary manors. Henceforth only very outstanding towns are added to the lists in Appendix IV.

Henry's exaction of 1173–74 is styled *assisa;* that of 1177, *auxilium.*[1] Nevertheless, the contribution of Colchester in this last year is called *tallagium,* and beginning in 1187, that designation becomes regular, with *donum* and *auxilium* as variants.[2] Henceforth the tax is merely continued according to the precedents set by Henry II. Persisting throughout the thirteenth century, it is not superseded until the completion of parliamentary organization forces the adoption of new fiscal expedients.[3]

Thanks to the unbroken series of Pipe Rolls under Henry II, we thus have the extraordinary privilege of tracing step by step the inauguration and perfection of a twelfth-century tax — and the one that proved to be the most profitable of any for the strongest monarchy of western Europe. The current doctrine of the texts has been that the tallage was an essentially servile obligation; that the king tallaged his burgesses because they were resident on his demesne and in some fashion continued to share the legal inferiority of peasants.[4] So far as the royal tallage was concerned, the exact contrary was true. According to the unimpeachable evidence of the records just examined, the tax was developed out of a system of borough aids. It was only in the later reign of Henry II that the exaction was extended downwards to include mere villages. Instead of beginning as a servile impost, the tallage began as a contribution by freemen.

This does not imply that no servile tallage existed in England, but merely that the latter had nothing to do with the royal tallage. Indeed, as has elsewhere been shown in detail,[5] even the familiar tallage of the manorial extents was originally, like the Continental *taille,* an imposition on all classes of seignorial dependents, not merely on serfs. In the earlier period the exaction was much vaguer than legal doctrine eventually made it out to be; and the vagueness of the institution was reflected in the names which it commonly bore. By *tallagium, auxilium, donum, assisa,* and on the Continent *tallia, demanda, questa, petitio,* etc., was denoted a contribution, occasional or regular, sometimes voluntary and sometimes

---

[1] To this latter aid Hastings, Winchelsea, and Dover contributed 100*m.* each, and Hythe 20*m.* (*P.R. 23 H.II,* pp. 192, 207) — the only time during the entire reign when any of the Cinque Ports paid any such tax. The one possible explanation is that the sums were requested and received from these towns as quite exceptional offerings.

[2] See Round, in *P.R. 33 H.II,* pp. xxix ff. The general formula is usually *De tallagio dominiorum regis et terrarum que tunc erant in manu eius per. . . .* But the individual payments are often called *donum* or *auxilium.*

[3] See S. K. Mitchell, *Studies in Taxation under John and Henry III* (New Haven, 1914).

[4] On this and the following subjects, see 'Taxation and Representation in the Middle Ages,' *Haskins Anniversary Essays,* pp. 296 ff.

[5] 'The Seignorial Tallage in England,' *Mélanges d'Histoire Offerts à Henri Pirenne* (Brussels, 1927), II, 465 ff.; 'The Origin and Nature of the *Taille,*' *Revue Belge de Philologie et d'Histoire,* v, 801 ff.

not, solicited by a superior from a subject. Henry II's levies were originally as informal as most; there is no point in attempting meticulous definition. Behind them lay the political authority to make them valid; to the king and to his contemporaries that sufficed. More abstruse justification was left to the legal talent of a subsequent generation.

Knowing the practical statesmanship of Henry II, we cannot doubt that his tallage was deliberately framed to tax the increasing wealth of the bourgeois class. The *auxilia* of Henry I continued to be associated with the ancient Danegeld, an agrarian impost, and were themselves apparently assessed on separate borough lands. The list of aid-paying boroughs remained essentially a list of the greater Domesday boroughs.[1] But under Henry II all this was changed. His subsidies were never allowed to deteriorate into a series of fixed payments; each levy was separately negotiated and separately assessed. From the outset his tallage was a flexible tax, bearing rather on cash resources than on real property. In the fiscal development of the English kingdom it marks the beginning of a new epoch.[2]

This system, as will appear below, involved certain administrative practices of high importance for municipal organization. But it also produced a mass of statistics from which may be drawn a particularly useful method of rating the boroughs in the later twelfth century; for by averaging the aids paid during the reign of Henry II, we obtain a direct indication of their financial capacities over an extended period.[3] Such procedure at once reveals striking changes from the similar estimate made for the time of Henry I. London, of course, retains first place, paying almost three times as much as its nearest competitor, York. And that city is followed at a considerable distance by Norwich, Lincoln, and Northampton. Although Lincoln remains relatively a great town, it is passed by York. Norwich advances two places on the list and Northampton four. Sixth position goes to Dunwich, which had risen as rapidly as it was later to decay. Exeter slips back from sixth to seventh, and Winchester — a noteworthy decline — from second to eighth. Then come Gloucester, Oxford, Canterbury, and Cambridge — all ancient boroughs. But out of the next fifteen names nine are new, and of these nine towns seven are on the east coast.

Indeed, it is this growth of very youthful trading centres that makes Henry II's list so widely different from Henry I's. The latter at most had included less than thirty-five places, but if we take that same number un-

---

[1] Compare Appendices III and V.

[2] On the assessment of the tallage, see below, pp. 170–71.

[3] See Appendix VI. It should be remembered that Bristol, Leicester, and Chester were not in the king's hands, and that the Cinque Ports were exempt from the tax.

der Henry II, they are all found to be paying a tax of at least 20*m*.: more than half of them twice that amount, with Winchester contributing six times, Northampton ten times, York sixteen times, and London almost fifty times as much.   Of these thirty-five names fourteen are unknown to Henry I's list, while about a dozen boroughs of the earlier period no longer rank at all, being exceeded in taxable capacity by a score of simple manors.[1]

These ratings, of course, are not to be taken in too absolute a fashion but there can be no doubt that in general they are truly indicative of relative prosperity and consequently of relative importance to the crown. And the conclusions just drawn from tables of figures are in many ways confirmed by the evidence of the charters.[2]   Our next task, therefore, must be to examine the political privileges held by these same boroughs from the kings who so thoroughly taxed them.

3. The Nucleus of the Municipality

According to the nature of their foundation, we have seen that the boroughs may be divided into two groups: new and old, those created by charter and those whose charters merely confirmed ancient liberties.   But fundamentally there was no difference.   In so far as they were both boroughs, Beverley and York were the same.   Nor did the Channel mark any true line of differentiation, for on the two sides bourgeois status was identical.[3]   In both regions, moreover, social and economic freedom tended to produce a demand for local self-government, and to the extent that it received satisfaction, an upper class of towns arose, characterized by some degree of political autonomy.   Thanks to the thorough study of Mr Tait, supplementing the earlier work of Ballard, it is now apparent how very exceptional throughout the twelfth century were grants to boroughs of formal self-government.   Even concession of the *firma burgi* was relatively rare under Henry II.   At his death only five royal towns were farming their own revenues, and none of them held the privilege in fee.[4]

---

[1] In the case of a few boroughs, notably Stamford, the figures seem to indicate actual retrogression; but such towns as Thetford and Winchester sank in relative importance rather because others grew more rapidly than they did.   Wallingford likewise made no progress, in spite of the extraordinary favor shown the community by Henry II (see above, p. 130; and below, p. 169).   In other respects, also, the tabulation serves to correct false impressions gained from studying other sources.   From the charters we might guess that Newcastle-on-Tyne was an important borough under Henry II; but we should never suspect the new-grown prosperity of Dunwich, Grimsby, Doncaster, Berkhampstead, Lothingland, Scarborough, Corbridge, Caister, etc.

[2] See above, pp. 128 ff.

[3] See above, pp. 143 ff.

[4] Tait, 'The *Firma Burgi* and the Commune in England,' *E.H.R.*, xlii (1927), 352.   Mr Tait lists Lincoln, Cambridge, Northampton, Shrewsbury, and Bridgnorth; but Colchester should probably be recognized as a sixth (see below, p. 168).

So far as election of magistrates is concerned, positive evidence in the charters begins under Richard and increases under John. By 1216 at least a dozen boroughs had received the right to elect reeves or bailiffs and twice that number the fee-farm.[1]

These figures at once raise an interesting question: could a community enjoy the *firma burgi* and still remain under royal officials, or did that concession carry with it the power to install elected magistrates? Mr Tait holds with Ballard that the former grant always included the latter;[2] but if so, it is hard to understand why the two are kept so distinct in official documents. No extant charter of Henry II allows the election of magistrates, and yet nine boroughs are known to have been self-farming at one time or another during his reign.[3] Under Richard and John we have seen that concession of the *firma burgi* was about twice as frequent as the authorization to elect magistrates; and the same disparity continues throughout the thirteenth century, when the practice of chancery enrollments largely precluded the possibility of lost charters.[4] Such evidence establishes at least the presumption that neither right could be implied in the other. There are, however, additional sources; our fullest information with regard to the *firma burgi* comes, not from the charters but from the Pipe Rolls, which occasionally afford hints concerning borough officials also.

As Mr Tait has pointed out, the burgesses of Cambridge, Gloucester, and Grimsby held the privilege of farming their own revenues for brief periods, but in these cases the rolls contain nothing of any value for the problem in hand.[5] Nor is much forthcoming in connection with Shrewsbury and Bridgnorth. Identical entries in the Pipe Roll of 16 Henry II state that the burgesses have fined to gain control of their farm, and in succeeding years they render account of it at the exchequer.[6] In 1189

---

[1] *B.B.C.*, I, 221 ff., 241 ff.

[2] *B.B.C.*, I, lxxxvi.

[3] *E.H.R.*, XLII, 350 ff.

[4] *B.B.C.*, II, lvii.

[5] *E.H.R.*, XLII, 350–52. In the case of Grimsby, the men of the town are once entered as rendering account of the farm (*P.R. 7 H. II*, 17). The burgesses of Cambridge, similarly, are recorded as owing their farm for the last three years of Henry II (*P.R. 32 H. II*, p. 32; etc.). For Gloucester an incidental entry (*P.R. 24 H. II*, p. 57) refers to the time when the borough was in the hands of the burgesses. Earlier a certain *Osmundus prepositus* had accounted for the farm during a period of ten years — a fact which would indicate that he was not elected. Perhaps the remark in the roll of 24 Henry II was a slip. At any rate, the burgesses are reported to have gained the right under Richard, and henceforth they render account (*P.R. 6 R. I*, p. 232; etc.).

[6] *E.H.R.*, XLII, 351. For the first six years the burgesses paid their farms to the sheriff with an increment to the exchequer; after that they rendered account direct. Under Richard the rolls continue the same formula as before, without regard to the new charters. We may imagine that at Shrewsbury events took the same course as at Ipswich (see immediately below).

Richard gave Shrewsbury the fee-farm and in 1200 John conferred the right to elect reeves.[1] So, if this last privilege had been enjoyed earlier, the fact is not brought out by the extant records.

The case of Lincoln is more interesting. The second ranking town under Henry I, it logically secured, along with London, special treatment from the king. According to a famous statement in the Pipe Roll of 1130, the burgesses were given the *firma* in that year, and we know that they continued to hold it at the rate of 140*l.* under Stephen and Henry II.[2] Thus the rolls of 1156–57 show the citizens rendering account. Then, after a lapse of six years, during which the sheriff has the town in his hands, it regains its privilege. From the tenth to the thirty-fourth year of Henry II the reeves of Lincoln, usually two in number, account for the farm. The fact that these men are styled *prepositi* does not, of course, prove that they were elected by the citizens. But the names are obviously bourgeois and they change very frequently — nineteen variations out of a possible twenty-five. And yet during all this time only twenty different names appear.[3] Such an effect could hardly have been produced except by a system of local election in which the offices were constantly passed about within a narrow group. But we have no charter that refers to the matter until 1194, when Richard gives Lincoln the farm in fee together with the right to elect a reeve.[4]

Meanwhile similar evidence comes from Colchester and Northampton. The former town, after being farmed for a long period by a royal appointee, is taken over by burgess reeves in 1178, who continue to render account under Richard.[5] Northampton also is separately farmed, at first by a royal reeve, and then by the sheriff. But from 31 Henry II onward the account is rendered by local men, serving in pairs and constantly changing as at Lincoln.[6] If the case of that borough stood alone, we might conclude that the formal grant of the *firma burgi* included permis-

---

[1] *B.B.C.*, I, 223, 245.

[2] *E.H.R.*, XLII, 337, 341 ff.

[3] The general effect may be seen from the beginning of the list: (10 H. II) Willelmus de Paris, Ailwinus Net; (11) Walterus f. Radewi, Warnerus; (12–13) Willelmus de Paris; (14) Warnerus f. Turgari, Willelmus f. Ailsi; (15) Walterus f. Redwi, Radulfus Villanus; (16) Willelmus de Paris, Warnerus; (17–19) Warnerus, Radulfus Villanus; (20–21) Aulfwinus Net; etc.

[4] *B.B.C.*, I, 221, 244.

[5] *E.H.R.*, XLII, 349. The reeves of Colchester who accounted for the farm were unquestionably burgesses, serving singly or in pairs and constantly changing as at Lincoln. At Southampton, on the other hand, single persons held the contract in succession, each for a considerable period. Mr Tait remarks (p. 353) that Richard's charter to Colchester allowing election of reeves would not have been necessary if the borough had earlier had the right. But that is surely a dubious argument to advance in connection with any borough charter; cf. particularly those to Lincoln and Northampton.

[6] *E.H.R.*, XLII, 352.

sion to elect magistrates. But so far as our records go, neither Northampton nor Colchester received any charter from Henry II conferring
the former right; and those from Richard confer both privileges.[1] We
can therefore suppose that both, either informally or by written grants
subsequently lost, were separately allowed under Henry II.

Such a conclusion, moreover, is supported by the facts known of Wallingford. Henry II's charter of 1156, though generous, does not mention
the *firma burgi* and clearly contemplates a royal reeve.[2] Yet at that very
time the men of Wallingford are recorded as rendering account of the
farm.[3] Subsequently men described as reeves appear in this connection,
but whether they were elected or not can hardly be decided from the entries.[4] There is at least no reason why their election should be thought
to have been necessitated by the holding of the farm. And at Ipswich
we may be sure that the *firma burgi* was secured by the burgesses six
years before they first chose their own magistrates.[5]

On the whole, therefore, the sources do not bear out the idea that the
only way in which a town could farm its own revenues was by electing its
own officials. Instead, if we stop to analyze the situation, distinction between the two functions will offer no insuperable difficulties. The king's
interest was primarily that of any lord anxious to get as much as he could
from the management of his property. When the borough revenues were
incorporated with those of the shire, the sheriff was, of course, liable for
the whole *firma comitatus*, no matter how much or how little he got from
any one item. When the borough was separately farmed by a reeve or
other person, the latter became legally responsible and the king was immediately concerned only with the payment of what was due. In either
case the farmer could sublet all or a portion of his contract without in the
least affecting the royal rights, and he seems often to have done so. Thus
we infer from Domesday that the men of Northampton were farming their

---

[1] *B.B.C.*, i, 222, 236, 244.

[2] Above, p. 130.

[3] *E.H.R.*, xlii, 350.

[4] The entries in the later rolls (*P.R. 24 H. II*, p. 99; *P.R. 29 H. II*, p. 138) indicate the election of
local reeves, but the record is very confusing and the royal charters that were issued in this connection have been lost. Henry's treatment of Wallingford was always extraordinary. By 1197 the
town had piled up a deficit of over 231*l.* (*Chancellor's Roll 8 R. I*, p. 16).

[5] *P.R. 6 R. I*, pp. 47, 63: 'Homines de Gipeswiz r. c. de lx marcis pro habenda villa sua in manu
sua per crementum c sol. per annum de firma et pro confirmatione domini regis de libertatibus suis.'
Norwich (p. 64) gave 200*m.* for the same two purposes, but its charter of 1194 granted the election
of reeves (*B.B.C.*, i, 244) — a privilege which was already held by Lincoln, Northampton, and Colchester, and which was extended to Ipswich in 1200. Henceforth the farms of Norwich and Ipswich were rendered at the exchequer by their respective burgesses. Presumably the former also
elected magistrates at once, but the latter did not do so till after 1200 (see below, pp. 174 ff.).

borough from the sheriff as early as 1086[1] — and if we had later sources that dealt with such informal matters, we should probably hear of many similar arrangements.[2]

By agreement of this sort local men would merely bind themselves to pay a fixed annual sum, covering certain regular charges, but the royal officer would remain liable for that revenue. Furthermore, he would still collect all taxes and extraordinary dues, preside over the borough court, and perform the dozen other administrative duties connected with his office. And if the town later secured the *firma burgi* in chief, actual practice would be changed but slightly. The king would merely establish direct relations with an organization that had already proved its efficiency under a subordinate. But what sort of organization could it have been? As yet the burgesses had no formally constituted government of their own. There is every reason to suppose that the assumption of financial responsibility by a group of substantial citizens would suffice.[3] For although the whole body of burgesses was legally liable, the burden must actually have been borne by the few.

Nor is this an isolated problem. The same kind of query arises in connection with the tallage. The system of variable *dona* developed by Henry II necessitated constant negotiation between borough and crown. The *Dialogus de Scaccario* says that the royal justices, while reserving the right to assess the tax on separate inhabitants, were in the habit of accepting the offer of a lump sum from the community, in which case the money was raised by the burgesses themselves through a local levy.[4] And this statement is borne out by the Pipe Rolls. Individual assessment was apparently first used by the government for the *auxilium ad filiam maritandam* of 1167–68, when, also for the first time, demesne manors were generally made to contribute.[5] But the normal practice in

---

[1] Above, p. 110.

[2] Cf. the case of Shrewsbury and Bridgnorth (above, p. 167, n. 6). It has frequently been remarked that burgesses who received the *firma burgi* from the king were said to hold the borough *in capite* (*H.E.L.*, I, 650 ff.). Was not the force of this usage derived from the fact that boroughs were often farmed by the burgesses under subordinates? In this connection it may be noted that an ordinary manor might be farmed by the men of the vill; e.g., Whatley, Rawreth, and Wickford (*P.R. 30 H. II*, pp. xxxii, 135).

[3] Altogether, it would seem that control of the *firma burgi* was primarily a matter of financial administration and did not imply any great political authority when it was taken over by the burgesses. Indeed, a group of local capitalists might undertake the borough farm as a speculation, as was sometimes done in connection with a lesser contract. For example, see *P.R. 31 H. I*, p. 142: 'Burgenses de Caerleolio r. c. de c sol. de veteri firma mineirie argenti.' *P.R. 30 H. II*, p. 138: 'Cives Londonienses r. c. de VIII lib. et XVI sol. et VIII den. de veteri firma Heðe Regine.'

[4] *S.C.*, pp. 237–38.

[5] For examples see *B.B.C.*, I, lxxx ff. The aids raised by individual assessment can usually be distinguished also by the oddness of the sums that resulted from the practice. The method of negotiation by which select committees met the justices is portrayed in the later writs (e.g., *Close Rolls 1227–31*, p. 280).

the boroughs remained that of composition and self-taxation. How could this system have worked without the informal organization in each of at least the prominent citizens?

Again, similar conclusions would seem to be necessitated by the facts known of the Cinque Ports. When Edward the Confessor granted the men of Dover certain customs in return for specified service of ships, with whom was the agreement made? And what persons, year after year, saw to the due performance of the contract? In the particular case of Dover we know that a royal reeve still held office;[1] but it was the community, not he, who enjoyed exemption from geld and toll, collected the necessary funds, and on royal demand sent the fleet to sea. This whole arrangement is quite unintelligible unless we presuppose a permanent local organization co-operating with the royal administration. None of the charters to the Cinque Ports throughout the twelfth and thirteenth centuries authorized the election of magistrates, but long before the customals came to describe the government in detail, each town in the confederacy was administered by a board of twelve jurats.[2] To explain the origin of this institution we obviously have to deal with the beginnings of communal privilege and obligation.

In the course of our investigation we have thus been led through the subjects of borough taxation and borough service back to the conclusion of the previous chapter, that the germ of the later municipality is to be found rather in the mercantile than in the judicial organization of the borough. The prevalence throughout England of the gild merchant during an age when formal self-government was denied most towns is a striking fact which immediately suggests that the one was a sort of substitute for the other.[3] And when it is realized that the chief interest of the borough community was trade, the significance of this substitution is at once apparent. Thanks to the gild organization, the men of the average borough really enjoyed considerable local autonomy. As Gross pointed out, the regulations of toll found in the charters imply some sort of financial arrangement between gild and royal officials,[4] and this may help us also to understand the early provisions with regard to the *firma*. Surely, in

---

[1] Above, p. 119. As pointed out by Mr Tait (*E.H.R.*, xlii, 349), reeves of Dover who were apparently royal appointees, are heard of as late as 1183–85.

[2] For the literature on the jurats see Tait, in *E.H.R.*, xliv, 200. The government of the separate Cinque Ports has never been adequately studied. From what is known of the Continental *jurés* and of similar officials in England (see below, pp. 175 ff.), it would seem probable that the jurats of the Cinque Ports originated as groups of men sworn in by the various communities to manage local affairs; that the practice was taken for granted from the outset and was consequently never made the subject of formal grant.

[3] See above, pp. 150 ff. Mr Tait's admirable discussion of this subject (*E.H.R.*, xlv, 533 ff.) leaves nothing more to be said on it.

[4] *Gild Merchant*, i, 44, 93, n. 1.

any matter involving a money offer, the arbiters of local action would
be the leading business men of the community.   All that we know of
mediaeval town politics makes us suspect that the popular court in the
churchyard merely ratified what had been determined by caucus in the
gild-hall.[1]

As is well known, however, the gild merchant may not be taken as the
sine qua non of municipal development.   We have no record of such gilds
at London, Northampton, Colchester, Norwich, or the Cinque Ports, and
no mention until the reign of John of any at Ipswich, Yarmouth, Dunwich, Nottingham, and Derby.   We certainly cannot take for granted
that gilds originally existed in all these boroughs.   The sources at our
disposal are very scanty, but they seem to indicate that the importance
of the gild varied from place to place.   Perhaps the existence of a strong
gild organization tended to delay the establishment of a formally elected
magistracy.   Of the four towns — London, Lincoln, Northampton, and
Colchester — which earliest secured this privilege, Lincoln was the only
one, so far as we know, to have a gild.[2]   And there must be more than
coincidence in the fact that the Cinque Ports were exceptional alike in
lacking gilds and in possessing advanced liberties at a remarkably early
time.   But in the absence of more certain information, further conjecture
in this direction is futile.   With or without a gild, the twelfth-century
borough appears in the records as a community led, if not governed, by
an influential group of citizens; and they, to judge from the privileges
which they sought and obtained, were normally traders.

The cumulative effect of the evidence just reviewed, vague and incon-
clusive as it may be on many points, is decidedly impressive.   It all runs
counter to the idea that the true origin of the English municipal system
is to be found in the sudden adoption of a foreign system.   Examined

---

[1] See especially the proceedings at Oxford cited by Mr Tait (*E.H.R.*, xlv, 531).

[2] See above, p. 150; *B.B.C.*, i, 202 ff.   In spite of all that has been written on the gilds, many
obscure problems remain in connection with them.   One is the relation between the gild and political
organization.   The gild appears all-important at Winchester and non-existent at London, and yet
various boroughs were given the trading rights of both at once (above, pp. 128 ff.).   Oxford, Lincoln, Norwich, and Northampton enjoyed the liberties of London; but the former two had gilds and
the latter two apparently had not.   In this connection Miss Cam (*V.H.C. Northampton*, iii, 7) has
suggested that the freemen of Northampton were equivalent to gildsmen elsewhere, and herein may
lie the solution of the mystery.   Normally, as noted above (pp. 132–33), enjoyment of the town
liberty was equivalent to being in scot and lot with the burgesses, and this with membership in the
gild.   But actually the same result could be secured by giving the town government control of trade
and restricting the liberty of the town to the trading class.   Although both systems confront us in the
later period, we cannot be sure that they were of equal antiquity.   If the borough had no gild, who
regulated local trade before the borough received rights of self-government?   It was assuredly not
exclusively the royal officials.   And if they allowed an informal combination of burgesses to act in
such matters, what was it but a gild?   The history of London should provide the answer, but as
yet it has not been forthcoming.   See below, p. 183, n. 5.

from many points of view, our earliest sources for the history of the free borough constantly lead to the conviction that the emergence of formal self-government toward the close of the twelfth century had been long prepared by an obscure but vital evolution. What, then, are the facts that have been interpreted to produce another conclusion?

4. THE BOROUGH AND THE COMMUNE

Quite recently Mr Tait has re-examined the much controverted question as to the origin of borough self-government in England. As noted above, he has expressed the opinion that a grant of *firma burgi* carried with it the right to elect reeves; but neither privilege, he concludes, was the germ from which developed the thirteenth-century municipal constitution. Although the history of the borough reveals the gradually developing *communitas* rather than the revolutionary *communa*, the influence of the latter in England, exerted indirectly through the example of London, was very considerable. The election of mayors, as distinguished from royal officials like bailiffs, the organization of regular councils, as contrasted with older courts turned to new functions, and the beginnings of formal incorporation were all due to the example of the foreign commune.[1] Thus Mr Tait, though with numerous reservations and qualifications, on the whole backs the well known thesis of Round, as opposed to the doctrine of Maitland, Gross, Mary Bateson, and others, who argued for the evolution of municipal institutions out of the ancient borough court.[2]

Now the preceding inquiry, while throwing considerable doubt upon this latter theory, has brought little support to Mr Tait's contention. Comparative study of urban liberties on the Continent has led to mistrust of any argument that attributes decisive influence to the commune as a *seigneurie collective populaire*.[3] And it has shown that no great significance can be attached to municipal titles. Neither function nor origin distinguished mayors from magistrates with other names. Mayors were not peculiar to communes, and all communes did not have mayors. They were no less seignorial or royal than other officials. Nor can we, without appeal to arbitrary logic, rigidly define a municipal council as distinct from a municipal court. The normal system of government in the Continental town was that by a group of variously designated selectmen, within which there was at first no differentiation of executives, legislators, and judges.[4]

[1] *E.H.R.*, XLII, 353, 358 ff.; 'The Origin of Town Councils in England,' *E.H.R.*, XLIV, 177 ff., 192 ff.; 'The Borough Community in England,' *E.H.R.*, XLV, 529 ff., 545 ff.

[2] Above, pp. 146 ff.

[3] Above, pp. 14 ff., 27 ff.

[4] Above, pp. 37 ff., 46.

In England we have already noticed indications of a similar system;[1] and further comparison of the charters merely serves to strengthen the impression thus obtained.   When elected magistracies became common, it certainly made no difference whether a borough had one reeve or several.   Moreover, we fail to detect any distinction between reeves (*prepositi*) and bailiffs (*ballivi*).[2]   Eventually it was usual for a borough to have a mayor, who might or might not be superimposed over previously existing magistrates.   But many great towns had no mayors, and those which did have them almost never received special authorization to that effect.[3] It is quite impossible to make any useful classification of the boroughs according to the titles either of their chief or their subordinate magistrates. The presence of a single office seems to have mattered as little as the election of a particular person; for the actual government was that of an influential group.   The one constant feature of early borough government was the existence at its base of a select body, whose titles varied, but who really constituted a permanent council.[4]

Nor is this largely a matter of conjecture.   A famous record of 1200 provides remarkably clear evidence on the point.[5]   The story has often been told, but because it provides our single full account of borough political activity in the formative period, it will stand one more repetition. By royal charter, dated 25 May 1200, Ipswich had been authorized, like various other boroughs, to elect reeves and coroners.[6]   So, on 29 June

[1] Above, pp. 168 ff.

[2] *B.B.C.*, I, 241 ff.; II, 351 ff.; and cf. Ipswich, immediately below.   Innumerable entries in the Close Rolls use the two titles indiscriminately, but in general 'bailiff' was the more popular in the thirteenth century.

[3] Mr Tait has shown (*B.B.C.*, II, lvii) that, except for London's grant of 1215, no extant charter authorized an English borough to elect a mayor before 1284; but that at least a dozen towns had 'copied London and provided themselves with mayors' before the death of John — most of them, in fact, before 1215 (*E.H.R.*, XLIV, 198).   Are we to believe that revolutions in legal status were thus effected, and without formal authorization, or that a mere change of fashion in titles took place?   A glance at the Close Rolls also tends to discredit the idea that the establishment of a mayor made any profound change in the borough constitution.   See, for example, John's letters to Winchester, in *Rotuli Litterarum Clausarum*, I, 144, 145, 150, 156, 157, 162, 178, 185, 206, 207, 214, 259; where it seems to make no difference whether the writ is addressed to the mayor and reeves, the reeves alone, or the mayor alone.   And any number of similar documents may be cited for other boroughs, in which the presence or absence of the mayor's title is obviously a matter of indifference.

[4] Mr Tait has cited all the earliest evidence, and it shows the council of twelve or twenty-four virtually universal, no matter what officials headed the administration.   The latter, we know, were generally royal appointees till late in the twelfth century; so any urban self-government that existed earlier must have been developed through co-operation with local groups of citizens.   On such matters, of course, the sources give us practically no information; but whatever hints they supply all point in the same direction.   They indicate that the germ of the municipal constitution was the council, rather than the individual magistrate (see above, pp. 170 ff.).

[5] Gross, *Gild Merchant*, II, 114 ff.   For comment see *ibid.*, I, 23 ff.; *H.E.L.*, I, 658, 664.

[6] The grants to Ipswich, Gloucester, Lincoln, and Shrewsbury were modelled after that to Northampton, on which see Miss Cam's comment in *V.H.C. Northampton*, III, 5.

following, the whole borough assembled in the churchyard of St Mary at the Tower and unanimously (*de communi assensu et una voce*) chose two good and lawful men, to wit, John Fitz-Norman and William de Belines, who were thereupon sworn in as bailiffs, to keep the reeveship of the said borough and well and faithfully to treat both poor and rich.[1]   In the same way they elected and installed four coroners, to hold the pleas of the crown and to attend to other matters there pertaining to the crown, and to superintend the acts of the bailiffs; but among the four chosen were the bailiffs themselves.

'Likewise on the same day it was ordained by the common counsel of the said town that henceforth there should be in the said borough twelve sworn chief portmen, as there are in other free boroughs of England, and that they should have full power, for themselves and for the whole town, to govern and maintain the said borough and all its liberties, to render the judgments of the town, and also to keep, ordain, and do in the said borough whatever should be done for the well-being and honor of the said town.'[2]   And it was announced by the magistrates that for this purpose the whole town should reassemble in the churchyard on the next Sunday.

At the appointed time, therefore, the election was held. By the consent of the town, the four bailiffs and coroners chose four good and lawful men from each parish of Ipswich, and they, having been suitably sworn, named the chief portmen *de melioribus, discrecioribus, ac potencioribus ville predicte ad ordinandum pro statu ville ut predictum est*.   The twelve thus selected were the four magistrates and eight others, who were then put on oath to guard and govern the borough of Ipswich, to maintain its liberties, to render just judgments, and to do whatever else needed to be done.[3]   And thereupon the twelve had the burgesses raise their hands toward the Book and together solemnly swear with all their power to respect, assist, and obey their bailiffs, coroners, and portmen and to defend and maintain the honor and liberties of the town of Ipswich in all places and against all men, saving the lord king and his royal authority.

[1] Gross, *Gild Merchant*, II, 116: 'qui iurati sunt ad custodiendum preposituram predicti burgi, et quod bene et fideliter tractabunt tam pauperes quam divites.'

[2] *Ibid.*, II, 117: 'Item eodem die ordinatum est per commune consilium dicte villate quod de cetero sint in burgo predicto duodecim capitales portmenni iurati, sicut in aliis liberis burgis Anglie sunt, et quod habeant plenam potestatem pro se et tota villata ad gubernandum et manutenendum predictum burgum et omnes libertates eiusdem burgi, et ad iudicia ville reddenda, ac eciam ad omnia [custodienda], ordinanda, et facienda in eodem burgo que fieri debeant pro statu et honore ville memorate.'

[3] 'Qui iurati sunt coram tota villata predicta quod bene et fideliter custodient et gubernabunt burgum Gippeswici, et ad manutenendum secundum eorum posse omnes libertates . . . , et ad iudicia curiarum eiusdem ville iuste reddenda . . . , et insuper ad omnia alia ordinanda et facienda que pro statu et honore ville predicte fieri contingent, et ad iuste et legittime tractandum tam pauperes quam divites.'

On future occasions various other decisions were made by the community assembled under the presidency of its officers. The town revenues were to be collected and the king's farm was to be paid by the two bailiffs and four other lawful men of the borough. It was ordered that no merchant of Ipswich should be quit of custom unless he were in scot and lot with the burgesses.[1] Two beadles were to be sworn to make attachments and distresses and to carry out the other commands of the magistrates; and one of them, under proper security, was to guard all prisoners placed under arrest by the town authorities. A common seal was to be manufactured and placed in the custody of three or four men whom the town should appoint. The king's new charter was to be read in the county courts of Suffolk and Norfolk and likewise entrusted to official keepers. Also a fit man was to be elected as alderman of the gild merchant, with four others to act as his associates.

By October 12 all this work was completed. The same two men were chosen to serve as bailiffs for the next year and four others (not of the twelve) were named as assistant collectors of customs. The two beadles (likewise not of the twelve) were installed. The seal was made and, together with the town charter, placed in charge of three men, viz., the two bailiffs and one of the remaining coroners. Another of the portmen was chosen alderman of the gild and as his associates four more of the twelve. And they were sworn well and faithfully to administer the gild merchant and all matters pertaining to it, and well and lawfully to treat all brothers of the gild. And afterwards it was announced by the alderman and his four associates, in the presence of the townspeople, that all who were of the town liberty should come before them on a day to be announced in order to put themselves in the gild and pay to it their *hanse*.[2]

The graphic account contained in this most remarkable document has many features that deserve special attention. In the first place, it is shown that the king's charter authorizing the election of magistrates resulted in no mere administrative variation, but in the formal inauguration of a complete municipal government endowed with a common seal. Secondly, this government is by specific repetition declared to be that of a group rather than of individuals. The bailiffs are merely the two most

---

[1] *Ibid.*, ii, 120: 'Item ordinatum est quod nullus burgensis predicte ville sit quietus de custuma in eadem villa de merchandisis suis, videlicet, si sit mercator, nisi sit lottans et scottans in communibus auxiliis et negociis villa.' See above, p. 133.

[2] *Ibid.*, ii, 121: 'qui iurati sunt simul cum aldermanno quod bene et fideliter gubernabunt gildam mercatoriam in burgo Gippeswici et omnes articulos ad gildam pertinentes, et quod bene et legittime tractabunt omnes fratres gilde. Et postea dictum est per aldermannum et quatuor socios suos in presencia populi ville quod omnes qui sunt de libertate ville veniant coram aldermanno et sociis suis ad certum diem, quando et ubi eis scire facient, ad ponendum se in gilda et ad hansam suam eidem glide dandam.'

prominent of the twelve portmen, all of whom are endowed with full powers, judicial and executive.   Thirdly, the actual working of the mediaeval
'democracy' is beautifully illustrated.   The naïve recital of the proceedings at Ipswich brings out with surprising distinctness that all efficient
action was taken by the influential citizens and that the rôle of the assembled populace was to agree *una voce* with all that its leaders proposed.
And beyond a doubt these leaders were the same men who assumed the
government of the town, the twelve portmen, eight of whom held some
fourteen offices in borough and gild.   Furthermore, we are again confronted with a burgess community practically equivalent to a gild merchant.   Not only were the two governed by a sort of interlocking direc-
torate, but all who shared the town liberties were commanded at the outset to enroll in the gild.   So far as actual power and privilege were concerned, all *burgenses* were *mercatores*.   And lastly, we are given a very
pretty example of a lawful commune.   The assembled town makes itself
into a sworn association by taking a solemn oath of fidelity to the borough, its liberties, and its constituted authorities.

In spite of its repute and its clarity, this document does not find favor
in Mr Tait's eyes.   The story of the twelve chief portmen he brands as
'either a wild misstatement or a later interpolation'.[1]   But he gives no
real reason for doubting the authenticity of the account beyond its inherent improbability, and that is a matter on which opinions may differ.
Nor does the alleged exaggeration rest on more than Mr Tait's translation of *alii liberi burgi* as 'all free boroughs.'[2]   Similar practice in the few
towns then authorized to elect magistrates would entirely justify the Latin expression.   And why should we not believe that the action taken at
Ipswich merely followed established custom?   It agrees remarkably with
what we know of early towns on the Continent and is contradicted by no
evidence in England.   Its improbability disappears entirely with the
abandonment of Mr Tait's peculiar theory regarding the origin of town
councils.

This theory, as we have seen, attributes decisive influence to the French
commune; but Mr Tait has considerable trouble with his thesis.   He ad-

---

[1] *E.H.R.*, XLIV, 194.

[2] Mr Tait first translates the phrase (*ibid.*, p. 182) as 'other free boroughs in England'; but in his
note on the following page finds it 'incredible that all free boroughs had a sworn council under any
name at the end of the twelfth century.'   And this is the interpretation repeated on p. 194.   As to
the suggested interpolation, Mr Tait thinks that the expression *capitales portmenni iurati* 'has a
later ring.'   But we hear of a *portmannemot* at Bury St Edmund's in 1121–38 (*B.B.C.*, I, 116) and
at Oxford in 1147 (*E.H.R.*, XLV, 533).   In an age when *jurés* were so common in towns, twelve
iurati at Ipswich do not appear at all extraordinary, and the adjective *capitales* is surely insufficient
to discredit the passage. On the whole it would seem impossible to throw out the Twelve—whatever
their title — without throwing out the whole document.

mits that 'the new councils were merely the old *potentiores* more closely organized and with wider functions.' They were new neither in numerical composition, in titles, nor in other minor respects. It was only 'the general idea of a council emanating from the community and sworn to serve and uphold its interests' that 'seems to have been derived from foreign example'.[1] The normal council of the later mediaeval period was an advisory body, subordinated to the mayor, 'a new officer created by the town itself to express its new unity and independence and free from all financial entanglement with the Crown.'[2] Such a system, however, is not found in those towns, notably Ipswich and the Cinque Ports, which continued under governing boards without mayors. And at London, where the mayoralty made its English début, the councillors were the time-honored aldermen.[3] The plain fact is that at the opening of the thirteenth century, when the invasion of the commune was allegedly taking place, the constitutional arrangement described by Mr Tait was non-existent.

Aside from Ipswich, the clearest information on municipal custom under John comes from Northampton. This town, as we have seen, had long been one of the most flourishing in England. As early as the reign of William I the burgesses had apparently held the *firma* of the sheriff, and by 1185 had secured it from the crown direct — since when they had apparently been allowed also to elect their own reeves.[4] In 1189 Richard had confirmed these rights in perpetuity, and in 1200 John had given Northampton the charter that served as the model for that to Ipswich.[5] Presumably, therefore, the action taken by the men of the latter borough followed a precedent set at Northampton, but on this point we have no direct evidence. It is certain only that in 1215 John issued letters notifying the burgesses that he had received William Thilly, their newly elected mayor, and instructing them to choose twelve *de discrecioribus ad expedienda simul cum eo negocia vestra in villa vestra.*[6] The men of Northampton had thus, presumably by virtue of the liberties of London which they enjoyed, put a mayor at the head of their administration. But can we doubt that the council of twelve merely continued an existing practice, in which the chief officers shared power with a group of *discreciores?*[7]

---

[1] *E.H.R.*, XLIV, 198–201.

[2] *E.H.R.*, XLIV, 192. But the idea that the mayor had no financial responsibility is contradicted by many writs; see, for example, those cited above, p. 174, n. 3.

[3] *E.H.R.*, XLIV, 191, 199, 200.

[4] Above, p. 168.

[5] Above, p. 174.

[6] *Rot. Litt. Claus.*, I, 188; *E.H.R.*, XLIV, 183 ff.

[7] Cf. the case of Dublin cited by Mr Tait (*E.H.R.*, XLIV, 185–86). In 1229 the citizens received permission to elect a mayor by a charter modelled after that of London in 1215, and they immediately

As Mr Tait says, 'in the communal age an elected chief magistrate, whether new mayor or old bailiff, must be assumed to have had for his necessary complement an elected body of twelve or twenty-four. Both represented the community, and the earliest conception of their relation seems to have been one of co-operation rather than of subordination.'[1] And which was more significant, the addition of an official with a new title or the political tradition into which he was fitted? The answer seems obvious, but before drawing more definite conclusions, we should give further attention to the institutions of the capital.

No problem connected with the controversial subject of the English borough has produced more widely divergent opinions than the mediaeval constitution of London. While the prominence of the city has naturally made its development a topic of general interest, the pertinent sources are at once fuller and more perplexing than for most towns. And especially the intermittent appearance of the commune in London has added to the difficulty of understanding its history. Thanks to the admirable reviews already made of this controversy,[2] it will not be necessary here to do more than mention the outstanding points.

First to appreciate the importance of the London commune was Stubbs, but his comments were vague and his conclusions halting.[3] The real pioneer in the field was Round. Brilliantly rewriting the entire history of Norman London, that keen scholar advanced the argument that the year 1191 opened a new epoch for the development of the English towns. It was the recognition of the London commune, he contended, that gave the city its first true municipality — a corporate constitution patterned after that of Rouen. The mayoralty and council that spread throughout the Anglo-Saxon world were French importations.[4]

Since its presentation in 1899 Round's thesis has been subjected to considerable amendment and criticism. George Burton Adams attempted to supplement it by applying the theory of the commune to the taxation of London, but his argument has met with scant favor and must be rejected as baseless.[5] Mary Bateson's suggestions have fared better. Since

---

installed also a council of twenty-four. For the influence of London on Dublin *via* Bristol, see above, p. 134.

[1] *E.H.R.*, XLIV, 192.

[2] Petit-Dutaillis, *Studies*, ch. ix; F. M. Stenton, *Norman London* (Historical Association Leaflet no. 38, London, 1915): M. Weinbaum, *Verfassungsgeschichte Londons* (Stuttgart, 1929); Tait, in *E.H.R.*, XLIV, 178 ff.

[3] Above, p. 16, n. 3.

[4] *Geoffrey de Mandeville* (London, 1892), pp. 347 ff.; *The Commune of London* (London, 1899), pp. 219 ff.

[5] G. B. Adams, *The Origin of the English Constitution* (2nd ed., New Haven, 1920), pp. 385 ff. The whole argument of Adams rested on the assertion by Giry and Luchaire that communes paid only feudal aids; see above, pp. 14, 28 ff., also Appendix I. On the taxation of London see especially *Haskins Anniversary Essays*, pp. 296, 305, and immediately below.

her publication of new evidence in 1902,[1] it has been at least difficult to believe that London's mediaeval constitution was remodelled in imitation of the Rouen *Etablissements*.   But the extent to which it was influenced by the commune in general has remained an open question, to be treated most recently by Mr Tait, whose main conclusions have already been noted.[2]

Writing in the 1890's, it was natural that Round should accept Giry's doctrines, which were then being popularized by Luchaire.   Mr Tait's concept of the commune, in spite of all that has since then appeared on the subject, is the same.   But if the exception taken to that concept in the preceding pages is well founded, speculation as to the feudal status of any commune in England would seem distinctly unprofitable.[3]   More-over, if we dissociate the commune from any one form of government, Round's thesis concerning the London municipality loses its remaining substance, and the constitutional history of the capital must be ap-proached from another angle.   The essential facts are already familiar; it remains only to put them in new alignment.

Anglo-Saxon London, like other boroughs at the time, was governed, not by its citizens, but by royal officials.   The outstanding local pecul-iarity was that the portreeve of London was also sheriff of Middlesex — a combined office that passed unchanged to a Norman baron after 1066.[4] For a while the sheriffs of London, as we know from their names, con-tinued to be of the feudal class, but after 1100 they were displaced by Londoners.[5]   Perhaps originally appointed, at least after 1129 they were elected, and this right was finally guaranteed in perpetuity by Henry I's famous charter.   Among the towns of England, London was thus, so far as we may tell, the first to have an elected magistracy — the privilege fundamental to the establishment of formal self-government.

---

[1] *E.H.R.*, xvii, 480 ff.

[2] Above, pp. 173 ff.

[3] In the feudal age all sorts of ideas were likely to be expressed in the more or less suitable language of feudalism.   Liberties might be granted in fee to a town or to the freemen of England (*H.E.L.*, i, 674).   A borough farmed by the burgesses was said to be held in chief of the king — a usage that, according to Luchaire's definition, should have implied a commune, but certainly did not (above, p. 170, n. 2; Tait, in *E.H.R.*, xlii, 352).

[4] Round, *Geoffrey de Mandeville*, pp. 37, 354, 439; W. Page, *London: Its Origin and Early Develop-ment* (London, 1923), pp. 81, 200.

[5] *Ibid.*, pp. 204–08.   This fact is clearly brought out by Mr Page, though he has another interpreta-tion of its significance.   In general his thesis (see p. 83) minimizes the effect of Henry's charter and throws the origin of London's constitution back into Anglo-Saxon times — a conclusion based upon various ideas which the present study is written to refute.   The view here taken coincides rather with that expressed by Mr Stenton in his *Norman London;* and more recently by Dr Weinbaum (*Verfassungsgeschichte Londons*, ch. ii).   The latter essay, in particular, owes much of its clarity to the author's understanding of contemporary institutions on the Continent.

When subsequently granted to the ordinary borough, authorization to elect a reeve was taken to include that to choose all municipal officials, subordinate as well as superior, to differentiate functions of administration, and to adopt a common seal.[1] Was this the case at London also? Unfortunately, we have no direct evidence on the point, but there can be no doubt that Henry's charter was an epoch-making grant. The citizens received the farm in fee, again the earliest known example of such a concession. Another article guaranteed exemption from arbitrary taxation, and by implication entitled the Londoners to grant voluntary aids.[2] Trials of citizens were restricted to the city; even royal pleas were to be held there, and under the presidency of an elected justice, the prototype of the later coroner. Thus the folkmoot and husting of the charter, no matter what they had earlier been, became municipal courts to the fullest degree then known.[3] And although nothing is said of them in the document, the aldermen must in some fashion have been brought under control of the community.

No mention either of aldermen or of wards is to be found before the twelfth century. But since at that time the wards were primarily military districts, they were presumably of Anglo-Saxon origin, like the wards of other boroughs mentioned in Domesday.[4] And it would seem to follow that the aldermen, who were in charge of these districts, were originally military officials, subordinates of the portreeve.[5] At the opening of the twelfth century, certainly, there were at least twenty — twenty-

---

[1] See the case of Ipswich, above, pp. 174 ff.

[2] *G.*, I, 523; *S.C.*, p. 129: 'Et sint quieti de scot et de danegildo et de murdre, et nullus eorum faciat bellum.' Cf. Saint-Omer, above, p. 35, and references there given. That the Londoners' exemption included more than Danegeld seems certain. In Domesday *scot* appears occasionally as the equivalent of *geld*, but in the twelfth century appears as a general term for tax, like *tallage* or *taille*; cf. *scot* and *lot* (*B.B.C.*, I, 107 ff.; *G.*, II, 646). Unfortunately, the effect of the charter on London's liability for *auxilia* cannot be determined; for the charter was issued after the Pipe Roll of 1130 was drawn up and was cancelled before the accession of Henry II.

[3] See above, pp. 137, 147 ff. In the twelfth century the folkmoot met three times a year for extraordinary matters, and thus corresponded to the great court or full hundred of the other boroughs (Bateson, *Borough Customs*, II, cxlv ff., and in *E.H.R.*, XVII, 487, 502; *G.*, II, 522, 572). The husting, presumably through pressure of routine business, met weekly, as did also the Bristol hundred (above, p. 134); while the ordinary borough court met monthly. That the husting had long been concerned with mercantile affairs is indicated by the fact that the London husting weight had been standard from the days of Aethelred, when the city first appears as a prominent centre of overseas trade: Liebermann, under *Gewicht*, 8ᵃ (*G.*, II, 473); above, p. 72. There is much that we should like to know about the earlier history of these courts, but in the absence of all definite evidence, speculation seems rather useless.

[4] Ballard, *Domesday Boroughs*, p. 52; cf. Bury St Edmund's in the time of Stephen (Round, in *A.H.R.*, II, 689).

[5] H. W. C. Davis in *Essays presented to T. F. Tout*, pp. 45 ff.; Round, *Commune of London*, pp. 103 ff., 241 ff., 255 ff.; Page, *London*, pp. 173 ff., 212; Stenton, *Norman London*, p. 6; Weinbaum, *Verfassungsgeschichte Londons*, pp. 18 ff.; *G.*, II, 565–66.

four, we should expect — who were distinctly of the old landed aristocracy and tended to hold their offices by hereditary right.   They were
plainly men who before 1066 would have been called thegns or *cnihtas;*
in fact, some of them were members of the famous *cnihtengild* that was
soon to die a voluntary death.[1]   In this respect, and as holders of *sac* and
soc, they resembled the lawmen of the older boroughs.   Because they
helped to render judgments in the husting, Mary Bateson declared that
they were lawmen.[2]   Nevertheless, the fate of the latter in the other boroughs must make us wary of such a conclusion.[3]   And the fact that the
aldermen had judicial functions in the time of John does not prove that
they had always had the same functions, or that by virtue of such functions they were in all respects like the ancient lawmen.[4]   We know too
little about the aldermen to be sure of Mary Bateson's identification.
Was it under Henry I that they, like the sheriffs, became distinctly bourgeois?   Were they then, as later, elected by the citizens in the wardmoots?[5]

However this may be, the new régime was short-lived.   After securing
as complete self-government as that enjoyed even by the greater towns of
France, London suffered from the feudal reaction under Stephen.   That

[1] See above, p. 150.   It seems quite impossible to find in the *cnihtengild* any features of significance
either for the municipal or the mercantile organization of the capital.   If London ever had a gild
merchant, it was not the *cnihtengild*.   Nor was the latter in any way identical with the aldermen as
an official body (Round, *loc. cit.*).   It is also perfectly clear that the aldermen were holders of *sac*
and *soc* as individually privileged landlords, and not by virtue of their common office (Weinbaum,
p. 18, as opposed to the view expressed by Davis).

[2] *E.H.R.*, xvii, 481 ff., 786; *S.C.*, p. 313.

[3] On the lawmen of Domesday see above, p. 111, n. 4.   The survey shows no connection between
lawmen and wards.   At Stamford there were twelve of the former and six of the latter; at York there
were eight *iudices* and seven shires.   The only lawmen who are heard of in the later age were those of
Stamford (Maitland, *Domesday Book and Beyond*, p. 24; Ballard, *Domesday Boroughs*, p. 52).   If
they had kept any real connection with municipal government, their office would not have become
the forgotten honor described by the Hundred Rolls.   Stamford failed to make any progress in the
twelfth century (above, p. 166, n. 1).   Was it not for that reason that the antiquated arrangement
persisted there while being entirely superseded at Lincoln, York, Cambridge, and Chester?   See
Tait, in *E.H.R.*, xliv, 195.

[4] Groups of doomsmen commonly appear in all popular courts of the twelfth century; in the
boroughs the law was regularly defined by a group of chief men and not by the presiding official
(above, p. 137).   These men might be called lawmen or aldermen or anything else; but they held
their position because they represented the burgess community and could state its custom.   When
the borough was essentially mercantile, they would be of the merchant class.   Lawmen of the old
agrarian aristocracy, whose titles were hereditary or attached to particular sokes, could not possibly
continue to have real authority in the growing town.   Consequently, the fact that the aldermen continued as municipal magistrates is itself proof that they were essentially different from the lawmen
of Domesday.

[5] The wardmoots must have been a familiar institution under Henry I, or the famous mistake of
wardemota for *vadimonia* would not have been made at so early a time (*G.*, i, 525; *B.B.C.*, i, xxxvi).
Cf. the election of *magistri civium* (*Bürgermeister*) at Cologne *c.* 1112 (Koebner, *Köln*, pp. 276 ff.).

this king, in spite of the city's support at his coronation, broke its liberties is proved by his recognition of Geoffrey de Mandeville as sheriff.[1] And it is at the same time that we hear of the commune — plainly a sworn association set up by the Londoners during civil war to maintain or recover their freedom.[2]   To such a hope the Angevin succession proved fatal.   Henry II, who had rewarded the loyalty of Rouen by confirming its commune,[3] punished the city that had driven out his mother by refusing to restore its earlier liberties.   By the charter of 1156, indeed, London kept its more elementary privileges; but the fee-farm, the election of magistrates, and fiscal exemption were all dropped.[4]   Until Henry's death the city was held under royal administration, burdened with an extortionate farm, and subjected to arbitrary taxation of unprecedented severity.[5]

Inevitably, when the royal grasp was relaxed in 1190, the cry of commune was again raised and a fresh attempt made to regain the lost liberties.   This time, thanks to an era of troubled politics, it succeeded, and London once more became self-governing.[6]   Henceforth the head of the administration bore the prouder title of mayor, but that seems to have been the extent of foreign borrowing.   Probably, as Mary Bateson thought, the *échevins* of the communal oath to Richard were merely the aldermen in French translation.[7]   In any case, it was the aldermen who

[1] Round. *Geoffrey de Mandeville*, pp. 140, 153, 367.

[2] *Ibid.*, pp. 116–17, 247; *Commune of London*, pp. 223–24.

[3] Above, pp. 40 ff.

[4] Round, *Commune of London*, pp. 224 ff.

[5] See Appendix IV.   For reasons that will be fully explained in his forthcoming publications, Dr Weinbaum believes (I quote from a letter) 'that Henry did no more than deprive the city of the outward forms of self-government.'   Except that 'the financial relations between the crown and the city were no longer those of two partners,' conditions really remained about the same.   In particular, the king did not object to the citizens' activity in economic matters.   Thus, although London had no gild merchant, the actual government of the city, under the supervision of the royal magistrates, devolved upon a clique of influential citizens, presumably including the aldermen and others who controlled the husting.   Was it not, I should add, exactly such an informally organized group that, with or without a legalized gild, formed the basis of every municipal administration in the early twelfth century?

[6] The interpretation here adopted is that also of Mr Stenton (*Norman London*, p. 9) and of Dr Weinbaum (*op. cit.*, p. 46).   The one great privilege that the Londoners failed to regain was exemption from arbitrary taxation; hence their demand during the barons' rebellion *de omnibus taillagiis delendis nisi per communem assensum regni et civitatis* (*E.H.R.*, XVII, 726).   See the works cited above, p. 179, n. 5; and cf. other claims, including restriction of military service, made in the *Libertas Londoniensis* (*G.*, I, 673).

[7] *E.H.R.*, XVII, 510.   On the Flemish *scabini* see above, p. 36.   For the better part of a century the word had been used to denote the members of a municipal administrative board.   Whether the aldermen of 1191 could naturally be so called would depend upon their contemporary position in the city.   If they were still what they had been in 1128, we should hardly expect the usage.   But by the thirteenth century the aldermen were elected from the wards.   Had that been temporarily established under Henry I?   And had a reactionary system been restored under Henry II?   Evidence

continued, despite temporary innovations, to act as associates of the city's chief in court and council.[1]

The history of London was thus far from abnormal. The capital, though in many ways exceptional, was not so through being more subject to spasms of foreign imitation. French influence there assuredly was; but what English borough had not felt its force since the Norman Conquest? The constitution of London was as much, and as little, a gradual development as that of the average mediaeval town. After 1191 the city might well have borne the permanent title of commune. That it did not was probably accidental, and in any case is a matter of indifference. The name would not have changed its status one jot.[2]

For the reasons stated, it would thus appear difficult to follow Mr Tait in his argument concerning the origins of the English municipal corporation. The evidence that he cites with regard to early borough seals is interesting and important, but hardly proves the necessary connection of commune and corporateness. What it does prove is that the notion of the town as a body politic emerged in England, as it had on the Continent, along with the formal establishment of municipal self-government.[3] But for England the epoch-making event in that connection was Henry I's charter, not the commune of 1191. For the latter, though adding a few refinements, only restored to the Londoners part of what they had peaceably secured before 1135.[4] Nor did the commune mark the beginning of a new era for the other boroughs. As early as 1189 at least

to decide the matter is at present lacking. We may be sure only that the fate of the aldermen was in some way determined by the explosion under Richard. Between 1128 and 1216 the status of aldermen was revolutionized.

[1] Tait, in *E.H.R.*, xliv, 179 ff., 196, 199.

[2] Mr Tait seems to imply that the London commune of 1191 remained a permanent institution, although, as pointed out by Adams (above, p. 179, n. 5), the city's continued subjection to arbitrary tallage cannot be reconciled with Luchaire's definition (see especially *E.H.R.*, xlv, 530, n. 3, 541). The 'communes' at Gloucester and York, for which fines are recorded in the Pipe Rolls of 16 and 24 Henry II (*E.H.R.*, xlii, 353–4) were undoubtedly associations regarded by the government as unlawful conspiracies, but the objects for which they were sworn are not reported. It may be noted that the latter instance appears in the roll alongside many cases of traitorous correspondence (*communiones*) with the enemy.

[3] *E.H.R.*, xlv, 529 ff. The clearest evidence is contained in the Ipswich record (above, p. 176). Other examples of borough seals dating from the reigns of Richard and John are cited by Mr Tait, but they vary remarkably: *Sigillum burgensium de gilda mercatorum Gloucestrie* (p. 537); *Sigillum civium Eborac'* (p. 542); *Sigillum prepositorum de Northampton* (p. 545). And at Oxford (p. 541) the common seal of the *universitas civium* seems to have been the seal of the alderman of the gild, who was actually the chief officer of the town. Did this variation imply the finely drawn legal distinctions sought by Mr Tait? Did not the variety of seals merely reflect the variety of ways in which the will of a newly constituted municipality was actually expressed? From such evidence, at any rate, it is impossible to prove the existence or non-existence of a *seigneurie collective populaire* according to Luchaire's definition.

[4] Above, p. 183, n. 6.

three of them had already secured written authorization to elect magistrates, and this action seems, in two cases, to have been a mere confirmation of what had informally come to be enjoyed under Henry II.[1]

Accordingly, it is impossible to regard the dramatic events in the capital as in any sense marking the turning-point in the constitutional history of the borough.   Municipal incorporation did not depend upon the application of a legal technicality; rather it was the final stage in a slow evolution of self-government that can be traced back to obscure beginnings under the Norman kings and even earlier.   And in this evolution the controlling factor was a social transformation, to summarize which will be the final task in the present study.

[1] Above, p. 168.

VII

THE GROWTH OF THE BOROUGH

1. Topographical Study: Roman Foundations

IN THE foregoing pages the problem of urban development in England has been approached by examining the principal groups of sources in their chronological order. As a result, it may be hoped that various stages in the history of the borough have been pictured with as great an accuracy as the evidence permits. Many gaps stand in the account, because many are left by the documents. To some extent, perhaps, they may be filled in by imaginative reconstruction, but that is a hazardous undertaking to be postponed as long as possible. And in the meantime greater continuity can be brought into the story by supplementing the written records with data of a quite different sort.

On the Continent, as noted above, a striking effect of the mercantile settlement theory has been to stimulate the topographical study of urban expansion.[1] Such research has now been carried on for over a quarter of a century, and with splendid results. Thanks to the new approach, the history of Roman cities like Paris and Cologne, of tenth-century burgs like Ghent and Erfurt, and of newer foundations like Etampes and Lübeck has been revealed with a clarity and distinctness otherwise unobtainable. The lack of similar work in England is only too apparent, and the cause for it is equally plain. Boroughs generally have been regarded as towns without regard to the age in which they existed. Whatever difficulty has been encountered in explaining the origin of the borough, none has been felt in describing its subsequent development; it merely continued to be what it had been. With careful re-examination of the sources, however, this alleged continuity tends to disappear; and once the essential newness of the Norman borough is appreciated, the problem of its relationship to the old Anglo-Saxon borough challenges investigation.

Such an enterprise obviously requires the attention of the trained archaeologist. The vestiges of urban growth are not the documentary sources of ordinary historical research. Rather they are the remains of walls, gates, and buildings; traces of ditch and embankment; lines of streets, market places, and parish boundaries. To the skilled observer all these things, combined with information drawn from ancient records

[1] Above, pp. 21, 23 ff.

and maps, tell an eloquent story. But few besides local antiquaries have the opportunity for profitable study of this kind, and up to the present their efforts have rarely been concentrated on borough growth.

Certain related subjects, it is true, have always proved fascinating. Roman antiquities have been meticulously studied, and thanks to able work like that of Haverfield, the outlines of most British *civitates* are well known. The castle also has attracted many investigators, and the researches of Round, Hope, and Mrs Armitage have, as already remarked, had an important bearing upon the problem of urban origins.[1] Furthermore, a scholar of the older generation occasionally became interested in the topography of an ancient borough and so, without perhaps entirely realizing the significance of his discoveries, would hit upon facts of great moment for the present inquiry. And more recently various students of local history have produced studies that reveal the possibility of brilliant advance in subjects that have been somewhat neglected.

Even a rank amateur in the field of topographical study may take the results of specialized investigation and, combining them with other data of a rather elementary sort, formulate tentative conclusions. No more than this will be attempted in the following pages. The object is not to present an exhaustive discussion, or to offer definitive opinions. It is intended merely, by way of illustration, to review the facts that have been established for a few boroughs and, through comparison with what has been done on the Continent, to indicate certain problems that deserve the attention of the expert.

While previously considering the tenth-century boroughs, we saw that they fell into two main divisions: those whose fortifications dated back to Roman times and those constructed during the Danish war.[2] Of the places that can be classified in the former group, and which continue to stand upon the list of boroughs in the twelfth century, London, with a walled enclosure of 330 acres,[3] was the largest; and Bath, with one of less than 23,[4] was the smallest. Next above Bath was Rochester, with slightly more than 23 acres;[5] while Winchester, with 138,[6] ranked next to the top. Canterbury, Chichester, Colchester, Exeter, and Leicester were all about the same size, between 100 and 125 acres.[7] And in the

---

[1] Above, pp. 52 ff.

[2] Above, pp. 55 ff.

[3] Royal Commission on Historical Monuments, *An Inventory of the Historical Monuments in London*, iii (London, 1928), 35.

[4] Haverfield, in *V.H.C. Somerset*, i, 227.

[5] G. Payne, in *Archaeologia Cantiana*, xxi (1895), 11. The elaborate plan by G. M. Livett, opp. p. 17, shows a slight extension by the Normans to include the cathedral.

[6] Haverfield, in *V.H.C. Hampshire*, i, 285 ff.

[7] Haverfield, *The Romanization of Roman Britain* (Oxford, 1923), p. 62, n. 2; Merivale, in *Quarterly*

case of all these towns the mediaeval walls seem to have been built on Roman foundations. In other words, the fortified area of each was sufficient to accommodate practically all increase of population during the Middle Ages.

For example, as late as the thirteenth century, the old London walls included, not only thickly settled quarters, but considerable vacant land as well. To the north, where the Walbrook yet flowed above ground, lay marshes available for pasture; and the properties of great ecclesiastics and other prominent persons regularly included garden plots and orchards.[1] To the south, it is true, the wall that had once paralleled the Thames had been torn down to make way for new streets and business houses, while small suburbs had risen along the main roads to east and west.[2] But in general mediaeval London still occupied the site of the ancient Londinium and, according to present-day standards, was a decidedly small town, smaller even than the City that forms the heart of the modern metropolis. And yet it was three times the size of such boroughs as Canterbury and a dozen times as big as Rochester. Judged even by Continental practice, the original *enceinte* of London was extraordinarily large; it was much greater than those of Cologne and Mainz, and they exceeded practically all similar constructions in northern Gaul.[3] If, therefore, the English capital was eclipsed by French and German cities in Norman times, it was because the latter had been enormously extended since the tenth century.

It thus appears that those walls which the Romans had erected to meet the needs of urban centres were ordinarily not outgrown during the mediaeval period. But the case was otherwise with constructions of a more purely military character. For example, the city of Eburacum stood on the triangle of land formed by the junction of the Ouse and the Foss. Its wall, as had been definitely established by careful research, was nearly square, with towers at the four corners and at certain other points along the sides. The total area of the enclosure, since that was originally intended for a military post, was only $52\frac{1}{2}$ acres; and by the fourth century

---

Review, xcvii (1855), 95; E. L. Cutts, *Colchester* (London, 1888), p. 34; W. Somner, *The Antiquities of Canterbury* (Canterbury, 1703), p. 8, and cf. *Archaeologia Cantiana*, xv (1883), 340; R. G. Collingwood, *The Archaeology of Roman Britain* (London, 1930), pp. 92 ff.; G. Macdonald, *Roman Britain, 1914–28* (London, 1931), pp. 73 ff.

[1] Page, *London*, p. 270.

[2] *Ibid.*, pp. 178, 272. No definite evidence has been presented to show just when the southern wall was torn down, except that it must have been after the time of Alfred. The first extramural territory to share the liberty of London was the Portsoken, mentioned in Henry II's charter (*ibid.*, p. 277). See above, p. 51, n. 3.

[3] A. Blanchet, *Les Enceintes Romaines de la Gaule* (Paris, 1907), especially p. 283; and see the reference cited above, p. 187, n. 3.

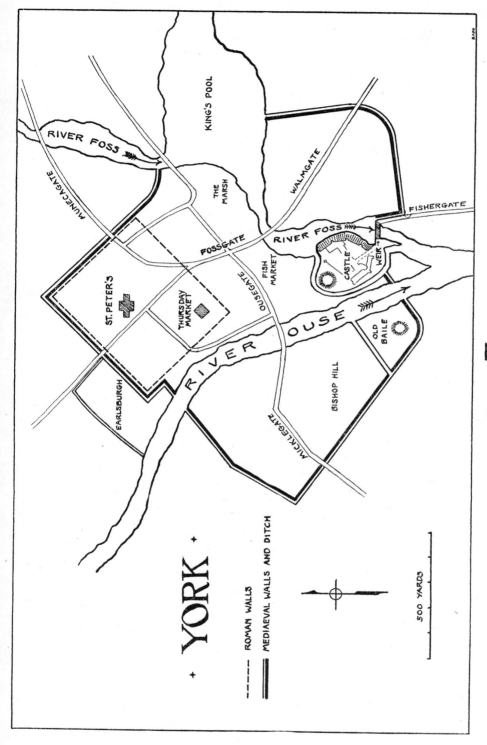

+ YORK +

‑ ‑ ‑ ‑ ROMAN WALLS

▬▬▬▬ MEDIAEVAL WALLS AND DITCH

500 YARDS

PLATE III.

extensive suburbs had appeared outside the walls.   Across the Ouse, in
particular, lay a prosperous residential quarter that included temples,
baths, and many luxurious villas.[1]   Then came the Saxon invasion.
York, like other cities of Britain, lost the bulk of its population and sank
into obscurity.   Aside from its ecclesiastical prominence, little is known
of the city for five hundred years.   Its walls still stood and they were
presumably made use of by the Saxon invaders, but no details of the
fighting that surged about them have come down to us.

In the ninth century York was captured by the Danes and, as earlier
noted, became one of their great military and political centres.[2]   And
when it was taken over by the English, the city kept its administrative
importance, standing at the head of what eventually became known as
Yorkshire.   Meanwhile York had undoubtedly profited by the development of Baltic trade.   Its geographical location naturally tended to make
it the greatest port of the Danelaw, and by the eleventh century, according to the vague remarks of a chronicler, had come to rival London in
prosperity.[3]   But at this point Domesday provides us with much more
valuable information.

According to the survey, York before the Conquest included six shires,
besides that of the archbishop, but one of the six has been destroyed *in
castellis*.   In these five shires there were 1,418 *mansiones hospitatae*, and
in the archbishop's shire 189.   The latter now, in addition to the episcopal palace and the homes of the canons, contains only 100 *mansiones
hospitatae*, big and little.   In the other five shires the king now has 391
mansiones rending all custom, 400 that pay a penny each or less, and 500
so waste that they produce nothing — in all 1,331.   Individual barons are
then described as holding 86½ *mansiones* which they had taken over from
Saxon predecessors; and so we find, except for a lost half, the original 1,418
mansiones accounted for.   Moreover, there has been considerable new
construction.   The king has 145 *mansiones* occupied by Frenchmen, and
since their haws are not reckoned in the 1,418, they must all have been

---

[1] See especially George Benson, *An Archaeological Plan of York* (Cooper and Swan: York, 1926),
which by map and commentary summarizes all the results of recent investigation.

[2] Above, p. 56.

[3] J. Raine, *Historians of the Church of York and its Archbishops* (Rolls Series), I, 454: 'Est civitas
Eboraca metropolis totius gentis Northanimbrorum, quae quondam erat nobiliter aedificata et
firmiter muris constructa; quae nunc est dimissa vetustati; quae tamen gaudet de multitudine
populorum non minus virorum ac mulierum, exceptis parvulis et pubetinis, quam xxx millia eadem
civitate numerati sunt; quae inedicibiliter est repleta et mercatorum gazis locupleta[ta] qui undique
adveniunt, maxime ex Danorum gente.'   The quotation is from the *Vita Oswaldi*, which Raine
dated before 1005.   The author plainly indicates the existence of a Danish trading settlement in or
about the ancient *castrum*, which had been allowed to become somewhat ruinous.   His estimate of
an adult population of 30,000 is, of course, not to be taken seriously.

established in some freshly developed quarter.   Hamelin has one house *in fossato urbis*.   Earl Hugh has put up seven *minutas mansiones* on a fifty-foot lot.   Hugh Fitz-Baldric possesses twenty-nine *minuta hospitia;* Berenger de Todeni eight *mansiones ad hospitia*, half of them *in fossato urbis;* Osbert de Archis twelve *mansiones ad hospitia;* Odo Balistarius one *hospitium*.[1]

In all we thus hear of 204 newly built houses, at least some of which stand on the city ditch.   What ditch was that?   We cannot be positive in our conclusions from such scanty evidence, but it would seem probable that we here find reference to the abandonment of the old fortifications at the southern angle of the Roman city.   As noted above, the original walls of York contained a comparatively small area, which was obviously quite inadequate for the flourishing town of the eleventh century.   By that time the population had spread over a considerable portion of the triangle between the two rivers, and there can be little doubt that the new quarter was mainly a Danish trading settlement.[2]

From Mr George Benson's admirable map, it is perfectly clear that mediaeval and ancient York by no means coincided.   The Roman city, according to the standard plan, had been constructed where two highways intersected at right angles, and the civilian suburb had extended far across

---

[1] *D.B.*, I, 298; above, pp. 97, n. 7, 104.   In the survey the various properties are indiscriminately combined in one list.   It is only after classification that the Domesday arithmetic becomes apparent.

[2] The literature on the topography of mediaeval York is considerable.   T. P. Cooper's *York: The Story of Its Walls, Bars, and Castles* (London, 1904) contains much valuable material, but indulges in fanciful speculation as to the origin of the urban fortifications.   A much safer guide is provided by Mr Benson's two volumes, which are remarkable for their intimate knowledge of archaeological data and include a wealth of plans and illustrations: G. Benson, *York from its Origin to the End of the Eleventh Century* (Cooper and Swann: York, 1911); *Later Mediaeval York* (Coultas and Volans: York, 1919).   But the opinions set forth in these books have been considerably amended in Mr Benson's latest work, cited above, p. 189, n. 1.   See also F. M. Stenton, *York in the Eleventh Century* (York Minister Historical Tracts, no. 8); Harald Lindkvist, 'A Study on Mediaeval York,' *Anglia*, L (1926), 345 ff.   In this interesting paper Mr Lindkvist develops the thesis that the extent of Danish settlement at York may be determined by the prevalence in that locality of Scandinavian names, particularly those ending in 'gate' with the meaning of street.   That this approach to the problem has much to recommend it cannot be denied, but various considerations warn us that it must be used with caution.   In the first place, the word 'gate,' though originally Danish, unquestionably became good English throughout a wide region, and is so cited in Murray's *New English Dictionary* for as late a period as the sixteenth and seventeenth centuries.   The usage was common in many towns (cf. Lincoln, Nottingham, and Norwich) — too common to be entirely primitive. And in many cases the name proves that the street was a later creation (e.g., Castlegate).   As Mr Stenton says, the names of the main streets look old; those of the lesser streets do not. For York the oldest positive evidence is a document of 1080 (*Yorkshire Archaeological Journal*, XVIII, 412 ff.), which mentions *Munecagate*, *Walbegate*, and *Fiscergate*.   But the ending 'gate' no more proves that these highways were in the borough than would the ending 'street.'   Consequently I cannot follow Mr Lindkvist in thinking that Danish York embraced all the suburbs that are later found within Edward's wall.   The philological argument, to be valid, must be confirmed by archaeological evidence, and that is not forthcoming.

the Ouse to the west. But in the later city the northern angle was taken up by the minster and appurtenant lands — the *scyra archiepiscopi* of Domesday.[1] The market was in the extreme southern angle and formed the centre of a region that to a considerable degree lay beyond the walls. The one bridge across the Ouse led to this region, and so diverted the main highway of Micklegate away from the line of the ancient road to the northeast — a striking proof that the mediaeval town was essentially a new growth.

There is no evidence that the Danes made any extension of the Roman fortifications at York, but their settlement to the south was protected on three sides by water and on the north by the city walls and the entrenched estate of the earl.[2] All the other defenses would seem to have originated with the Normans. In the first place, William built two castles, one on either side of the Ouse; and thereby, as Domesday tells us, destroyed one of the city's seven shires.[3] Secondly, the fortifications of the city were greatly extended and improved. A ditch, connecting the Foss and the Ouse, was dug about the city to the north, and inside it a continuous rampart constructed.[4] The Bishop Hill quarter was similarly enclosed, and eventually the Walmgate suburb beyond the Foss was brought within the ring of defenses.[5] By the end of the thirteenth century the area of the city had thus been quadrupled, and under Edward I the entire expanse was surrounded by the magnificent stone wall that has so largely and so fortunately escaped destruction.

Meanwhile the southern walls of the old *castrum* had long since been obliterated. Apparently they were still standing in 1066; otherwise the

[1] All the historians of the city have expressed the opinion that the archbishop's shire lay across the Ouse — a conjecture which seems to rest on nothing besides the name Bishop Hill. But Domesday states that this shire included the archiepiscopal *curia* and the houses of the canons, and so must have adjoined the minster. See Plate III, which is based (with his permission) upon Mr Benson's *Archaeological Plan.*

[2] Mr Benson (as he has kindly informed me by letter) now considers all the embankments west of the Ouse to have been constructed after 1066. But the possibility remains that the Danes built some sort of works to connect the western corner of the ancient *castrum* with the Ouse, and its eastern corner with the Foss.

[3] This shire evidently had occupied the point of the triangle between the two rivers. The construction of the castle there not only destroyed a large number of houses but produced other topographical changes as well. To secure an adequate supply of water for his new ditches, the king dammed the Foss just below the castle and so created what Domesday refers to as *stagnum regis.* This inundation, says the survey, covered two new mills and at least a carucate of arable, meadow, and garden. Furthermore, it seems to have cut the main highway to the southeast, forcing Fossgate to be bent toward the castle. And the fact that the land to the east of that street was called the Marsh would indicate that it was not built over for some time after the Conquest. It is not improbable that this crowding of the old borough helped to produce the suburbs across the rivers.

[4] Benson, *York*, I, 68.

[5] Mr Lindkvist makes this region one of the seven shires mentioned in Domesday, but it would rather appear to have been a later addition fortified in the thirteenth century.

Domesday entries regarding the appropriation of the city ditch are hard
to understand.   But whenever it occurred, their disappearance was the
result of commercial expansion.   The York of the Middle Ages was essentially a mediaeval development.   Topographical study not only confirms but greatly amplifies the conclusions that may be drawn from documentary sources.   Between the Eburacum of the Romans and the York
of to-day there is little continuity.   The modern town can hardly be
traced back of a trading settlement that seems to have emerged in the
course of the tenth century, and by the middle of the eleventh to have
secured well defined liberties that already distinguished it from the countryside.[1]   With the Norman Conquest York suffered cruelly, but in spite
of all wastage, the economic recovery of the city is plainly attested by
Domesday, and during the next two hundred years its increasing prosperity is vividly illustrated by the map of its physical growth.   Although
certain details remain doubtful, the main outline of the city's history is
exceptionally clear.

York is thus our best example of a Roman city that expanded in the
Middle Ages.   To a certain extent Lincoln offers an interesting parallel,
but unfortunately that city still lacks a chronicler of its fascinating history, and in consequence we cannot be sure of any but the most salient
facts in its development.   The original Roman wall described a rectangle
of about forty-one acres on the crest of the great hill that rises abruptly
from the valley of the Witham.[2]   Subsequently the western and eastern
walls were extended down hill and connected on the south by another
straight wall running a hundred yards or so from the bank of the river.
As may be seen from the accompanying sketch, this addition more than
doubled the area of the city, and we should like to know exactly when it
was made.   Though proof is lacking, the extension was presumably Roman.[3]   That supposition is borne out, not only by the general design of
the enclosure, but by the known fact that Lindum, beginning as a military post, eventually became a great commercial town, with the status
of *colonia*.   As population became concentrated in the valley below the
original camp, the fortifications would seem to have been extended round
the newer settlement.

Through the lack of archaeological investigation, the subsequent his-

---

[1] Above, p. 91, n. 3, 117.

[2] Haverfield, *Ancient Town-Planning* (Oxford, 1913), p. 118.

[3] Haverfield considered it probable; although with his usual caution, he refused to accept the idea
as a fact until it had been verified by actual observation.   See Plate IV, which is based on William
Marrat's map of 1817.   For a photograph of this map, together with much information on local
topography, I am greatly indebted to Mr Frank Hill, who is engaged in collecting materials for a
much needed history of the early city.

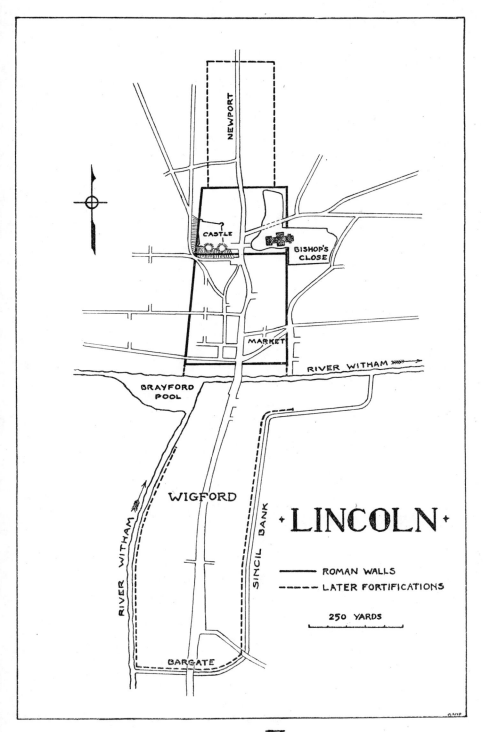

NEWPORT

CASTLE

BISHOP'S CLOSE

MARKET

RIVER WITHAM

BRAYFORD POOL

WIGFORD

RIVER WITHAM

SINCIL BANK

LINCOLN

——— ROMAN WALLS
----- LATER FORTIFICATIONS

250 YARDS

BARGATE

PLATE IV.

tory of Lincoln is even more obscure than that of York. As one of the Five Boroughs, Lincoln was an important place under the Danes; principally, we may be sure, because of its tremendously strong *castrum* on the hill-top. As to the fate of the lower city we know little; but if its walls still stood, it was large enough to accommodate all increase of population in the tenth and eleventh centuries. According to Domesday, the city *T.R.E.* contained 1,150 *mansiones hospitatae*, which by 1086 had been reduced to 910; and of the 240 waste *mansiones* no less than 166 had been destroyed for the castle.[1] These figures force us to believe that the mass of the inhabitants at the Conquest were living 'above hill.'

The actual area of the castle precinct is about one-sixth of the upper city, but we should probably assume that a somewhat wider expanse was actually laid waste. By assigning eight acres to the 166 mansiones, we obtain an average of 20 to the acre; which would imply one house for every 250 square yards or so — that is to say, on a lot 30 by 75 feet. Thus, even if we decrease our average to 15 or 16 *mansiones* per acre, we still have to imagine three-fifths of Lincoln's population about 1066 crowded into the oldest enclosure, while the lower city in large part lay vacant. Perhaps there was a separate mercantile settlement by the river, but on this point Domesday, which provides much detail concerning the holdings of burgesses in the surrounding fields, has nothing to say.[2] And as yet the silence of the records has not been made up for by research in other directions.

On the whole, it would seem incredible that so many men would have congregated at Lincoln, the site of a flourishing town under the Romans, except through the attraction of commercial advantage. The men of Torksey are described as enjoying rather unusual customs besides those held in common with the men of Lincoln.[3] Surely we shall not go wrong in imagining that the history of this city, like that of York, turned upon the establishment of a Danish trading settlement.

However that may be, the topography of Lincoln was revolutionized under William I. In addition to the extensive changes necessitated by the new castle, came now the enclosure of wide lands for the benefit of the recently installed bishop and the raising of his glorious minster. Between these two encroachments, the upper city was reduced to half its previous size. Was one consequence the construction of the new port to the north, with earthen ramparts attached to the ancient wall?[4] Again no defin te

[1] *D.B.*, I, 336[b]; Armitage, *Norman Castles*, p. 167.

[2] See above, pp. 95, 103.

[3] See above, p. 117.

[4] New Port, of course, meant new borough (cf. Norwich, below, p. 199). Marrat labelled it 'Saxon Town,' but that was merely an imaginative suggestion. Mr Hill tells me that traces of the

answer is forthcoming, but the extension could hardly have been earlier. Meanwhile great prosperity unquestionably came to the city 'below hill,' for it was in this region that the life of the mediaeval town came to be concentrated. Under Henry II, as we have seen, Lincoln ranked fourth among the king's boroughs;[1] and another proof of its increasing wealth and population may be seen in its southward expansion. On this side the old wall was razed, while those to east and west were extended to the river.[2] And eventually a new suburb, Wigford, was laid out beyond the bridge, protected throughout by embanked ditch or river.[3] Such, in conjectural outline, was the topographical development of Lincoln — a subject of vital interest to all students of British history. Soon, we may hope, it will be adequately treated.

Both York and Lincoln thus began as legionary fortresses, which, even in Roman times, grew into flourishing urban centres — one with an extension of the original walls and one without it. There were many other such constructions and, in the same way, their later history depended on local circumstances. Deva seems to have remained purely military to the end. Glevum, on the other hand, remained a town rather than a camp after army headquarters had been moved west to Isca Silurum. All three *castra* were built after the same plan and contained about fifty acres each.[4] The third, of course, has lain vacant since the fifth century, but the other two have been English boroughs for somewhat over a thousand years.

Thanks to the Anglo-Saxon Chronicle, we know that Chester was first occupied and repaired under Edward the Elder, but we are left to guess that the sudden prominence of Gloucester was due to similar action under his father.[5] In any case, both became shire boroughs and both inevitably prospered with the development of Irish trade. From the records alone we should judge that Chester and Gloucester, in the twelfth

---

northern wall are still visible, and that a court roll of the fourteenth century proves that there were lateral walls also.

[1] Above, p. 165.

[2] Cf. London and Cologne, above, pp. 24, 188. No attempt has been made to date these changes at Lincoln.

[3] Mr Hill tells me that there was certainly a stone wall along the bank of Sincil dyke between Great Bargate and Little Bargate. Marrat shows walls extending on both sides to the north, but whether they were of stone or not remains doubtful. This whole strip was evidently made from reclaimed marsh — when is not known. In the Middle Ages, as is proved by a court roll of the fourteenth century, Brayford Pool reached much farther south than it does at present. In connection with the age of the Lincoln suburbs, it should be noted that Henry II's charter (*S.C.*, p. 197) refers to *quatuor divisas civitatis*.

[4] Collingwood, *Archaeology of Roman Britain*, pp. 15–25: Chester, 56 acres; Caerleon, 50 acres; Gloucester, slightly less. Cf. York, $52\frac{1}{2}$ acres; Lincoln, 41 acres.

[5] See above, p. 56.

century the two greatest towns of the west coast after Bristol, must have outgrown such narrow defenses as they originally had.[1]   And this supposition is confirmed by recent archaeological research.   As yet, however, attention has been concentrated on the Roman walls, and it is impossible to say exactly when the additions were made.[2]   Until the matter is decided by experts, we may only assume that the expansion came under the Normans rather than at an earlier period.

Meanwhile London, Colchester, Exeter, Leicester, Canterbury, Winchester, and other thriving towns were still contained within their ancient fortifications.   For additional examples of striking urban development, as attested by the map, we must turn to Saxon and Danish foundations.

2. TOPOGRAPHICAL STUDY: MEDIAEVAL FOUNDATIONS

Of the boroughs known to have been built in the tenth century, all whose dimensions are ascertainable resembled Bath rather than London or even Canterbury.   As we have seen, the inner wall at Witham enclosed only $9\frac{1}{2}$ acres, and that of Eddisbury only a little more.[3]   Some important boroughs were larger, but the few of which we may be certain never reached an area of fifty acres.[4]   Consequently, whenever the borough came to attract an extensive population, it quickly outgrew its origi-

---

[1] See above, pp. 109, 129; also Appendices III, V.

[2] See the plan in G. Ormerod, *The History of the County Palatine and City of Chester* (London, 1882), I, 180, which shows mediaeval Chester approximately twice the size of the ancient *castrum*.   The enlargement was made by widening the city about one-third and extending the walls south to the castle and the river.   The course of the walls that were torn down clearly appears from the outline of the later streets.   For plans of Gloucester, see *Archaeological Journal*, LVII (1921), 266, and *Transactions of the Bristol and Gloucestershire Archaeological Society*, I (1876), 156.   The latter, in particular, shows that at Gloucester, also, an enlarged borough was created by removing a Roman wall and building new fortifications to include a settlement by the river.   The location of the cathedral and the castle would indicate that the extension was at least planned as early as the Norman Conquest.

[3] Above, p. 58.

[4] Above, pp. 56, n. 11, 58.   The well known earthworks at Wallingford and Wareham, though often attributed to Britons or Romans, are thought to be Saxon by Mrs Armitage (*Norman Castles*, p. 28).   There is certainly no reason for considering them Roman, and some evidence that they were not (see Hope, in *Archaeological Journal*, LX, 74, n. 4).   Both boroughs were assuredly Saxon fortresses, but we can hardly be sure that either now remains as it was in the tenth century.   The fortifications enclose more space than any known to date from that age — Wareham about eighty acres and Wallingford only slightly less.   Such an area, on the other hand, would be about right for either settlement in the twelfth century.   Wallingford, though not a town of first rank, was then important enough to receive extensive liberties from Henry II (see above, pp. 130, 169).   At the same time Wareham was held by the earl of Gloucester.   None of its early charters have come down to us, but it was undoubtedly a relatively prosperous borough, able to pay John a fine of a hundred marks to secure the town at fee-farm: J. Hutchens, *The History and Antiquities of the County of Dorset* (London, 1774), I, 18.   It would therefore seem more likely that the existing ramparts of Wallingford and of Wareham are the remains of subsequent, rather than primitive borough defenses.

nal defenses. And the normal Danish or Saxon fortification was merely a ditch and a timbered embankment, which could be easily levelled and soon forgotten. In many cases all vestiges of the old *enceinte* are lost beneath the streets and houses of a modern town, and only chance excavation, by revealing a filled entrenchment, may indicate the ancient boundary.

Such a happy chance led to discoveries of the most remarkable character at Nottingham. Here, the Anglo-Saxon Chronicle tells us, the Danes built a borough which in 919 was captured and repaired by Edward the Elder. Two years later the king built a second borough south of the Trent, but the historic Nottingham has always been the construction to the north.[1] This, according to Domesday, was a small affair. In the time of King Edward it contained less than two hundred households, and a third of them were lost at the Conquest. Its population appears to have been purely agricultural, including at the top an aristocracy of *cnihtas* and at the bottom a class of peasants — villeins and bordars.[2] The importance of Nottingham as one of the famous Five Boroughs must have rested on military strength, rather than on population and wealth.

Domesday, however, tells also of noteworthy changes effected by the Normans. In one brief sentence we have an obscure reference to the great new castle erected about half a mile from the centre of the old borough[3] — an unusual procedure, but one presumably dictated by the strategic advantage of the location selected. Was it because of the intervening gap that the sheriff, Hugh Fitz-Baldric, was then inspired to construct a new borough? At any rate, he did so, placing there thirteen new houses.[4] And by 1086 his action seems to have led others to follow his example. We are told that Roger de Busli, on land that previously contained three *mansiones*, has put up eleven houses and let them at 5*d.* each.[5] William Peverel, constable of the castle, besides certain *domus equitum*, now holds forty-eight *domus mercatorum*, from which he gets 36*s.* — i.e., 9*d.* each. And merchants are reported also in other houses, some of them the earlier property of *cnihtas*. 'Seventeen houses and six other houses are *in fossato burgi*' — a remark that makes us wonder if the addition of the new borough had not rendered part of the ancient fortifications obsolete.

---

[1] Above, pp. 55–58; Armitage, *Norman Castles*, pp. 44–46.

[2] Above, pp. 79, 92.

[3] *D.B.*, I, 280: 'Willelmo Pevrel concessit rex x acras terrae ad faciendum pomerium.' See Armitage, *op. cit.*, p. 176.

[4] 'Ipse tamen Hugo in terra comitis in novo burgo statuit xiii domus quae antea non fuerant, apponens eas in censu veteris burgi.'

[5] 'Rogerus de Busli habet in Snotingham iii mansiones in quibus sedent xi domus reddentes iiii sol. et vii den.'

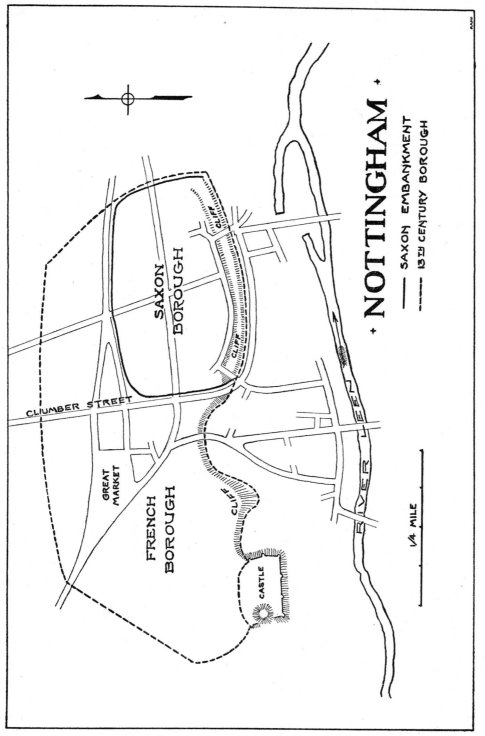

+ NOTTINGHAM +

———— SAXON EMBANKMENT

– – – – 13ᵀᴴ CENTURY BOROUGH

PLATE V.

This is all that Domesday has to tell, but much additional information has been uncovered through local research. Long before Maitland gave the matter fresh significance, it had been familiar to legal historians that in the Middle Ages Nottingham was divided between two customs, one for the French and one for the English borough.[1] Furthermore every student of the town's history knew that the boundary between the two boroughs was the line of a street anciently called Cow Lane, but later changed to the more elegant Clumber Street; and that the centres of trade and municipal government had from an early time lain to the west, in the French borough. But it was left for W. H. Stevenson first to determine the exact limits of the Saxon borough. Starting with the fact that a railway cutting in 1890 had disclosed a filled ditch, some ten feet wide by seven deep, he sought to trace the course of the embankment that had once stood inside it. Clues were provided by the peculiar arrangement of certain streets and by the names originally borne by others. And eventually he was able to show that the ancient Nottingham had been contained within a rectangular space of about thirty-nine acres, of which three sides were formed by an earthen rampart and the fourth by the cliff overlooking the Trent valley.[2]

Standing in a position of such commanding strength athwart the highroad from London to York, the military importance of Nottingham leaps to the eye. It is equally obvious, however, that the beginning of the famous commercial town was rather the new foundation by Hugh Fitz-Baldric. The original boundary of his French borough remains doubtful, but would most naturally have been formed by extending the northern rampart of the old borough southwest to the castle. In any case, the ancient earthworks were levelled and forgotten when a stone wall was later built to enclose a space some three times the size of the Saxon borough — and this in turn was finally razed to meet the needs of the present industrial town. A clearer example of urban growth induced by commercial expansion is hard to imagine.

To-day Norwich is quite eclipsed by metropolitan Nottingham, but in the Middle Ages the former was many times greater. For one thing, Norwich had become much more of a town before the Norman Conquest. Domesday, omitting London and Winchester, ranks it second only to York; as an aid-paying borough under Henry II it stands third, yielding precedence only to London and York.[3] In the time of King Edward,

---

[1] *H.E.L.*, I, 647.

[2] The main facts were stated by Stevenson in *V.H.C. Nottingham*, I, 297; but the details of his discovery remain hidden in the Nottingham *Daily Guardian*, July 23, 1901, together with the plan used as the basis for Plate V. See also his article, 'The Great Ditch,' *Transactions of the Thoroton Society*, xv (1911), 151 ff.

[3] See Appendices III, VI.

we are told, Norwich counted 1,320 burgess households; now, says Domesday, there are left only 665 that pay custom.[1] At least 98 houses have been destroyed to make room for the castle; some have been given to the newly installed bishop or to other men who refuse to render the old dues; many lie vacant for a variety of reasons. The Conquest and the subsequent revolt of the earl have apparently ruined the landholding class, a considerable number of whom have fled to outlying estates in the county. But to make up for some of the loss, the conquerors have added a French borough, which in twenty years has come to contain 1 5 households.

From Domesday alone we should therefore suspect that at Norwich, as at Lincoln and Nottingham, revolutionary changes were under way during the years following 1066. And when we turn to examine local topography, the suspicion becomes a certainty. Thanks to the scholarly labor of W. H. Hudson, the map of mediaeval Norwich is already familiar to a host of students.[2] Although his books were written too early to profit by the work of Round on the origin of castles in England, Hudson avoided the common error of attributing to Britons, Romans, or Saxons all the salient features of his native town. As the author of *How the City of Norwich Grew into Shape*, he showed a lively sense of historical evolution. The ancient borough, he demonstrated, centered at Tombland within the loop of the river Wensum. Thither the main highways originally converged and thither led the oldest of the bridges, Fye Bridge.[3] The exact limits of the tenth-century borough are unknown, but it presumably included the hill and excluded the marshes to the east. If not originally demanded, an embankment to defend the entire loop would be necessitated by such a population as that described in Domesday. And the natural line of fortification would be the ridge of Ber Street and the small stream known as the Cockey.[4]

[1] The Domesday statistics on Norwich utterly defy intelligent analysis. Repeated study merely tends to increase the suspicion that the returns were badly jumbled by clerks who had no understanding of the task before them. After the introductory statement concerning the 1,320 burgesses and the sokes to which they belonged *T.R.E.*, the figures cease to make sense. We should, in particular, like to know what happened to the 655 burgesses who have disappeared since 1066. We hear of 297 houses that lie vacant or have been destroyed, of various other *domus* and *mansurae*, from which the king gets nothing, and of 480 *bordarii* who render no customs. If we add the latter in, the total is too large; if we leave them out, it is too small. See above, p. 79, n. 7.

[2] See Plate VI. The most useful in the present connection of Hudson's numerous works is *How the City of Norwich Grew into Shape* (Norwich, 1896). The fact that Hudson, with all the authorities of his day, attributed the castle to the Saxon period threw his whole study out of perspective; for the hill, with no castle on its crown, may be seen as a natural position round which to construct an early borough.

[3] The antiquity of Fybridge was proved by the discovery of the piles on which it had once rested: Hudson, in *Norfolk Archaeology*, XIII (1898).

[4] J. Kirkpatrick, *The Streets and Lanes of the City of Norwich*, ed Hudson (Norwich, 1889), pp. 9,

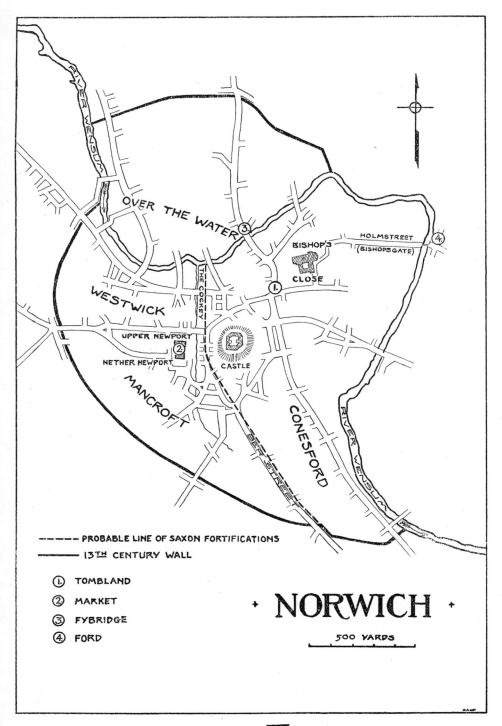

RIVER WENSUM

OVER THE WATER

③

BISHOP'S

HOLMSTREET
(BISHOPSGATE)

④

CLOSE

①

WESTWICK

THE COCKEY

UPPER NEWPORT

②

NETHER NEWPORT

CASTLE

MANCROFT

BERSTREET

CONESFORD

RIVER WENSUM

- - - - - PROBABLE LINE OF SAXON FORTIFICATIONS

――――― 13TH CENTURY WALL

① TOMBLAND

② MARKET

③ FYBRIDGE

④ FORD

✦ NORWICH ✦

500 YARDS

PLATE VI.

Certainly we cannot well suppose a wider Norwich in the eleventh century than would thus be contained in the river loop. Domesday tells us that 98 *mansiones* were destroyed for the castle, and we know that the latter with the outer bailey included at most eight acres.[1] At this same ratio the entire population of 1,320 households could have been accommodated within 110 acres — and considerably more than that lay between the Wensum and the Ber Street ridge. This conjecture, moreover, finds support from the location of the French borough just to the west of the Cockey. Though later organized as Mancroft Leet, it would seem originally to have been called New Port — as indicated by the two streets that led to the great market.[2] And as at Nottingham, it was this section that constituted the centre of trade and municipal activity in the twelfth century; for in the meantime the old borough had been completely transformed. The castle was placed squarely across its principal lines of communication and to the east of Tombland almost all of the river loop was devoted to the new cathedral and its clergy. Thereby that quarter gained a fresh loveliness, but the history of Norwich as a town became the history of the French borough. From there the customs founded by William I spread throughout Conesford, Westwick, and the suburb that eventually grew up on the other side of the river, all of which were enclosed within a new wall by the end of the thirteenth century.

Unfortunately, neither Domesday nor archaeological remains tell us much about the borough of Northampton, which was destined to make a sensational advance in the period following the Norman Conquest. Northampton also began as a fortified position of the tenth century and, as at Norwich, the original borough was apparently built round a commanding hill in the curve of a river. This hill the Conqueror appropriated for his castle and, again as at Norwich, local topography was rudely disturbed. In her recent chapter on the history of Northampton Miss Cam has pointed out that the older section of the borough lay west of the Roman road; that the thirteenth-century borough was centered rather to the east of it, about the market square.[3] After reading Domes-

---

101–104; Armitage, *Norman Castles*, p. 174. Hudson was inclined to regard both Conesford and Westwick as having lain within the primitive borough, but they may have begun as Danish settlements outside the original ramparts. And it should be remembered that the ending 'gate' is no more certainly a mark of Scandinavian creation at Norwich than it is at York. Altogether it would seem unlikely that the earliest borough could have included even the entire river loop, and as late as 1066 it could hardly have extended beyond the Cockey. Otherwise, there would have been no reason for a new borough in that direction.

[1] Armitage, p. 176.

[2] Kirkpatrick, *Streets and Lanes*, p. 106. The modern names are Bethel Street and St Giles Street, but originally they were known as Upper and Nether Newport.

[3] Helen M. Cam, in *V.H.C. Northampton*, III, 1 ff., 30. Miss Cam's description emphasizes topography and is illustrated by good maps.

day's casual remark about a *novus burgus*[1] and comparing the maps of
Northampton, Norwich, and Nottingham, it is hard to avoid the conclusion that urban development was much the same in all three.   Perhaps
local research will discover some means of testing an hypothesis that so
plainly obtrudes itself.   For the present nothing more can be done than
to suggest it.

Cambridge offers a somewhat different problem, but one that after all
involves the same fundamentals.   Across the river from the main part
of the modern town lie the remains of a considerable earthwork, which
from time to time has aroused the interest of many scholars, among them
W. H. St John Hope.[2]   As traced by Hope, it was an oblong rampart
with rounded corners, enclosing an area of twenty-eight acres.   He considered it a Roman work, but Mrs Armitage has classed it among the
boroughs of Danish origin.[3]   So far as the present study is concerned,
it is of little consequence who first designed the work; what is of greater
interest is its relation to the mediaeval town of Cambridge.   Considerably
before Hope wrote his paper on this subject, T. D. Atkinson had argued
that the original Cambridge was near the castle; although a village may
have existed south of the river, all ten wards described in Domesday lay
to the north.[4]   His contention, it is true, has against it the weighty opinion of Maitland and of Mr Arthur Gray;[5] but let us reconsider the problem.

Domesday tells us that there were ten wards in the borough of Cambridge, but that one ward, the sixth, has disappeared through the destruction of 27 houses for the castle.   The nine others are then described
in detail, totalling 373 houses, of which 49 are waste.[6]   Out of that number, however, we note that, while 14 are distributed among five wards,
11 lie in the third and 24 in the fourth.   Assuming, as would indeed seem

---

[1] *D.B.*, I, 219: 'Praeter hos sunt modo in novo burgo XL burgenses in dominio regis Willelmi.'

[2] W. H. St John Hope, 'The Norman Origin of Cambridge Castle,' *Proceedings of the Cambridge Antiquarian Society*, XI (1903–06), 340, 344; see Plate VII.

[3] *Norman Castles*, p. 55; above, p. 56, n. 5.   On the Roman origin of Cambridge, see particularly A. Gray, *The Town of Cambridge* (Cambridge, 1925), pp. 1 ff.   Mr Gray advances good reasons for identifying Bede's Grantchester with the Cambridge earthwork, but seems not to realize that the Saxon *burh* might be that same earthwork (pp. 6 ff.).   And how could there be a Saxon town that was not also the Saxon borough?

[4] T. D. Atkinson and J. W. Clark, *Cambridge Described and Illustrated* (London, 1897), p. 8.

[5] Maitland, *Township and Borough*, p. 99; A. Gray, *The Dual Origin of the Town of Cambridge* (Cambridge Antiquarian Society, 1908), pp. 24 ff., and *The Town of Cambridge*, pp. 21 ff.

[6] *D.B.*, I, 189.   The Domesday entry suffers from the obscurity that is chronic in that record, but the general meaning seems plain enough.   The first ward is given 54 houses, with the remark that it once counted for two, but that 27 houses had been destroyed for the castle.   Since the sixth ward is left out, it had apparently ceased to exist and the few remaining houses in it had been annexed to the first ward.

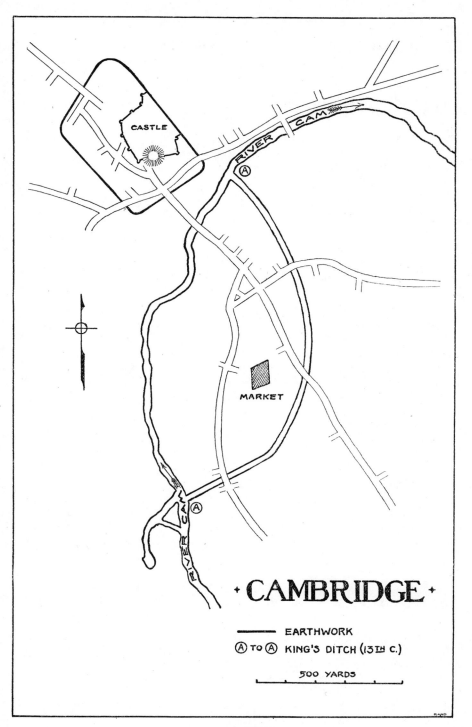

CASTLE

RIVER CAM

Ⓐ

MARKET

RIVER CAM

Ⓐ

• CAMBRIDGE •

——— EARTHWORK

Ⓐ TO Ⓐ KING'S DITCH (13ᵀᴴ C.)

500 YARDS

PLATE VII.

probable, that such extensive waste in two wards was likewise the result of castle-building, we obtain a total of 62 houses destroyed out of 400, or 15½ per cent. As to the wards, Domesday says that the ten lay *in burgo* — an expression by which the survey regularly means inside the walls.[1] We should therefore suppose that the wards were all contained within some fortified area, either that described by Hope or another. But the remains of the castle are still visible and Hope shows that it, together with the attached bailey, were entirely enclosed by the ancient embankment. The proportion of the former (4½ acres) to that of the latter (28 acres) is almost exactly 16 per cent; and we have just estimated the percentage of houses destroyed for the castle at 15½.

So, although these figures are by no means conclusive, the weight of the evidence would tend to support the contention that the Domesday borough of Cambridge was wholly contained within the earthwork beyond the river. And should any one consider fourteen houses to the acre impossible for an early borough, let him turn to the estimates for Lincoln and Norwich.[2] Furthermore, in dealing with matters of relative size in the Middle Ages we must apply the mediaeval scale. A borough of 28 acres at Cambridge compares well with one of 22 at Maldon, of 24 at Thetford, and of 39 at Nottingham. Contemporary York, with nearly five times the population, needed an area of over a hundred acres, but Cambridge did not. And since the wards were probably military districts connected with the defense of the wall,[3] they did not have to be of any particular size.

To-day Cambridge is not a large town, but it spreads over a tremendous area compared with that of the little earthwork beyond the bridge. The concept of a Cambridge so much smaller than the present town will doubtless be rejected by all who would carry urban life far back into the Saxon period, but in the face of the available evidence, that is hard to do. The sources seem to leave us no choice but to account for the Cambridge south of the river as largely a Norman development. Although Domesday gives us no details, it is not improbable that the conquest of 1066 produced as great changes at Cambridge as it did in many other boroughs. By the thirteenth century Cambridge centered to the south, where an earlier village may well have been absorbed into an expanding mercantile

---

[1] See above, p. 77.

[2] Above, pp. 193, 199. This evidence was not taken into account by Maitland (*Township and Borough*, p. 100), and it is the best that we have. Contemporary villages were not forced to contain their houses within walls, and later boroughs were often laid out with more space inside the fortifications than proved to be needed. It should be noted that the *minutae mansiones* at York did not each have a frontage of fifty feet, but that all seven of them were built on such a lot (above, p. 190).

[3] Maitland, *op. cit.*, p. 50; above, p. 181.

settlement. Its eastern boundary was the King's Ditch, which, in spite of all argument to the contrary, was evidently a new work constructed for the defense of a town that was hardly old.[1] To Maitland's eyes Cambridge at that time was a very rural community; but his description should not make us forget that, in the twelfth century, Cambridge was a ranking borough of no mean importance.[2] Though it may seem small to us, it was not then insignificant. That it enjoyed a monopoloy of trade along its slender stream is proved by Henry I's writ.[3] It was only after the founding of Bishop's Lynn that Cambridge slipped back in the race for material prosperity.[4] All admirers of its illustrious university are assuredly thankful that the town has not become another Nottingham, but the fact remains that there was a day when its future may well have appeared less academic.

By way of contrast we may now turn to a borough that can boast neither Roman foundation, a proud record in tenth-century combats, nor official recognition as the *chef lieu* of a shire; but which, none the less, seems to have been constructed before the Norman Conquest. Although documentary evidence on its early history is almost wholly lacking, local topography reveals the main facts of its development with amazing distinctness. Bristol is first mentioned in the Anglo-Saxon Chronicle under the year 1052, when Harold is said to have come thither by ship; and again in 1063 we are told that he sailed thence.[5] At that time Bristol was plainly a well known seaport; but it must also have been a borough, for it is so referred to in 1067. A son of Harold, says the chronicler, then crossed over from Ireland with a naval force and would have stormed the *burh*, but the *burhwaru* fought stoutly against him and he could gain nothing.[6] These sturdy men of Bristol were surely burgesses of the old type. Even if the Normans had had time to build a new borough at Bristol, its inhabitants could hardly have played the rôle described by the Anglo-Saxon historian. Nor had the defense of the country been taken over by French knights garrisoned in a French castle. Bristol castle, which first appears in the Chronicle under the year 1088, was presumably the work of Geoffrey, bishop of Coutances, whom Domesday

---

[1] T. D. Atkinson, in *Proceedings of the Cambridge Antiquarian Society*, XI, 251; J. W. Clark and A. Gray, *Old Plans of Cambridge* (Cambridge, 1921), p. xxiii. Mr Gray thinks that the ditch was old, but there is no evidence of its existence before the thirteenth century. It is said that Henry III intended to erect a wall along it and that the project was never carried out.

[2] See Appendices III, V, VI.

[3] Above, p. 131, n. 5.

[4] Above, p. 141.

[5] *A.S.C.*, II, 149 (1052), 161 (1063).

[6] *A.S.C.*, II, 173 (1067).

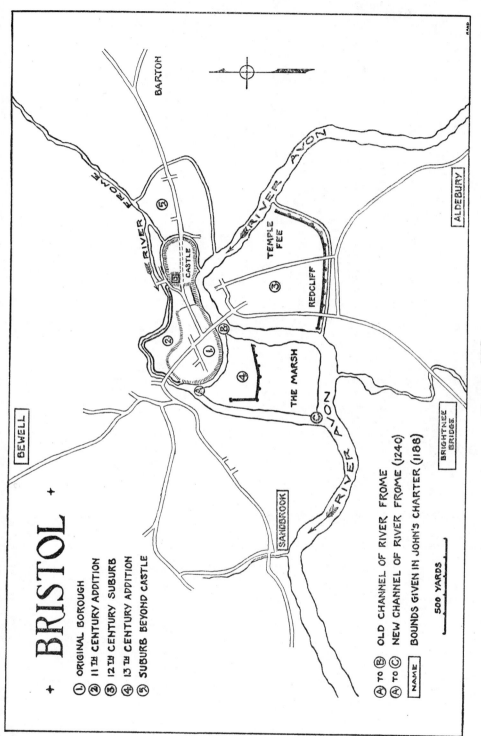

+ BRISTOL +

1. ORIGINAL BOROUGH
2. 11TH CENTURY ADDITION
3. 12TH CENTURY SUBURB
4. 13TH CENTURY ADDITION
5. SUBURB BEYOND CASTLE

(A) TO (B) OLD CHANNEL OF RIVER FROME
(A) TO (C) NEW CHANNEL OF RIVER FROME (1240)
BOUNDS GIVEN IN JOHN'S CHARTER (1188)
NAME

500 YARDS

BEWELL

BARTON

ALDEBURY

RIVER FROME

CASTLE

RIVER AVON

TEMPLE FEE

REDCLIFF

THE MARSH

SANDBROOK

RIVER AVON

BRIGHTNEE BRIDGE

PLATE VIII.

reports to be farming the borough as an appurtenance of the manor of Barton and rendering for the two 110 marks of silver.[1]

If from such paltry records we now turn to the map, we at once obtain additional information of first-rate importance. The old borough of Bristol is found to have occupied a headland of great natural strength, round which the Frome was forced to flow before reaching the Avon.[2] Within the small loop thus formed the old wall of Bristol enclosed all the high ground. And since this area was only about sixteen acres, the Conqueror was given the choice of destroying the borough or placing his castle outside the loop. He took the latter alternative, and as a consequence Bristol castle arose across the narrow neck between the two rivers, exactly like a stopper in a bottle. And it was apparently about this time that an outer wall was built along the Frome from the northeast corner of the castle to the middle of the eastern borough wall. But, even with this addition, Bristol was badly cramped. Across the Frome to the north the land was pre-empted by religious establishments, and to the south a great marsh extended to the Avon, the bank of which became precipitous shortly after it reached the borough wall. To the westward the way was blocked by the castle. Thus the natural line of growth led southeast across the Avon, where a considerable territory seems to have been thickly built over by the end of the twelfth century. Henry II extended at least some liberties of Bristol to his men dwelling in the marsh by the bridge, and Henry III confirmed the same privileges to the men of Redcliff. In fact, it was by royal command that these burgesses joined in the great Bristol projects of the thirteenth century.[3]

In the first place, a new channel for the Frome was dug southward through the Avon marsh, thereby providing an improved waterway and greatly extended wharves, as well as permitting the construction of a new urban quarter beyond the old riverbed. Next came the erection of a fine stone bridge across the Avon, and eventually the enclosure of the Redcliff and Temple sections with a wall and ditch. And by that time another suburb had been fortified — the town that had developed between the castle and the manor of Barton.[4] By the fourteenth century, consequently, the borough had increased five-fold and under Edward III was created a separate county, with a territory extending to the ancient metes

[1] Armitage, *Norman Castles*, p. 110; *D.B.*, I, 163. For analysis of the Bristol charters, see above p. 133 ff.

[2] See Plate VIII, based on the maps in W. Hunt, *Bristol* (London, 1887), where (chs. I–II) the general topography of the town is well described. Cf. E. W. W. Veale, *Burgage Tenure in Mediaeval Bristol* (Bristol Record Society, 1931), pp. 3 ff.

[3] *Bristol Charters*, ed. N. D. Harding (Bristol Record Society, 1930), pp. 4, 18, 22.

[4] The exact chronology of all these changes has never been worked out, but we may be sure that they all came between the Norman Conquest and Edward III's charter.

named in John's charter of 1188.[1]   Beginning as a walled enclosure half
the size of Danish Nottingham, Bristol under the Normans overtook and
passed the great city of York.   And this, in the absence of all prestige
either as a shire borough or a cathedral town, was accomplished by virtue
of the newly developed trade with Ireland.

These are only a few examples of burghal growth in England, selected
because the pertinent evidence has been made readily accessible.   They
are obviously inadequate as the basis for rigorous generalization concerning all boroughs; but such as they are, these bits of investigation indicate
certain probabilities which must be considered by every student of mediaeval English culture.   The fundamental similarity of urban growth,
whether from a Roman *civitas* or a subsequent construction, and whether
in Britain or on the Continent, is too striking to be overlooked.   In spite
of local variations, the development of York, as proved by the map, was
essentially parallel to that of Cologne, or of Paris, or of a host of other
cities; the growth of Bristol, or of Nottingham, was fundamentally the
same as that of Ghent or of Magdeburg.   In the case of all these towns
the crucial period was especially the eleventh century, when the revival of
European commerce brought the increasing population that henceforth
governed their destinies.   Thus, although we remain in doubt concerning
the particular histories of most boroughs, we are led to expect that on
examination they will fit into the same general pattern of development.[2]

---

[1] *Bristol Charters*, pp. 142–64, and frontispiece (Rocque's map of 1742).   The perambulation here
described obviously followed the *metas ville* referred to in John's charter, viz., Bewell, Sandbrook,
Brightnee Bridge, and Aldebury.   All persons dwelling within these bounds, as I understand the
grant, were not to be burgesses; but those who were burgesses were guaranteed their free tenures
and other liberties.   The territory thus described was certainly not the borough, and yet it somehow belonged to the borough.   Was it not the ancient hundred of Bristol?   The court of Bristol was
called the hundred — a custom that takes us back to the Domesday account of Chester.   See above,
pp. 111, 134.

[2] Most of the tenth-century boroughs remain unexplored for the sort of data that are here emphasized.   In particular, we should wish that local historians might follow up Mary Bateson's hints
with regard to Hereford and Shrewsbury (*E.H.R.*, xv, 305, 307).   The need of further research on
the Cinque Ports has already been remarked.   Some of them must probably continue to be mysteries,
but more can surely be learned about the early development of Dover.   From the famous story in
the Anglo-Saxon Chronicle it is evident that the original *burh* was on top of the cliff (Armitage,
Norman Castles, p. 139).   What was the relation between that and the port?   As an example of what
may still be done to explain the origin of a well known town, a few random observations may be made
on Oxford.   Mr Salter tells me that no study of the question has been undertaken, but that, if the
borough was once smaller than it was in the thirteenth century, its most likely boundary on the
east would have been Cat Street.   And when we turn to the splendid maps appended to Wood's
City of Oxford (Oxford Historical Society, 1889), vol. i, they at once suggest that the original wall
ran between Cat Street and Schools Street and probably excluded St Frideswyde's and the Grey
Friars on the south.   Under such conditions Oxford would constitute a borough of about forty acres
quite like ancient Nottingham — a rectangle with its centre at Carfax, where two main roads intersected.   Perhaps some one will consider this hypothesis to be at least worth the testing.

The validity of such an assumption is of course a matter to be determined by the intensive research that is so greatly needed. Investigation of local topography has commonly been carried out in isolation. The history of each community has been studied with slight reference to others of the same type either in England or on the Continent. To show how much may be gained by even an elementary comparison has been the chief object of the present chapter. Once the importance of the subject is appreciated by the many scholars equipped to pursue it, splendid results should quickly follow; for the admirable researches mentioned above have proved what can be done with sources that remain too little used.

In the first place, old lines of wall and ditch deserve special attention, since through the changing outline of the *enceinte* we gain direct evidence of urban growth in the Middle Ages. Secondly, not merely the fortified, but the populated area must be studied. And this problem has two phases: the age and size of extramural suburbs and, particularly within old Roman walls, the actual extent of settlement at a given time. Occasionally written records may supply hints for such an inquiry, but its chief basis must always be archaeology. Then too, a great deal more than has ever been attempted can be done with comparative urban topography. The arrangement of streets with regard to wall, market place, river, and highway is often eloquent. And how do these matters compare in old and new boroughs, or in England and on the Continent? Philology can also be made to contribute valuable testimony, for sometimes the derivation of local names will indicate facts that no other approach can determine. Lastly, much remains to be found out as to the antiquity of town churches. When and how new parishes came to be created in most boroughs is still an obscure problem, but one on which some definite information should reward the careful searcher.

Compared with what we should like to know, the scattered facts that have been assembled above seem few indeed. But they have an interest out of all proportion to their number, for they bring to our concept of the mediaeval borough a graphic touch otherwise unobtainable. And they will be seen to add much strength to the final conclusions that must now be drawn.

3. The Social Transition in the Boroughs

The twelfth-century borough is very familiar. We have no trouble in recognizing it as a town — such a town as was still to be met with in any English county down to the Industrial Revolution. It was, of course smaller and dirtier and more crowded than are most towns of to-day. It was hidden behind walls that have now largely disappeared. It was populated by men who wore strange clothes and carried stranger weapons.

But fundamentally it seems to us quite comprehensible, for its life was predominantly mercantile. Its shops and warehouses, its markets and wharves, its homes of traders and artisans, spread below an occasional church tower or feudal battlement, constituted a picture that we know, and know intimately.

It is true that the town-dwelling class was then much more sharply distinguished from the rural classes than is the case at present, but that fact does not prevent our feeling well acquainted with the burgess. Indeed, it is easier for us to understand his position in the world than to understand that of the villein, or even that of the baron, — so bourgeois is our modern society. We do not have to be told what is implied by free urban status. It is rather feudal than burgage tenure that has to be explained to us. We sympathize with the burgess in his insistence on what to us seem ordinary rights, and in his demand for a court to enforce them. We readily perceive why townsmen objected to seignorial exploitation and were willing to pay well for the chance to manage their own affairs.

The difficult problem for the student of mediaeval life, accordingly, has never been to describe the borough in the twelfth century, but rather to account for its sudden prominence. Thenceforth the town attained a constantly mounting importance in state and society. Why had it earlier been so obscure?

Since the majority of boroughs had long occupied well recognized positions on the map, it was at first asserted that the mediaeval towns, in all fundamental respects, were merely surviving Roman cities or newer foundations made in imitation of them. But this theory, when attacked by historians of the Germanist school, was shown to be based on little besides sheer assumption. It followed, therefore, that the borough was essentially a mediaeval product; that it somehow arose or was made in the period following the barbarian invasion of Britain. And the Germanist explanation hardly advanced beyond such a vague generalization; for every attempt to frame a simpler and more definite formula ended in confusion. To derive the twelfth-century borough from the borough-building activities of Dane and Saxon in the tenth century, despite all continuity of name, proved impossible. When one set of boroughs had been reasonably accounted for, it only became more apparent that another had not been. So Maitland's vivid picture of the old military borough left the mercantile borough an unsolved mystery. So Mary Bateson, by demonstrating the revolutionary nature of the new borough, made its connection with the original borough more obscure than ever.[1]

Meanwhile, on the Continent, similar sources had led to similar specu-

---

[1] See above, pp. 15 ff., 120 ff., 144.

lation, which had ended in a similar *impasse*. But eventually the difficulty was avoided by refusing to take for granted that an older structure,
whether called *civitas*, *urbs*, *burgus*, or anything else, was originally more
than it was proved to be by contemporary evidence.[1] The same procedure must be followed in dealing with the English towns. However natural it may be to regard the twelfth-century borough as a mere continuation of the earlier institution that bore the same name, such a
presupposition is unwarranted and misleading. The primitive borough
must be studied quite apart from all associations made familiar by later
usage.

This approach to the subject inevitably leads to the acceptance of
Maitland's central thesis.[2] The older sources clearly depict a borough
the essential importance of which was military. Some boroughs were Roman fortifications adapted to the needs of combatants in the ninth and
tenth centuries; others were new constructions. Many boroughs, particularly of the latter sort, were short-lived; but many, becoming identified with the freshly organized kingdom of England, continued as permanent centres of administration. And it would seem that the models for
these official boroughs were those of the old Roman cities which, because
of their strength, had continued to be used by the Saxon conquerors for
royal residences, courts, mints, and markets. But whatever the precise
origin of such administrative arrangements, it is they which appear to
have dominated the tenth-century borough, not mercantile activity.

Contemporary trade was virtually restricted to the petty exchange that
served to multiply local markets throughout the Dark Age; the most important transactions were in slaves and live stock. The commerce that
reached an English port from overseas was as yet too slight to differentiate the mass of its inhabitants from the population of the countryside.
As late as the reign of Edward Confessor we find almost no indication of
a socially distinct burgess class. On the contrary, the *burhwaru* of the
older type are revealed by the records to have been predominantly agrarian. The outstanding borough-dweller was the *cniht* — a man of thegnly
or semi-thegnly rank, an aristocrat who rode and fought, and who gained
a living from lands tilled by poorer dependents. If he had a house within
the walls, the location was dictated rather by gentlemanly preference than
by business opportunity. If a peasant came to reside there, he remained
a peasant. As yet there was no common borough privilege, no uniform
burgage tenure, no characteristic burgess law. Judicially and fiscally
burhwaru were still included under a territorial system devised for the

[1] See above, pp. 6 ff.
[2] See above, pp. 70 ff.

country at large. Such a borough lacked all the conspicuous features of urban life.[1]

Finding the original borough so widely and so profoundly different from the twelfth-century borough, we are constrained to suppose a transitional period when one was produced from the other. At what time, under what impetus, and by what process was the change effected? To formulate definite answers to all these questions is extremely difficult, perhaps impossible. Nevertheless, we are not without positive information on which to base a few intelligible conclusions.

That the later borough was fundamentally mercantile is beyond doubt. Commerce underlay its social structure, and on this, in turn, was built its legal and political constitution. To analyze the municipal charters is to be convinced that the boroughs to which they were granted were essentially trading communities. The typical burgess appears as a trader. His liberties, adapted to his own particular calling, serve to distinguish him from members of the military and agrarian classes. And when self-government emerges in the borough, it is so intimately associated with the bourgeois status of the new age, and so completely unknown in rural communities, that we are led to accept it as a peculiarly urban development.[2]

A borough of this sort could arise only in an age that had become extensively commercial. Such a complex institution could not be wrought by king or by army; it could not be created by official pronouncement. Nor could it grow from a mere cattle market. The development of urban life required commerce on a larger scale — on a European scale. That is why it is impossible to dissociate the history of English towns from the history of Continental towns. If in France and Germany trade was insufficient to permit extensive urban life before the later eleventh century, we should not expect flourishing towns in Britain during the ninth and tenth centuries. The burden of proof assuredly lies with those who assert that the early borough was more than a fortress and an administrative centre.

It is in this connection that Domesday Book is of inestimable value for the study of the towns. The great survey shows that the salient features of the old borough in 1066 were still military and agrarian. Exceptions there were, but the facts which Domesday emphasizes and reiterates on page after page are such as positively deny the existence of the twelfth-century urban system.[3] We are thus given no choice but to decide that

---

[1] See above, ch. III and pp. 73–74.

[2] See above, chs V–VI.

[3] See above, ch. IV.

in general the system was the product of the Norman period — whether through conscious reform on the part of the conquerors or through the effect of revolutionary forces stimulated by their conquest.

Neither factor can be ignored. The deliberate establishment by Norman barons of new boroughs after French models is incontestible.[1] And the same policy was followed by William himself. At Norwich, Nottingham, and Northampton it must have been he, rather than subordinates, who founded the French boroughs.[2] In such localities as these the new settlers are portrayed as the recipients of special privilege — the same kind of privilege that eventually came to characterize towns in all regions. At Hereford in 1086 this privilege was still restricted to the French colony; later it came to be shared by the whole borough. The twelfth-century custom of Shrewsbury seems to have been produced in the same way.[3] Moreover, there is excellent reason to suppose that a similar development took place at Nottingham; for the testimony of Domesday, together with the results of topographical study, leads us to believe that there also a new régime began in 1066.[4] Individually, the obscure references of the survey to French colonists in other boroughs prove little, but their cumulative effect is very considerable. If the establishment of 125 French traders at Norwich could lead to such tremendous results for the history of the town, what was the effect of the 145 who are reported at York?[5] And while these changes were being effected in lesser boroughs, what was happening at London? For every newcomer in any other single borough there must have been a dozen in the capital. Was their influence proportionately as great as it was at Hereford?

Altogether, the presumption is strong that in most old boroughs the establishment of uniform privilege came only under the Normans. The principal cause, we may well believe, was the insistence upon such guarantees by the mercantile class; but another fact powerfully contributed to the same result. Down to the Norman Conquest the borough remained the centre of political life in England. Saxon aristocrats not only owned land in the borough; they often lived there as well. We shall probably not be wrong in imagining the population of the old borough largely made up of an official, military class, together with its dependents.[6] But this situation was revolutionized by the Norman conqueror. After 1066 it was the castle which, as a fortress and as administrative headquarters

---

[1] See above, pp. 75 ff., 93, 120 ff.
[2] See above, pp. 196 ff.
[3] See above, p. 93.
[4] See above, pp. 79, 132 ff., 196 ff.
[5] See above, p. 189.
[6] See above, pp. 65 ff., 82, n. 2, 88 ff.; cf. p. 13, n. 2.

for the royal government, dominated the countryside.[1]   The feudal nobility did not live in boroughs, and these, consequently, were allowed to become exclusively bourgeois.

The change was not effected all at once. Years were spent in the erection of the new fortifications, the establishment of new tenants, and the organization of the new governmental system.   Many ancient arrangements were left to die a natural death together with the men who had upheld them.   As late as 1086 Domesday describes the boroughs as still being essentially what they were under Edward the Confessor.   And yet, by the time of Henry I, the old order has disappeared; the borough stands with its new social constitution complete.   Very likely we should attribute much to the energy and ability of that great king — notably the fixing of the *auxilia burgorum* and the perfection of the Cinque Ports confederacy.[2]   But more of the change must have come as the culmination of a slow process.   With the opening of the twelfth century, the older generation of men who had survived the Conquest was gone; and with it vanished the remnants of many an ancient and honorable institution.

William's inquest of 1086 asked for data on the comparative value of estates before and after 1066.   To secure the information, the king turned to the local courts, where juries were made up of men who knew the facts — largely therefore of the older inhabitants.[3]   Inevitably the final record stressed the easier régime of Edward and paid little attention to changes of custom under the Normans except those affecting agrarian arrangements.   In the boroughs, particularly, the reports seem to have been dictated by the dying generation, and what the jurors regarded as insignificant details are shown, in the light of later history, to have been matters of great importance.   If the juries had consisted of men with our appreciation of economic factors, the survey would undoubtedly have drawn a radically different picture.

The twenty years which Domesday passes over so lightly must have seen the beginnings of tremendous social changes.   The introduction of a feudal aristocracy affected, not merely the lords who were displaced, but likewise the mass of the people.   An event which could arbitrarily convert into villeinage the free tenure of thousands was no mere change of rulers.   And, as already remarked, the ultimate effect on the borough population was equally great.   Thegns and *cnihtas*, house-carls and *lidsmen*, disappeared from the scene.   Henceforth borough land, if possessed by a noble, was held by feudal tenure; if possessed by a townsman, was

[1] See above, pp. 52 ff., 155.
[2] See above, pp. 156 ff., 160 ff.
[3] See above, pp. 112 ff.

held by burgage tenure. As burgess status developed, a peculiar borough law emerged, which was enforced by a borough court of a different type. The gilds of the Saxon borough-thegns gave way to gilds merchant organized after a Continental pattern. *Burhwaru* became bourgeois.

To a considerable degree archaeological research has already confirmed the results of documentary study; has demonstrated that in physical aspect, as in social constitution, the boroughs were revolutionized under the Norman kings. The old Saxon *burh*, except when it was a repaired Roman city, enclosed a very restricted area — rarely if ever fifty acres, and often much less.[1] Nor was there usually, before 1066, any extension of the old ramparts. At York, to be sure, a Danish commercial suburb had appeared beyond the original walls by the middle of the eleventh century; but in this respect York was decidedly exceptional, and even there the new quarter seems to have remained unfortified.[2] In general, the boroughs of Edward the Confessor were still the defensible enclosures of the tenth century.

With the Norman Conquest there began a new era of construction in and about the old official centres. Some of it was necessitated by the devastation of warfare, but more was incidental to the ambitious projects immediately launched by the triumphant invader. Entire sections in the ancient boroughs were laid waste for the erection of churches and castles. For such purposes commanding positions were taken without regard for existing arrangements. But as old thoroughfares and markets were blocked, new ones were laid out, with new residential quarters to accommodate the ousted population, together with the immigrants whom commercial opportunity brought in constantly increasing streams. And to protect the enlarged settlements systematic fortification on an unprecedented scale was quickly undertaken.

It is, indeed, evident that this work of borough reconstruction was by no means a series of makeshifts. The map of a town like Nottingham or Norwich proves that to a large degree the future development of the community was consciously provided for.[3] Within the greater Roman cities, of course, there was no occasion for such extensive alteration. We as yet have very slight information as to the precise effect of the Conquest upon most of them, but there can be little doubt that for them, as for the other boroughs, the year 1066 inaugurated a period of amazingly rapid growth. The more one examines the subject, the more he tends to be convinced that, except for the outline of an occasional Roman wall, the domi-

[1] Above, pp. 58 ff., 195 ff.
[2] See above, pp. 190 ff.
[3] See above, pp. 197 ff.

nant topographical features of the mediaeval English town were more likely to be Norman than Saxon.

These conclusions are not intended to imply that the urban life of early England was exclusively or necessarily a Norman product. According to the view here advanced, it hardly mattered whether a given community was French or English, Danish or Irish. Such questions as who erected the fortifications, who owned the soil, or who ruled the district, can be generally ignored in accounting for the rise of a town. The burgage tenure of the twelfth century, by whatever name it was called, was more than a foreign importation. Its substance would probably have been the same if there had been no Norman Conquest. London's charter might well have contained the same major articles if it had been granted by a son of Harold, rather than by a son of William. We have every reason to suppose that many boroughs would have developed a mercantile population and secured uniform privilege under any dynasty. For the commercial revival that was sweeping Europe would have reached Britain in spite of all variations in its political history. Old cities were there destined to regain their prosperity and new settlements to appear as rivals, whether or not they received the laws of Breteuil.

Indeed, a beginning in this direction was already evident in England before 1066. We may doubt the organization of the Cinque Ports under Edward Confessor, but not the foundation of the Dover liberties.[1] Scandinavian trade had brought considerable population to York, Lincoln, and Norwich;[2] and London must have been greater than any of them. Droitwich seems to have grown from saltworks in Saxon times, and Dunwich from herring fisheries.[3] Some municipal privilege had certainly emerged in a few progressive localities, and may have existed in others concerning which we have no information.[4] But as yet it was exceptional and restricted. It had not come to characterize the ordinary borough.

Thus it was left for the Norman Conquest to continue a process which had barely started when William landed at Pevensey. The perfection of urban organization was impossible without the establishment of a new social grouping. This the invaders, though not entirely conscious of what they were about, accomplished with revolutionary speed and thoroughness. Results that might have demanded a century of slow development were achieved inside the lifetime of one generation. In an age when reviving commerce was just gaining headway on the continent, England was brought into close union with a Continental state, and all traditional in-

---

[1] See above, pp. 118 ff.
[2] See above, pp. 189 ff., 193, 198 ff.
[3] See above, p. 82, n. 2.
[4] See above, pp. 117, 119.

stitutions that might have hampered the complete triumph of the mercantile class in the boroughs were swept aside. The consequence was the sudden appearance in the twelfth century of a uniform urban system that Saxon England had never known. And if any one hesitates to believe that the span of a half-century was sufficient for so great a transition, he has only to remember how the same period affected other phases of English civilization. In the constitutional, ecclesiastical, military, and cultural history of the nation the Norman Conquest began a new era. To accept that event as crucial also for the development of the towns is merely to follow the results of long established criticism.

It is therefore submitted that the history of the English borough can best be understood by regarding the mediaeval town as essentially a mercantile settlement. To do so does not entail acceptance of a rigid formula; does not force us to believe that urban development always followed one pattern. In fact, we may be quite sure that it did not. The old military and administrative centres were of all shapes and sizes; when new inhabitants arrived, they might settle either inside or outside the existing fortifications, and might or might not form separate trading quarters. Documentary evidence for details of this sort is entirely lacking, and archaeological research has but rarely been brought to bear on the problem. More intensive study of local topography should eventually provide us with much fuller information, but as yet it is unsafe to make positive statements about the growth of population in the early borough.[1]

Nevertheless, while we may not know precisely how the borough came to be socially transformed, we may be reasonably sure that such a transformation took place, and we may even date it within comparatively narrow limits. The contrast between the borough pictured by the dooms and that pictured by the Norman charters is eloquent. The testimony of Domesday Book, such archaeological data as we have, and our deepening knowledge of urban development on the Continent, all support the conclusion that, in the latter half of the eleventh century, the population of the borough ceased to be predominantly military or official and became predominantly mercantile. This transition — it is here advanced — carried with it the revival of urban life in Britain and eventually established the equivalence of the terms borough and town.

---

[1] When the fortifications were of Roman origin, they usually enclosed sufficient space to accomodate all increase of population for many centuries (above, pp. 187 ff.). And many of the boroughs constructed in the tenth century, like the contemporary *Burgen* of Germany (above, p. 25, n. 3), contained market places toward which groups of professional traders would naturally tend to be attracted. M. Pirenne tells me that none of the Flemish burgs is known to have contained an official market, but the existence of such an institution would not be incompatible with their general character (see above, pp. 12, 23, 111, n. 4.).

Such a view avoids a dilemma of long standing.   Maitland's exposition of the early borough may be taken as thoroughly sound, without implying that any one created a town by laying out a fortified camp or defining a doctrine of *Burgfriede*.   At the same time Mary Bateson's portrayal of the new borough may be accepted and her principal conclusions extended even to the boroughs that were not baronial.   Comprehension of all later municipal development is made simpler and clearer, for the Norman borough may be considered new in all its essential features, no matter when or by whom its walls were raised.   Divorced from the origin of the borough, the origin of town life in England thus appears in its true character — a problem, not of legal interpretation, but of social history.

APPENDIX I

GIRY AND LUCHAIRE ON THE COMMUNE

ALTHOUGH the feudal theory of the commune has chiefly owed its popularity to the work of Luchaire, its formulation was largely due to Giry, with whom scholarly research on the mediaeval French town may be said to have begun. Giry's first book was his justly famous monograph on Saint-Omer.[1] In it the author very sensibly decided that the liberties of that town were the product of a gradual evolution, and so could not be considered as the peculiar result of a sworn commune.[2] The sharp distinction made by Warnkönig between *communes jurées* and *villes à loi* was not, he thought, borne out by the sources. All the Flemish towns were in some fashion members of the feudal hierarchy and conducted themselves like vassals toward their count.[3] It was not until he turned his attention to Normandy that Giry discovered what seemed to him a more distinctive type of commune.

After studying the history of Rouen and its *filiales*, he came to the conclusion that the Anglo-French communes were totally different from those made familiar by earlier writers. The English kings were not governed, as other historians had supposed, by the mere desire of earning bourgeois gratitude.

Dans l'organisation communale, ils ont surtout envisagé le côté militaire et pour ainsi dire féodal. Ils ont voulu, sans doute, s'attacher les villes, mais au sens féodal du mot, en créant entre elles et eux un lien de vassalité et en leur imposant les devoirs que comportait cet état. C'est pourquoi il leur est arrivé, non seulement d'accorder le droit de commune à toutes les villes qui le demandaient, mais encore d'enjoindre aux habitants de certaines villes de s'organiser en commune.[4]

The sworn communes of Normandy did not, like many in northern France, arise from insurrectionary organizations. In Normandy the communal oath was rather an oath of vassalage than of association. The town's new status was created by the king, who thereby endowed it with the rights and obligations of a baron.

Avec la fidelité, elle doit l'host et la chevauchée, c'est-à-dire le service militaire féodal complet, elle a comme un seigneur une part plus ou moins étendue de la justice, et enfin la taille est remplacée pour elle par de véritables aides féodales.[5]

It was consequently a mistake, said Giry, to consider the communal revolution essentially an anti-feudal movement. Although communes often fought

---

[1] A. Giry, *Histoire de la Ville de Saint-Omer et de Ses Institutions jusqu'au XIV⁰ Siècle* (Paris, 1877).

[2] *Ibid.*, pp. 55, 154.

[3] *Ibid.*, pp. 42–43, 81. The first clear expression of this idea that I have encountered was that of Thierry, *Recueil des Monuments Inédits de l'Histoire du Tiers État* (Paris, 1850), I, xxv–xxxvi.

[4] *Les Établissements de Rouen* (Paris, 1883), I, 439.

[5] *Ibid.*, I, 440.

against their lords, they did not fight against feudalism as a system; rather they sought to enter the feudal hierarchy as themselves *véritables seigneuries*. And these conclusions, though drawn for Normandy, might also be valid elsewhere: 'Ce caractère féodal n'est pas particulier, du reste, aux communes anglo-françaises.'[1]   But at this point Giry broke off his argument, leaving to the future the task of reconciling such a theory with what he had already written about the communes of Picardy and Flanders.[2]

Meanwhile Luchaire had been writing his *Histoire des Institutions Monarchiques de la France sous les Premiers Capétiens*, which must have been virtually completed before Giry published his work on Rouen.[3]   Among the king's men who received some sort of privilege various groups should be distinguished.   These, in particular, were rural colonists or *hôtes*, the inhabitants of the *villes neuves*, and the bourgeois of the *villes privilégiées*.

Au dessus de ces différents centres de population serve ou libre, mais toujours justiciable du prévôt royal, se placent les villes élevées à la dignité de *communes*, investies d'une certaine souveraineté, du droit de nommer leurs magistrats et de se gouverner elles-mêmes. Celles-ci, à vrai dire, ont cessé d'appartenir à la classe des roturiers ou des vilains. A titre de seigneuries collectives, elles sont devenues membres de la société féodale.[4]

These categories of men Luchaire then described in detail, repeating the argument that he had already stated.   The *villes privilégiées* were those that lacked the communal organization, *c'est-à-dire le lien fédératif et les libertés politiques*.[5] The richer towns were not satisfied with such mediocre rights.

Elles aspiraient à un degré plus élevé d'émancipation et tendirent à se consituer en *communes*, c'est-à-dire en municipalités plus ou moins maîtresses d'elles-mêmes, établies par association et par assurance mutuelle sous la foi de serment. Ainsi surgit, dans la région capétienne, comme partout ailleurs à la même époque, une classe de roturiers dotés de libertés judiciaires et politiques, et formant de véritables seigneuries populaires militairement organizées. Un nouvel élément féodal apparaissait au milieu des fiefs laïques et des principautés d'Église, et demandait sa place au soleil.[6]

In his first book Luchaire thus portrayed the communes in a clear and restrained fashion.   They were *seigneuries* because of the political authority that had been delegated to them; as a class, the communes were distinguished from the lesser towns by the self-government which made them more or less autonomous municipalities.   Luchaire cited Giry's monograph on Rouen with ap-

---

[1] This is all that he says on the subject; the sentence constitutes a paragraph.

[2] The weakness of Giry's argument in this book has recently been shown by Mr S. R. Packard (*Haskins Anniversary Essays*, pp. 231 ff.).   For reasons brought out above (see particularly pp. 40 ff.), I am inclined to consider the view entirely mistaken.

[3] The first edition was published at Paris in 1883 and Luchaire's references to Giry's book are restricted to the notes.   The second edition (Paris, 1892) makes no change in any of the portions here considered, and so citations will be made to it.

[4] *Institutions Monarchiques*, II, 119.

[5] *Ibid.*, II, 144.

[6] *Ibid.*, II, 158.

proval.[1] He adopted Giry's theory concerning the peculiar character of the Norman communes and himself used a similar argument to explain Louis VI's charter to Mante.[2] But as yet Luchaire made no attempt to explain all communal relationships in terms of technical feudalism, and his thesis remained fundamentally distinct from Giry's.

Seven years later Luchaire published his famous *Communes Françaises*, embodying a series of public lectures that he had in the meantime delivered at the Sorbonne.[3] The concluding chapter of Book I he called *La Seigneurie Communale*, and in it he elaborated all the ideas that have since become so familiar. The commune was a *seigneurie collective populaire*, bound by all the obligations of the vassal. It took a *véritable serment de foi et hommage*, and this was followed by the formality known as *l'aveu et le dénombrement*. It was liable for feudal aids on the three fixed occasions. It rendered military service through its militia. It constituted a feudal fortress. It exercised seignorial rights over its soil, levying taxes, administering justice, etc. And this authority was symbolized by possession of seal and belfry. These were much the same points as had earlier been emphasized by Giry; but Luchaire applied them, not to the 'peculiar' communes of Normandy, but to communes in general. And as proofs he cited half a dozen documents of the later thirteenth century, mostly collected by Giry, and several articles from the Saint-Omer charter of 1127.[4]

It was about this same time that Giry wrote his article on the mediaeval communes for *La Grande Encyclopédie*, citing Luchaire's recent book and supporting the views there set forth.[5]

On désigne dans l'histoire sous le nom de communes les villes qui avaient acquis vis-à-vis du seigneur ou du souverain une situation d'indépendance et d'autonomie assez analogue à celle dont jouissaient les fiefs.

The commune was a *seigneurie*, holding chartered privileges in return for homage, *ost et chévauchée*, feudal aids, etc. — all of Luchaire's argument was repeated in

---

[1] *Ibid.*, ii, 164, n. 2. Luchaire was in no doubt as to the scope of Giry's argument: 'Enfin, il a nettement défini la *commune jurée* des chartes anglaises en faisant resortir les différences qui la séparent de celles de la Picardie, de la Flandre ou de l'Ile de France.'

[2] *Ibid.*, ii, 173; see above, p. 44.

[3] *Les Communes Françaises à l'Époque des Capétiens Directs* (Paris, 1890).

[4] *Ibid.*, pp. 97 ff. In the charter of Saint-Omer Luchaire found examples of the *serment de protection du suzerain* and of the *droit de monnayage* (see above, pp. 34 ff.). The next oldest bit of evidence is the oath taken by Laon to the king in 1228; but this, like the other such oaths, affirmed only fealty. And fealty, Luchaire himself insisted (*Manuel*, p. 186), was essentially distinct from homage: 'A proprement parler, le fidèle est le *sujet*.' The other documents show that a certain amount of feudal ceremonial or feudal language was employed in the later age when dealing with some of the great towns, but no one has ever shown that such practices were restricted to those called communes or those which had arisen by means of the sworn association. As a matter of fact, all self-governing municipalities tended in some degree to attain corporate character. Eventually the town might be recognized as a fictitious person and so considered a *seigneurie*. But that was the culminating stage in urban evolution, not its starting point. In this respect the doctrine of Viollet (above, p. 15, n. 2) seems to me much preferable to Luchaire's.

[5] *La Grande Encyclopédie*, xii, 119; and see bibliography.

summary. And this *seigneurie*, it appears, was not the military establishment of Norman custom, but the old familiar commune based on the sworn association.[1]

Thus formulated, the doctrine was reaffirmed with additions by both writers. Giry stated it with the utmost rigor in the second volume of Lavisse and Rambaud, *Histoire Générale*,[2] and Luchaire developed it into a well known chapter of his *Manuel des Institutions Françaises*. There too the theory was maintained fundamentally unaltered, but the accomplishment had its difficulties. For Luchaire was no longer writing merely on the one class of communities; he was endeavoring to sketch the whole subject of municipal institutions in mediaeval France. Thus, as already noted, he abandoned the effort to distinguish the communes as self-governing towns and presented them as characterized solely by the sworn association.[3] And this feature he was compelled to attribute also to the southern consulates, which he had defined as a variety of *villes libres*. No evidence was forthcoming, but its absence was the more easily passed over because a handbook is expected to consist of generalizations without detailed citation of documents. Indeed, the whole exposition of the commune was simply a repetition of what had earlier been advanced as too evident to require proof. Luchaire was convinced of its truth, and that fact has sufficed for scores of writers who have adopted his argument.

Nevertheless, any one who will take the pains to follow the analysis outlined above can hardly fail to be struck by the remarkable way in which the doctrine came into being. What had been formulated by Giry to distinguish the Norman communes from the rest was applied by Luchaire to the latter rather than the former, and as such was eventually adopted by Giry himself. That scholar, who had begun by minimizing the importance of the sworn commune for municipal evolution, ended by affirming its primary importance. And Luchaire, after originally describing communes as those towns endowed with political autonomy, was led to assert that self-government had nothing to do with the case. On what was this amazing development of ideas based? Not on Giry's original study of Rouen, for his conclusions in that connection were later ignored by both writers.[4] Not on the materials cited by Luchaire to illustrate his popular lectures, for they were obviously inadequate. The doctrine seems to have been

---

[1] *Ibid.*, p. 122. Giry, ignoring his earlier argument, says that in most towns the commune began as a sworn association.

[2] See above, p. 15, n. 1. In this chapter it harmonized very badly with the description (apparently by Réville) of the communal revolution as an international phenomenon due to economic causes.

[3] See above, pp. 14 ff. But note particularly *Manuel*, p. 402: 'Le trait distinctif, essentiel, de la vraie *ville libre*, n'est pas dans la possession d'une municipalité élective, à la formation et à la gestion de laquelle l'autorité seigneuriale serait absolument étrangère; est n'est pas non plus dans l'exercice de la pleine juridiction de tous degrés. . . . La ville libre est avant tout celle qui, organisée sur la base de l'association assermentée, est devenue vassale du seigneur au lieu de sujette qu'elle était auparavant, constitue une entité politique, une seigneurie collective, jouissant de la plupart des attributs de la souveraineté.'

[4] In his last work (*Manuel*, p. 407, n. 1) Luchaire explained the difference between the communes of Normandy and those of Picardy by declaring that the former were *de la seconde couche* — i.e., princely imitations of the true and original communes, which had been founded through insurrection.

materialized from a mist of vague opinions and to have owed its remarkable success to its own superficial attractiveness. It was a thoroughly nice theory — so nice that it could induce excellent historians to forget that it was not supported by contemporary evidence.

The theory will not stand careful scrutiny. Luchaire's final version of it leaves the heterogeneous class of *villes franches* distinguished solely by the allegation that they were not *villes libres*, and the latter group tends to disintegrate as soon as it is closely examined. The consulates, says Luchaire, were essentially the same as communes, but many towns with consuls were merely *villes franches;* for it was only the *grandes républiques consulaires* that were based on sworn associations.[1] And even their *coniurationes* seem to have been rather a matter of logical necessity than of actual fact.[2] Luchaire's inclusion of the consulates was plainly an afterthought; the true centre of his theory was the northern commune, whose services alone he was able to describe as those of a vassal.[3] On this crucial point his enumeration at first glance seems imposing, but what does it actually amount to? After all, to assert that a commune was a vassal and then to designate its obligations as feudal may be arguing in a circle. If these attributes really distinguished the communes from other towns, they may be accepted as constituting a valid test of communal character; otherwise not.

Neither oaths of fealty nor reciprocal promises of protection were in any way peculiar to communities of one technical sort.[4] All free towns were normally exempted from arbitrary taxation and military service. If the communes occasionally furnished troops or money to their lords, so did the others, and in precisely the same way. The militia of Soissons was no more feudal than that of Bourges; the aids of Laon were no more feudal than those of Lorris.[5] The *ville franche* was hardly less of a fortress than the *ville libre*. Did all communes, and they alone, have seals and belfries? Did they come to hold land, administer property, make grants, issue ordinances, or collect local taxes in any fashion peculiar to themselves? In view of the facts cited above, it may be positively stated that they did not. These functions were normally those of the self-governing town everywhere, whether secured through a sworn association or apart from one.

The feudal theory of the commune is condemned, not only by its incompatibility with any general explanation of municipal development throughout western Europe, but by its own inherent weakness. It has never rested on more than a certain plausibility, which on careful analysis proves to have been an illusion.

---

[1] *Ibid.*, p. 407: 'L'élément générateur de la ville libre a été partout l'*association des habitants conclue sous la garantie du serment mutuel*.' In the appended note Luchaire says that Thierry was wrong in implying that the great consulates were not similarly constituted, but he gives no references.

[2] See above, p. 28, n. 2.

[3] *Manuel*, pp. 413 ff.

[4] Cf. Freiburg im Breisgau (above, p. 33) and Ipswich (above, p. 175); also Luchaire's own remarks, *Manuel*, p. 384.

[5] C. Stephenson, 'Les Aides des Villes Françaises aux XII⁰ et XIII⁰ Siècles,' *Le Moyen Age*, XXIV (1922), 274 ff. In this article will be found many references to other writers who have had something to say about the taxation of towns in France and their representation in the Estates.

APPENDIX II

TABLE OF ANGLO-SAXON BOROUGHS

Name italicized = *ceaster*

First column: a=borough in Anglo-Saxon Chronicle (aa=two boroughs); b=listed in Burghal Hidage; c=mint in tenth century or earlier; d=gives name to shire or hundred

Second column: *=called borough or equivalent in Domesday (**=also new borough); §=otherwise designated in Domesday

Third column: *=chartered

Borough	Century			Borough	Century		
	10th	11th	12th		10th	11th	12th
Axbridge	b	*		Maldon	acd	*	?
Barnstaple	b	*	*	Malmesbury	b	*	*
Bath	abcd	*	*	Marlborough²	?	§	*
Bedford	aacd	*	*	Milbourne²	?	*	
Bridport	?b	*		Northampton	ad	**	*
Bridgnorth	a		*	Norwich	cd	**	*
Bristol¹	?	*	*	Nottingham	aacd	**	*
Bruton²	?	*		Oxford	abcd	*	*
Buckingham	aabcd	*		*Pevensey*	d	*	*
Calne²	?	*		Reading³		*	
Cambridge	acd	*	*	*Rochester*	acd	*	
Canterbury	acd	*	*	Romney³		*	*
Chester	acd	*	*	Salisbury²	?	§	*
Chichester	abc	*	*	Sandwich	ad	*	*
Colchester	ad	*	*	Seasalter¹	?	*	
Cricklade	b	*		Shaftesbury	bc	*	
Derby	ad	*	*	Shrewsbury⁴	?acd	*	*
Dorchester	ad	*		Southampton	abcd	*	*
Dover	cd	*	*	Southwark	b	*	
Droitwich³		*	*	Stafford	ad	*	*
Dunwich³		*	*	Stamford	aac	*	
Exeter	abc	*	*	Steyning³		*	
Fordwich	d	*	*	Sudbury³		*	
Frome²	?	§		Tamworth	ac	*	
Gloucester	acd	*	*	Taunton⁵	d	*	*
Guildford¹	?	*		Thetford	acd	*	
Hastings	abd	*	*	Torksey	a	*	
Hereford	acd	*	*	Twineham	b	*	
Hertford	aacd	*		Totnes²	?	*	
Huntingdon	acd	*	*	Wallingford	bc	*	*
Hythe³		*	*	Wareham	abc	*	
Ilchester	c	*	*	Warwick	abcd	*	
Ipswich	cd	*	*	Wilton	bcd	*	*
Langport	bc	*		Winchcombe	d	*	
Leicester	acd	*	*	Winchelsea	c		*
Lewes	bc	*	*	*Winchester*	abc	*	*
Lidford	b	*		*Worcester*	abd	*	*
Lincoln	acd	*	*	Yarmouth³		*	*
London	ac	*	*	*York*	acd	*	*

¹ Doubtful antiquity; probably old in eleventh century.

² Antiquity indicated by recording of third penny in Domesday.

³ Probably new in eleventh century.

⁴ Doubtful reference in Anglo-Saxon Chronicle.

⁵ Antiquity also attested by royal charter to the bishop of Winchester.

APPENDIX III

TABLE OF RANKING BOROUGHS IN DOMESDAY

Rank	Borough	Mansiones		Rank	Borough	Mansiones	
		T.R.E	T.R.W.			T.R.E.	T.R.W.
1.	York	1,890[1]	1,181[2]	24.	Hythe		231
2.	Norwich	1,320	1,270[3]	25.	Torksey	213	103
3.	Lincoln	1,150	910	26.	Maldon	198	180
4.	Oxford	990	409	27.	Nottingham	192[8]	133
5.	Thetford	943	720	28.	Stafford		184
6.	Ipswich	808	210[4]	29.	Dorchester	172	88
7.	Gloucester	614	508	30.	Hertford	146	
8.	Wallingford	487[5]	479	31.	Dunwich	120	414[9]
9.	Chester	487	226	32.	Steyning	118	123
10.	Huntingdon	436[6]		33.	Winchcombe	115	
11.	Leicester		414	34.	Bridport	120	100
12.	Stamford	412[5]	407	35.	Totnes		110
13.	Cambridge	400	332	36.	Lidford	109	69
14.	Colchester		c.400	37.	Hereford	103	
15.	Exeter	333[5]	285	38.	Chichester	c.100	160
16.	Sandwich	307	383	39.	Fordwich	96	73
17.	Northampton	290	295	40.	Guildford		75
18.	Wareham	285	135	41.	Malmesbury		83[10]
19.	Canterbury	263	252	42.	Bath		74
20.	Shaftesbury	257	177	43.	Yarmouth	70	70
21.	Shrewsbury	252	151	44.	Barnstaple	72	49
22.	Warwick		244	45.	Taunton		64
23.	Derby	243	140[7]	46.	Buckingham		39[11]

[1] Includes 283 houses allowed for the waste shire (above, pp. 189 ff.).
[2] Does not include 540 houses wholly waste.
[3] Includes 480 *bordarii;* also the French borough (above, pp. 198 ff.).
[4] Includes 100 *pauperes burgenses* (above, p. 79).
[5] Tabulation doubtful; should perhaps be larger.
[6] Includes 100 *bordarii* and 20 haws 'under the burgesses' (above, p. 78).
[7] Includes 40 *burgenses minores.*
[8] Includes 19 *villani.*
[9] Includes 178 *pauperes homines.*
[10] Includes 9 *coscez.*
[11] Includes 11 *bordarii* and 2 *servi.*

APPENDIX IV

TABLE OF BOROUGH AIDS IN THE TWELFTH CENTURY†

County	Borough	*29 Hen. I	*30	*31	*2 Hen. II	2	4	5	6	7	*8	11	14–15	19	20	23	33
				aux.	aux.	don.	don.	don.	don.	don.	aux.	aux.	aux.	ass.	ass.	aux.	tall.
Devon	Exeter			?	30			395+		120	30		200	60		100	[1]40
Somerset	Ilchester				50s.			37		15	5l.		11+	5l.		10	12+
Dorset	Boroughs		odd	[2]15l.													
Wiltshire	Boroughs			17l.													
	Marlborough				1l.									40		40	60
	Calne							10		10		3	3l.	3	3	3l.	13+
	Salisbury							2		3		3	10+	1l.	1l.	20	7+
	Wilton											5l.	15+	5l.	5l.	20	38+
Berkshire	Wallingford	15l.	15l.	[3]15l.									15				15+
Hampshire	Winchester	odd	odd	120	4			170+		178	[2]5l.	[5]60	163+	80		150	140+
	Southampton									10			44+			30	49
Sussex	Chichester							5		5		20	13l.			20	39+
Kent	Canterbury			30	[6]20	20		[7]40		40	[8]30	40	109	70		100	[7]30
	Rochester			5l.	15	5		5l.		5l.	[9]15	10	14+			40	11+
Surrey	Southwark	odd	odd	5l.	[10]5l.			10		5l.	5l.	10	19			20	19+
	Guildford				[11]5l.			10		10		8	13			20	14+
Middlesex	London	odd	odd	180	180			1,043l.		1,000	[12]150+	[13]500	926l.	10		1,000	
Essex	Colchester	odd	30	30	[14]12l.+			20		10	[16]30		48	50		[16]30	20
	Maldon											3	10+		22+	7	15+
Suffolk	Ipswich			7l.	[1]75	?		5l.		25	5l.		80	70		20	24
	Dunwich												200		300	150	100
	Lothingland												45			40	45
	Orford													20		15	31+
Norfolk	Norwich			[18]45	50		[19]300	622		300	45	[20]150	300	200		100	140+
	Yarmouth				6					3		[21]3	15	20		20	38+
	Thetford			[22]15				10		10	5l.	5	40	35		20	4
	Caister												41+		48+	2	47
Huntingdon	Huntingdon			12	12			15		15	12	?	10	40			54+
	Godmanchester												24+		30	30	31l.
Cambridge	Cambridge			18	[22]18	15		30		30	18	?	50	60		30	110+

† Compiled from the Pipe Rolls and exhaustive within the limits indicated above, pp. 161 ff. Unless otherwise indicated, sums are given in marks. * Years when Danegelds were collected.

Table reproduced from a rotated page (boroughs listed by county; columns are numbered fiscal categories with their type — aux. = auxilium, don. = donum, ass. = assisa, tall. = tallagium). Best-effort transcription; some cell alignments are uncertain.

County	Borough	*29 Hen. I	*30	*31 aux.	*2 Hen. II aux.	2 don.	4 don.	5 don.	6 don.	7 don.	*8 aux.	11 aux.	14-15 aux.	19 ass.	20 ass.	23 aux.	33 tall.
Hertford	Hertford		odd	^{24}15	^{25}5l.						15	5l.	27+	10		20	
	Berkhampstead												75+	33		59	
	Newport											5	9+			20	18+
Bedford	Bedford			5l.	10						15	3	25	24	30	100	
Northampton	Northampton		odd	15	40			40		40	30	20	200	300	25	300	
Oxford	Oxford		odd	^{26}30	^{27}30	30?		200		160	15l.	^{21}100	75	60		100	
Gloucester	Gloucester		odd	15l.	15l.			^{28}117		^{29}80	^{32}5l.	50	109	108	50	100	
	Winchcombe			3l.	^{31}5l.	30?		100	30	100		^{21}60	3+		50	4	
Worcester	Worcester				15l.	20		60		50	^{33}15l.		40		3	40	2
	Droitwich				5l.						5l.				10	40	30
Hereford	Hereford				15	^{34}10		50	30	20	15		30	15	10	40	15
Shropshire	Shrewsbury				^{35}5l.	10		50	40	25	5l.		28		60	20	68+
	Bridgnorth							10	12	5			6+		15	20	15
	Newport								1l.				6+		4		
Stafford	Stafford		odd	5	5	^{34}5		15	18	10	5		48	15		20	42s.
	Newcastle		^{36}25s.	25 8s.						2½			6+	35		5	13l.
	Tamworth				^{25}8s.	5l.		5l.	7	2½			3			3½	23
	Tamworth				^{30}8s.					?			2			1½	3
Warwick	Derby (together)		odd	15l.	15l.	5l.		10		?	15l.	20	30		30	21	
Derby																	
Nottingham	Nottingham						100	20		?		40	40		^{37}58+	150	264+
Lincoln	Lincoln			80	^{38}80	100		200+		^{39}300	^{41}975	200	350	400	79+	20	68+
	Stamford			5l.									21		32+		
	Grimsby												44+				
	Horncastle																
York	York		odd	60	60	40?	667	200		200		^{21}300	500		100	200	339+
	Doncaster						20	60		15		20	50			40	54
	Scarborough							10				20	60			20	70
Northumberland	Newcastle							20		15		40	70			55	43+
	Corbridge						30			10		30	70	70		31+	60
Cumberland	Carlisle							20		10		30	50			31	

223

NOTES TO APPENDIX IV

[1] Paid in 32 Henry II.

[2] St Edwards pardoned 2*l. pro paupertate;* Dorchester 2*l.* These and other small boroughs of Dorsetshire only reappear in the rolls when, beginning in 14 Henry II, manors of ancient demesne are made to contribute to royal aids. Dorchester pays 17*l.* in 14 Henry II and 15*l.* in 33 Henry II; the others less.

[3] Aids for all three years pardoned.

[4] Roll damaged.

[5] Called *assisa.*

[6] 20*m. de auxilio* owed this year and paid next year; the other 20*m. de dono* paid this year.

[7] Name omitted in the roll.

[8] Pardoned 7*l. pro paupertate.*

[9] Pardoned 5*l. pro paupertate.*

[10] Besides 100*s. de auxilio,* the sheriff accounts for 5*m. de hominibus de Suthwerch'.* Next year 15*s.* 8*d.* of the former is reported waste.

[11] Next year 35*s.* waste.

[12] Roll torn; odd sums totalling over 100*l.* would seem to indicate the figure 120*l.*

[13] Called *assisa civitatis* and *auxilium exercitus.*

[14] 12*l.* 14*s.* 8*d.* paid; no debit given. Account remains unfinished and does not reappear.

[15] 10*l.* 10*s.* unpaid *pro paupertate.*

[16] Called *tallagium.*

[17] The sheriff accounts for 15*l.* 17*d. de assisa comitatus et de auxilio de Gipeswiz,* perhaps arrears; then for 80*l. de asisa comitatus* and for 5*m. de asisa de Gipeswiz.*

[18] Pardoned 5*l.*

[19] Perhaps amercement, as a similar sum seems to have been collected at Ipswich; but in the latter case the roll is damaged.

[20] *Pro navi.*

[21] *De exercitu.*

[22] Pardoned 3*l.*

[23] Both sums reported *de auxilio.*

[24] Pardoned 5*l. pro paupertate.*

[25] Waste 40*s.*

[26] Pardoned 10*l.*

[27] Waste 10*m.*

[28] Pardoned 10*m.*

[29] Includes *donum* from moneyers.

[30] 109*m. de dono comitatus et civitatis et de murdris et placitis.*

[31] Waste 4*l.* 8*s.*

[32] Next year 15*s.* waste.

[33] Called *donum.*

[34] *De alio auxilio.*

[35] Waste 50*s.*

[36] Pardoned *pro paupertate.*

[37] 31*l.* 20*d. de assisa burgi de Notingeh';* 8*l. de assisa Francisci burgi de Notingeh'.*

[38] Waste 25*l.*

[39] Called *assisa.*

[40] 333*l.* 2*s.* 8*d. de dono comitatus et civitatis.*

[41] May include other items.

APPENDIX V

TABLE OF RANKING BOROUGHS UNDER HENRY I

(DANEGELD AIDS)

RANK	BOROUGH	MARKS	RANK	BOROUGH	MARKS
1.	London	180	9.	Hereford	15
2.	Winchester	120	9.	Thetford	15
3.	Lincoln	80	9.	Hertford	15
4.	York	60	9.	Nottingham[1]	15
5.	Norwich	45	10.	Huntingdon	12
6.	Exeter	30	11.	Ipswich	10½
6.	Oxford	30	12.	Shrewsbury	7½
6.	Canterbury	30	12.	Bedford	7½
6.	Colchester	30	12.	Southwark	7½
7.	Gloucester	22½	12.	Guildford	7½
7.	Worcester	22½	12.	Derby	7½
7.	Wallingford	22½	12.	Stamford	7½
8.	Cambridge	18	12.	Droitwich	7½
9.	Northampton	15	12.	Winchcombe	7½
			13.	Stafford	5

[1] Allowing Nottingham two-thirds of the 15*l.* rendered together with Derby.

APPENDIX VI

TABLE OF RANKING BOROUGHS UNDER HENRY II

(AVERAGE OF AIDS)[1]

RANK	BOROUGH	NUMBER OF AIDS ASSESSED	AVERAGE IN MARKS	RANK	BOROUGH	NUMBER OF AIDS ASSESSED	AVERAGE IN MARKS
1.	London	6	997	19.	Worcester	7	41
2.	York	7	334	20.	Nottingham	4	40
3.	Norwich	8	264	21.	Bedford	7	39
4.	Lincoln	8	246	22.	Scarborough	4	39
5.	Northampton	6	210	23.	Corbridge	7	38
6.	Dunwich	4	188	24.	Ipswich	6	38
7.	Exeter	6	153	25.	Carlisle	5	38
8.	Winchester	7	124	26.	Southampton	4	33
9.	Gloucester	7	90	27.	Caister	4	33
10.	Oxford	6	76	28.	Marlborough	5	32
11.	Canterbury	7	61	29.	Colchester	6	30
12.	Cambridge	6	52	30.	Godmanchester	4	29
13.	Grimsby	4	47	31.	Huntingdon	5	27
14.	Newcastle on T.	7	46	32.	Hereford	8	26
15.	Doncaster	5	45	33.	Orford	3	22
16.	Berkhampstead	4	43	34.	Stafford	7	21
17.	Lothingland	3	43	35.	Derby	6	20
18.	Shrewsbury	7	42				

[1] Excluding Danegeld aids levied in second and eighth years.

INDEX OF AUTHORS[1]

[1] Restricted to those authors whose works are, to some extent, given critical treatment either in the text or in the notes. Throughout the indices figures refer to pages and footnotes, the latter indicated in parentheses.

INDEX OF PLACES[1]

---

[1] For more complete lists of boroughs, see Appendices II-VI.

INDEX OF TECHNICAL TERMS AND SUBJECTS[1]

aid, see *auxilium*.
aldermen, of London, 178, 181 ff.
allodia, 90.
amercement, limitation of, 29 ff., 45, 93, 121 ff., 122(3), 124, 129 ff., 141 ff.
appurtenance, in *D.B.*, 82 ff.
assisa, 161 ff.
auxilium, 155, 157, 160 ff., 170 ff., 179(5), 181(2), 210.
avouérie, 35.

bailiffs, 166 ff., 174 ff.; see reeves.
bastide, 30(2), 32.
bordarii, 79 ff., 198(1).
borough court, early, 63 ff., 66, 68 ff., 111 ff.; twelfth century, 129 ff., 137, 146 ff., 173 ff.
bourg, bourgeois, 11, 18, 30(2), 32, 121 ff.
Burg, in Germany and Flanders, 8 ff., 11, 23 ff., 70, 213(1).
burgage tenure, 88 ff., 121 ff., 134 ff., 138 ff., 148 ff., 212.
burgagium, 142 ff.
burgaria, 143(3).
burgenses, on the Continent, 11; in *D.B.*, 77 ff., 82, 109, 152.
Bürgermeister, 42, 182(5).
burghal district, 60 ff.
Burghal Hidage, 61 ff., 74.
burgus, on the Continent, 11, 207; in *D.B.*, 18, 75 ff., 201; twelfth century, 128 ff., 138 ff.; see *liber burgus*.
burh, origin and early nature, 52 ff., 57, 59, 211; = *port*, 65 ff.
burh-bot, 81, 97(7), 101, 156.
burhgemot, see borough court.
burhwaru, 54, 60, 61, 156, 202, 207.
-bury, 54.
buzecarli, see house-carls.

capitouls, 32.
carucates, assessment in, 97 ff.; see hides.
castle, on the Continent, 7, 10, 30(2); relation to the borough, 55 ff., 58, 156, 209 ff.; York, 189 ff.; Lincoln, 193 ff.; Nottingham, 196;

Norwich, 199 ff.; Northampton, 199; Cambridge, 200 ff., Bristol, 202 ff.
castellum, 30(2), 48; see castle.
castrum, on the Continent, 23, 25; in England, 48 ff., 53, 59, 66, 191 ff., 194.
ceaster, 48 ff., 54 ff., 67.
château, see castle.
-chester, 48 ff., 54.
chevage, 35, 39.
chevauchée, see *ost et chevauchée*.
cité, of Paris, 26.
civitas, on the Continent, 7, 8, 25; in England, 48 ff., 54, 77, 187.
cniht, 89, 91, 92, 150, 182, 196, 210.
colonia, 48, 192.
communal ownership, 90 ff., 111.
commune, on the Continent, 13 ff., 27 ff., 35 ff., 37 ff., 40 ff., 215 ff.; in England, 16, 173 ff., 179 ff.
coniuratio, 27, 42, 219.
coniuratores fori, 33(1).
consuetudines, in *D.B.*, 96 ff., 101, 108 ff., 118 ff., 154.
consuls, consulates, 14, 41(6), 42, 218.
corvée, 29 ff., 45.
council, see municipal council.
County Hidage, 62.
court, see borough, hundred, shire.

Danegeld, see geld.
Dialogus de Scaccario, 170.
domus, in *D.B.*, 82, 152.
donum, 162 ff., 170; see *auxilium*.
dooms, Hlothere and Eadric, 51 ff.; Edward the Elder, 65; Aethelstan, 63 ff., 65; Edmund, 68; Edgar, 68 ff., 111; Aethelred, 69, 71 ff.; Canute, 69.

échevins, 35 ff., 41, 42, 111(4), 183.
equites, see *cniht*.
entertainment, restriction of, 29 ff., 35 ff., 45, 124 ff., 128 ff.

faesten, 55 ff.
farm, see *firma*.

---

[1] For more general subjects, see the Table of Contents.